The Rise and Fall of Boeing
And the Way Back

The Rise and Fall of Boeing

And the Way Back

By **Scott Hamilton**

author of
AIR WARS:
THE GLOBAL COMBAT
BETWEEN AIRBUS AND BOEING

LEEHAM
COMPANY LLC

ISBN-13: 978-1-7376405-3-0 (paperback)

Edited by Melissa Twomey
Design by Michael Brady Design

Cover photo of clouds © iccup, Unsplash contributor
Cover photo of Boeing 787 © Carl Court/Getty Images

Contents

Author's Note

IN MEMORIAM

ROBERT SPINGARN

DIED APRIL 7, 2025

Rob Spingarn died after a five year battle with a rare blood cancer that is believed to have originated with the 9/11 terrorist attacks. Rob was the aerospace analyst for Credit Suisse, with offices in lower Manhattan. In my opinion, and that of many of his peers, Rob was one of the best analysts in his field. Rob was one of those rare analysts who wrote what he believed, not what the companies he covered wanted him to write. He was one of my best friends in business. All of us who knew Rob miss him greatly.

ACRONYMS USED IN THIS BOOK

Acronym	Meaning
ADIRS	Air Data Inertial Reference System
AGM	Annual General Meeting
AOA	American Overseas Airlines; also Angle of Attack
BA	Stock Symbol for the Boeing Company
BCA	Boeing Commercial Airplanes
BCC	Boeing Capital Corporation
BDS	Boeing Defense, Space & Security Division
BGS	Boeing Global Services
BOAC	British Overseas Airways Corp.
BWB	Blended Wing Body (type of airplane design)
CEO	Chief Executive Officer
CFM	CFM International (a 50-50 joint venture between GE and French company Safran)
CFO	Chief Financial Officer
COO	Chief Operating Officer
DOD	Department of Defense
DHC	De Havilland Canada
DOJ	U.S. Department of Justice
DPA	Deferred Prosecution Agreement
EMD	Engineering and Manufacturing Development (a design process)
EIS	Entry Into Service
ETOPS	Extended Twin-Engine Operations (overwater)
EVP	Executive Vice President
FAA	Federal Aviation Administration
FAL	Final Assembly Line
FCF	Free Cash Flow
FSA	Future Single-Aisle (airplane)
FMS	Flight Management System
GATT	General Agreement on Tariffs and Trade
GE	General Electric
GEAE	GE Aircraft Engines
GECAS	GE Capital Aviation Services
H2	Hydrogen (green, alternative way to power airplanes)
IATA	International Air Transport Association (a global trade group for airlines)
ICAO	International Civil Aviation Organization (a global policy organization approved by governments)
IDS	Boeing Integrated Defense & Security (renamed to Boeing Defense, Space & Security [BDS])
KLM	KLM Royal Dutch Airlines
Lav	Lavatory

Table continues   →

Acronym	Meaning
LCC	Low-Cost Carrier
MAX	Boeing 737 MAX, the successor to the Boeing 737 NG (Next Generation)
MCAS	Maneuvering Characteristics Augmentation System
MDC	McDonnell Douglas Corporation
MHI	Mitsubishi Heavy Industries
MOM	Middle of the Market (the name for a market segment re: Size of Aircraft)
MOU	Memorandum of Understanding
MRO	Maintenance, Repair, and Overhaul
MRTT	Multi-Role Tanker Transport (based on the Airbus A330-200)
NBA	Next Boeing Airplane
NG	Next Generation or Next Gen (the Boeing 737, 1994–2018)
NGAD	Next Generation Air Dominance (New Air Force Sixth Generation fighter platform type)
NLRB	National Labor Relations Board
NM	Nautical Miles
NMA	New Midmarket Aircraft (a Boeing concept about the size of the 767 family)
NSA	New Small Airplane; also New Single-Aisle Airplane (see FSA, Future Single Aisle Airplane)
NTSB	National Transportation Safety Board
OEM	Original Equipment Manufacturer
P&W	Pratt & Whitney
Pan Am	Pan American
PBH	Power by The Hour (type of contract)
PD	Product Development (department within Boeing)
PFS	Partnering for Success (Boeing program)
PNAA	Pacific Northwest Aerospace Alliance
R&D	Research and Development
RLI	Reimbursable Launch Investment
RR	Rolls-Royce, Plc
SAF	Sustainable Aviation Fuel
SB	Service Bulletin (issued by Airbus, Boeing, and others to address an anomaly)
SEC	U.S. Securities and Exchange Commission
SM	Statute Miles
SMS	Safety Management System (approved by the FAA and used by U.S. airlines, Boeing, et al.)
SSA	Safety Systems Assessment (a process required by the FAA)
SST	Super Sonic Transport
TTBW	Transonic Truss-Braced Wing (an aircraft design)
TWA	Trans World Airlines
WTO	World Trade Organization

LIST OF AIRCRAFT MENTIONED IN THIS BOOK

Aircraft	Description
247	Boeing 247 (1933), considered the "first modern airliner" of the era.
307	Boeing 307 Stratoliner. A four-engined aircraft, it was the first pressurized airplane. Based on the B-17.
377	Boeing 377 Stratocruiser, Boeing's first post-war airliner. Based on the B-29/50 bomber.
707	Boeing's first commercial jet. Based on the KC-135 aerial-refueling tanker.
717	The McDonnell Douglas MD-95, renamed after the 1997 Boeing–McDonnell Douglas merger.
720	A slightly shorter version of the Boeing 707.
727	Boeing 727, a tri-jet short-to-medium-range airliner designed to replace propeller airliners.
737	The Boeing 737, a twin-engine, originally a short-range model, revised over the decades into the MAX.
747	The Boeing 747, the industry's first jumbo jet, nicknamed the Queen of the Skies.
757	The Boeing 757, designed to replace the 727.
767	Boeing 767, the first twin-engine, twin-aisle jet widely used on trans-Atlantic routes.
777	Boeing 777, a twin-engine, twin-aisle jet larger than the 767, designed to replace the DC-10 and the L-1011.
787	Boeing 787, the first airliner with an all-composite wing and fuselage.
880	Convair 880, a medium-range jet entering service in 1960.
990	Convair 990, a larger Convair 880 designed to be the world's fastest airliner.
737 Classic	The unofficial name for the 737-300/400/500 series.
737 MAX	The official name of the current 737-7/8/9/10 family.
737 NG	The official name of the 737-600/700/800/900/900ER series.
737 Original	The unofficial name for the original 737-100/200 series.
777X	The developmental name for the new 777-8/9 and 777-8F series awaiting certification.
A300	Airbus's first airplane, the twin-engine, twin-aisle 250-passenger medium-range aircraft.
A310	A "shrink' of the Airbus A300 for more range; equivalent to the Boeing 767-200.
A320	Airbus's first single-aisle airplane; competed with the Boeing 737 and McDonnell Douglas MD-80. Includes the A318, A319, and A321.
A320ceo	The new marketing name for the original A320, reflecting the "current engine option."
A320neo	The marketing name for the A320 with new engines, the "new engine option."
A330	Airbus's successor to the A300.
A330ceo	The original engines on the A330.
A330neo	With new engines on the A330.
A340	The long-range companion to the medium-range A330, the A340 is a four-engine model.
A350	Airbus's answer to the 787 and to replace the Boeing 777, the A350 has composite wings and fuselage.

Table continues →

Aircraft	Description
A380	Airbus's answer to the Boeing 747. It's about one-third larger.
B-17	Boeing B-17 bomber designed before World War II; became legendary during the war for its ruggedness.
B-2	Northrop Grumman bomber, a "flying wing," with an all-composite airframe.
B-29	Boeing bomber best known for dropping the first atomic bombs in history, ending World War II.
B-47	Boeing designed, the first jet bomber in the world, post–World War II.
B-50	A modified, improved derivative of the Boeing B-29, post–World War II.
B-52	Boeing's successor to the B-47.
BAC-111	A twin-engine 69-passenger airliner from British Aircraft Corp. Competitor to the DC-9 and 737 Original.
Caravelle	Sud Aviation (France) twin-engine short-to-medium range jet entering service in 1959.
Comet	de Havilland Comet, the world's first commercial jet airliner.
Constellation	Lockheed four-engine airliner with a triple tail. Competitor to the Douglas DC-4/6/7.
DC-1	Prototype developed by Douglas to compete with the Boeing 247.
DC-2	Production model of the DC-1.
DC-3	Successor to the DC-3, more than 10,000 built.
DC-4	First Douglas four-engine piston airliner.
DC-6	Improved, pressurized version of the DC-4.
DC-7	Successor to the DC-6.
DC-8	Douglas's four-engine jetliner competitor to the Boeing 707.
DC-9	Douglas's twin-engine design to serve short-and-medium range routes. Competitor to BAC-111 and Boeing 737 Original.
DC-10	Designed by Douglas just before its merger with McDonnell, the DC-10 is a tri-jet with U.S. domestic and international ranges.
Electra (1930s)	Lockheed's 10-passenger competitor to the Boeing 247.
Electra (1959)	Lockheed's four-engine, 99-passenger jet-prop designed to replace DC6/7s and Constellations on medium-range routes.
L-1011	Lockheed's competitor to the DC-10.
MD-11	McDonnell Douglas successor to the DC-10. Competitor to the A340 and 777.
MD-80	Further derivative to the DC-9, with stretch and new engines. Originally called the DC-9 Super 80, rebranded to reflect merger.
MD-90	Re-engined MD-80 with another stretch.
MD-95	Shortened MD-80 about the size of the DC-9-30, with Rolls-Royce–BMW engines.
TriStar	Another brand name for the L-1011.
VC-10	Vickers jet airliner with four jets clustered on the tail. Competitor to the 707 and DC-8.
Viscount	Vickers four-engine jet-prop, the first airliner to use jet-powered engines.

Air Wars: The Global Combat Between Airbus and Boeing

Air Wars covers the intense, competitive battle between Airbus and the Boeing Company that lasted for thirty-five years, beginning with the career of Airbus super-salesman John Leahy. Sales, market, and product strategies are detailed in the book, which features interviews from industry leaders, salesmen, and customers of Airbus and Boeing. The book covers the successes and failures of both companies. It follows Boeing through the 737 MAX crisis and the COVID-19 pandemic, ending while these crises were still underway.

Air Wars is available on Amazon and at Barnes & Noble.

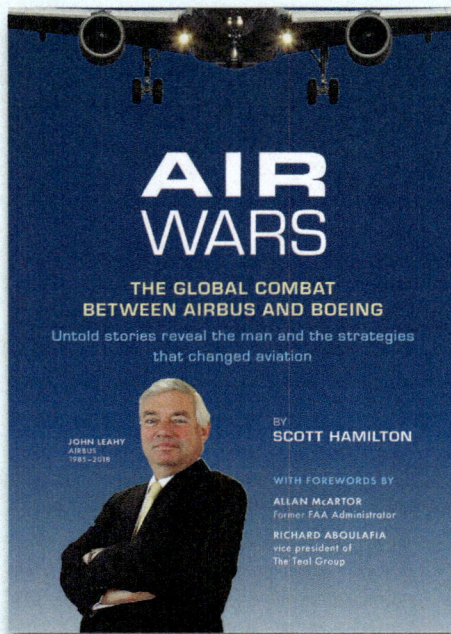

The Rise and Fall of Boeing is essentially a sequel to *Air Wars*. Boeing's existential crises didn't end when the MAX returned to service or when the pandemic was over. Self-inflicted wounds emerged at the company and continued through the writing of *Rise and Fall*. The new book recounts Boeing's rise to dominance and its fall from its position as a global engineering leader to a company pushed to the brink of bankruptcy.

Air Wars, by Scott Hamilton

https://www.amazon.com/Air-Wars-Global-Combat-Between
/dp/1737640503

Prologue

Boeing's word was gold. Until recently.

"Looking back twenty years, Boeing used to be the leader, introducing airplanes like the 747, the Triple Seven, the 787. I feel like in the last five or six years, they've allowed Airbus to spend more money on R&D and basically take market share away from them, particularly in the narrow-body, the single-aisle family."

—Steven Udvar-Hazy, Chairman, Air Lease Corporation, June 9, 2021, on CNBC.

The Rise and Fall of Boeing
And the Way Back

INTRODUCTION

Existential Crisis

"Alaska Flight 1282, Declaring an Emergency."

DAVID CALHOUN AND BRIAN WEST, the chief executive officer (CEO) and the chief financial officer (CFO) of The Boeing Company, were upbeat. It was November 2, 2022, and Boeing held its first investors day briefing since 2018.

The intervening years had presented existential threats to Boeing. First, the 737 MAX ("737" or "MAX") suffered two crashes five months apart in October 2018 and March 2019. Regulators across the globe grounded the airplane. It would be twenty-one months before the Federal Aviation Administration (FAA) recertified the MAX for a return to service. Boeing had billions of dollars tied up in 450 MAXs that had been built and stored before production was suspended during the grounding. Bringing these airplanes into compliance with the necessary fixes and software updates, and simply "waking" the planes up from being stored so long, took weeks per airplane. Boeing wrote off more than $5 billion dollars for costs and customer compensation. The 737 is the company's biggest money-maker. In any given normal year, 737 sales account for between 80 and 85 percent of Boeing's orders.

In March 2020, just two months after becoming CEO, Calhoun was hit with another existential crisis: the new, mysterious deadly disease called COVID-19 became a global pandemic. Airlines worldwide slashed service by up to 90 percent. West had to raise an additional $25 billion to carry Boeing through the grounding and the pandemic. The additional debt nearly doubled Boeing's long-term debt to more than $50 billion. Boeing's credit rating was reduced, which made borrowing more expensive. Boeing's deliveries of widebody planes ground to a halt. It would be two years before the pandemic was under control, after millions died.

The pandemic was not Boeing's only problem in 2020. In October of that year, production flaws in the company's 787 model were discovered during inspections. Paper-thin gaps were found between fuselage barrel sections. Deliveries were suspended for twenty months. Reworking the 787s to shim these gaps and to fix other problems discovered during the inspections would take three to four months per airplane. Boeing built 110 787s that were stored during the delivery suspension. For the first time in the 787's program, the company took a billion-dollar-plus write-off as costs and customer compensation mounted.

The FAA revoked Boeing's ability to certify each 737 and 787 as airworthy, a step required before any aircraft could be delivered to a customer. This "ticketing authority" was assumed by the FAA, which had to staff up to perform its duties, adding another step to the certification process and causing public embarrassment for the company. There was no telling when, or even if, the FAA would return ticketing authority to Boeing.

Certification of the 737-7 and 737-10 MAXs was stalled once the MAX was grounded because of the lengthy time needed to make design fixes, validate them, and implement them. The MAX 7 was already in flight testing, which ground to a halt. The MAX 10's first test airplane rolled out of the factory during the grounding and straight to a parking place while all the work required by the FAA was underway. (Unknown at the time: neither derivative would be certified during the next six years.)

The grounding, inspections, discovery of new technical problems, and the scandal surrounding the FAA's assumption of the certification process of the MAX caused one delay after another. Boeing and the FAA were embarrassed by the revelations that emerged from multiple investigations. Certification of the giant 777X had been in process when the MAX crashes happened. After the accidents, the FAA began a review that involved looking at every step Boeing had undertaken on the plane's production and certification steps to date. The negative halo effect of this oversight indefinitely stalled certification of the 777X. Boeing estimated at the time that certification would happen in 2024, nearly five years after it had been expected. Even this would prove optimistic.

On top of these issues, the company's defense and space programs were running years late and up to billions of dollars over budget.

But by investors day in late 2022, Calhoun and West were sufficiently confident that the end of the company's trials and tribulations was in sight. The inventories of the stored MAXs and 787s should be cleared by the end of 2024, they said. Profits and positive cash flow would return as the inventory airplanes, with concurrent increases in production of the 737 and 787 lines, were delivered. The executives predicted that by the end of 2025, the production rate for the 737 would return to fifty per month (still below the pre-grounding rate of fifty-two per month). Boeing was already alerting its supply chain that higher production rates were imminent. The 787's production rate, reduced to a mere 0.5 per month during the delivery pause, would be back to five per month by the end of 2023 and ten a month by the end of 2025. This was well below the pre-pandemic peak of fourteen per month, but nevertheless a healthy rate for a widebody airplane.

Calhoun and West told aerospace analysts that November 2 that by

2025/2026, free cash flow should reach $10 billion a year. The analysts, more concerned about near-term shareholder value than long-term company health, were pleased. More pleasing was Calhoun's announcement that Boeing would not "introduce" a new airplane until the middle of the 2030s. Technology, he said, would not be ready before then to produce the 20 to 30 percent improvement in cash operating costs the airlines needed to justify a new airplane.

The analysts loved hearing this. A new airplane meant a jump in spending for research and development (R&D). A jump in R&D spending meant less money for stock buybacks and dividends, i.e., shareholder value. Boeing's stock price jumped on November 3, 2022. Within a week, it was up 18 percent and climbed further as the year ended.

For Boeing, the year 2023 was not without hiccups. Production ramp-up for the 737 was falling behind plan, and meeting announced production rates was a struggle for the company. The supply chain still hadn't recovered from the pandemic; shipping parts was also falling behind schedule. Quality was a problem. After Boeing laid off thousands of workers during the grounding and the pandemic, thousands of new people were hired. Training and a learning curve were necessary for an efficient assembly process. Mistakes happened. Boeing was plagued by poor quality products, which it calls "quality escapes." Planes were rolled out of the factory with missing parts because the supply chain couldn't deliver on time. While this "traveled work" is normal (and happens at Airbus and other manufacturers), it's annoying and inefficient. If severe enough, it causes delivery delays.

Despite these setbacks, Boeing's stock price continued to climb. By the end of 2023, the price was more than $250 a share. This was well below the $440 a share before the March 2019 grounding of the MAX fleet but well above the five-year low of $95 per share at the start of the pandemic in March 2020.

Thus, as 2023 shifted into 2024, there was nothing but optimism at Boeing that its main troubles were behind it.

Then, on January 5, 2024, at 5:06 p.m., Alaska Airlines flight 1282 took off from Portland, Oregon, for Ontario, California. There were 177 passengers and crew aboard the ten-week-old 737-9 MAX. There were only seven empty seats on the flight. Two of these seats were 26A and 26B.

Six minutes later, the plane was passing 14,830 feet on climb-out when the cabin pressure dropped from 14 pounds per square inch (PSI) to 11.64 PSI. The plane was flying at 271 knots. In the cockpit, a warning light flashed that the cabin-pressure equivalent was now greater than 10,000 feet, the altitude considered safe for humans. Within seconds, the cabin pressurization went to zero. The cabin completely depressurized. The cockpit door blew off its hinges, oxygen masks deployed, the shirt of a teenager in seat 25A was ripped off, and his mother in 25B grabbed her son and held him to prevent him from being sucked out a hole in the fuselage next to seat 26A. Had this seat been occupied, this passenger probably would have been sucked out despite being buckled in with a seat belt.

"Alaska 1282, declaring an emergency," the co-pilot radioed. The pilots landed at Portland at 5:26 p.m., fourteen minutes after the depressurization. There were no fatalities and only minor injuries. There was damage throughout the cabin. It was a terrifying experience, but the passengers and crew were lucky. It could have been far worse.

A part of the fuselage had separated from the airplane. It was a "door plug" that fit into an opening designed to be an emergency exit for the high-density version of the MAX 9. Alaska Airlines, United Airlines, and others that configured their cabins for a lower density didn't need this emergency exit, so instead of a removable door to allow emergency egress, a plug is installed. The plug reduces weight (63 pounds vs. 150 pounds for an emergency door) and eliminates the need for some structural components, which saves fuel. Without the emergency exit, seat pitch didn't have to be expanded to allow unimpeded egress in the event of an evacuation.

It was sheer luck that nobody was seated in 26A or 26B and astounding luck that the mom was able to hold onto her son in seat 25A. Flight attendants in the forward cabin didn't know what had happened, only that the cabin depressurized. Communications between the cockpit and the flight attendants were severed due to cabin and cockpit damage. At 16,000 feet, the peak altitude of the event, the differential between the cabin air and outside atmosphere was far less than what it would have been had the event occurred at cruising altitude. At 16,000 feet, passengers were still buckled in. Had the event occurred at cruising altitude, passengers might have been moving about the cabin, flight attendants could have been serving food and beverages, and seat belts might have been loosened. Anyone standing in the cabin or sitting with a loosened seat belt could have been sucked out of the airplane. The explosive decompression at that altitude may have been too much for the airplane to withstand; the plane could have come apart, killing all aboard.

When the door plug separated from the fuselage, it missed hitting any other part of the airplane. Had it hit the horizontal or vertical tail, the structural damage could have made the plane uncontrollable. The plane could have crashed, with deaths—perhaps to all aboard—likely.

The pilots reacted as they were trained. The air traffic control recordings available on YouTube reflect a calm response to the emergency. The co-pilot, handling the radio, was communicating through her oxygen mask, which distorted her voice somewhat. This led some misogynists to claim that the female pilot was rattled and unqualified to be in the cockpit and that she was there only because of diversity policies. The claims were nonsense, of course. The co-pilot had 8,300 hours of experience, including

1,500 in the MAX. (The captain had 12,700 hours of experience, including 6,500 in the MAX.)

After the flight landed, all anyone knew was that the door plug had separated from the airplane. Within hours, Alaska Airlines grounded its MAX 9 fleet of sixty-five aircraft.[1] United, which had seventy-nine MAX 9s, followed suit the next morning. The FAA officially grounded the 171 MAX 9s flying in the United States shortly after United's action. Foreign operators of the MAX 9 with the door plug instituted groundings of their own.

Within days, the "why it happened" narrative began to emerge. Boeing was responsible for yet another quality escape when assembling the Alaska Airlines airplane—one that could have been fatal. The FAA descended on Boeing with new factory inspections. It capped production rates and blocked the establishment of an entirely new 737 North Line at the company's Everett, Washington, factory. The FAA rejected Boeing's first inspection-and-repair process and kept the MAX 9 grounding order in effect for three weeks while Boeing revised the process and completed inspection of at least forty aircraft.

The company's stock price plunged from 2023's close of $261 to $217 (17 percent) when Boeing's culpability became clear. Certification of the MAX 7, expected to occur early in 2024, was put off again, this time by at least nine months if not longer. Southwest Airlines, the principal customer for the 737-7, took the airplane out of its scheduling plans for 2024. Certification of the MAX 10, which Boeing hoped would take place in early 2025, was to be delayed, probably by a year. United took the MAX 10 out of its scheduling plan indefinitely.

A new crisis was underway for Boeing. Another crisis in confidence began.

Once considered the gold standard in aerospace engineering and production efficiency, many wondered how Boeing had experienced such a precipitous fall from grace. The company once commanded about 60 percent of the global airliner market. Today it's about 40 percent and falling. Again, how did this happen?

The Rise and Fall of Boeing examines how the company became a poster child for inefficiency and quality escapes. Many of the events leading to Boeing's fall were self-inflicted wounds; the oft-repeated accusation that illegal subsidies to Airbus were to blame is untrue. *Rise and Fall* tells the story.

Can Boeing recover and become a leader in the sector once again? *Rise and Fall* explores this question.

---

1. The smaller, standard 737-8 MAX doesn't have the emergency exit or door plug, so it was not affected.

PART 1
THE RISE

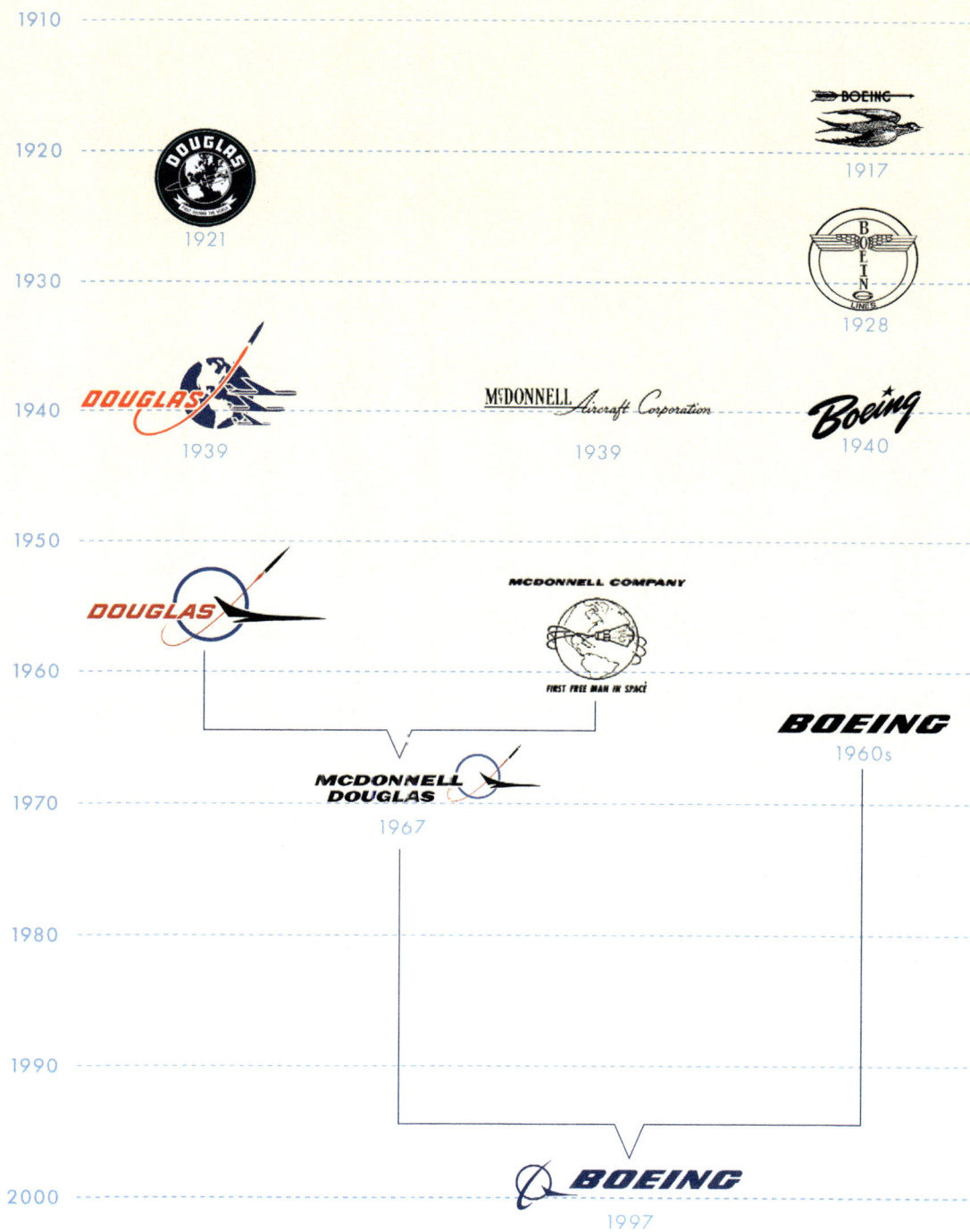

		BOEING 1917
DOUGLAS 1921		
		BOEING LINES 1928
DOUGLAS 1939	MᶜDONNELL Aircraft Corporation 1939	Boeing 1940
DOUGLAS	MCDONNELL COMPANY FIRST FREE MAN IN SPACE	
		BOEING 1960s
	MCDONNELL DOUGLAS 1967	
	BOEING 1997	

Credit: Guilhem Renier

Figure 1. Boeing's first airplane was the biplane B & W Model 1 seaplane. This is a replica. Museum of Flight photo.

1

Humble Beginnings

The First Modern Airliner—and a Tactical Mistake

THE BOEING COMPANY WAS FOUNDED IN 1916 in Seattle by William Boeing. Bill Boeing made his fortune logging in the Pacific Northwest. Bitten by the emerging aviation bug, the first Boeing airplane, the Model 1, was a single-seat biplane (a fixed-wing aircraft that has two wings, one situated above the other) also known as the B & W Seaplane. The "W" stood for co-designer George C. Westervelt. Only two were built. The airplane was offered to the U.S. Navy, which declined the offer. The two airplanes were sold to buyers in New Zealand, where they were first deployed at a flying school. Later, they were used to carry mail. A replica of the Model 1 hangs in the Museum of Flight at Boeing Field in south Seattle.

Through the 1920s, passenger air service began to take hold in Europe and the United States. Small, single-engine airplanes were built, including Boeing's Model 40. About eighty of these biplanes were sold. The pilots of Model 40s worked in an open cockpit. Four passengers were carried in the plane's closed cabin. In 1927, Boeing introduced the tri-motor Model 80, also a biplane. Twelve passengers were carried in the cabin, and Model 80

9

Figure 2. Boeing's Model 247 was considered the first modern airliner in the early days of aviation. Museum of Flight photo.

Figure 3. Douglas responded to a request from TWA for an airplane to compete with the Boeing 247. Credit: Getty.

pilots worked—finally—in a cabin-accessible closed cockpit. Only sixteen Model 80s were built; one survives at the Museum of Flight.

The Ford Motor Company built 199 TriMotors, a metal airplane introduced in 1926. A carbon copy of the Fokker TriMotor, a wooden airplane introduced in 1925, legend has it that Henry Ford took measurements of a Fokker overnighting in Detroit to design the Ford TriMotor. The Fokker plane carried twelve passengers. Its wooden construction proved to be its fatal flaw. A wing spar on a TriMotor operated by Transcontinental & Western Airlines, the forerunner of Trans World Airlines (TWA), rotted through and the plane crashed, killing Notre Dame's famous football coach, Knute Rockne. The crash led manufacturers to produce only all-metal airplanes.

While single-engine biplanes and planes produced from old designs plodded around the U.S. and the world, Boeing took the plunge and created the first "modern" airplane, the Model 247. The 247 was the first passenger aircraft that was a low-wing monoplane. It was metal, it was a twin-engine design, and it carried ten passengers. The 247's wing spar—metal, after the Fokker crash—ran right through the cabin. A step was needed for passengers to climb over it. For its day, it was aerodynamically clean. There were no stringers on the wings, and its design was sleek compared with the clunky aircraft from Boeing, Ford, Fokker, and others that preceded it. For the day, it was also fast.

The 247's first flight was in February 1933. Airlines loved the plane. There was only one problem: Boeing couldn't sell it to any airline but United. Boeing had become part of a consortium that owned Pratt & Whitney and United, which had been given exclusive purchase rights to the first sixty 247s. This prompted United competitor TWA to issue a request for proposals (RFP) to other manufacturers to design and build

Figure 4. Boeing designed the B-17 bomber for the U.S. Army Air Corp (later the U. S. Army Air Force). Credit: Getty.

Figure 5. Boeing followed the B-17 with the civilian B-307 Stratoliner, using the engines, wings and tail. Credit: Getty.

a plane to rival the 247. Among those responding was the small-sized Douglas Aircraft Company.

Douglas designed the DC-1 prototype, which begot the DC-2 model. The DC-2 carried four more passengers than the 247 and had more powerful engines, greater range, and was faster. Perhaps more importantly, it was available to purchase.

In response to TWA's RFP, the Lockheed Corporation designed the Model 10, also known as the Electra, in 1934. Another ten-passenger airplane, it was faster than the DC-2. The Electra entered service in 1935; the DC-2 came on the scene in 1934. Sales were respectable for the era: 149 for the Electra and 198 for the DC-2. Sales for Boeing's pioneering 247 stopped at 75. It wouldn't be the last time Boeing's industry-leading designs came up short in sales competition.

While Boeing worked to fill United's order for those sixty 247s, Douglas sold to all comers. Boeing made history with the "first modern airliner," but it made a huge strategic mistake by blocking out the first sixty sales for United. Douglas quickly became the number one commercial-airliner producer. American Airlines wanted an improved DC-2. Douglas designed the even better, twenty-one-passenger DC-3, the iconic airplane that, thanks to demand for the model in World War II, saw more than 10,000 built. Boeing was for all practical purposes put out of the commercial aviation business because of its miscue on the 247 sales. The company later built the long-range B-314 Clipper, a large flying boat for Pan American Airways (Pan Am). Only a dozen of these models were built, however, before World War II made flying boats obsolete.

Boeing's engineering prowess was on display with its next civil airliner. The company attempted to leapfrog to the next level with the B-307

Figure 6. The Boeing B-29 was designed for the long distances over the Pacific Ocean. It's most famous for dropping the world's only atomic bombs on Japan to end World War II. Credit: Getty.

Figure 7. During the latter part of World War II, Boeing developed the C-97 freighter based on the B-29. Post-war, the C-97 was turned into the B-377 Stratocruiser. The similarities with the B-29 are obvious. The Stratocruiser was not successful as an airliner. Credit: Getty.

Stratoliner. Based on the early B-17 bomber, the Stratoliner used the wings, tail, and engines from that airplane. The cigar-shaped fuselage could seat thirty-three passengers, which was huge for the era. The B-307 was the first airliner to offer pressurization. It was highly advanced for its day. Pan Am bought five and TWA bought four. TWA's principal owner, Howard Hughes, bought one. Only ten were built. The B-307 had a range of only 1,750 miles, eliminating it from use for transoceanic service, something the B-314 provided. Sales prospects for the B-307 were hurt when a prototype Stratoliner crashed during a demonstration flight for KLM Royal Dutch Airlines, which had personnel on board. Demonstrating how the airplane would fly with two engines feathered on the same side, the pilot lost control. An investigation of the incident concluded that the plane's vertical tail was too small to provide directional stability with two engines out on one side. The Stratoliner finally entered service with Pan Am on July 4, 1940. World War II was already underway, however, and the Stratoliner would soon be eclipsed.

While Boeing pursued the Stratoliner, Douglas designed the DC-4E (the "E" was for "Experimental"). This four-engine airplane, unlike the tail-dragging Boeing, sat on a tricycle gear. It had a triple tail to fit in low-rise hangars and forty-two passenger seats. It was also pressurized. The prototype was the only DC-4E built, and it was, in 1938, considered too big by the airlines. Also, the many systems innovations on this experimental aircraft were thought to be too complex by the airlines. Nevertheless, the DC-4E proved to be useful in that it led to the simpler DC-4 that went into production at the start of World War II as the C-54. This became the staple of long-haul cargo and VIP transport during the war, and the first four-engine airplane to carry passengers after the global conflict. The DC-4 became the forerunner of the highly successful DC-6 and the less successful but still useful DC-7.

Lockheed also pursued a four-engine, pressurized airplane, the Constellation (also known as the Connie). With its shark-like fuselage and triple tail, the Connie entered service with the military in 1943 as the C-69. It, too, migrated to the airlines after the war.

That the Stratoliner was based on the B-17 illustrated Boeing's shifting emphasis to military development. Boeing's B-17 was succeeded by the B-29 Stratofortress. With pressurization and very powerful if temperamental piston engines, the B-29 had long range for use across the Pacific to bomb Japan. It cruised at high altitudes.

Once more using a bomber as a base, Boeing developed the B-367 cargo airplane. The baseline B-29 model was used as a foundation: wings, engines, tail, and lower fuselage. Another fuselage was placed on top, creating the so-called "double bubble." The military designation for the B-367 was the C-97, which first flew in late 1944. After the war, William Allen, who succeeded Bill Boeing as CEO, decided that Boeing needed a product to herald the company's return to commercial aviation. He ordered the development of a civilian version of the C-97. Identical to the cargo airplane except for a taller tail, the B-377 Stratocruiser ("Strat") was launched.

The B-377 was an ungainly looking airplane. Its blunt round nose made it look like it was pushing, not gliding, through the air. Its powerful engines were cranky. Failures were frequent, and it wasn't unknown for the vibration from a failed engine to rip it from the wing. The plane's exposed flat firewall made it difficult to stay airborne. At least one or two crashes were thought to be caused by the increased drag of such a failure. The B-377's operating costs were far higher than those of the competing DC-6s and Constellations. (The DC-7 would come a few years later.)

The B-377 Stratocruiser was huge by the standards of the day. It could carry up to eighty-three passengers, more than all other airplanes until well after it entered service in 1947. The Strat had a lower-deck lounge that gave it a panache not seen on any other post-war airplane and which wouldn't be seen until the advent of the Boeing 747 design, with its upper-deck lounge, in the mid-1960s. The B-377 had more range than the DC-4s, DC-6s, and Connies of 1947–1952. But it was its lounge that gave it romance.

Pan Am ordered twenty Strats for its transatlantic and Hawaiian services. Northwest Orient Airlines, United, American Overseas Airlines (AOA), and British Overseas Airways Corporation (BOAC) placed orders. So did Scandinavia's SAS, but it canceled before taking delivery. United sold its small Stratocruiser fleet to BOAC in 1954 after only four years in service. AOA's B-377 fleet went to Pan Am in a merger. Trans Ocean Airlines, a successful charter carrier, bought a fleet of Stratocruisers as they were retired from mainline carriers. Trans Ocean promptly went bankrupt after acquiring the costly, temperamental airplanes.

Only fifty-six Stratocruisers were built, including the prototype. But Boeing built 888 KC-97s, ensuring financial success for the company's combined civilian-military program and further cementing its long history of cross-overs between its military and commercial divisions. The Stratocruiser, operational dog that it was, served its purpose. It kept Boeing in the commercial aviation market. Even as the aircraft struggled in service, Boeing was designing a commercial jet, code-named the 367-80 to hide its studies. Recall that the original C-97 had the internal designation B-367. The -80 suffix was said to represent the 80th design iteration of the jet. Indeed, some early drawings illustrated a C-97 fuselage with swept wings and podded-engine clusters.

With developments in Europe bringing jet-powered airliners forward and its own experience with the B-47 and B-52, Boeing naturally turned to the development of a jet-powered airliner. The jet age was about to dawn in the United States.

2

The First Jet Age

"It was a big, hairy-chested airplane."

—D. P. DAVIES, CHIEF TEST PILOT FOR THE UK'S CIVIL AVIATION AUTHORITY

THE RISE OF THE BOEING COMPANY in commercial aviation began with the jet age. The company's 707 model entered service in October 1958. Boeing would hold the top spot in the industry for nearly fifty years, eclipsing Douglas in the jet age as the number one producer of airliners. Lockheed, which had shared dominance in the piston era, took a pass on offering a jet and instead chose to design a second Electra model (see Chapter 1), this one a four-engine turboprop. But for all of Boeing's innovation in the field of jets (which began with the jet-powered B-47 and B-52 bombers), European aircraft manufacturers initially were the leaders in the commercial jet age. The Soviet Union's Tupolev designed the twin-engine TU-104 jet, which entered service in 1956.

During World War II, Britain's airplane industry concentrated its efforts on fighters and bombers. While America's industry pursued fighter and bomber development, it also developed transports and cargo airplanes. Thus, after the war, Britain converted World War II bombers—notably the Lancaster—to civil airliners. The fuselages of these planes were cramped and, because they were "tail draggers," passengers had to climb uphill to reach their seats. These planes were hardly the ideal solution to postwar travel. The Americans had the tricycle-gear DC-4 and the Lockheed L-049 Constellation, followed by the later-improved DC-6, DC-7, and multiple Constellation models. Boeing had the unsuccessful Stratocruiser (see Chapter 1).

Some debate exists over who developed the first jet engine. Britain's Frank Whittle developed a jet engine concept in 1929, obtaining a patent a short time later. The Royal Air Force (RAF) had no interest in the engine initially, and the design languished on paper. It wasn't until 1936 that the RAF showed interest and Whittle's engine approached the prototype stage.

In Germany, jet engine development was underway more or less on a similar timetable. Hans Von Ohain, an engineer at the airplane manufacturer Heinkel, filed for a patent for an engine in 1935 after reviewing Whittle's early work, and Spain's Virgilio Leret Ruiz filed his own engine patent in 1935. None of the engines were produced when World War II began on September 1, 1939. But with the Allies regularly overwhelming the Luftwaffe, the world's first operational jet airplane, the Messerschmidt Me-262 fighter, entered service in April 1944. Faster than the fastest Allied fighter, Luftwaffe Me-262 pilots shot down more than 500 fighters and B-17 bombers by war's end.

The Germans designed other jet-powered warplanes, but none reached production. And it's here that Boeing got its jump over Douglas and all other U.S. aerospace companies. Boeing engineers were part of a U.S. postwar contingent that swept up German war records, including secret plans for new weapons, submarines, and airplanes. Germany's swept-wing concepts and design papers made their way back to Boeing in Seattle. This research became the basis for the world's first all-jet bomber, the Boeing B-47. A follow-on design, the B-52, came a few years later. The first B-52 flight was in 1952, and the plane entered service in 1955. The B-52 proved to be so robust that it is still in service today.

B-47s and B-52s needed aerial-refueling tankers to fulfill their intended missions. The piston-powered Boeing KC-97, itself a basic derivative of the famed Boeing B-29, was too slow to accomplish this task. The jet bombers had to slow down to speeds barely above stall at the refueling altitudes. Even after the U.S. Air Force added jet engines to supplement piston power, the KC-97s clearly had to be replaced.

The Air Force ran a jet tanker competition. Forgotten to history, Lockheed won with a design that embedded four engines—two on either side of the aircraft—next to the fuselage. Named the Constellation II, after the C-69 military and L-049 civilian Constellation models, the L-193-44 (as the internal designation was named) beat out Boeing's tanker concept. The reason why is lost to history.

Boeing's tanker design had four engines in pylons across the aircraft's wings, similar its B-47 and B-52 models. The plane, called the C-135/KC-135, was ready to fly. Boeing had a close relationship with General Curtis LeMay, the first commander of the new Strategic Air Command (SAC), in no small part because the company's B-47s and B-52s were becoming the mainstays of SAC and its KC-97s were refueling them. With the L-193-44 still a paper concept, LeMay turned to Boeing for the KC-135. Once Boeing was in the door, Lockheed was out, and it never produced the L-193-44, either in military or civilian form.

Boeing's prototype 707 first flew in 1954. As early as this was, however, the Brits hit the skies first with jet power for an airliner.

The British-designed Vickers Viscount first flew in July 1948, three years after the end of the war in Europe. The Viscount was designed around jet-prop engines. The plane was small, seating just forty-four passengers in its original version and up to eighty in its subsequent stretched Viscount 810 model. The plane's range was a mere 1,400 statute miles—plenty for intra-European routes but well short of the vast distances of planes operating in the United States. Capital Airlines and Northeast Airlines were the original operators of Viscounts in the U.S. The systems of these airlines were largely confined to areas east of the Mississippi River and up and down the East Coast, respectively. Continental Airlines ordered a small number of the largest model 810, but its system ended in Chicago and Texas. Still, the Viscounts, with their oversized passenger windows, nearly vibration-free flight experience, and relatively quiet engines were a big hit with airlines and passengers alike. The Viscount was easily the most successful of all British airliners, with 445 built during a fifteen-year production run ending in 1963.

As successful as the Viscount was, Britain placed its commercial airliner bet and prestige on the de Havilland Comet jetliner. The first flight of this aircraft followed the Viscount by a year almost to the day. The Comet entered into service nearly three years later. Like the Viscount, the Comet was too small. It, too, carried a little more than forty passengers, and, like the Viscount, its range was too short, just

Figure 8. Lockheed proposed a jet tanker for the U.S. Air Force with the internal name L-193. Jets were buried next to the plane's fuselage. A commercial version called the Constellation II was floated. Neither went into production. Credit: Lockheed.

Figure 9. The de Havilland Company of England designed the first commercial jet airliner, the Comet. It first flew in 1949 and entered service in 1952. The Boeing 707 prototype did not fly until 1954. Credit: Getty.

1,750 miles. This shortcoming was a function of the fact that the engines were new and had a thrust of only 5,000 lbs. The plane's wings were small, limiting fuel capacity. The Comet I, as the initial model became known, only had a cruising speed of 400 knots, or about 450 m.p.h. In 1952, the skies were dominated by DC-6s, Constellations, Stratocruisers, and converted British bombers that plodded along at 300 m.p.h. on a good day. The slower DC-4s and oldest Connies cruised closer to 200 m.p.h.

BOAC was the launch customer for the Comet. It placed the airplane on routes to the Middle East, South Africa, and, eventually, Singapore. The plane's short range meant frequent stops on the longest routes. But the

Comet still beat the piston airliners to its destination by hours and some-times by days. As much as passengers liked the Viscount, they liked the Comet even more. While the Viscount's Rolls-Royce (RR) engines were much quieter and virtually free of vibration compared with piston en-gines, the Comet's Ghost jet engines were quieter and had less vibration. The Viscount could cruise above 20,000 feet. The Comet could cruise up to 40,000 feet, well above all but the most extreme weather.

In October 1952, a mere five months after entry into service (EIS), a BOAC Comet crashed on takeoff in Rome. Everyone on board survived. The fol-lowing March, a Canadian Pacific Airlines Comet on a delivery flight from the UK to Canada crashed following a fueling and rest stop in Karachi, Paki-stan. Five crew members and six passengers died. In each case, pilot error was found to be responsible. The plane's over-rotating on takeoff was found to have caused a loss of lift, contributing to the crashes. Leading-edge wing modifications were adopted to prevent this from happening again.

Two months after the Canadian accident, a BOAC Comet crashed in Cal-cutta, India, shortly after takeoff into a major thunderstorm. Observers saw the Comet, wingless, falling from the sky, indicating a structural fail-ure. Investigators concluded that the airplane was stressed beyond design limits. All forty-three people on board died.

De Havilland made history with its breakthrough technology. But its ground-breaking airplane was destined for tragedy. The company, through no fault of its own, pushed the scientific envelope farther than the known science at the time. In 1954, two BOAC Comets blew apart over the Med-iterranean Sea at high altitudes. At the time, before the advent of flight data, cockpit voice recorders, and widespread radar coverage, the caus-es of the two events were hypothesized to be sabotage or perhaps blades thrown from the engines buried next to each other in the wing roots.

The weather for each BOAC accident was clear and radio communica-tion during each flight was routine. There was no obvious reason for the airplanes to come apart at or near cruising altitudes. The British indus-try regulator, the Air Regulation Board (ARB), grounded the airplanes until more information could be gathered. The wreckage of the planes lay deep on the Mediterranean's seabed. A massive recovery effort was launched. Bodies floating on the surface of the water showed signs of blunt-force trauma consistent with catastrophic depressurization, which could possi-bly be explained by sabotage or uncontained engine failure. The two air-planes had logged low flying hours and a low number of cycles (each cycle is a takeoff and landing). Surely, many thought, the planes didn't simply blow apart on their own. But after recovering enough wreckage for exam-ination, investigators believed that was precisely what happened. Signs of metal fatigue along the aircraft's navigation windows on top of the fu-selage were unmistakable. De Havilland and the British government took a BOAC Comet with similar flight time, dunked it into a giant water tank, and rapidly pressurized and depressurized the cabin, simulating flights from takeoff-to-altitude-to-descent and landing. Eventually, the structure of the cabin and the navigation windows failed. Without a doubt, the Comet's fatal flaw was metal fatigue. Even though de Havilland used state-of-the art testing processes for the time, unknowingly, it didn't go far enough.

While the Comet drama was unfolding, Boeing was developing the four-engine, swept-wing jets that would become the U.S. Air Force's aerial-refueling tanker and its all-cargo sibling, the KC-135/C-135, along with a commercial airliner that would become the 707. Douglas, meanwhile, began design on the 707's rival, the DC-8. Boeing wanted to use the tanker tooling for the 707 to save costs. The tanker's fuselage was wide enough to accommodate five passengers abreast in the coach section. Douglas, with no such restriction, designed its cabin for six abreast, a requirement from customer United Airlines. When the two commercial jet programs were launched, Boeing initially jumped to the lead. In a scenario reminiscent of Boeing's lead with the 247, which went on to be overtaken by the DC-2 and DC-3, the company refused to widen the 707's fuselage for six-abreast seating. Douglas's orders soon surged ahead. Fearing a repeat of the piston-era rivalry, Boeing made the costly decision to widen the 707's cabin with the associated new tooling. With an EIS advantage of one year, airlines flocked to Boeing, which never looked back—at Douglas. But arrogance, poor decisions, and complacency would one day relegate Boeing to a distant second to a different rival.

The aviation industry learns lessons from every accident. The Comet tragedies were no exception, and the lessons learned benefitted commercial aviation. Boeing, Douglas, and every other jet airliner manufacturer learned more about metal fatigue in high altitude, high pressurization operating environments from the Comet accidents and investigations. Thicker skin was selected, and stringers or stoppers were designed into the fuselages to prevent cabin tears from ripping to the point of destruction. For the most part, the industry succeeded. Although metal fatigue in various forms and in various components, structures, or engines would bring airplanes down in the coming decades, nothing along the lines of the Comet accidents would plague the industry again.[2]

---

2. The closest incident happened on Aloha Airlines flight 243 in 1988 when the upper half of the forward fuselage of an aging Boeing 737-200 ripped off while the plane was cruising at 24,000 feet. Fatigue was found to be the culprit, but the fact that the plane operated in a very high-cycle, corrosive salt-air environment in Hawaii, combined with the bonding method used on planes at the time, was to blame for the fatigue—not a design flaw, per se, by Boeing.

Figure 10. The United States Post Office issued an airmail stamp in July 31, 1958, with the image of a jet aircraft strongly resembling the Boeing 707. Public domain.

By the time de Havilland redesigned the Comet, naming it the Comet IV, Britain's industry lead had vanished. (Production of the Comet II had been halted, with modified airplanes going to the Royal Air Force instead of to airlines, and only one Comet III had been produced.) BOAC inaugurated trans-Atlantic service with the Comet IV in October 1958, only a few weeks ahead of Pan Am's new jet service with the Boeing 707. The introduction into service of the Douglas DC-8 would follow in September 1959. Sud Aviation's Caravelle, a twin-engine jet airliner, entered service in April 1959, following a four-year flight-testing program. The Caravelle used the nose/cockpit section of the Comet. The Caravelle was a short-to-medium range transport in a different category than the medium-to-long-range Comet, the 707, and the DC-8.

In the end, de Havilland only produced 114 Comets. Boeing produced more than 1,000 707s/720s. Douglas built 555 DC-8s. Sud Aviation sold 282 Caravelles. After the successful Vickers Viscount, no other British-produced airliner came close to the Viscount's sales success.[3]

A FAMILY OF AIRPLANES

A key factor in Boeing's march to leadership in the jet age was a decision to offer a variety of versions of the 707 in a bid to win orders.

To win over Braniff International Airways, which had hot-and-high air-

---

3. The British Aircraft Corporation's BAC-111, the first twin-engine jet of the 1960s, which came ahead of the Douglas DC-9 and the Boeing 737-100/200, saw only 244 sales. The DC-9-10 through the plane's Series 50 won nearly 1,000 sales; the 737-100/200 saw more than 1,000 sales. De Havilland designed a plane called the tri-jet Trident but, like so many British jets, it was too small and had too short a range. Only 117 Tridents were sold under the Hawker Siddeley brand, into which de Havilland was forcibly merged by the UK government. The Trident beat the Boeing 727 into the air and into airline service, but sales of the more flexible 727, which shared commonality with the 707/720, reached 1,832. The British Aerospace regional jet, initially branded as the BAe 146 and later the Avro RJ, saw 394 sales, the most successful of the British jets, despite being a miserable airplane for passenger experience and initially equipped with balky Lycoming jet engines.

ports in South America to serve, Boeing offered a hot-rod version, the 707-227, with more-powerful engines. Only five were built. To win the business of Qantas Airways, the flag carrier of Australia and a long way from everywhere, Boeing shortened the 707's fuselage while keeping its standard wing and engine designs to produce another hot-rod, long-haul version, the 707-138B. BOAC needed RR engines to "buy British," so Boeing offered this, too, in the 707-420.

When United wanted a medium-haul jet in 1960, Boeing offered the 707-020 with a shorter fuselage (which was still slightly longer than the Qantas model). United didn't want to call it the 707, so Boeing named it the 720. Eastern Airlines, Northwest Airlines, Aer Lingus, and several other carriers ordered the 720 and its fan-jet version, the 720B. Douglas stubbornly resisted making these specialized versions, although it did offer a RR-powered model for Trans-Canada Airlines (after all, it was a British Crown country). No shorter fuselages. No hot-rod versions.

In December 1960, Boeing launched the 727. The 727 was designed for short- and medium-range routes and was intended to replace the Constellations, DC-6s, and DC-7s that were displaced by jets for long-haul routes and to replace the Viscounts and turboprop Lockheed Electra for short-to-medium routes. The 727, with its three engines and wing design that made it possible to land at airports serviceable to propeller airplanes but not four-engine jets, was an engineering marvel. Its commonality with the 707/720 made the decisions by airlines to stick with Boeing easy.

Douglas responded with the DC-9, a twin-jet designed for short-to-medium, small-airport service. The DC-9 wasn't as versatile as the 727, however, and it didn't have the commonality with Douglas's DC-8 the way the 727 did with Boeing's 707.

Eventually, Douglas created the DC-8 Super 60 series. The -61 could seat up to 250 passengers. The -62 had a slight stretch over the standard DC-8, and better engines and aerodynamic cleanup gave it superior range. The DC-8-62 was an "ultra long-haul" airplane with a range of some 6,000 miles. The -63 combined the capacity of the -61 with the improvements of the -62. Even so, DC-8 production ended with 555 sales. Boeing sold more than 1,000 707/720s. There were ninety-three military models that came off the commercial 707 line. More than sixty C-135 Transports and more than 700 KC-135s were built.

EARLY DEFECTS OF THE 707 AND THE DC-8

As the story of the de Havilland Comet showed, the transition from prop planes to jets was difficult. Boeing, Douglas, and Convair—the third U.S. airliner manufacturer of the day—suffered early, fatal crashes. Some occurred during training flights (this was before simulators became widely avail-

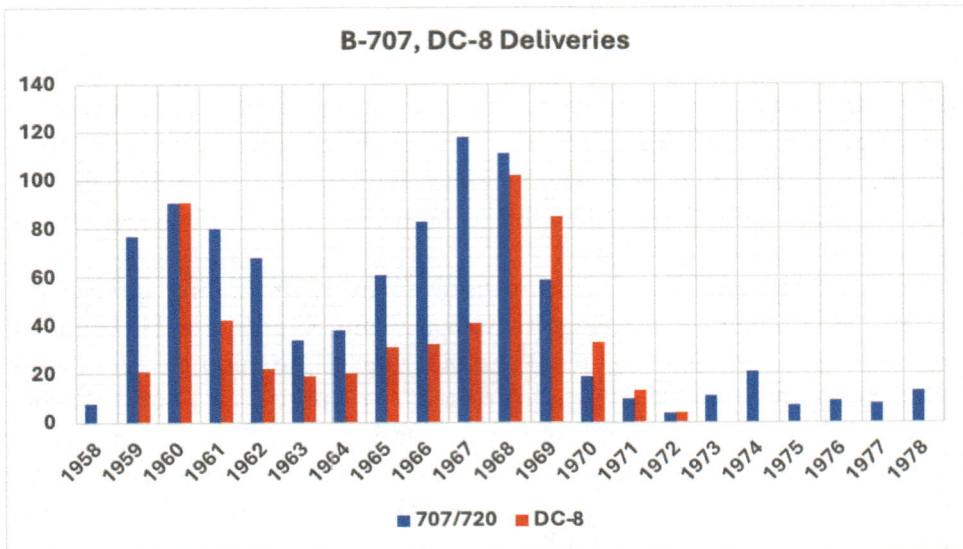

Figure 11. Douglas Aircraft Company dominated the piston airliner era, with Boeing a very distant third (after Lockheed's second place). But in the jet age, Boeing leapt to a big lead and didn't give it up for forty years. Credit: Company data. Chart by Scott Hamilton.

able for jets). Others occurred for weather-related reasons. Some occurred due to pilot error. Jets are unforgiving, especially for pilots transitioning from pistons to jets, and mistakes that might be correctable in prop models quickly spun out of control in jets. The DC-8's defects were related to power units that caused a loss of control. The 707 had larger issues.

Boeing's 707 drew scrutiny from Britain's regulator, the Air Registration Board (ARB). The original tail on the 707 was shorter than people might remember today. The ARB was concerned that in an engine-out situation, the 707's rudder in its short tail was insufficient to give pilots enough control over the aircraft.

D. P. Davies, the ARB's Chief Test Pilot, explained these concerns in a speech before the Royal Aeronautical Society on September 16, 2017. Davies recalled his battle with the ARB and his boss, Sir Robert Hardingham, over the certification of the Boeing 707, a plane that had major stalling problems. In a lecture, Davies was asked, "Why do the Americans build better airplanes than we [the Brits] do?" Davies replied, "I can give you one reason. When you build an airplane, your own pilots fly it and they tell you whether it's good, bad, or indifferent. They might even tell you you've got a bloody great snag on it. You can have big problems. In the States, the difference is the attitude of the chief designer. In America, a chief designer listens to his pilots. If they say, 'holy smoke, you've got a snag, you'll never get away with it, you've got to fix it[,]' . . . they fix it. It doesn't matter what it costs or the delay. They fix it there and then. They would work like mad. They'd put a new wing on. They'd do anything to fix it. In the UK, the chief designer says, 'oh, I've got a big problem.' When he's asked what he's going to do about it, he says, 'oh, I don't know.' They're hoping the problem will quietly go away. But it doesn't go away." Then, Davies said, the pressure campaign starts to accept the airplane.

"The Boeing 707 really was one of the leaders in big transport airplanes for its day. The first 707 bought by BOAC was one of the Intercontinentals, the 707-436 [with RR engines]. It was a big, hairy-chested airplane. But it was unreasonably demanding to fly. The primary flight controls were fundamentally manual . . . supported by power spoilers for roll and a boosted rudder. But the airplane was very heavy to fly on all axes and lacked precision over small angles," he said.

"The flight trials at Boeing Field went reasonably well in a lot of areas. The stall qualities were immaculate. But it became clear there were large problems in directional stability and control. Fundamentally, the fin [vertical tail] was too small. This led to all the problems associated with it—divergent Dutch roll, violent rolls following engine failure, and high minimum-control speeds. It was compounded by high foot forces (180 pounds) in engine-out conditions and extremely high foot forces (220 pounds) in two engine-out conditions. It was all made worse by the unachievably low minimum-control speeds on takeoff and go around." Davies said that Boeing's 747 required a foot force of 70 lbs.

Davies continued: "I was appalled when I finished flying the airplane. It didn't take any wit on my part to turn the aircraft down [for certification] on all these grounds. The unfortunate circumstances were that the machine was already FAA-certificated and the FAA test pilot had not been supported by Washington in his attempt to reject the airplane. The machine was literally potentially dangerous in the event of engine failure, particularly at the speeds quoted in the FAA flight manual. Boeing simply couldn't believe that we were turning the airplane down. In an attempt to limit the damage to their reputation and knowing in their hearts that the machine was much too demanding, they promised a fix within twelve months if we would accept the airplane temporarily.

"Having been caught before by promises not kept, and truly fearful of an airline pilot failing to control the machine in the event of engine failure on takeoff, I said no, and I came home. It caused an awful fuss. BOAC were furious. The BALPA[4] and the airline pilots in general were all with me. My chairman at the time, Lord Brabazon, who I heard later from his wife, quote, loved to fight, unquote, stuck with me, and together we persuaded the then-permanent secretary of the ministry to refuse the machine's certification. Some months later, I was recalled to Seattle to fly the improved model. The

---

4. British Air Line Pilots' Association.

improvements were a much larger fin (it was increased in height by forty inches), an additional ventral fin, and a powered rudder," Davies said.

Davies recalled that these physical improvements, coupled with realistically achievable minimum-control speeds, significantly improved the airplane and brought it within acceptable limits in all areas of directional stability and control; also, rolls and rolls following engine failure in flight were greatly softened. Rudder forces in the engine-out cases came down within limits, although with two engine-out cases, they were still very heavy.

"To their credit, Boeing issued these modifications free to all users," Davies said. The ARB had resisted commercial and political pressures to approve the 707. "To be honest, I didn't find anything particularly praiseworthy in sticking to a set of rules giving the pilot a reasonable chance of surviving a known, quite probable single failure case."

It may be coincidence, or not, that the short rudder on the 707 and its directional control were not limited to the 707. The famed B-17 bomber, designed and flying before World War II, had a small tail. The B-17-inspired B-307 Stratoliner used the same tail. When Boeing was performing a demonstration flight for KLM, with an engine-out scenario, the plane crashed, killing all on board, including the KLM visitors. The B-307 was modified with the larger tail installed on the B-17. The B-29 and B-29-inspired C-97 had short tails. Following the war, Boeing refined the B-29 into the B-50 with a taller tail, which the post-war C-97, KC-97, and B377 Stratocruiser used. The B-52 jet initially had a short tail. It was later replaced with a taller one. Although a short tail never appeared on the 737 or the 747, each had rudder problems. Crashes resulted in the 737. But for superb flying skills by Northwest Airlines pilots, a rudder issue on the 747 could have led to a fatal accident.

The first 707-436 was delivered to BOAC in May 1960, a year after the model's first flight, a delay of several months because of the controversy outlined above.

Decades later, Boeing would come under withering fire for what many criticized as the company's bullying of and battling with the FAA and its representatives who were embedded in Boeing's factory. In addition to the original certification battle involving the 707, Davies pointed to other issues involving Boeing and industry regulators.

The next 707 model was the -320 (the -336 for BOAC), which had a leading-edge modification to give it more lift. Boeing put these new devices close to the plane's fuselage. By doing so, a lot of lift was achieved, but the airplane pitched up and approached a stall, Davies said. As the plane got close to a stall, the pilot had to push on the yoke to bring the nose down. "This is a complete denial of all the longitudinal stability requirements," which were identical in the U.S. and the UK. "I came along in all innocence to do the -336. The rest of the airplane was conventional. It flew like a bird.

It was great. But when we came to the stalls, to my absolute astonishment, it started to pitch up. I had to push to stop it. Not madly, but ten or twelve pounds of stick force. When I got down, I said, 'Look, you've done it again. You are not supposed to have that quality. Why does it happen?'"

Boeing said that the pitch-up happened because of the modification to the leading-edge devices. "I took a deep breath and said we're in trouble again. And I said I'm always the fall guy. You guys build these airplanes and you certificate them. You bully the FAA into certificating them. I come along and I turn them down and I am always in odium in North America."[5] Davies got hold of an FAA test pilot who tested the 707 and asked him why he agreed to the certification. "We cleared it on equivalent level of safety," the FAA pilot replied. Equivalent level of safety is the concept that a plane's level of safety may not have to meet the exact wording of controlling requirements provided an equivalent level of safety is met through other processes, an approach used now and then. But when pressed as to how this applied in the case of the 707, Davies said the FAA pilot was unable to respond.

Davies noted that when the 707 stall resulted in a nose-down situation, recovery was perfect. The UK's Federal Air Regulations required longitudinal stability up to the stall, and Davies concluded that the 707-336 didn't comply. He went back to London with his findings. "There was a big row again. BOAC was upset. My boss was upset. I had a different boss then, and we had a big row."

Boeing had a fix, but it initially chose to send all its top men to London for a big meeting that devolved into a big row, Davies said. "In the end, even my own boss deserted me. He said that I couldn't turn certification down if the FAA staff said the plane is safe. I said, yes, I can, because you are compromising a fundamental level . . . of stability in the requirements." His boss replied that Davies would have to argue with the ARB's counsel.

Eventually, Boeing installed what was called a stick nudger. It triggered a stick shaker, winding up a spring that put a "little, gentle push force into the control column. It takes out the pitch-up and created a pitch-down. That's all it did," Davies said. "You could set the aeroplane up to do a stall and instead of pitching up, it would pitch down and recover." After listening to Davies, the ARB turned down certification of the unmodified 707.

The process sounds eerily familiar. Fifty-seven years later, Boeing created a system called the Maneuvering Characteristics Augmentation System (MCAS) for the 737 MAX.

---

5. Odium: general or widespread hatred or disgust directed toward someone as a result of their actions. Oxford Dictionary.

3

The Second Jet Age

"Will the last person leaving Seattle please turn out the lights?"
—A BILLBOARD APPEARING DURING BOEING'S STRUGGLES

THE FIRST JET AGE, beginning in October 1958 with the BOAC Comet IV and Pan Am's 707 service, was not even six years old when the second jet age began.

The U.S. Air Force was the underlying impetus for the new era of innovation, just as it had been with the Boeing KC-135 tanker that kicked off the first jet age. The Air Force needed a giant airlifter for troops, tanks, and equipment. Requests for proposals (RFP) were issued, and Boeing, Douglas, and Lockheed responded to produce the airlifter. Pratt & Whitney (P&W), Curtis Wright, and the General Electric Corporation (GE) replied to produce the giant, new engines needed to power the airlifter. The plane would be named the C-5A.

The C-5A was a huge airplane. It was 247 feet long; its wingspan was 223 feet; and it measured 65 feet to the top of the tail, the equivalent of a six-story building. The largest 707 model, the -320C, had a length of 152 feet, a wingspan of 146 feet, and a tail height of 42 feet. The C-5A had a maximum takeoff weight of 840,000 pounds, compared with the 707-320C's 333,600 pounds. Lockheed and GE won the competition to build and power the C-5A in 1964. The schedule was ambitious. The first flight was due in 1968, and entry into service (EIS) was planned for 1970.

Boeing and Douglas had invested time and money in research and development on the C-5A. Now what?

Boeing likes to say that the 747 was developed independently from the C-5A. But the similarities in the fuselage design and the broad concepts of the two models are unmistakable. It also defies logic that what was learned within Boeing for the C-5A project didn't find its way over to the 747.

Development of the 747 began in 1965. Concurrently, the United States was pursuing development of a Super Sonic Transport (SST) in competition with the British-French Concorde. Just as the Concorde received funding from the two European governments, the SST had U.S. government backing. Lockheed, North American Aviation, and Boeing squared off in the SST competition. Boeing won the government contract.

It is said that Boeing's "A" teams of engineers were on the SST, the "B" teams were on the 747, and the company's "C" team was developing the 737. This is too simplistic, but in the coming years, when issues emerged on the 737, critics would point to this, myth or not.

In 1966, Pan Am placed an order for twenty-five 747-100s, powered by P&W engines. If the 707 wasn't really a "bet the company" project, the 747 surely was. Boeing had to construct the world's largest building under a single roof in order to build the airplane. The program launched in April 1966 and faced a first-flight target of 1969 and an EIS date (with Pan Am) of 1970.[6]

The original 747-100's cabin was twenty feet wide, allowing for two aisles instead of the 707's single aisle and for ten seats across instead of six. Multi-class passenger capacity was 336, compared with 141 on the 707-320C. The 747 had an upper-deck lounge behind the cockpit, a late addition to the plans requested by Juan Trippe, the CEO of Pan Am. The 747 would radically transform the airline passenger experience.

The original development budget ballooned as problems, design creep, and delays converged. In the midst of a recession, Boeing teetered on the edge of bankruptcy. Tens of thousands of employees were laid off. Reflecting a creative, if macabre, sense of humor, someone bought a billboard and posted a sign that read: "Will the last person leaving Seattle please turn out the lights?"

The 747's problems weren't confined to building infrastructure and de-

---

6. The typical launch-to-EIS period is seven years. For the 787, four years was the goal.

Figure 12. The Lockheed C-5 (right) dwarfed the Boeing 707-based KC-135. The KC-135 is conducting engine icing tests on the C-5A in this photo. Credit: Getty.

Figure 13. Boeing's proposed 2707 SST was to carry 300 passengers 5,000 miles. Environmental and government subsidy objections eventually killed the project. Credit: Getty.

sign issues. P&W's engine development was equally if not more troubled. By 1968/69, there was a line of 747s on the ramp at Boeing's new Everett, Washington, plant with yellow-painted concrete blocks hanging from the engine pylons. P&W was late delivering the engines. When they finally arrived and went into flight testing, the engines tended to overheat. This happened on Pan Am's inaugural flight from New York's John F. Kennedy Airport. Anticipating such an event, Pan Am had another 747 standing by.

While Boeing struggled under the strain of the 747's issues, its engineers and others were proceeding with development of the SST. Technical challenges also presented themselves on this project, but Boeing faced additional political and social problems. Having been down-selected by the government for the SST in 1967, Boeing continued to work on the SST project while simultaneously developing the 737 and 747. Unfortunately, opposition to the SST was building and gaining strength.

The environmental movement was in its infancy at this time and was picking up steam. The SST (both the Concorde and Boeing's version of the plane) was viewed as a threat to the ozone layer.

Additionally, some members of Congress, as well as other critics, objected to Boeing receiving government funding. Government subsidies were standard in Britain and France, but the Congressional subsidies for Boeing were unusual. Wisconsin Senator William Proxmire was Boeing's leading congressional opponent. The irony of Boeing's later complaints about government subsidies flowing to Airbus shouldn't be lost on anyone. The fact that Boeing was two years behind schedule on its SST (known as the 2707), having abandoned its swing-wing design for a traditional delta-wing concept, did not help matters.

Within Boeing, there was a view that the SST was probably a losing proposition. Phil Condit, a Boeing "lifer" and engineer who rose to become the company's CEO, told me years later that the plane couldn't make money catering to economy-class passengers. Designed to carry 300 people versus the Concorde's 100, and with true trans-ocean range compared to the Concorde's barely serviceable trans-Atlantic range, Boeing concluded that the 2707 just wasn't economically feasible. In 1971, Congress cut funding for the SST despite support by the Nixon Administration. Boeing shelved the project. Congress' rejection of further subsidies was a disappointment for many who had envisioned the SST as Boeing's prestige aircraft, and the funding termination came at a difficult time for Boeing. In the end, however, the loss of the SST was probably for the best.[7]

COMPETITION

Boeing was the industry leader in creating the "jumbo jet" with the 747. But it wasn't going to be alone in the sector for long. Along with many airlines, the McDonnell Douglas Corporation (MDC, formed when McDonnell Aircraft merged with Douglas in 1967) and Lockheed recognized that the 747 was too big for all but the biggest markets. A smaller jumbo jet, providing comfort levels similar to those offered by the 747 and better suited for the U.S. domestic market and other global markets, was needed. There was also a need for smaller jumbos for international routes that couldn't support the capacity of the 747.

MDC designed the DC-10, a three-engine, 250-passenger, twin-aisle airplane that still bore the Douglas moniker. Lockheed designed a similarly sized aircraft, also with three engines. Its name was the L-1011 TriStar (the plane continued Lockheed's custom of naming its aircraft after stars, e.g., the L-10 and L-188 Electras, the Constellation, and so on). Both names (L-1011 and TriStar) were commonly used by the airlines. The main physical difference between the L-1011 and the DC-10 was that the DC-10's number two engine was mounted on the top of the plane's fuselage at the base of the tail with a straight-through inlet and exhaust. The TriStar's Number 2 engine was mounted at the rear of the fuselage (it made for easier servicing), with the inlet at the base of the tail with a giant S duct to the engine's inlet.

The DC-10 came in a U.S. domestic version, the DC-10-10; a hot-and-high model for AeroMexico and Mexicana de Aviación called the DC-10-15 (which featured the -10's airframe and wings and had higher-thrust engines); and two intercontinental models, the GE-powered DC-10-30 and the P&W-powered DC-10-40. The L-1011 initially came only in medi-

---

7. When Boeing first began work on the 747 and the SST, some believed that the 747 would have a short life in passenger service, as it would be supplanted by the SST. Once it was replaced, engineers believed that the 747 would be converted to a life as a freighter. This thinking informed the choice of the 747's fuselage diameter: two LD3 cargo containers could fit side-by-side on the plane's main deck.

um-range versions of the same size with different designations, reflecting the very first variant (the L-1011-1); subsequent versions (the L-1011-50 and -250) reflected increased gross-weight models. Lockheed's intercontinental TriStar model, the L-1011-500, which was to feature a shorter fuselage and a longer range, had to wait.

Rolls-Royce (RR), which provided the engines for the TriStar, ran into development problems so serious that it filed for bankruptcy. The UK government had to bail the company out.

The RR engines were late in getting to Lockheed. Lockheed's concurrent development of the C-5A was running late and over budget. The development programs of both firms were so delayed and costly that Lockheed nearly filed for bankruptcy. As a major defense contractor, the U.S. government didn't want the manufacturer to tank. After a stiff political fight, Congress approved a loan guarantee that saved Lockheed. But the bailout couldn't save the L-1011. While technically superior to the DC-10 (it had the industry's first automated landing system), the TriStar was so hamstrung by RR's difficulties and the negative halo effect of the C-5A problems that only 250 planes were sold. MDC sold 444 DC-10s and another sixty KC-10 aerial-refueling tankers to the U.S. Air Force. The two virtually identical aircraft lost money for both Lockheed and MDC because they split the narrow market.

In 1970, Airbus introduced the twin-engine A300 twin-aisle airplane. Not as versatile as the DC-10 or even the L-1011, the A300 was the first airplane of a new European consortium created to compete with the Americans. The diverse group of aerospace companies in the UK had been consolidated previously, usually by government mandate. The British Aircraft Corporation (BAC) was the principal remaining company, along with BAE Systems, which designed and manufactured wings. In France, Sud Aviation was the surviving entity of a similar consolidation. Germany's tiny commercial aircraft industry hadn't yet gained any traction. Spain was the junior partner when it came to aircraft manufacturing. Its commercial aviation industry was predominantly controlled by CASA, a small airliner manufacturer.

Airbus Industries, as the group was known, wasn't even a company in a strict corporate sense. It was a French *groupement d'intérêt économique* (GIE). The partner companies kept their own books and experienced their own profits and losses. Airbus, the GIE, didn't report its own profits or have its own balance sheet. The governments of the member countries provided subsidies to the companies for their participation in Airbus. Years later, after Boeing led the U.S. aerospace industry's complaints against these funding schemes, the subsidies were renamed Reimbursable Launch Investment, or RLI.

Airbus's A300 challenged the DC-10 and the L-1011 on shorter- (but not short-) and medium-range routes in Europe and Asia. Its smaller size but similar capacity (250 passengers) actually made it better suited for these routes than the planes made by its two competitors.

The A300 competed on routes up to 3,000 miles long against the MDC and Lockheed airplanes. The smaller A310 competed with Boeing's new 767-200, a twin-aisle airplane carrying up to 189 passengers in a multi-class configuration. Boeing's larger model, the 767-300/300ER, carried another thirty to forty passengers and proved to be the best airplane of its class. However, the early big engines powering the twin-engine A300 were somewhat underpowered, an affliction that didn't affect the DC-10 and L-1011 because both of these planes had three engines.

Backed by the European governments that also controlled state-owned flag carriers, Airbus sold the A300 within France and Germany. (BOAC stubbornly refused to buy the aircraft. Privately owned British Caledonian Airways and Laker Airways did, however, thus supporting BAE Systems' participation in the GIE.) Airbus also had success in selling the A300 in Asia. Penetrating the all-important U.S. market was much more difficult. To sell the A300 to financially troubled Eastern Airlines required loaning four A300s to the carrier for six months to prove the value of the airplanes. Eastern later placed an order for twenty-three planes, but it would be years before Airbus became a real player in the U.S.[8]

Boeing dominated the global market, with MDC a distant second and Lockheed an even more distant third. Airbus in these days trailed Lockheed. Fokker of the Netherlands was a niche player with the F-27 turbo-prop and the F-28 regional jet. BAC would eventually disappear into British Aerospace PLC (BAE), which created the BAe 146 regional airliner.

Boeing recovered from its brush with bankruptcy in the 1970s. It launched the 757 and 767 models in 1978. EIS for both planes happened four years later. The twin-aisle 767 and the single-aisle 757 were developed simultaneously. The 757-200 and 767-200 each carried about the same number of passengers. The 757 was to replace the 727. The 767 competed with the Airbus A310. The initial models of these two planes, the 767-200 and A310-200, were similar in range and capacity. The 767-200ER (Extended Range) opened the first trans-Atlantic twin-engine non-stop service between the U.S. and the European continent.

Airbus added fuel tanks to its A310-200, calling the longer-range model the A310-300. But the 767 proved to be a superior airplane. When Boeing stretched the 767 into the higher capacity -300 and its mate, the -300ER, Airbus's A310 and the larger, longer-range A300-600R couldn't successful-

---

8. The full story of Airbus's success in the U.S. is detailed in the author's previous publication, *Air Wars: The Global Combat Between Airbus and Boeing and the Man Who Influenced Both.*

ly compete. Boeing built 121 767-200s and 687 passenger -300ERs. The -300ER freighter version remains in production (slated to end in 2027). There were 222 767F orders as of 2024. The 767-200ER lives on as the KC-46A U.S. Air Force aerial-refueling tanker, with 179 initially ordered and a follow-on order of more than 100 expected. Airbus built 816 A300/A310s.

Boeing's position as the preeminent supplier of commercial airlines from the start of the jet age and for more than thirty years thereafter—1958–1989—was plain to see.

By 1989, MDC was a shadow of its former self. Lockheed withdrew from the airliner business for the second and last time. Airbus had not yet become a force. This would not happen until the 1990s, when John Leahy, who came to be known as the industry's super-salesman, landed a key order with United Airlines and Airbus developed the A330 successor to the A300 and two more models of the A320 to create a small, medium, and large family of single-aisle airplanes. Yet Boeing and MDC stubbornly refused to take Airbus seriously.[9]

While Boeing came roaring back in the 1980s, Airbus was beginning to develop successors to its A300/A310 family of aircraft. What would become the A330/A340 program was announced in 1987. The A320 program was announced in 1984. The A330 and the A340 were essentially identical airplanes, with the former being a medium-range, twin-aisle aircraft and the latter, a four-engine long-haul airplane. The A340 was pushed by Lufthansa, which hadn't bought into the emerging idea of using twin-engine planes over water (called Extended-Range Twin-Engine Operations Performance Standards (ETOPS) aircraft). The German flag carrier wanted four-engine safety for its long-haul routes. Airbus planned to use the new SuperFan engine proposed by International Aero Engines (IAE), a joint venture led by P&W and RR. The SuperFan was the forerunner of today's Geared Turbo Fan (GTF), offering up to 25 percent better economics than the engines then in existence. However, due to technical concerns and politics between P&W and RR, development of the SuperFan was terminated. Airbus suddenly had a glider on its hands. Ultimately, the A340 was powered by CFM 56 engines made by CFM International.[10] The A340 became "just another airplane" with OK economics and a slower cruising speed. It took up to an hour longer to go across the Atlantic than the 767, which became the first of the modern twin jets to be used in trans-ocean flying.[11] The forthcoming 777 would cement ETOPS operations.

---

9. *Air Wars* provides fuller detail on the companies' miscalculation.

10. More information on this topic can be found in *Air Wars*.

11. The Sud Aviation Caravelle and the Boeing 737 were used on charter flights with multiple stops.

Widebody Deliveries
1970–1979

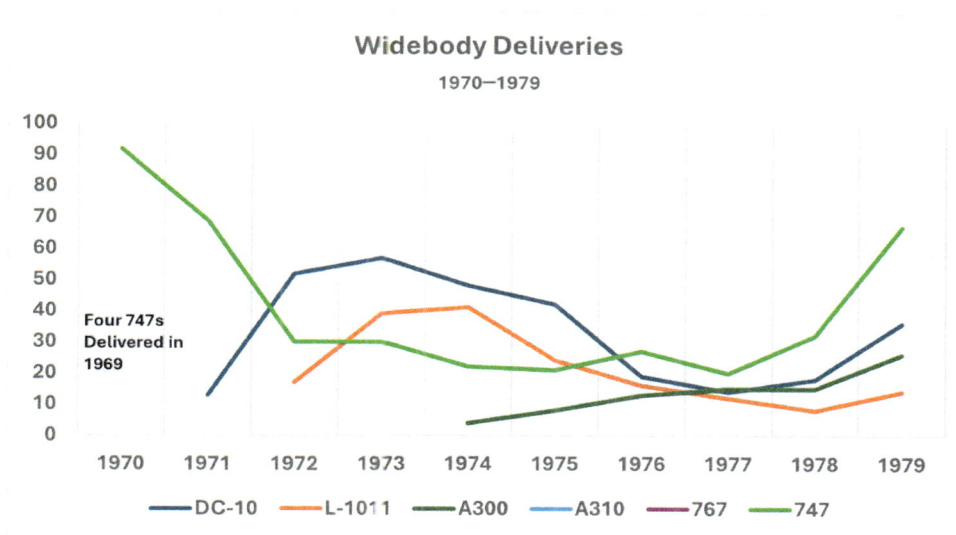

Figure 14. Throughout the 1970s, Airbus, Boeing, Lockheed, and McDonnell Douglas offered six widebody aircraft. Credits: Company data. Chart by Scott Hamilton.

In many ways, the introduction of ETOPS can be viewed as the start of the third jet age. The 767 was originally designed with the U.S. domestic market in mind. United was an early sponsor and TWA also ordered early. TWA later modified its 767-200s to have some overwater capabilities, calling this version of the plane the EM. But it was the development of factory-produced 767 "ERs" (Extended Range) that truly opened the trans-Atlantic market to the 767. With Boeing's development of the 777, launched in 1990, ETOPS became standard and widely accepted.

ETOPS was the death knell for the A340, however. Airbus valiantly tried to promote the airplane as "4 Engines 4 the Long Haul," but the economics of four engines versus two and the plane's slower cruising speed were fatal disadvantages. Even creating the longer-range A340-500 and the super-stretch A340-600, both equipped with RR engines, failed to boost sales. In the end, only 377 of all A340 models were sold. Airbus's twin-engine A330 was steadily improved until its range was more than 7,000 nautical miles. More than 1,000 A330s were sold, and the A330neo (re-engine) model was still in production well into the 2020s.

Throughout the 1990s, Boeing dominated the widebody market. By 1997, MDC was no longer a factor and it disappeared into Boeing in a merger that year. Except for Russia's aerospace industry and its captive market, Boeing and Airbus were now the Big Two of commercial aviation, with Bombardier and Embraer serving regional markets.

4

9/11

"It's outta control."

—TOM MAHR, FRIEND OF THE AUTHOR

"What is?"

—THE AUTHOR

SEPTEMBER 11, 2001, was a beautiful day throughout the United States. In the Seattle suburb of Sammamish, I was up by 7:30 a.m., checking e-mail and the news headlines on America Online (AOL), then a much more dominant service than it is today. I saw a headline that referred to airplanes, the World Trade Center, and terrorists. Pulling the story up, I read what it said and didn't believe it. The audacity of it all! Surely a hacker had gotten into the system and was perpetrating a hoax.

Tom Mahr, a good friend and a long-time member of the airline industry, was an AOL Instant Message buddy. He popped up with the message, "It's outta control." "What is?" I replied. I still didn't get it. Tom quickly realized that I didn't know what was going on (despite the AOL news story on the screen staring me in the face) and urged me to turn on CNN. At that moment, my mother in Wheaton, Illinois, called. It was 7:45 a.m.

Like the rest of the nation, I spent the next several days glued to the television set, disbelieving even as I watched the footage of the United Airlines 767 hitting the North Tower of the World Trade Center, even as the buildings collapsed, even as the Pentagon went up in flames.

The horror of it all, and what airline employees must have been going through, was unimaginable.[12] The general public has little understanding of what it means to airline employees to lose an airplane—one with their own friends and perhaps family members crewing the plane or present as pass-riders—and the passengers who entrust their safety to them. All too

---

12. The families of the passengers on the four airliners who would be distraught under circumstances surrounding an "ordinary" crash must have gone through a special kind of hell when they realized that their family members had all been murdered. Ditto for the relatives of the Trade Center and Pentagon victims.

often the media, and often attorneys, characterize airline employee "go-teams" as unfeeling people whose sole mission is to screw plane-crash survivors into small insurance settlements. As someone who has been on the ground at two accidents before the smoke cleared and the bodies were removed,[13] and as a person who has flown directly over a third crash site,[14] I've seen first-hand the sadness of employees following a crash. But how can an outsider begin to imagine the realization of co-workers being murdered, flights being taken over, and trusting passengers becoming pawns in the hands of terrorists bent on killing perhaps tens of thousands and destroying the White House or the Capitol?

Because the crashes on 9/11 became criminal investigations from the minute the realization dawned that these were terrorist acts, information about what had happened became tightly controlled. The cockpit voice- and flight-data recorders on three of the four flights were destroyed by intense fires. The recorders from United flight 93, the Pennsylvania flight, were recovered but impounded by law enforcement authorities. Still, a fair amount of information emerged to paint a grim picture of what happened on the airplanes. We know details from cell and air phone calls placed by passengers to people on the ground, with the heroics of the passengers of Flight 93 gaining the most attention.

The first news of the hijackings came from American Airlines flight 11, from Boston to Los Angeles, when flight attendant Betty Ong called American's flight operations center. She reported that four hijackers had taken over the plane.[15]

There is a gripping—and chilling—account of the hijackings and 9/11 in the book, *Body of Secrets*.[16] This book is about the super-secret National Security Agency, which intercepts and collects intelligence data worldwide. In a chapter devoted to the events of 9/11, the book states that those on flight 11, the American jet that crashed into the World Trade Center, were all seated in first class.[17] The two American pilots were quickly killed as the hijackers took over the airplane. This scenario was repeated on Amer-

---

13. The first was American Airlines flight 191, involving a DC-10 in Chicago in 1979; the second involved a Delta Air Lines 727 flight in Dallas in 1987.

14. Delta flight 191, Dallas, 1985.

15. This detail is from an excellent recounting of the day's events in the *Wall Street Journal*, October 15, 2001.

16. By James Bramford, Anchor Books and Random House, c. 2001, 2002.

17. In a remarkably detailed account, the book says that lead hijacker Mohammed Atta had, in addition to the well-publicized box cutter, a plastic knife for use as a weapon. If true, this made the federal rules enacted immediately after 9/11 permitting plastic knives on meal-service trays suspect.

ican's flight 77 (which slammed into the Pentagon), United's flight 175 (another Trade Center missile), and United's flight 93.[18]

American and United officials immediately moved to ground their airlines as events unfolded, even before U.S. Secretary of Transportation Norman Mineta issued an order to ground all planes in U.S. airspace. A few hints of what might have happened emerged in the days after the grounding. A pair of Middle Eastern men was detained on a train from St. Louis after their flight had been grounded; they were found to have thousands of dollars in cash and box cutters in their possession. A Delta Air Lines 767 that was sent in for maintenance was found to have a box cutter taped underneath a first-class seat. Information emerged that perhaps the Sears Tower in Chicago and the Embarcadero Center in San Francisco were targets. One source told me that maybe as many as twenty-one airplanes were to be hijacked that fateful day.

Al Qaeda's plans for 9/11, whether confined to four aircraft or as many as twenty-one, while audacious, were not the first terrorist plans to target civilian airliners. In 1995, authorities broke up a plot to hijack at least three and perhaps as many as twelve U.S. airliners and blow them up over the Pacific.

IMPACT ON AIRLINES—AND ON BOEING

The events of 9/11 were disastrous for the airline industry. The immediate effect was the grounding of the airlines for four days while new, emergency security procedures were put in place. The airlines were losing hundreds of millions of dollars a day while their planes were idle. Wholesale bankruptcies were very real possibilities. So, the airline industry went to Congress seeking a bailout package. $5 billion in grant monies were immediately awarded to the airlines, distributed based on available seat miles flown. A $10 billion loan guarantee program was also authorized. The $5 billion in grants were not controversial. The same could not be said about the loan guarantee program. The Bush Administration opposed it, many of the major airlines feared it would be used by failing carriers, and many in Congress didn't want to put taxpayer dollars at risk.[19] There was also a sense of inequity in it all: if the airlines benefited from government largess,

---

18. United flight 93 crashed into a field in Pennsylvania. Months later, intelligence determined that this plane was destined for the White House. Others concluded that the Capitol was the target. *Body of Secrets* reported screaming and scuffling in flight 93's cockpit as heard on control-tower tapes. Previously, only snippets of conversation had been released to the press.

19. Loan guarantees are nothing new. Lockheed and Chrysler each received loan guarantees, for example, in the 1970s and 1980s.

why not the hotel and other travel-related industries also hurt by 9/11?

There was, nonetheless, an overriding sense that the airlines required special aid. Administration misgivings notwithstanding, President Bush signed the legislation establishing the Air Transportation Stabilization Board (ATSB) to administer the applications for loan guarantees. The first applicant was America West Airlines (AWA), based in Phoenix, which made no bones about the fact that it would be forced to file bankruptcy without a guarantee. AWA filed its application in December 2001 and, after jumping through some hoops, was granted a $380 million guarantee (on a $429 million loan) in January 2002.

AWA had the advantage, and disadvantage, of being first in the queue. The ATSB didn't have any solid rules and policies and was feeling its way. This cut both ways for the airline. Since it was first, AWA was a test case of how the ATSB would handle applications. If AWA was turned down, this would not bode well for future applications. Indeed, initially AWA was turned down. Its CEO, Doug Parker, would later recall flying back to Phoenix dejected, thinking his airline was doomed. But he tried again, and this time was successful. The terms and conditions of the guarantees could not be too lenient or be seen as too onerous.[20]

AWA was probably helped by the fact that one of the legislative sponsors of the loan program was powerful Arizona Senator John McCain, a long-time champion of the airline in Washington. Critics said that AWA was failing anyway and therefore should not be granted a loan. AWA CEO Parker deserves the highest praise for pulling this deal off, although it is widely believed that the carrier's political connections were equally or more responsible for the approval.

Most other applications were rejected.

The next applications to the ATSB were from Frontier Flying Service of Alaska, cargo airline Evergreen International Aviation, Vanguard Airlines of Kansas City, and Spirit Airlines of Florida. Back then, Spirit was a far different airline than the one flying today. In 2001, Spirit was a traditional low-cost carrier in the mold of Southwest Airlines. Today's Spirit is an ultra-low-cost airline. Except for Spirit, the other applications on their merits seemed silly.

---

20. Views are split as to whether America West got off easy or whether the terms and conditions were too stiff. Continental Airlines Chairman Gordon Bethune called the terms usurious under Texas law (where Continental was based); America West said that the price was too high but that there had been little choice; Joe Adams, former executive director of the ATSB, said that for what was essentially a bankrupt company, the level of warrants granted the government (equal to 33 percent of the common stock when converted) was too low.

Of the fourteen airlines and one specialty carrier (MedJet, an air ambulance service) that applied for loan guarantees, the ATSB approved only six.

By far, the most controversial loan guarantee denial was that for $1.8 billion for United. The carrier immediately filed for bankruptcy. The sheer size of United's bankruptcy, the largest in airline history and one of the largest in American business (along with WorldCom and Enron), made the ATSB's denial an instant political target, especially considering the political pressure exerted on the board by United's labor, congressional, city, and affiliated constituencies to approve the loan.

The application had been troubled from the start. United's underlying business fundamentals were considered by most of the industry, and by analysts who covered the airline, to be just awful. Although largely considered to have the best route system of any airline, United's labor costs and corporate governance structure were considered to be fatally flawed. The company's management team was considered at best to be mediocre. Not only was the application for the loan guarantee widely derided as being poorly put together, but United's revenue assumptions were also criticized by its opponents (and, ultimately, by the ATSB) as overly optimistic (some said totally unrealistic). Labor cost cuts were not enough in the application, nor were other cost-cutting measures.

The ATSB's conclusions on the United application were widely criticized. But when United filed for bankruptcy a few days later, buried deep in the paperwork were pleadings from the carrier saying that banks and lending institutions had reached the same conclusions, which is why United did not have access to capital markets—one of the criteria set forth by the ATSB before it would approve an application. In other words, private industry had already concluded that United's business plan was unworkable, a conclusion that the ATSB could hardly be faulted for also reaching.

United, in bankruptcy, went after the cost cutting that was required for ATSB loan approval. Labor costs were reduced by about a third, and other costs, most visibly aircraft debt and rent, was dramatically cut. Other vendors had to cut costs as well, including the carriers supplying services for United Express: SkyWest Airlines, Atlantic Coast Airlines, and Air Wisconsin.

US Airways applied for $900 million in loan guarantees before filing for Chapter 11 protection. The government had conditionally approved the application before US Airways entered bankruptcy. A major difference between US Airways and United, however, was that US Airways had a good business plan that was realistic and that included a well-defined path for the future. Once US Airways completed its reorganization and exited bankruptcy in March 2003, a mere seven months after filing under Chapter 11, the ATSB signed off on the loan guarantee.

There were some curious omissions from the applicants for loan guarantees. American seemed to be a natural applicant. It was, along with United, one of the targets of 9/11 and, therefore, was disproportionately hurt by these events. American also suffered an accident the following December, when an Airbus A300-600R crashed shortly after takeoff from New York's John F. Kennedy Airport. The event was unrelated to terrorism but, coming only three months after 9/11, terrorist fears naturally reemerged. It was revealed quickly to be "just" another airline accident, but American nonetheless suffered short-term negative effects. Losses continued to mount well into 2002 (and beyond, as it turned out), as the deadline for loan applications approached. And with American's biggest rival, United, filing an application, it seemed to make sense that American would, too.

American's management philosophically opposed bankruptcy and the effect it would have on employees, shareholders, and stakeholders. While admirable in theory, this approach proved to cripple American for years until it finally succumbed in 2011.

9/11 affected Airbus and Boeing, too. Each was faced with order cancellations or deferrals. Airbus, then still closely tied to government funding, was less affected. Boeing, a true capitalist firm whose order book was heavily weighted toward U.S. carriers, faced a much more dire near-term future. But, more ominously, 9/11 set in motion of chain of events that would bring shame on the company, the wrath of one of the most cantankerous and powerful men in the U.S. Senate, and an international controversy that lasted for twenty years.

With far less market share in the U.S. in 2001 than Boeing, Airbus was somewhat insulated from the negative impacts of 9/11. Outside the U.S., while there was a decline in passenger traffic, airlines weathered 9/11 far better than America's airlines. Accordingly, so did Airbus. It was in the near-term post-9/11 years that enabled Airbus to overtake Boeing in orders and, soon, in deliveries. By 2004, Airbus began to eclipse Boeing.

TANKER SCANDAL

Boeing's post-9/11 collapse in customer demand had a profound impact on its finances. One way to offset this impact was to fall back on its defense unit, enlarged by the acquisition of McDonnell Douglas. The U.S. was going to war, and all its defense contractors were going to benefit. It was a solid affirmation of then-CEO Phil Condit's vision to diversify Boeing's revenue and customer base.[21]

Boeing as a matter of routine always had its eye out for market oppor-

---

21. This is further detailed in Chapter 8.

tunities. One of these was the aging aerial-refueling tanker fleet used by the U.S. Air Force. Entry into service (EIS) of the tanker was in 1957. The last KC-135 was delivered in 1965. Eight hundred and twenty-five tankers were delivered over the life of the program. Many updates were incorporated into the fleet, including re-engining some with CFM 56 engines from CFM International. Even at the time of this writing in 2025, KC-135s continue to serve the Air Force and will do so for years to come.

In 2001, Boeing looked at the aging tanker fleet and correctly recognized that the Air Force needed to think about replacements. This is called recapitalization in Pentagon-ese. But with the majority of the defense department's budget committed to other things, and now with a war to fund, there really wasn't going to be room in the budget to buy a fleet of new tankers. Boeing came up with an unusual solution: build a fleet of 100 tankers based on the Boeing plane closest in size to the KC-135, the 767-200ER, and lease them to the Air Force for ten years. At the end of this time (basically in the 2010–2020 decade), so the thinking went, the Air Force could either buy the airplanes or the tankers could be sold to the private sector and converted to pure cargo airliners.

On its face, it was an innovative idea, a creative solution for the budget-strapped Air Force, and a shot in the arm for Boeing and its Commercial Airplanes (BCA) division because of the 767 connection. A closer look at the concept did reveal some flaws, however. First, at that time, no U.S. defense service had leased airplanes in this manner. Second, the idea that the 767-200ER would be an attractive freighter at the end of the lease term was (to put it charitably) ridiculous. By the 2010s and into the 2020s, freighters would be using larger aircraft like the 767-300ER instead of the smaller -200ER.[22] Third, but likely not finally, de-militarizing the KC-767 (the name adopted for the effort) would be costly. Second-tier cargo airlines wouldn't want to absorb this cost, and first-tier cargo carriers would want the larger freighter and likely would order new aircraft. Leasing aircraft (or cars, for example) ultimately costs more than purchasing them outright.

Setting aside these flaws, under the circumstances driven by the Pentagon budget, Boeing's idea wasn't outrageous.

Boeing worked its sources on Capitol Hill (Congress), in the Air Force, and at the Pentagon. A procurement process was begun by the Air Force under the leadership of an Air Force officer named Darleen Druyun, the principal Deputy Undersecretary of the Air Force for Acquisition. Airbus would later claim that Druyun excluded it from consideration, implying this was improper. Whether she did or didn't, and whether such exclusion

---

22. This is exactly what happened. The freighter of choice was indeed the 767-300ER.

was improper, was not relevant to the realities of the day. Airbus had not created a tanker at the time; the A330 MRTT came later. Boeing had the long history of the KC-135, and the MDC side of the company developed the KC-10, the last of which was delivered in 1987. Boeing was rusty, to be sure, but on paper Airbus simply wasn't qualified.

Regardless, the procurement process turned out to be fatally flawed. Boeing was awarded its lease deal in 2003, and Druyun was given a job at Boeing shortly after. She was given a salary of $250,000 (nearly $430,000 in 2025 dollars) and a signing bonus of $50,000 ($86,000). Boeing's chief financial officer at the time, Mike Sears (a former MDC officer), was the point man on this endeavor. On its face, this move raised all sorts of questions. The lease deal also was criticized as being more expensive than purchasing the aircraft.

The deal caught the attention of Arizona Senator John McCain, a Republican. A key member of the powerful Senate Armed Services Committee, McCain was the son of an admiral of the same name and the grandson of another admiral, also named John, who served in World War II. McCain was a carrier pilot during the Vietnam War. He narrowly escaped death on the *USS Forrestal* when a missile separated from another plane, skidded across the deck into a group of parked aircraft, and exploded into a ball of fire. McCain had been in the cockpit of one of these aircraft, awaiting his turn for takeoff. Later, he was shot down over Hanoi, held captive for six years, and refused offers for early release because of his father's position in the Navy. Badly injured when he was shot down, and tortured by his captors, McCain had permanent injuries that prevented him from raising his arms above his shoulders.

Elected to the U.S. House of Representatives in 1982, he ran for Senate in 1986. Accused of being a carpet bagger in Arizona during one of his campaigns, McCain noted that he had been out of the country for six years in the "Hanoi Hilton," the name given to the infamous POW prison in which he and others had been held captive.

In his first term in the Senate, McCain naïvely became a participant in a scandal involving a group of savings and loans in which an Arizona man named Charles Keating was involved. McCain tried to help him. The scandal erupted, and McCain, along with several other members of Congress, was tainted. McCain was deeply embarrassed by the affair and the resulting stain on his honor and integrity, virtues that had been instilled in him by his service in the Navy and the heritage of his father and grandfather. He became a stickler for honor and integrity in the perpetually challenged Congress. As a result, when he looked at the Boeing tanker deal, McCain saw red.

McCain criticized the deal's economics as a taxpayer rip-off and attacked Boeing's hiring of Druyun. Eventually, Druyun and Sears, who hired her, pled guilty to criminal charges and served several months in jail. Boeing was fined hundreds of millions of dollars but avoided being barred from defense work. The KC-767 tanker contract was cancelled. Condit wasn't implicated in the scandal, but the embarrassing events happened on his watch. He resigned. Boeing's board appointed Harry Stonecipher to replace him. Stonecipher had retired as president and chief operating officer of the company but had continued to serve on the board.

The Air Force still needed to replace its aging KC-135s, so a new tanker-procurement program was created. By this time, Airbus and its parent the European Aeronautic Defence and Space Company (EADS, later renamed Airbus Group) developed a tanker concept based on the A330-200 called the A330 MRTT (Multi Role Tanker Transport). Boeing, for its part, again offered the KC-767. EADS, recognizing that its then-present U.S. defense work was miniscule compared with Boeing's, partnered with Northop Grumman to offer the MRTT. Northrop was one of the Pentagon's largest contractors, with decades of experience. Northop was to be the prime contractor and EADS its principal sub-contractor.

This time, Airbus (EADS) was a serious contender. Boeing pulled out all the stops to oppose the Northrop-Airbus bid, correctly pointing out that the A330 was much larger than the 767-200ER, which was somewhat larger than the KC-135. Logistics and ramp footprints would be issues for the Air Force. The larger A330 used more fuel than the 767, so operating costs would be greater. (This was true but not nearly to the extent Boeing claimed.) Airbus had no experience designing and building a tanker. Its plans to construct a production plant in Mobile, Alabama, and hire brand-new workers couldn't compare with Boeing's skilled work force. This was true as far as it went, but Boeing ignored (though Northrop didn't) the fact that legacy Boeing hadn't built a tanker since the 1960s and MDC hadn't done so since the 1980s. Boeing's designers and workers were essentially fresh as well.

But Boeing placed its biggest effort on tearing down Airbus and the subsidies it received from its member states for airplane development, including the A330. Boeing began the refrain, picked up by its supporting politicians and others, that Airbus shouldn't be rewarded for receiving "illegal" subsidies.

Stonecipher, having succeeded Condit as Boeing's CEO, in 2004 persuaded the U.S. government to renounce a 1992 trade agreement covering subsidies and file a complaint with the World Trade Organization regarding government money going to Airbus. Some believed this was to distract attention from Boeing's own scandals, and there could be some truth to this. But in retrospect, the moves appear to be part of the larger strategy to tar Airbus in the tanker competition. Details of the trade wars are in the next chapter.

Few gave Northrop-EADS a serious chance of winning the contract. Part of the EADS strategy was to establish its bona fides for future Pentagon work, although EADS was sincere in its efforts to win the tanker deal. Thus, everyone, including Northrop-EADS, was shocked when the Air Force awarded the contract to Northrop.

During the debriefing the Air Force gave to Boeing about why Northrop won the tanker deal, a standard procedure, Boeing learned that in making the award, the service had given extra credit for the A330's greater capabilities over the 767. For all the disadvantages the larger airplane had that were cited by Boeing, the A330 has greater range and troop and cargo transport capabilities than the 767. One of the factors considered was a war game involving China. China had publicly talked about one of its strategies if a U.S. conflict that involved neutralizing Guam, where a U.S. base was located, were to break out. Guam is 1,800 miles from the China coast. Other bases in Japan would also be neutralized. The vast distances involved in flights from base alternatives in Australia and Hawaii gave the longer range of the A330 the advantage.

The problem was that the Air Force hadn't included these metrics in the specifications for the tanker procurement. Boeing didn't know these existed. The company protested the award, which was upheld. A third procurement process became necessary. Northrop decided to skip the next round. EADS, now with additional Pentagon business in other sectors and having designed the MRTT, decided to go it alone for round three.

In the meantime, Boeing had sold eight KC-767s, four each to Japan and Italy, but the airplanes suffered from wing flutter and other issues. Boeing revised the design to update the 767 in several respects. It added a glass cockpit from the 767-400 and updated several systems, and illustrations showed the airplane with winglets that would improve fuel consumption. Airbus offered essentially the same MRTT in the third round of the procurement process. As was the case in the second round, Boeing's primary focus in the third round of the competition was not about how its airplane was better and its workforce more experienced. Boeing once more placed heavy emphasis on the illegal subsidies that Airbus received in general and for the A330 specifically. As an industry observer, writer, and commentator at the time, I thought the fact that Boeing wasn't placing its focus on an airplane versus airplane comparison but was spending more time running down Airbus spoke volumes about the company and the shortcomings of its own offering.

At the urging of Washington Congressman Norm Dicks, one of Boeing's biggest supporters, Boeing aggressively bid its pricing. This time, the Air Force's top criteria was what's called a Technically Acceptable, Lowest Price (TALP) process. Only if the submitted bids were within 1 percent of each other would a model's extra capabilities be factored in. The Air Force awarded Boeing the contract under TALP. The company's bid was 10 percent lower than Airbus's, a price nobody could understand. Jim McNerney, Boeing's CEO at the time, told Wall Street that the tanker program would make money in the long run based on anticipated foreign sales and contracted maintenance work. It was a "tell" that the initial contract for 179 tankers would be a money-loser, though nobody could predict just how costly the program would prove to be.

Boeing also appeared to misjudge foreign sales. While the Air Force clearly was the biggest market for tankers, North Atlantic Treaty Organization (NATO) allies and other countries were also buyers. Japan and Italy were already in the Boeing camp, having purchased KC-767s. Israel was also a solid Boeing customer. But Airbus won over every other country: France and Germany (no surprise there); the UK, the Netherlands, Australia, Saudi Arabia, the United Arab Emirates, Singapore, South Korea, and others. Through 2024, Airbus sold sixty-one MRTTs. In 2024, Airbus announced that future MRTTs would be based on the A330-800, the upgraded version of the -200 model, which has newer engines and a revised wing for better fuel economy.

The Biden Administration Pentagon said that it was going to consider a procurement for a follow-on tanker order, but it was unclear whether there would be a competition. Initially, it said yes. Then it said no, it would be a sole-source procurement of more KC-46s (as the revised KC-767 was named). Then it said no, it would wait for an advanced tanker of an entirely new design.

The Trump Administration hasn't yet said what it plans to do regarding tanker procurement.

As for the controversial reliance by Boeing on trade complaints, this is a story of its own.

5

Trade Complaints at the WTO

"Subsidies to Airbus—now a successful and profitable company—
must cease."

—HARRY STONECIPHER, CEO OF THE BOEING COMPANY, OCTOBER 6, 2004

THE BOEING COMPANY'S NARRATIVE blaming Airbus's success and its own loss of market share on "illegal subsidies" isn't entirely without merit. But it's overstated and is a classic case of playing the victim while not taking responsibility for one's own shortcomings. There is no question that Airbus had sweetheart deals with its member governments, whether at the federal or local level. The World Trade Organization (WTO) eventually found that Airbus had illegally benefited from subsidies in the amount of $7.5 billion. The WTO also found that Boeing had benefited through illegal funding and tax-benefit schemes to the tune of more than $4 billion.

Boeing persuaded the Office of the United States Trade Representative (USTR) to file a complaint with the WTO in 2004. Airbus persuaded the European Union (EU) to file a counter-complaint a few months later. The WTO issued its findings in 2017, the first year of the first Trump Administration. After more years of back and forth, including imposition of tariffs by both sides, the Biden Administration in its first year (2021) and the EU agreed to suspend tariffs and turn their attention to China's funding of state-owned COMAC, which was in flight testing for the C919, a competitor to the A320 and the 737. However, in the remainder of the Biden Administration, no visible action toward filing a formal complaint with the WTO had been taken by either the United States or the EU.

When Trump assumed office again in 2025, the WTO case officially remained suspended, twenty-one years after the USTR first filed the complaint. But the trade dispute at issue didn't actually start in 2004. The true date of the beginning of the conflict went back more than a decade.

An international agreement called the General Agreement on Tariffs and Trade (GATT) was reached in 1992. It emanated out of discussions at the United Nations. The purpose of the pact, the agreement stated, was to have a "substantial reduction of tariffs and other trade barriers and the elimination of preferences, on a reciprocal and mutually advantageous

Subject: Fwd: RE: RE: Question for Aug
    23 Town Hall Meeting
From: "Piasecki, Nicole W" <nicole.w.
    piasecki@boeing.com
To: "'Donald Shuper'" ---Cc: "Mulally,
    Alan" <alan.mulally@boeing.com
Subject: RE: RE: Question for Aug 23
    Town Hall Meeting
Date: Thu, 7 Nov 2002 18:53:17 -0800
Don,
Our strategy is to help the ailing
airline industry become healthy and
profitable again so that we can
stimulate demand for new Boeing
aircraft.
Because most of the US airlines
operate a mixed fleet of Boeing and
Airbus products, a Countervailing Duty
(CVD) or Antidumping tariff would
result in further negative impact
to our own customers who fly Boeing
aircraft as well as Airbus. We believe
this puts Boeing at higher risk for
additional cancellation of Boeing
aircraft deliveries than we already
experiencing from a very fragile
marketplace. And unprofitable airlines
do not order aircraft. To that end we
advised SPEEA that filing a case at
that time was not in the best interest
of the Boeing Company nor the aviation
industry.
Having said that, it is our
obligation to ensure Boeing's overall
competitiveness. We are committed
to achieving a rules-based trade
system with the Europeans that does
not advantage them and are taking
necessary actions to achieve this.
It is unacceptable that Airbus, who
will likely be the industry leader
in deliveries next year, is receiving
government support of up to 33% to
develop a new aircraft that is not
otherwise commercially viable.
For your information, Mr Rudy de Leon
will visit Seattle on November 18th to
discuss this topic further with SPEEA.
Nicole
Nicole Piasecki
Boeing Commercial Airplane

basis." The 1992 GATT agreement limited the amount of subsidies Airbus and Boeing could obtain from governments, whether federal or local.

The agreement was a compromise. Subsidies to Airbus (and those to other manufacturers) were limited to one-third of launch expenses. It wasn't long before complaints resurfaced, mostly from Boeing and McDonnell Douglas (MDC, then a separate entity), since Airbus was eating into their market shares (primarily at the expense of MDC). When Airbus was talking about developing a "very large aircraft" that eventually emerged as the A380, Boeing's president (he wasn't yet CEO) Phil Condit warned Airbus that if it proceeded, Boeing would file a formal complaint about the illegal subsidies Airbus received before the giant airplane program and, undoubtedly, subsidies associated with the A380. At the time, this threat turned out to be an empty one. Airbus launched the big airplane without any formal complaint being made.

Don Shuper was a Boeing employee and a member of the engineers union, the Society of Professional Engineering Employees in Aerospace (SPEEA). Even today, Shuper complains that Boeing could have, and should have, filed formal complaints back then. He believes Boeing's failure to do so enabled Airbus to grow into a viable competitor that saw MDC disappear into Boeing and the demise of Lockheed's commercial ambitions.

A 2002 email (reproduced at left) that Shuper provided from Nicole Piasecki, senior vice president of marketing and business strategy in Boeing's Commercial Airplane Division, addressed to him, which was copied to Alan Mulally, CEO of Boeing Commercial Airplanes (BCA) at the time, succinctly sums up Boeing's position. Shuper and SPEEA had been pushing Boeing for years to ask the U.S. government to file a countervailing duty (CVD) complaint under the GATT. Piasecki's email was dated not quite one year after 9/11. U.S. airlines were still struggling to recover from the devastating effects of that terrorist attack.

De Leon was Boeing's vice president of government relations in Washington, DC.

By 2004, things had changed. Condit was gone because of the procurement scandal over the 2001 leasing agreement between the U.S. Air Force and Boeing for 100 aerial-refueling tankers (see Chapter 4). Allegations of illegal subsidies to Airbus played a big part in the tanker competition. But this was the sideshow to the main event at the WTO.

It's a complex subject that could fill a couple of books. It's mind-numbing and would easily make a reader's eyes glaze over. But it's an important part of the Airbus-Boeing story. Throughout the history of the trade war, the antagonists were identified in the media and political circles as Airbus and Boeing. This is certainly true, but legally, the complainants are the United States (through the USTR) and the EU. For ease of discussion, this chapter will refer to Airbus and Boeing rather than the EU and the USTR, except when distinctions are needed.

In 2004, Boeing was also caught up in a trade-secret theft scandal after hiring key people from Lockheed. After Jim McNerney succeeded Stonecipher as CEO in 2005 following yet another scandal, this one involving a sex dalliance between Stonecipher and a subordinate, Boeing paid $615 million in penalties to the government to resolve the tanker and trade-secret theft scandals. At the time, it was a record fine.[23]

By 2004, Airbus' A330 had pretty much run the 767 out of the passenger-aircraft market. The A340, while not much of a threat, was the only Airbus product competing directly with the 777. Although it entered service a few years ahead of the 777-200, the four-engine A340 had nearly 300 orders by the end of 2004, compared with 500 for the 777. Boeing viewed those 300 orders in the context of illegal subsidies. The 777-300ER entered service in 2004. Its success drove the A340 out of business; production ceased in 2011.

There's no doubt that the trade complaint rallied members of Congress to Boeing's side as the tanker scandal unfolded. But the history of Boeing grievances over Airbus subsidies was long and well-established.

Boeing did much of the legwork for the USTR before the complaint was filed with the WTO, and probably most of it thereafter. Areas of interest

---

23. When it was discovered that Boeing could deduct the fine from its income taxes, some members of Congress objected. Boeing said it would not do so.

included subsidies provided by Airbus "member states" France, Germany, Spain, and the UK.[24] In addition, aid from local jurisdictions (state and local governments in U.S. parlance) was identified as suspect.

Outright financial contributions were the basis of Boeing's biggest grievance. Boeing and the USTR called these illegal subsidies under WTO rules. Airbus called them permissible Reimbursable Launch Investment (RLI) funds under the 1992 GATT agreement. RLI was limited to 33 percent of a program's cost. While disputing the legalities of RLI, Boeing argued that Airbus exceeded the one-third limit as well. Tax breaks, land grants, favorable rents, and other financial benefits offered by federal and local jurisdictions also came under complaint from Boeing. Every program Airbus had ever launched, from the A300 through the A380, was identified and included in the complaint.[25]

Boeing, which engaged in an aggressive media and political campaign, calculated that the total benefit to Airbus over the programs in which it took part exceeded $100 billion, a figure most considered to be preposterous. Boeing arrived at the number by taking commercial interest rates (as opposed to the lower, favorable rates granted by member-state governments) and multiplying them over the years.

Airbus responded by pointing out that it had paid royalties on the airplanes it produced. Critics pointed out that these royalties were paid only after the break-even point was reached on a given airplane program. Break-even points are highly guarded secrets. Generally, but not always, 400 sales were considered break-even in the world of aircraft manufacturers.[26] At the time, most observers concluded that the only program on which Airbus paid royalties was the A320.

Airbus's A300/310 programs eventually sold a total of 816 aircraft, but individually, did each cross that break-even threshold? The A340 is widely agreed to have been a loss-making venture for Airbus, but cost allocation

---

24. The UK wasn't a formal partner in the Airbus Industries *groupement d'intérêt économique* (GIE, a type of organization), but it did provide aid to British company BAE Systems, which made the wings in Broughton, Wales.

25. Airbus's A350 had not been launched when Boeing's WTO complaint was filed in 2004. The A350 was launched at the Paris Air Show in 2005. Despite the WTO complaint, Airbus obtained another round of RLI for the A350. Airbus disclosed this in its 2005 annual report. The amount was modest compared with funds received for other programs. Trade publication *Leeham News* found the detail in the footnotes of the annual report and published the number. The information disappeared from the next year's annual report. The A350's launch aid would become the subject of follow-on complaints by Boeing and the USTR.

26. That was then. Today, the break-even tends to be more than 1,000 aircraft.

can be a tricky thing. By the end of 2004, Airbus had delivered 329 A330s. As a co-program with the A340, was the A330 a profitable enterprise yet? By 2004, the A380 was still in development, so clearly it was not a profitable effort.

The Airbus counter-complaint was filed six months after Boeing's complaint, in October 2004.

In addition to the litany of similar government subsidies that Airbus claimed went to Boeing, the EU claimed that Boeing improperly benefited on the commercial side from research and development programs for defense and NASA. Of note, Airbus claimed that $3.2 billion in tax breaks that Washington state granted Boeing for the final assembly line at Boeing's Everett plant were illegal.[27] Tax breaks granted to Boeing by Kansas and Illinois were also among those pointed out by Airbus.

Boeing bitterly complained that Airbus sold aircraft at a loss and that financing also played a major role in sales, inferring that below-market financing deals (fueled by government subsidies to Airbus) enabled sales that Boeing couldn't afford. Financing certainly played a big role, but Boeing did more customer financing than Airbus, a legacy of the McDonnell Douglas Finance Corporation inherited by Boeing in the companies' 1997 merger. Airbus successfully resold nearly all its customer debt on the secondary markets, while Boeing shifted much of its debt to subsidiary Boeing Capital Corporation (BCC).

Consequently, when the airline industry in the U.S. (and elsewhere to some extent) sank into financial chaos post-9/11, Airbus had limited financial exposure while BCC had several very sick airlines to deal with, with billions of dollars of exposure. Boeing also stepped up to finance virtually every 717, a legacy of the MDC-bred MD-95. As an "orphan" airplane (that is, not part of a family of airplanes like the 737), few financiers were willing to lend money against the aircraft. Thus, BCC's largest financial exposure at one point was to relatively tiny AirTran Airways, which ultimately took delivery of eighty-six MD-95/717s.

Airbus initially had a great deal of financial exposure to United Airlines (for the A319/A320) and US Airways (for the A319/A320 and the A330). But Airbus resold this debt, as it did earlier with American Airlines financings (for the A300-600R). When these three carriers went through financial turmoil in 2002 and 2003, Airbus only had a few million dollars of exposure for things like spare parts. Investors who bought the airplane debt had to deal with bankruptcies and consensual restructurings.

---

27. The WTO eventually agreed. Despite being found illegal, in 2013 these tax breaks were extended in the amount of $8.3 billion to land the 777X wing plant and final assembly line at Everett.

The WTO found that subsidies allowed Airbus to offer low prices on its planes, thereby defeating Boeing sales campaigns. One example was a campaign with Europe's easyJet, which had been a Boeing customer but had switched to Airbus. There were other examples cited by the WTO as well. The WTO also found that subsidies to Boeing allowed the company to win sales at Airbus's expense.

Boeing often accuses Airbus of offering uneconomical deals to win an order. In doing so, Boeing speaks with a forked tongue. The so-called exclusive contracts that Boeing struck with American, Continental, and Delta to buy only Boeing planes for twenty years were done at prices that probably allowed little profit.[28] The deals were done to preserve Boeing's market share. When MDC thought it had won an order from Scandinavia's SAS to launch the MD-95, Boeing countered with the 737-600 at a price undercutting the MD-95's price of $18 million or less. Every 737-600 delivered to SAS cost Boeing money.[29]

One agreement that came out of the USTR WTO complaint was that, going forward, launch aid to Airbus had to be made on arm's-length commercial terms. Boeing and the USTR continue to assert that launch aid in any form is illegal, but as of this writing, no new complaint has been filed with the WTO over launch aid provided since the original ruling.

Boeing hardly approached this subject with clean hands either.

Boeing's cross-pollination between its 707 and its C/KC-135, its Stratoliner and its B-17, and its Stratocruiser and its B-29/B50, as well as its C-5 research and its 747 program, helped boost the company's commercial division. Composite experience on the B-2 bomber aided Boeing's Commercial Airplanes division and its 787 program. Long before Airbus was even a gleam in someone's eye, Boeing fed at the taxpayer trough. Bill Boeing threatened to move from Seattle to California unless the city built him an airport. (It's called Boeing Field.) In 1996, Boeing announced that it would offer the V-22 Osprey, a Marine helicopter developed jointly with Bell Textron Inc., for commercial use. This troubled chopper, which was then roughly $1 billion over budget, was developed entirely with government money.

Five years later, in 2001, Boeing proposed a complex program to keep its C-17 production line alive. The plane, then priced at $200 million, was designed as the successor to the Air Force's C-5. Boeing would offer it to

---

28. American CEO Robert Crandall famously said of the deal, "I don't care what it costs Boeing. I only care what it costs me."

29. In fairness, however, this was before the Boeing-MDC merger. Prior to the merger, Boeing indeed placed great importance on market share. After the merger, the John McDonnell–Harry Stonecipher view of shareholder value became more important than market share, a view with which a great many people would not take issue.

airlines for $170 million with a guarantee that the planes would be used 20 percent of the time by the armed services. (How Boeing could have guaranteed this utilization was left unsaid.)

When Boeing was in the early stages of developing the 757, in the late 1970s, it negotiated with BAE Systems to have that firm take a developmental role in the production of the airplane. Among the elements under consideration at the time would have been a subsidy to BAE by the British government. Also, with Rolls-Royce (RR) in contention to become the lead engine supplier for the 757, the British government also was geared up to provide a subsidy to RR.[30] It seems that Boeing wasn't above accepting government subsidies when they involved Boeing airplane development.

Asked about the subject years later, Phil Condit told me that Boeing would be remiss not to take advantage of tax breaks and government largesse.

A more overt and direct government subsidy appeared in the competition among states to land the assembly site for Boeing's new 7E7 airliner, which was intended to replace the company's 757 and 767 models. The state of Washington offered a $3.2 billion tax break to Boeing to keep the site in the state; the WTO eventually found this to be an illegal subsidy. Kansas offered a $500 million taxpayer-funded bond package, Texas anted up $265 million, and about twenty other states offered various tax-funded incentives. The Japanese government funded the so-called "Japanese Heavies," Mitsubishi and other industrial partners on the 7E7 program, with billions of dollars.[31]

A 2010 study by the Institute for Wisconsin's Future, entitled *Boeing's Cash Cow*, detailed how Boeing watered at the taxpayer trough all over the country, seeking tax breaks and other financial incentives.

A definitive figure never was revealed, but local press added up the state and local incentives that South Carolina and the greater Charleston area offered Boeing to locate the second 787 final assembly line there: nearly $1 billion. The Export-Import Bank of the United States (EXIM) was often called "Boeing's Bank" because most of its funding went to support the sale of Boeing airplanes.

This isn't to say that Airbus hasn't continued to seek financial incen-

---

30. The source for this piece of interesting history is Howard Banks' *The Rise and Fall of Freddie Laker* (Faber and Faber, 1982).

31. In its complaint against Boeing, the EU (Airbus) did not list the Japanese subsidies. Airbus had a small market share in Japan and dearly wanted to sell the giant A380 and the A350 to Japan Air Lines and All Nippon Airways, thus it kept quiet about the subsidies for fear of offending Japan by dragging it into the WTO case. The 7E7 competition stands as a clear example of how Boeing benefited from government subsidies.

tives outside of the WTO cases. The city of Mobile, Alabama, and the state of Alabama offered more than a quarter billion dollars to support the construction of a final assembly line for the production of Airbus's A320. Just as Boeing had EXIM at its disposal, Airbus had several European Credit Agencies (ECAs) on its side. While Boeing had the one bank, Airbus had ECAs from the UK, France, and Germany to support sales of its airplanes.

Of a more esoteric nature, the WTO in 2000 ruled that a tax scheme called Foreign Sales Corporations (FSCs, pronounced "Fisks") amounted to an unfair tax break for Boeing and was therefore an unfair subsidy. The ruling also applied to Microsoft and scores of other companies, including U.S. and non-U.S. airlines alike, the latter financing Boeing aircraft using FSCs. (Non-U.S. airlines finance planes through U.S. companies that take advantage of the FSC tax structure.) The structure is complex, but basically, a U.S. company, such as a bank or airline, creates a company in a tax haven like the Cayman Islands. The machinery, an airplane or something else, is owned by this foreign sales corporation and tax benefits flow to the parent company of the FSC. The savings can be substantial.

The WTO ruled that FSCs, since they applied only to U.S. companies, amounted to unfair competition to European companies (like Airbus) and ordered the U.S. to close this loophole. The propriety of a supra-national body ordering a country to change its laws is a debate for another time and another place. However, the WTO did nothing about French and German tax laws that are used solely for the benefit of Airbus, although the monies involved with these were relatively minor compared to the amounts involved in FSCs.

In the arcane world of aircraft finance, there is the leveraged lease. Japan at one point was a leading player in this market. The U.S. uses these leases, as do France and Germany. In the U.S., any airliner may be financed using a leveraged lease. In France, only Airbuses, turboprops manufactured by ATR (a French-Italian company), and the Boeing 737-300 and -900 series (the latter only because the engines are built by a 50-percent-French-owned company) can be financed using leveraged leases. In Germany, only Airbuses can be financed by leveraged leases. This is the sort of protectionism that the WTO is supposed to redress but doesn't, putting Boeing at a disadvantage.

Airbus and Boeing occasionally trade charges of government interference in the free marketplace. Both are probably right on this one, but so what? Boeing has groused that European governments will award coveted airport slots to airlines that order Airbus products. Airbus complains that U.S. government officials strong-arm governments that benefit from U.S. foreign aid on behalf of Boeing. Boeing claims that the French government does the same thing. But, as a former Airbus official pointed out, if you were a developing-country official, would you be more impressed by pressure to buy aircraft from the U.S. or from France?

In 2012, Wikileaks published secret U.S. diplomatic cables revealing that the U.S. Department of Commerce and the president of the U.S. lobbied foreign governments to buy Boeing aircraft. This was reported by some to be a scandal. However, aren't Commerce and the president supposed to promote U.S. business interests? The French, British, and German governments do the same thing—and they do it better than the U.S. government.

Against this backdrop and that of the tanker competition, Boeing convinced the U.S. government to renounce the 1992 GATT agreement governing subsidies. Airbus offered several times to negotiate (technically, the EU representative suggested the times), but Boeing (technically, the USTR) demanded that Airbus first give up subsidies before negotiations could occur. This was a non-starter; in fact, Boeing had no desire to negotiate. So, Airbus (the EU) filed its own complaint with the WTO.

The entire process is ridiculous. The WTO can conclude whatever it wants, but it has no enforcement powers. And parties to the complaints aren't bound to honor them. The WTO can authorize the aggrieved party, or parties, to impose tariffs if the offending party (or parties) don't comply with a WTO ruling to remedy the issue. But the imposition of a tariff is optional, and, more bizarrely, a tariff doesn't have to be applied to the product or even the industry at issue. This means, in the case of Airbus versus Boeing, that the U.S. doesn't have to impose tariffs on Airbus products, nor does Europe have to do the same on Boeing airplanes. Tariffs may be imposed on *any* industry. Europe could impose tariffs on U.S. cars, apples, clothes, electronics, or anything else. Likewise, the U.S. could impose tariffs on French wines, German beer, and so on.

The WTO previously found that Canada and Brazil had violated WTO rules when it came to export financing support for Bombardier and Embraer airplanes. But neither country imposed any penalty on the other's industries or imports, and life moved on.

The WTO previously found the U.S. to be in violation of WTO rules with respect to FSC tax breaks. Congress changed the law, but the WTO found the changes illegal, too. Airbus (the EU) claimed that Boeing was still benefitting from the FSC rules, or at least had not remedied the offense, when it filed its complaint that Boeing benefitted from illegal subsidies from the U.S. Defense Department and NASA, as well as from state and local tax breaks and other incentives.

Fifteen years after the USTR filed its complaint, the WTO finally authorized the U.S. to levy tariffs against the EU. The U.S. was authorized to levy up to $7.5 billion in tariffs, at a rate of up to 100 percent on EU products, including Airbus airplanes. The WTO determined that Airbus and the EU had not cured violations relating to the A380 and A350 aid.

By then, in 2019, Donald Trump was president of the U.S. Having made unfair trade practices against the U.S. a centerpiece of his 2016 presidential campaign, Trump's administration in October of that year levied a 10 percent tariff on Airbus airplanes imported into the U.S. The A320 family of airplanes assembled in Alabama were exempt. (Perhaps not coincidentally, Alabamans consistently provided Trump with his highest approval ratings.)

With most of 2019 over by the time the Trump Administration levied tariffs, there were few imports affected. Only $22 million was collected from Airbus.[32] The balance of the $277 million collected in connection with the WTO case was from other industries from nearly thirty EU member states. The tariff was increased to 15 percent in March 2020.

The WTO in the fall of 2019 authorized the EU to begin levying tariffs on Boeing airplanes, and on other U.S. goods, for a total of up to more than $4 billion. The EU imposed a 15 percent tariff on Boeing aircraft, effective November 15—just days before the FAA lifted a grounding order on the MAX and recertified the airplane.

Boeing, hoping to head off tariffs, in February 2020 asked the Washington State Legislature to void the tax breaks adopted for its 787 and 777X models. It did so in April, and Boeing predictably crowed that it now was in compliance with the WTO rulings.[33] Airbus followed a few months later by making changes to its A350 RLI, claiming that it was now in compliance with WTO rulings. Boeing pointed to the A380 and said that the illegal subsidies had not been cured. Airbus previously said that because it was terminating its A380 program, compliance was no longer required. There were still the matters of the Kansas and FSC tax breaks to address, and the WTO had to review Washington state's action and decide whether compliance was achieved. In the meantime, the EU could impose tariffs.

---

32. Scott Hamilton, "US Imposed $22m in Airbus Tariffs in 2019," *Leeham News and Analysis* (March 3, 2020), https://leehamnews.com/2020/03/04/us-imposed-22m-in-airbus-tariffs-in-2019/.

33. The question of whether there may have been another motive for discontinuing the tax breaks arose when, in July 2020, Boeing said that it would study whether to consolidate 787 production in South Carolina due to dropping demand for the airplane. If Boeing moved 787 production out of Washington, the tax breaks went away anyway under the terms of the company's agreement with the state. Scott Hamilton, "Pontifications: Did Boeing Telegraph Its Decision in February Consolidating 787 Production?" *Leeham News and Analysis* (Aug. 24, 2020), https://leehamnews.com/2020/08/24/pontifications-did-boeing-telegraph-its-decision-in-february-consolidating-787-production/.

6

Legacy Boeing's Last Hurrah

"Working Together."

—THE 777 FAMILY

IN 1985, AIRBUS, BOEING, AND MCDONNELL DOUGLAS (MDC) were planning for the next round of twin-aisle jets. Boeing toyed with the idea of building a larger 767. One concept included a partial double deck, but it was a very odd design. Instead of a 747-like hump at the front of the airplane, the upper deck began at about the wing and went aft. MDC considered a stretch of its DC-10 with initial working titles of Super 50, Super 60, etc. Airbus, still in the development phase on the A320, was already planning twin-aisle, two- and four-engine aircraft under the code names TA-6 and TA-7. These would become the A330 and A340.

Boeing's humpback 767 design was short-lived. It soon gave way to a wider twin-aisle, larger-capacity airplane that eventually became known as the 777. United Airlines was one of the leading contributors to Boeing's customer input process. The initial design became known as the 777-200. There was a shorter-range "A" model and a long-range "B" model. Both seated about 301 passengers in a mixed-seating configuration. The A model's range was 5,240 nautical miles (nm); the B model, which later was named the ER (for Extended Range), had a range of 7,065 nm. The planes' dimensions were identical.

One proposed feature for the 777 was the inclusion of folding wing tips to allow the plane to use some of the ramp and gate space of smaller widebody aircraft. Boeing eventually dropped the idea for weight-related and other reasons. But the idea would resurface decades later and become a key component for the next-generation 777.

Boeing was going to be last on the market with the 777. The MDC MD-11 and Airbus's four-engine A340 would precede the 777. The three-engine MD-11 was essentially a stretched DC-10 with new engines, a glass cockpit, and split winglets. Even with such features, however, when the airplane went into service with American Airlines, it was a big disappointment. American ordered MD-11s and planned a major overseas expansion from its prime hub at Dallas–Fort Worth Regional Airport (DFW). DFW, situated in north Texas in the southern-middle of the United States, presented range challenges for American's ambitions across the Pacific. When the airline received route authority from DFW to fly to Tokyo, for example, American's long-range DC-10-30s couldn't make the hop non-stop. The airline acquired two ex–TWA 747SPs for the route. As a shrink, the plane wasn't as efficient as the standard 747, but it could make the 6,500-mile trip non-stop.

The MD-11 was supposed to be able to make the trip from DFW to Hong Kong, but it burned more fuel than expected, and its actual range was less than its designed range. DFW–Hong Kong was out, and the economics on other long-haul routes within its reduced range strained airlines' ability to make these runs profitably. MDC worked diligently to make up for the shortfalls but, in the end, engineers couldn't recover 100 percent of the deficiencies. With MDC already on the decline, the shortcomings of the MD-11 didn't help sales. Eventually, only 200 MD-11s were sold.

Over at Airbus, super-salesman John Leahy did everything he could to jump on the MD-11's shortcomings. The third engine sitting on top of the MD-11's fuselage at the base of the tail was, he sniffed, just a big aerodynamic drag. Leahy's rhetoric was seen for what it was. But his company's A340 had its own problems, which were not insignificant: the plane was designed around the SuperFan engine that Rolls-Royce (RR) and Pratt & Whitney (P&W) ultimately killed, destroying the planned economics of the aircraft. Airbus executives met with P&W executives and pressured them unsuccessfully to reverse the decision. So, Airbus's next stop was CFM International, the 50-50 joint venture between GE and what was then known as Snecma (now Safran Aircraft Engines), a French company. The CFM 56 powered the re-engined MDC DC-8 Super 60 series (rebranded the -70) and the Boeing 737-300/-400/-500, later called the 737 Classic. It had been a monumental mistake by P&W to cede the 737 market from the original 737-100/200/200A models to the re-engining of the -300/-400/-500 series models. The Classic series put CFM on the map. Like an amoeba, CFM's dominance in the small jetliner market spread across the world. Airbus initially chose the CFM 56 to power the A320. International Aero Engines (IAE) later joined this market with its V2500 engine, but CFM products ruled.

When Airbus went to CFM, hat in hand, to power the A340 Glider, CFM exacted its pound of flesh. Airbus had no choice but to take it. The result was an airplane that was overweight to the power provided and slow compared with other trans-ocean airliners. Leahy, well after he retired in 2018, put it in his typically direct way: The A340 was prone to bird strikes from the rear. With four engines, maintenance costs were naturally higher. Fuel economy wasn't as good as some of its competitors, either.

Airbus tried mightily to overcome the A340's operational and economic disadvantages. In those days, ETOPS aircraft, and the Extended-Range Twin-Engine Operations Performance Standards (ETOPS) that applied to them, which were developed and implemented by the International Civil Aviation Organization (ICAO), were both still fairly new. Qualifying for ETOPS certification was complicated, and some of the less-sophisticated airlines found that doing so strained resources. A four-engine airplane didn't require the same level of training, support, and sophistication as other models did, so the A340 fit nicely into airlines' systems. The A340, being lighter than the 747 and with less restrictive engine-out performance than a twin-engine widebody airplane, also could serve challenging airports more easily. For example, South African Airways found the A340 a better fit for its hot environment than the early 777s. The A340 could operate out of the French/Dutch island of St. Maarten in the Caribbean, with its short runway and mountains near one end of the runway, more easily than the 747.

Airbus produced the A340 in four versions—the original -200, with its underpowered CFM engines; the -300, with an upgraded engine; the -500 ultra-long-haul model; and a stretched -600 version, the last two featuring RR engines. Nevertheless, Airbus sold only 377 A340 models, a poor showing but still better than the MD-11.

Boeing's 777, with its subsequent versions, proved an out-of-the-park winner. Only eighty-eight of the base model -200s were sold, with United Airlines being a principal customer. The longer-range -200ER saw 422 sales. The ultra-long-range -200LR, the same plane dimensionally as the -200 and the -200ER, added sixty-one sales. Boeing stretched the airplane into two versions of the -300: the base model and the extended-range -300ER. These typically models seated around 365 passengers in a mixed-class configuration. The base -300 traded a little range (about 100 nautical miles) for capacity. The -300ER recovered the original ranges and added about 300 nautical miles more. It proved the most popular model, with sales of 837 aircraft.

Even then, Boeing wasn't through. It took the -200LR and made a freighter out of it. As of 2025, the freighter was still in production, with a total of 321 orders. The 777LRF is to remain in production until 2027, when new noise and emissions regulations will render the model obsolete. The 777 became one of Boeing's best-selling jetliners of all time. Production peaked at a rate of 8.6 a month, a record for a widebody airplane up until then. The 777 and 737 carried Boeing's Commercial Airplanes division (BCA) through future industrial snafus with the 787 and the delays of the poor-selling 747-8.

The program manager for the 777 was Phil Condit. A lifetime Boeing employee and an engineer, Condit and former BCA CEO Alan Mulally are credited with ushering in a major transformation in the way Boeing designed airplanes. The 777 was Boeing's first computer-designed aircraft. Its entry into service (EIS) was in 1994. The 777's development budget of $6 billion ballooned to nearly $12 billion (about $25.95 billion in 2025 dollars). But the airplane's reliability and performance over the following decades was unmatched. So was its safety. The first 777 hull loss didn't happen until 2008, fourteen years after the plane's introduction, when a British Airways 777-200ER lost power in both engines on a short final approach to London's Heathrow Airport. Through marvelous piloting, the plane crash-landed short of the runway. There were no fatalities and only forty-seven injuries, most of them minor. The power failure was traced to a freak icing condition that blocked fuel to both of the plane's RR engines. The 777 itself came away with a rather enhanced reputation for its strength.

The second hull loss happened to a 777-200ER when a cockpit fire broke out while the plane was parked. There were no injuries, and the fire damage was such that the airplane was written off. A third hull loss occurred when an Asiana Airlines 777-300ER crashed on landing at the San Francisco airport. Pilot error was blamed. Although the plane split in two upon the crash landing and spun around before coming to rest, only three of the 310 people on board died. They were the first fatalities of a 777 accident.[34]

How did legacy Boeing succeed so spectacularly with the 777 Classic? The reason is ironic, considering the future criticism that would come Boeing's way on the very same topic: culture.

"I believe that it was primarily the culture that we built essentially for the program," Condit recalled in 2023 in an interview for this book. "I had an advantage. I was coming from being executive VP so I could pick my team for the Triple Seven. I had the experience with the 757 program. We learned a lot on the 757 program. For example, what I discovered on the 57 program was that while we had a really good core team when we started, the developmental team, when the program got authorized, engineers started coming on the program at 200 to 300 a week. The culture very quickly shifted to what I call a traditional culture, because the core team was the minority all of a sudden. Everybody, in my words, set up camp the way they had always set up camp.

"On the 777 reset, when people come on to the program, everybody goes through what we call boot camp. Everybody got introduced to the program and got introduced to the culture. We actually took the whole initial team

---

34. Two more 777 hull losses occurred, resulting in fatalities to all on board the planes: Malaysian Airlines flight 370, which mysteriously disappeared in the ocean near Australia on a flight from Indonesia to China, and another Malaysian 777, which was shot down in a mistaken combat action by Russia during fighting in Ukraine. There have been a couple more hull losses, but no passengers died in these other accidents.

offsite on a Saturday and spent a whole Saturday crafting an eleven-word mission statement for the program very, very carefully. Every word in that mission statement had a really important meaning."

This was in 1990. Condit remembered that the theme then was people working together to produce the preferred new airplane family. "The first word in there was 'people'. The whole program had a very strong focus on people, how important they were in the program, how critical they were to the program. 'Working together' became the buzz phrase, if you will, for the program." Boeing had a tradition of putting a pilot's name under a plane's flight deck window on the left side, and a co-pilot's name on the right side of the airplane. At the time, "Working Together" was printed under the left side of each cockpit window.

"It was people working together," Condit recalled. "Working together to produce. We had a great, long debate. Not surprisingly, the engineers said it ought to be 'design.' The factory guys said it ought to be 'built.' The support people said, 'Well, how do we get it there?' The word[s] we settled on w[ere] 'to produce.' It included design, build, all of the pieces together. Next, 'the preferred.' We had another debate. We were looking at one, at the word[s] 'quality,' 'performance,' 'customer satisfaction.'"[35]

As with other Boeing 7-Series airplanes, with the exception of the 757, the 777 was going to be a new airplane family. "That was very intentional," Condit said. "We looked at a lot of derivatives that had potential for that program. [The 777] really changed the world. The whole program was designed with the intent that there would be a family of airplanes. We talked about that mission statement with everybody who came on the program, what it meant, why were we doing it. We said, for example, that 'working together' wasn't just internal, it was external. It meant that working together, we would work together with suppliers. We were going to work together with airlines. We actually had airlines on the team."

Condit's description of "working together" at all levels, internally and externally, is a marked contrast to how things evolved at Boeing over the next thirty-plus years, when confrontations with labor, suppliers, and even customers became the rule rather than the exception.

The 777 program was launched in October 1990. The original 777 entered service in June 1995. The highly successful 777-300ER, in 2004. The 777 "Classic" was the last airplane designed and developed by Boeing before its 1997 merger with MDC. In many respects, the 777-300ER was probably the best airplane Boeing ever designed. Through 2024, more

---

35. In 2024, when Kelly Ortberg was named by Boeing's board of directors to succeed departing CEO David Calhoun, Ortberg began using the phrase "working together" when meeting with employees.

than 1,700 of all sub-types had been delivered. As a widebody airplane, the 777-300ER paled in comparison to the 737. The company's 787 model had higher gross sales. But unlike the troubled 737 and 787 programs, the 777 Classic proved to be a superb program.

It was legacy Boeing's last hurrah.

PART 2

THE DECLINE

"A lot of GE leaders were thought to be business geniuses. But they were just cost cutters. You can't cost cut your way to prosperity."

—BILL GEORGE, FORMER CEO, MEDTRONIC

7

The GEntrification of Boeing

gen·tri·fi·ca·tion / ˌjentrəfəˈkāSHən /

NOUN: GENTRIFICATION; **PLURAL NOUN**: GENTRIFICATIONS
THE PROCESS WHEREBY THE CHARACTER OF A POOR URBAN AREA IS CHANGED
BY WEALTHIER PEOPLE MOVING IN, IMPROVING HOUSING, AND ATTRACTING
NEW BUSINESSES, TYPICALLY DISPLACING CURRENT INHABITANTS IN THE
PROCESS.

"GENTRIFICATION is a nuanced phenomenon along these characteristics, but most people engaged in any gentrification fail to acknowledge the nuances." (*Business Insider*, August 17, 2014.)

Gentrification is normally associated with changing neighborhoods. But change a few words here and there in the definition above, and it may be argued that this is the type of influence that the General Electric Corporation had on Boeing beginning in 1996 and continuing for the next twenty-eight years, when events converged to bring down an American icon. The GEntrification of The Boeing Company began to become visible within months of the company's 1997 merger with the McDonnell Douglas Corporation (MDC). In reality, the process began the year before the merger.

It's an article of faith among legacy Boeing employees, their families, and thousands of others that the merger of Boeing and MDC was really a takeover of Boeing by MDC. The thinking continues that MDC took over Boeing with Boeing's money, although this was a stock deal. Shareholder value rose to the top under the influence of MDC executives after the merger, displacing the engineering culture at Boeing.

It's conventional wisdom that Boeing's decline is the fault of Harry Stonecipher and, by extension, Phil Condit. It was Condit, after all, who was CEO of Boeing when MDC was acquired and who brought Stonecipher in as president and chief operating officer. Everything that followed happened because of these events, legacy Boeing employees and others believe. There's certainly some truth to this—but it's not the whole truth. Any CEO after Stonecipher could have plotted a different course than the one established by Stonecipher. He was officially the number two in the corporate hierarchy to Condit, who remained CEO and chairman following the merger.

Without diminishing Condit's culpability (if you want to call it that) in pursuing the merger with MDC and leaving Stonecipher to run day-to-day operations, Condit was viewed by some as ill-suited for the role of overseeing daily operations. His strength lay in the fact that he was a visionary. It's hard to criticize him for the mergers that occurred under his tenure (with MDC, with Rockwell Aerospace's defense and aerospace units, with Hughes Aircraft Company's Space and Communications Group, and others). The decision to expand Boeing's military business was a sound one.

Whatever criticism is leveled at Condit, it is only a piece of the puzzle. In the end, Boeing's board of directors must bear some of the responsibility. Board members approved the MDC merger. Board members appoint C-Suite officers (that is, top-level corporate management). Board members approve the nominations of other board members.

With a lifetime of service at GE and under Jack Welch—who was GE's CEO for twenty years—during the twilight of his career there, Stonecipher was clearly an advocate of cost cutting to boost profits and shareholder value. After going to the Sundstrand Corporation in 1984 and becoming its president and CEO in 1989, he moved to MDC in 1994. Stonecipher asked MDC's Douglas Aircraft unit to assess how the company might become competitive again in the three-way competition between itself, Airbus, and Boeing. Studies were undertaken and after about eighteen months, Stonecipher said that it would take S15 billion (nearly $32 billion in 2025 dollars) to get MDC back in the game. That was a non-starter for the McDonnell family, who never understood the commercial aircraft business and had little interest in it. By the time the merger with Boeing was announced in 1996, Douglas Aircraft Corporation was a shadow of its former self.

As part of the merger, MDC got the right to name one-third of the expanded Boeing board for the combined companies. As a result, Stonecipher's GE influence and the McDonnells' lack of understanding of the commercial sector entered the C-Suite on East Marginal Way, across from Boeing Field, where the company's headquarters were at the time. Stonecipher came aboard as president and COO, running day-to-day operations while Condit focused on the Big Picture. As will be detailed in the pages that follow, Stonecipher began upending Boeing's culture as an engineering company and converting it to one focused on financial returns. "When people say I changed the culture of Boeing, that was the intent, so that it's run like a business rather than a great engineering firm," Stonecipher famously (or infamously) said. Stonecipher was president only a few years before he retired. But he returned after Condit resigned in connection with a tanker scandal (chronicled in Chapter 4). He would last only fifteen months before he, too, resigned over a scandal (an affair with a Boeing officer).

Boeing's board in 1995—the last year before the merger with MDC was proposed—was filled mostly with old men (there was one woman) and with two insiders, Frank Shrontz and Condit. The average board member's age was nearly 65. The board's composition was largely unchanged in 1996, when Shrontz was elevated to Boeing's Chairman Emeritus and Condit was now firmly in control as chairman, president, and CEO. Including Condit and Shrontz, 50 percent of the members on the ten-person board were from the Seattle area. Another member was from Chicago, one from Detroit, and one from Boston. There wasn't a person with a GE background on the board then. It was this board that approved the MDC merger (see the Appendix).

John McDonnell and Stonecipher joined Boeing's board upon the consummation of the merger in August 1997. They became, respectively, the first- and second-largest individual stockholders in Boeing. John Biggs, the chairman of the Teachers Insurance and Annuity Association (TIAA), and Ken Duberstein, chairman of his own company, joined at the same time. They migrated from the MDC board to Boeing's board. Duberstein served in the Reagan White House, so his political connections were probably well received at Boeing. William Perry, the former Defense Secretary under President Clinton, joined the board in November 1997. With Duberstein a high-profile Republican and Perry a high-profile Democrat, Boeing was well represented in Washington political circles. Thus began the slow shift from a Seattle-centric board of directors to one with key political connections that came to dominate future boards.

The board debated throughout 2003 about whether to launch its first new airplane (the 787) since the 777's launch in October 1990 and entry into service (EIS) in 1994. Development costs for the 777 were two times over budget. This fact hung heavily over the board's debate on whether to go forward with the 787. The pernicious neglect of the Douglas Aircraft Company by the McDonnells following the two companies' 1967 merger also hung heavily in the air. The aviation industry seriously doubted whether the McDonnell-influenced Boeing board would greenlight a new airplane program.

Condit's influence had been diminished after the MDC merger as he handed authority for day-to-day operations to Stonecipher. After the tanker scandal referenced above erupted, Condit offered to resign. The offer was initially declined. He finally did so in December 2003.

There were plenty who doubted that Stonecipher would launch a new airplane. Pointing to Stonecipher's two years at MDC as "proof" that such doubts were warranted is probably unfair. MDC by then was already down to a single-digit market share. Selling the faltering company to anybody was already in the cards, and Boeing came out the winner. But Stonecipher was crucial in demanding that the industrial model for the 787 be outsourced at unprecedented levels compared to Boeing's usual practices. Financial risk was to be shared. Instead of following a build-to-print process, partners were assigned design-and-build responsibilities. Boeing failed to backstop the plan with its own oversight, leading ultimately to tens of billions of dollars in cost overruns and three and a half years of delays. Despite a white paper warning how similar practices at MDC had failed, and despite a warning by Boeing board member Jim McNerney about an overemphasis on cost cutting, Stonecipher forged ahead. The result was an industrial disaster.[36]

After Condit resigned, many believed that Stonecipher's return would doom the 787. But within a month, Stonecipher approved its launch, announcing the go-ahead in December 2003. (The official launch came the following April, with an order of fifty planes from Japan's All Nippon Airways (ANA).) Stonecipher was but one vote on the board of directors, however; the entire board had to approve the airplane and its business model. It's true that a company's board of directors must rely on the expertise of the company's executives and relevant underlings before making what is presumed to be an informed decision. The ten-member Boeing board had three people with aerospace experience: John McDonnell, Stonecipher, and McNerney. A fourth member, John Shalikashvili, was the retired chairman of the U.S. Joint Chiefs of Staff. A four-star General in the Army, Shalikashvili knew his way around procurement. McDonnell and Stonecipher believed in massive outsourcing. McNerney, having worked with Jack Welch at GE, did, too. The board was briefed on the risks of the new industrial model. Alan Mulally, then the president of Boeing's Commercial Airplanes division (BCA), being the highly regarded engineer that he was, signed off on the industrial model. Mike Bair, who became the 787's program manager, was also on board. One can imagine that the board had little reason to doubt the program's soundness.

Industrial outsourcing was a prerequisite to launching the 787, says one person knowledgeable about the program's decision-making. And the direction of the program wasn't driven by Stonecipher alone—the push to outsource came from the board as well.

GE AND SHAREHOLDER VALUE

Shareholder value became, in the words of one critic, priorities Number 1, Number 2, and Number 3 at Boeing Headquarters and with the company's board of directors. Certainly, Stonecipher and the McDonnells—as the company's largest individual shareholders—pushed it. But so did Wall Street analysts and institutional investors, who can't see past their own portfolio numbers for the long-term, greater good. However, the term

---

36. Full details of this story are discussed in *Air Wars*.

"shareholder value" didn't just appear after Boeing's merger with MDC was announced. It also appeared in the company's federal Securities and Exchange Commission (SEC) filings before the merger was announced. And Stonecipher was in, then out, then in and out again before he could do the damage that was yet to come.

For all the fingers pointed at Stonecipher, it was Jim McNerney who doubled down on the GE influence. McNerney's impact far outweighed Stonecipher's. McNerney was Boeing's CEO for ten years, compared with Stonecipher's fifteen-month tenure as CEO, plus his four-year stint as president and chief operating officer under Condit.

That McNerney followed the GE handbook is not surprising. He spent a good portion of his professional career at GE, including in the executive ranks. He was one of the top three candidates considered by Jack Welch to be his successor. Welch's management policies were essentially all McNerney knew. And cost cutting, including battling unions, was one area for which "Neutron Jack" Welch was very well known.

When McNerney ascended to the CEO position in 2005, Boeing already was headed for trouble with the 787, though the magnitude couldn't be imagined at that point. Before long, McNerney was faced with a *requirement* that costs at Boeing had to be cut in the face of growing cost overruns on the 787. The 747-8, launched in November 2005 (just five months after McNerney became CEO), would eventually run into billion-dollar cost overruns and delays. Cost cutting became a must at the company.

None of this, however, takes away from McNerney's predilection in this area. Like Welch, McNerney laid off thousands of workers in the heavily unionized Seattle area and transferred jobs to non-union states or to contract workers. Thousands of engineering jobs were outsourced to Russia and India. He set out to break unions. Shareholder value in the form of stock buybacks and dividends were prioritized. When he became CEO, McNerney, according to some analysts, was given a directive to bring Boeing's share price up to $200. He didn't succeed by the time he retired ten years later.

Robert Spingarn, a Credit Suisse analyst at the time McNerney was CEO, observed in hindsight, "I think people have really jumped on this bandwagon, but it was a cash flow–driven, cost-takeout atmosphere. While you were watching it happen, you didn't necessarily recognize that this was going to come at the expense of engineering. We very quickly ended up with McNerney coming on board. I don't know if this is the GE element or not, but we very quickly ended up seeing Boeing changing the way it did things in a number of different dimensions. GE management style was something new for Boeing, which today you look back and say that's a mistake because of underinvestment.

"There were folks who felt that McNerney had underinvested in research and development at 3M [where he went after GE and before Boeing]. Some more of that was to come, and maybe that's the case. When I talk about multiple dimensions, this segues into that there were two critical decisions made regarding what was then the 7E7 and became [the] 787 that turned out to be problematic." Speaking in Boeing's voice, Spingarn said, "One was we're [Boeing] going to go all carbon fiber with this airplane for the first time on a major aircraft. At the same time, we're going to significantly change the design paradigm and we're going to outsource the majority of the aircraft and along with it, the majority of the design."

One retired Boeing official said that McNerney was a more astute businessman than Stonecipher. "Harry was, 'Beat it with a stick until it's dead, no matter what.' I think Jim was a lot more nuanced in how to approach things, but the other difference was that McNerney certainly had the same focus on financials that Harry thought he had. I'm not sure Harry really had it, but it was definitely a financial focus with McNerney." The GE influence was the financial bottom line. "That was the name of the game."

Dennis Muilenburg became president and COO of Boeing in December 2013 and succeeded McNerney in July 2015, adding Chairman and CEO titles. A Boeing lifer, Muilenburg was already considered a cost cutter during his leadership positions within Boeing's defense unit and as CEO of the Boeing Defense, Space & Security division. He eased relationships with the International Association of Machinists District 751 (IAM 751) union and with the Society of Professional Engineering Employees in Aerospace union (SPEEA) but continued with McNerney's cost-control policies and upped the game on shareholder value. Muilenburg appeared to be fully GEntrified.

On Boeing's third-quarter 2016 earnings call, Muilenburg said, "It's important again to reiterate the principle that Greg[37] mentioned, and that is we're very focused on making sure we're returning to cash to shareholders and investing for the future. Investment in the future organic investment continues to be important, too. Along with that, returning roughly 100 percent of free cash flow to our shareholders. A balanced approach between share repurchases and dividends continues to be important to us. You can see our track record on share repurchase. Over the last three years, we have also increased dividends by 125 percent . . . . We understand that there is significant value associated with dividend . . . . [Y]ou can rest assured that we're very committed to returning cash to our shareholders, and we consider dividends to be a very important part of that."

During the July 26, 2017, earnings call for the second quarter, Boeing's chief financial officer Greg Smith told analysts, "We continue to expect op-

---

37. The reference is to Greg Smith, Boeing's chief financial officer.

erating cash flow to grow annually through the end of the decade. And we remain committed to returning approximately 100 percent of free cash flow to investors."

Smith addressed the doubts that emerged even then about future investment. "When we look at uses of cash, we consistently see our priorities as being [the] first, most important use is organic investment. And we are making good use of that today. We are bringing more innovation to the marketplace today than we ever have. And that spans our entire business, not to leave out our defense business. It certainly includes things like the 787, the 737 MAX, 777X, but it also includes investments that we're making in programs like T-X, our satellites business, and the autonomous systems that we're developing. We are making organic investments across the board. That's still our number one use of cash. And that's with the purpose of out-innovating our competition."

Returning cash to stockholders was not the first priority, Smith said—something that consultant Richard Aboulafia often took issue with. He repeatedly criticized Boeing for spending too much on shareholder value and not enough on research and development.

"Secondly, we're going to continue to return cash to our shareholders," Smith said. "Approximately 100 percent of free cash flow being returned through [stock] repurchases and dividends continues to be our second priority."

In another call, Muilenburg said that following the years in which Boeing faced billions of dollars in cost overruns on the 787 and 747-8 programs, shareholders were patient. "Now was the time to reward them."[38]

Under McNerney, Boeing's stock peaked at about $151 per share. In the days before the Lion Air MAX accident on October 29, 2018 (detailed more fully in later chapters), the stock price under Muilenburg peaked at $386. The stock dipped slightly after the crash; it was not known at the time that there was a flaw in the MAX, and Lion Air's poor safety record was viewed as the most likely cause of the crash. By March 1 of the next year, the stock price hit $442 per share. Boeing's cash flow, stock buybacks, and dividends were on an upward trajectory. MAX production rates were fifty-two per month, and Boeing was gearing up to hit fifty-seven by year's end. 787 production was humming along and, aside from some delays in the 777X program identified mostly as issues with the giant GE9X engines, there was nothing to suggest this program was going through anything other than normal testing.

---

38. The 787 and 747-8 programs weren't the only ones with cost overruns across Boeing, but as the two highest-profile programs, these were the ones most often cited.

Jack Welch's shareholder-value-driven philosophy was alive and thriving at Boeing. Visions of $500 share prices were sugar plums dancing in heads on Wall Street.

And then the Ethiopian MAX crash happened on March 10, 2019. Even then, the company's stock price remained a little north or south of the mid-$300 range until the bottom fell out of the global economy when the COVID pandemic began in March 2020. The rest is history.

PLIANT DIRECTORS

In theory and legally, members of a company's board of directors are supposed to be representatives of the company's shareholders. They are also supposed to be checks on management. All too often, however, board members seem to be more about get-along, go-along, good-old-boys clubs than questioning overseers. In recent decades, interlocking relationships, where executives serve on each other's boards or sit on common boards, became a growing concern among corporate governance groups and (usually) minority shareholders. In the long era of Jack Welch and his influence over corporate America (usually couched as a good example to follow), director compensation soared while employees suffered job cuts, outsourcing, reduced pension and health care benefits, and stingy pay hikes. Boeing's board was no different.

Being a director of a Fortune 500 company is a prestigious position. It's also lucrative. In 1995, Boeing paid directors $36,000 a year ($75,000 in 2025 dollars); $10,000 was in stock. (The average wage for workers was $26,000 in 1996 according to the Social Security Administration.) There was also a "committee retainer" for all committee service. This was $10,000 a year for committee chairs and $6,000 for committee members. A daily per diem of $2,000 was paid for each day of attendance at a board meeting, and a $1,000 per diem was paid out on days a board meeting was not held. By 2021, the fees increased dramatically. Outside directors earned an annual cash retainer fee of $135,000, an increase of 275 percent of the 1995 numbers. (The average wage in 2021 was $60,575, a 133 percent increase since 1996, according to Social Security.) Additional fees were paid as follows, reported in Boeing's 2022 Proxy Statement; directors in leadership positions were paid on a pro-rated basis reflecting time in the position.

- Chair of board: $250,000;
- Aerospace Safety Committee Chair: $50,000;
- Audit Committee Chair: $25,000;
- Compensation, Governance and Public Policy, and Finance Committee Chairs: $20,000; and
- Special Programs Committee Chair: $15,000.

Outside directors could defer all of part of their cash compensation into stock and could elect at certain dates to take payouts in lump sums or defer payouts for up to fifteen years.

Boeing shifted from staggered three-year director terms to annual terms in 2006. Recommended by various corporate governance groups, one-year terms in theory avoid director entrenchment and make it easier to change board members. In practice, one- or three-year terms don't matter with respect to entrenchment. If a board recommends election or reelection, it's rare that a director is rejected. Institutional stockholders hold sway and, unless a board is deeply underwater, an insurgence is very rare though not unheard of. In fact, it can be argued that one-year terms make it easier to kick a pesky member off the board. Prestige and cushy money are great incentives to be a pliant board member.

Under harsh criticism for its board composition, Boeing by 2022 had changed out eight members who were in place in 2018 when the MAX crisis began.

But in 2018, this changed board was years in the future.

8

The Man from Berkeley

"He was probably one of those hippies."

—ONE OF PHIL CONDIT'S EXECUTIVES

PHIL CONDIT WAS BORN IN BERKELEY, CALIFORNIA, IN 1941. Among the colleges he attended was the University of California at Berkeley, from which he graduated in 1963. It was the beginning of the Flower Child era in the 1960s, and for many, Berkeley was its epicenter. How much influence this had on Condit's persona is anybody's guess. But one of Condit's future associates would point to this history when he critiqued Condit's performance as The Boeing Company's CEO.

Condit joined Boeing in 1965, working on the company's Super Sonic Transport (SST) proposal, an effort that was undertaken in response to the Concorde SST joint program between the UK's British Aircraft Corporation and France's Sud Aviation. He stayed with this program only a few years before moving on to the 747 program.

The SST at the time was the top prestige program at Boeing. The 747 was viewed by some as an interim passenger airplane situated between the 707 and the 2707, as the SST was named. The thinking at the time was that the 747 would become a freighter while passengers jet-setted at high speed around the globe in the SST. The 2707 program was so costly that Boeing received government funding to carry it out (an inconvenient truth that Boeing ignored when, two decades later, its officials began complaining about Airbus subsidies). In 1971, Congress cut funding and the SST was dead.

Ironically, in 2023, Condit told me that the SST was never going to be commercially viable. The Concorde was a 100-passenger aircraft catering to businesspeople. The 300-passenger 2707 was intended to serve both business flyers and leisure passengers. Economy fare–pricing would never support an SST, Condit said. At the time of our conversation, Condit was serving as an advisor to Boom SST, which was developing an eighty-eight-passenger business-oriented SST. Boom's concept was largely derided by industry, even though Japan Air Lines, American, and United (among others) signed letters of intent or highly conditional orders for the airplane. None of the established engine manufacturers would consider developing an engine for it. Boom cobbled together a three-member group to design an engine, but few were impressed.

In addition to the SST and 747 programs, Condit worked on the 727, 737, and 757 programs in various capacities. In 1986, he became executive vice president (EVP) and general manager (GM) of Boeing's Commercial Airplanes division (BCA) and EVP and GM of the 777 program. In 1992, Condit was named president of Boeing and elected to its board of directors. Frank Shrontz remained chairman and CEO until 1996, when Condit became CEO. He moved up to chairman and CEO the following year when Boeing merged with McDonnell Douglas (MDC), a deal that was negotiated at the end of 1996 and completed in August 1997.

The 777 was legacy Boeing's last hurrah. The 777-300ER was the best twin-aisle airplane produced before current-technology aircraft, and it is the last model that the Boeing "family" designed before the controversial Harry Stonecipher took over the company. The 777 program theme, "Working Together," is what Kelly Ortberg emphasized when he became CEO in August 2024, having been hired by the board to replace the disgraced David Calhoun. Alan Mulally succeeded Condit as GM of the 777 program when Condit moved up the executive chain.

Condit credited the success of the 777 to the culture that was created around it. Some give Condit the credit (he certainly claims it), and others credit Mulally. They undoubtedly share the credit. It was 1990 when the program got underway.

The 777 family was one of Boeing's most successful lines of aircraft. By 2013, when Boeing was forced to create the 777X family to compete with the Airbus A350-1000, around 1,500 777s of all sub-types had been ordered. After the 777X was officially launched in November 2013, another 300 "Classics" were ordered. Production of the 777-200LRF is to continue through 2027, when new emissions regulations prohibit production of freighters using GE Aviation GE90 engines.

With little doubt, the 777 could be considered Condit's career high point. But it was not without its critics. After Condit resigned in 2003 as Boeing's chairman and CEO, *Business Week's* aerospace reporter Stanley

Holmes wrote a long critique about Condit's tenure at the company. It was brutal.[39] Holmes painted a picture of a laid back, disengaged chief executive whose own personal conduct interfered with his professional duties. Holmes wrote that Ron Woodard, the president of BCA, was fired by Condit as a sacrificial lamb when Condit was nearly dismissed by the board over production issues that shut down the 737 and 747 lines, leading to Boeing's first loss since World War II.[40] Even Condit's stewardship of the 777 program, considered his crowning achievement and one that put him on the path to become president of the corporation, was flawed, Holmes wrote. The program cost twice its $6 billion budget. The overruns had an influence on the development of the 787 that lasted long after Condit resigned.

But this is getting ahead of his story.

When Condit became president of the corporation, critics say he was in over his head. He pursued a course of expanding Boeing's defense business to offset the cyclicality of the commercial division. The OPEC oil embargo during the Carter presidency hit U.S. airlines hard, affecting Boeing's business. The 1991 invasion of Kuwait by Iraq spiked oil prices again, once more clobbering U.S. airlines, still a mainstay for BCA. President George H. W. Bush assembled a broad coalition of nations to join forces and take Kuwait back from Iraq. Nobody could predict how long the expected military action would last. Several U.S. airlines entered bankruptcy, and some ceased operations altogether. At the peak of this crisis, 40 percent of U.S. airlines' capacity was operating in bankruptcy, as pointed out by American Airlines. These airlines were pricing for cash, not profits, dragging down the others that were struggling to avoid bankruptcy. Boeing was hammered again because its largest customer base couldn't order airplanes and couldn't take delivery of those it did order.

Condit correctly envisioned a larger Boeing with a better balance of defense versus commercial products. In quick succession, Boeing acquired Rockwell Aerospace, Hughes Aircraft Company's Space and Communications Group, and the biggie, in 1997, McDonnell Douglas. Revenues expanded from $23 billion to $54 billion annually as a result. The Rockwell and Hughes acquisitions came off smoothly. The MDC merger changed Boeing in ways that reverberated for the next two decades and came close to bringing down the company, beginning with the 2018–2019 MAX crash-

---

39. Boeing: What Really Happened," *Bloomberg Businessweek* (December 14, 2003), by Stanley Holmes. https://www.bloomberg.com/news/articles/2003-12-14/boeing-what-really-happened.

40. Boeing tried to ramp up production on the 737 line too quickly at the same time it was transitioning to a new supply-management tracking system that didn't go well. *Air Wars* addresses some of the details of this story.

es that revealed just how deeply the shifting culture had affected how BCA did business.

The MDC merger came with Harry Stonecipher, who was the CEO of McDonnell Douglas at the time. He became president and chief operating officer of the combined companies. Condit relinquished the president's title to concentrate on strategy. Stonecipher dived into Boeing's day-to-day operations. It was a culture shock that will be more fully described in the section covering the Stonecipher era.

Legacy Boeing employees blame Stonecipher for the culture shift. There is no question that he exacerbated a focus shift away from engineering and toward shareholder value. In fact, there was a hint of this before the MDC merger was consummated in 1997.

Boeing's culture had begun changing from one based on engineers to one that emphasized shareholder value and profits after the company's merger with MDC was announced. In the 1996 Boeing 10K federal Securities and Exchange Commission (SEC) filing, the words "shareholder value" appeared for the first time. The merger was completed the following year.

GE's CEO Jack Welch told Condit that the way to run a company is to beat the street by a nickel every quarter, a Boeing executive with direct knowledge told me. Peter Lemme, a retired Boeing engineer who worked at the company in 1996, remembers that was the year, under Condit, in which the theme of shareholder value first showed up, rewarding key employees with stock. Condit lays the blame on Stonecipher and his GE heritage rather than on the MDC merger itself.

This brings us to the next complaint about Condit from legacy Boeing people, namely, that he abdicated his oversight of Boeing to Stonecipher while he, Condit, focused on strategy. "There is always a division of responsibility," Condit said in my interview with him. "The COO, who is the operating officer, and the CEO, who is the strategic officer. At a most fundamental level, the answer is my focus was long-term. Harry was focused on short-term operations. I think that he brought that GE culture with him. I think that happened."

Figure 14. GE's CEO Jack Welch (left) introduced the strategy of shareholder value to Boeing CEO Phil Condit (right). Credit: Getty.

Regardless of who was responsible for the introduction and implementation of shareholder value as a point of priority, the MDC merger was fortuitous. Just four years after the merger closed, on September 11, 2001, Saudi terrorists associated with Al Qaeda flew two airplanes into the North and South Towers of the World Trade Center in New York, one into the Pentagon, and a fourth was crashed in Shanksville, Pennsylvania, enroute, apparently, to the U.S. Capitol. President George W. Bush retaliated in Afghanistan and then expanded the war into Iraq. The Afghan fighting against the Taliban didn't end until twenty years later, when President Joe Biden withdrew forces (in a disastrous execution) under an agreement negotiated by President Donald Trump that some have called ill-conceived.

9/11 proved even more disastrous for U.S. airlines, including Boeing, than the oil embargo or the 1991 Gulf War. Boeing's commercial business was decimated, as it still had an overreliance on U.S. airlines. But it looked like the military side of its business was going to benefit from Bush 43's retaliation against Al Qaeda and the Taliban. (Bear in mind, though, that it was the military side of Boeing that produced the tanker scandal that led to Condit's resignation in December 2003.)

Boeing needed a shot in the arm for its commercial division, and the U.S. Air Force needed to begin replacing its aging KC-135 aerial-refueling tankers. Boeing offered to lease the Air Force up to 100 tankers whose design was based on the company's 767-200ER commercial airliner. The lease deal went through in 2001, and Boeing's then–chief financial officer, an MDC import, hired the Pentagon's procurement officer, who had worked on the deal, shortly thereafter, paying her a huge salary and a big signing bonus. The officer was later found to have acted improperly on the lease arrangement. The optics for Boeing were awful, as was the fact that the law had been broken. The officer and the CFO both went to jail over the incident.

In his post-mortem of Condit's resignation, aerospace reporter Stanley Holmes tells a different story. Condit was already on thin ice with Boeing's board of directors because of the 1996 production debacle for which Ron Woodard, president of BCA, had been fired by Condit. The snafu resulted in a shareholder lawsuit filed in 1997 over allegations that Boeing hid production-line problems in 1996–1997, leading to shut down of the 737 and 747 lines for a month. The suit was settled for $92.5 million (about $157 million in 2025 dollars). For a company the size of Boeing, the amount was peanuts.

Condit's hands-off management style was a little too hands off for many. The tanker scandal was the final straw; Holmes reported that Condit was ousted after this. In typical Boeing fashion, the company announced his resignation in December 2003, and his retirement was effective the following March.

In interviews for this book, Condit was described by some of his former BCA engineers as an idea man, a visionary. He wasn't a good operations guy, and he was the most risk-adverse executive one of his engineers had ever seen, one of his former colleagues said in 2022. Condit was the cliché nice guy, said one of his top salesmen. Few would accuse Stonecipher of being a nice guy, and one characterized him as a "pompous ass."

One story about Condit's out-of-the-box thinking is illustrative.

John Feren, who joined Boeing with the MDC merger, recalls that Condit told him to visit Walmart headquarters and talk with executives. The puzzled Feren noted that the retailer wasn't likely to start an airline, so why go?

"Because I want us to think differently, and I want us to talk to people that we wouldn't ordinarily talk to," Feren said Condit replied. So, Feren was off to Bentonville, Arkansas, where Walmart was headquartered. The excuse was to talk about Boeing's new 737-based business jet. Feren took a model of the 7E7, then a concept, to show the Walmart executives and he did a show-and-tell.

"We spent two and a half hours talking about the world and economics," Feren recalled. "I wrote a trip report to Condit. Condit wrote a personal handwritten note on [the report]. He goes, 'This is exactly what I want. Keep doing it.' We did a lot of things that Phil told us to do that appeared to be wise for Phil, that most of us wouldn't have taken for granted. We kind of took that impression with the 787 in the front of the cabin. If we're going to put in these fancy business class seats, we're going to have to be able to get the revenue for that because otherwise, we should just build an airplane that optimizes the amount of cheap seats we can put in. So, Phil was on the right path. That was kind of a different way of getting there, but I think the airlines spend enormous amounts of time today trying to figure out how to optimize the real estate on their appointment."

Feren said that Condit was very approachable and that he would never resist giving more insight if he thought it was wanted or needed.

"His visionary instincts were well documented. Without any debate you'll find people in agreement on that. His engineering skill was really superb. He really did understand detailed engineering and airplane design," Feren said. Condit and Stonecipher had different styles. "Harry didn't mind being gruff and didn't really care whether he ruffled your feathers. Phil was very congenial and likable, but I don't know if that really translates to good cop–bad cop. I don't think people ran to Phil to get him to overrule Harry or people went to Harry to have him sabotage [Phil].

"I thought that they had a reasonably functioning relationship [for] two guys that came together from a merger. When you bring two formidable CEOs together, it'd be unusual [for them to] have exactly the same style and [for] everything [to be] harmonious. But I didn't feel any unusual animosity or friction. Maybe I was just oblivious," Feren said.

Another retired Boeing engineer had this critique:

"Phil was brilliant. He was my mentor for a long time. When he was CEO and before I really got anywhere, I'd go over once a month and spend a couple of hours talking to him about stuff. He was a fantastic engineer. He would do anything to avoid conflict. He is probably one of the most conflict-averse people I've ever known. He was a long-term thinker. He focused on three, four, or five years out. He didn't have a lot of stomach for details or what's going to happen next day or day-to-day running operations. In some ways, he was probably the textbook definition of a CEO, but he needed a chief operating officer. He needed somebody to run the business."

One of Boeing's top salesmen during the Condit era said that Condit was "a dreamer. He was very smart. He was a very poor judge of character. I would probably say he was naïve. A nice guy. He and I and all of us were from the same generation and the same age." This employee views Condit's CEO tenure as a failure. "I think he did not have a strong personality." His multiple marriages, including to his first cousin, were "another illustration of his character. I hate to say this, but he's a product of California. He went to Berkeley, and he was probably one of those hippies."

The Stonecipher Era

HARRY STONECIPHER

Tenure at The Boeing Company: 1997–2005.
Titles: President and COO, 1997–2002;
Vice Chairman, Board of Directors, 2001–2002;
President and CEO, 2003–2005.

9

Changing the Culture

"We had a sense right then that there was an alpha dog in the room, and it wasn't Phil Condit."

—LARRY BROWN, A UNION MEMBER, UPON SEEING PHIL CONDIT AND HARRY STONECIPHER TOGETHER FOR THE FIRST TIME

HARRY STONECIPHER didn't become the chairman and chief executive officer of The Boeing Company until 2003. However, as president and chief operating officer to Phil Condit, Boeing's strategy-chasing chairman and CEO, Stonecipher lost no time staking his leadership claim.

Stonecipher's impact on Boeing was immediate. As one former employee recalled, Stonecipher came in and immediately brought the "Jack Welch approach" to several aspects of the company, from employee performance reviews to a laser focus on quarterly earnings. "The joke that surfaced towards the end of our existence as a separate company [before Boeing's merger with McDonnell Douglas (MDC)] was that we had navigated our way through thirteen quarters of continuous profitability to irrelevance by the time of the sale. We did manage to be profitable for the majority of the time that Harry was running the company because that was the focus. That carried over into the merged company. I remember my first few months in Seattle, [when] the merger transition for the sales marketing and contracts organizations [was going on] . . . [as] quite fascinating."

Within the first few months of Stonecipher's tenure at Boeing, it was very clear that the company was already being run very much like McDonnell Douglas was run before an early 1990s crisis which saw it start to lose market share, mostly to Airbus. Boeing employees were slow to understand the changes. MDC was on its fatal decline in the early 1990s, and

Airbus still wasn't taken seriously. There was a sense of invincibility within Boeing at the time. There was a sense that Boeing had the economic might to win any campaign it wanted to win.

"It didn't take very long for the kind of financial discipline Harry wanted to start making it harder for those decisions to be made," said an MDC salesman who transitioned over to Boeing's Commercial Airplanes division (BCA). "There was a system of deal approvals in place when the merger occurred that was based on one single individual. There was one individual with two assistant vice presidents at the time that had access to the economics of each aircraft model." These officers would have the economics of a proposed sale on a sheet of paper. The figures would be presented at an approval meeting. The sales director and his or her team would present their idea of a customer deal offer in a meeting that at the time was called an REC, Request for Extension of Credit. The REC meeting was basically a presentation to one individual heading the credit committee. This person "would look at his piece of paper and he would say, nope, can't do that price." The committee head would give a cap on the discount Boeing could offer. (In those days, discounts to the list price of an airplane were far lower than the 50 to 60 percent discounts that are common in the twenty-first century, depending on the airline and the size of the deal.)

Larry Brown joined Boeing in 1979 and remained an employee until 1997, just as the company's merger with MDC was consummated. That same year, he became an employee of the International Association of Machinists District 751 (IAM 751) union, remaining with until 2019 in various capacities, including as liaison to the Washington State Legislature. Thus, he was able to see the before-and-after effects of the merger.

"We had a national summit with the company" shortly after the merger, Brown recalled more than twenty years later. "We were at the Edgewater Hotel (an upscale hotel on the Seattle waterfront) in the big second-floor ballroom that had the beautiful panoramic view of the Puget Sound. In attendance were machinists union reps from across the country. Phil Condit and Harry [Stonecipher] were both there. Condit barely said a word. Stonecipher was the only real voice in the room for Boeing. We had a sense right then that there was an alpha dog in the room, and it wasn't Phil Condit."

Brown recalled that Stonecipher's message was that Boeing was no longer a family. "We used to talk about the Boeing family. Stonecipher said that this was a business and that those who got with the program would thrive and those that didn't, wouldn't. He said we would be ruthless in maintaining core competency and shedding the company of non-essential work." This was straight out of "Neutron Jack" Welch's GE playbook. IAM 751 members weren't sure what the new Boeing president meant by "non-essential work." "It was a pretty stark message for most of us. We probably weren't fully appreciative of the road we were heading down but yes, the message was clear. We're in charge and don't think we're not."

Stonecipher left Boeing's employ in 2001 when he reached the mandatory retirement age of 65, but he remained on the company's board of directors. Condit was still CEO. A short time later, the United States came under attack by terrorists who flew two Boeing airplanes into the World Trade Center towers in New York and another one into the Pentagon in Washington, DC. A fourth plane, also a Boeing, crashed into a field in Pennsylvania when passengers tried to take command back from terrorists, who flew the 757 into the ground rather than be overwhelmed by the passengers. For the first time, U.S. skies were closed to all but military aircraft and other selectively authorized airplanes for four days. U.S. airlines verged on bankruptcy—many were forced to file bankruptcy petitions and some ceased operations altogether. Boeing, whose business then was overweight with U.S. carriers, was hard hit.

"It probably was a situation where we were going to fly into the ground irrespective of who management was. It seemed to be less concerning to the new management folks than it had been before," Brown said.

Stonecipher began his career at the Allison division of General Motors (GM) in 1955 as a laboratory technician; he remained in this position through 1959. The Allison division provided the engines for Lockheed's C-130 military cargo plane and its Electra passenger airline, along with engines for smaller airplanes. After leaving GM, Stonecipher took time off to return to college to obtain a degree in physics. In 1962, he joined GE's Aircraft Engine division. He would remain at GE for the next twenty-five years. From 1962 to 1979, he was a program engineer. He was a general manager from 1979 to 1984. From 1984 to 1987, he was a division head. In 1987, Stonecipher joined the Sundstrand Corporation as executive vice president; he was named president in 1987, CEO in 1989, and chairman in 1991. Stonecipher was named president and CEO of MDC in 1994, holding this position through the company's merger with Boeing in 1997.[41]

Adam Pilarski, an economist with the Douglas Aircraft Company side of MDC, said that Stonecipher was brought in to sell the company.[42] Like many, Pilarski didn't view Stonecipher favorably. A contrary view is offered by Feren, a career employee at Douglas and later at Boeing after the merger. Feren was a salesman and later worked within the McDonnell Douglas Finance Corporation (MDFC), the company's commercial aircraft leasing/financing arm.

"I had known Stonecipher a little bit from his days at GE" and later,

---

41. "Harry C. Stonecipher, 1936– " *Reference for Business* (2006), https://www. referenceforbusiness.com/biography/S-Z/Stonecipher-Harry-C-1936.html.

42. This matter is discussed further in *Air Wars*.

when he moved to Sundstrand, Feren recalled in 2022. "Not realizing that Harry was eventually going to be my boss's boss someday, I just treated him like a normal guy. I don't know that Harry exuded a lack of confidence in McDonnell Douglas, but Harry's signature phrase when he was at GE [was] he'd rather be hit over the head with a baseball bat than launch this stupid CFM 56 engine."

The CFM 56 first appeared on commercial aircraft when the Douglas DC-8 Super 61 and 63 models were re-engined with the CFM International product in 1982.[43] In time, a group of Boeing KC-135s (which were based on the 707) were also re-engined with the CFM 56. Boeing selected the CFM 56 to power the 737-300/400/500 (later to become known as the Classic) models, a major upgrade to the 737-100/200 planes.

If Stonecipher didn't recognize the potential of the CFM 56–powered 737, he wouldn't be alone. Pratt & Whitney (P&W), which supplied the engines for Boeing's 737-100/200 models, also failed to recognize the future of the re-engined 737. P&W withdrew from consideration by Boeing for the project, instead placing its bet on the new, larger 757 then in development. It was a bad bet. P&W split the market for the 757 with Rolls-Royce (RR), which went on to power a majority of the 1,049 757s delivered. CFM, with a monopoly on the 737 Classic, later powered the 737 NG and 737 MAX models. Nearly 12,000 737s of all versions were delivered through 2024; all but about 1,000 were powered by CFM engines. At the end of 2024, Boeing's MAX backlog was nearly 4,800, all powered by CFM.

Looking back with the benefit of hindsight, Stonecipher's outlook about the CFM 56 is mind-boggling.

"We all get it wrong from time to time," Feren said. "I don't know that there's an executive out there that every decision they made was right and certainly on highly successful programs. There're never 100 percent of the people who thought it was going to be a roaring success. There were probably other people on the other side of the fence. I don't think Harry was blessed or particularly a deep student of the market and market trends, so Harry knew what he knew and thought what he thought, and he trusted his instincts."

Despite Stonecipher's background in commercial airplane engines, Feren said he didn't really understand the airline industry or even technology.

"I never considered him a scholar of RPMs or RPKs or supply and demand or technology per se.[44] He was much more about financial metrics

---

43. A few DC-8-62s also were re-engined, but nearly all of the 110 conversions undertaken were made to the -61 and -63 models. The re-engined aircraft were rebranded the -71, -72, and -73.

44. RPMs = Revenue Passenger Miles, and RPKs = Revenue Passenger Kilometers. Both are basic metrics of airline operations.

in the firm and holding people accountable and providing incentives to get certain kinds of behavior. I just don't think that was his stock-in-trade. Some people are really gifted in that area and other people, they know what they read," Feren said.

"When Harry left GE and went to Sundstrand, he got a plaque with a baseball bat on it and the inscription . . . said, 'I'm sure glad we didn't listen to you, Harry,'" Feren recalled.

REINVIGORATING DOUGLAS AIRCRAFT COMPANY—OR NOT

By the time Stonecipher joined MDC as president and CEO in 1994, the Douglas Aircraft Company was a shadow of its former self. Throughout the piston-airliner era, beginning with the DC-2 and cemented with the DC-3, Douglas was by far the world's leading aircraft manufacturer. Lockheed was number two, especially post-War, when its beautiful Constellations were Douglas's main competition with the DC-4, DC-6, and DC-7. Britain's Vickers hit the jackpot with the turboprop Viscount model, and France's Sud Aviation had modest success with its twin-jet Caravelle. But, in developing the DC-7 at the request of C. R. Smith of American Airlines instead of moving from the highly successful DC-6B straight to jets, Douglas made a huge strategic mistake. Initial plans were to go from the DC-6B to a jet-powered DC-7. The piston-powered DC-7 may have been what C. R. Smith wanted, but Douglas's delaying development of a jet gave Boeing the upper hand—though Boeing nearly blew its lead, as we saw in Chapter 1.

Boeing's failure in the commercial sector in the post-war piston era freed it to concentrate on jet development. As already recounted, Boeing got the jump on Douglas and never truly looked back. Benefitting from jet technology and designs from wartime Germany and the jet-powered B-47 and B-52 bombers, Boeing won the federal contract for a jet-refueling tanker, the KC-135. This development spread the company's risk of producing a commercial jet airliner, the 707.

Airbus, which was created in 1970 and put its first transport, the A300B2, into service in 1974, surpassed MDC in the 1990s. American Airlines, which ordered more MD-80s than any other customer, switched to Boeing, which offered the airline a twenty-year exclusive supplier deal in 1996. MDC, reduced to the MD-11, a shrinking MD-80 order book, an unsuccessful re-engining development of the MD-80 into the MD-90, and arguably a retro-development of the MD-95, by 1997 had only a 7 percent market share.

Stonecipher studied whether to reinvigorate Douglas. Industrial partnerships were explored, including a proposed MDF-100 project between MDC and Fokker, a Korean partnership, and even a collaboration with Airbus. Nothing came of any of it. A double-deck, super-jumbo aircraft called the MD-12 was considered as well. Except for the nose section, which had the classic McDonnell Douglas DC-10/MD-11 look, the MD-12 is very similar to what the Airbus A380 looked like when it was launched in 2000.

THE BEGINNING OF BOEING'S DECLINE

In a 2001 profile by *The Economist,* Stonecipher was characterized as the hard cop to Condit's soft cop.[45] Condit, *The Economist* reported, wouldn't even be at the 2001 Paris Air Show. Stonecipher would lead the Boeing team in France. This spoke volumes about who was who and what was what at Boeing. "When he first took over the day-to-day running of Boeing after the merger [with MDC], what Mr. Stonecipher saw horrified him. Boeing's civil-jet business was a mess. Ron Woodard, the ebullient salesman who ran the division, had started a price war to block the rise of Airbus, Boeing's European rival, in a booming market," the magazine reported. "Boeing quickly got into difficulties, its factories choked with half-finished aircraft because suppliers could not keep up with production. In the autumn of 1997, the production lines had to be stopped so as to catch up. Airbus continued to advance, and the price-war policy proved [to be a] costly shambles. As the civil-jet division continued to struggle and Boeing's shares dived, Mr. Stonecipher nudged Mr. Condit to get rid of Mr. Woodard, if only to signal a change. Mr. Condit understood the case, and Mr. Woodard duly left. The dismissal shattered Boeing's old executive culture, which had ensured that bosses were never fired, just shuffled."

Soon after the Boeing-MDC merger, Stonecipher asked his new team at legacy Boeing how much it cost to build the airliners coming out of Seattle. Nobody could give him an answer. Stonecipher demanded that within a week, BCA had to come up with an answer—reported out by tail number. The tail number demand was a ridiculous order. But the idea was not altogether ridiculous. However, coming up with an answer wasn't easy, either. Boeing used program accounting to assess the cost of building airplanes, rather than unit accounting. (Even unit accounting probably couldn't have come up with a cost-by-tail-number figure.) Program accounting, still used to this day, allows Boeing to average the cost of building airplanes over an accounting block for the life of a given program. All the upfront development and production costs and the learning curve get averaged out over hundreds or a few thousand airplanes. Instead of reporting huge losses up front as the first few hundred units are produced, Boeing can report profits despite the surge of up-front costs. The concept was hardly new to Stonecipher.

---

45. "Hard Man Harry," *The Economist* (June 7, 2001), https://www.economist.com/business/2001/06/07/hard-man-harry.

Stonecipher's view toward Boeing as an engineering company also was displayed early after the merger. In short order, Stonecipher said that Boeing had to become a company focused on profits, not engineering. After Woodard was fired by Condit at Stonecipher's urging, the COO took aim at Woodard's successor, Alan Mulally. It wouldn't be the last time.

"When I arrived, Alan was a great engineer and team leader. Now he is a fine businessman as well," Stonecipher told *The Economist*. He also threw out another observation to the media at the time. "When people say I changed the culture of Boeing, that was the intent, so that it's run like a business rather than a great engineering firm."

This sentiment was like fingernails on a blackboard to members of the Society of Professional Engineering Employees in Aerospace union (SPEEA). The sales force wasn't enamored of the concept, either. Before the merger, customers viewed Boeing's word as the gold standard. MDC was on a downhill trajectory, and Airbus—fishing for market share—was making promises that even airlines questioned. But after the merger, the MDC influence over Boeing quickly emerged. And it wasn't confined to Stonecipher's "hard cop" attitude. Stonecipher had spent twenty-five years at GE, where Jack Welch ruled with an iron fist aimed at profits and shareholder value. "Neutron Jack" ruthlessly cut costs and headcount in his quest for shareholder value. It was an example followed by Stonecipher (and later, another GE alumni who would head Boeing, Jim McNerney, and still later, David Calhoun).

In 2001, Stonecipher hit Boeing's mandatory retirement age. He stayed on as vice chairman of the board, where mandatory retirement ages didn't exist. As vice chairman, he had no power. But as the second-largest individual shareholder after the McDonnell family, he wielded strong influence.

Under Phil Condit, Stonecipher had been in many ways the de facto CEO, but he didn't have full power until Condit resigned in the wake of the 2001–2003 scandal over Boeing's proposal to lease 100 KC-767s to the U.S. Air Force.

Stonecipher was asked by Boeing's board of directors to succeed Condit. It was a logical choice, given he had been Boeing's president and COO as well as president and CEO of McDonnell Douglas. He became Boeing's CEO in December 2003. He faced an immediate decision about whether to greenlight Boeing's conceptual airplane, code-named the 7E7 (E for Efficient). Many doubted he would approve the project, given his history at MDC, where new airplane programs were denied in favor of derivatives of aging aircraft. At MDC, the DC-10 became the MD-11. The MD-80 went through several iterations, ending with the MD-90 (a re-engined version) and the MD-95 (a shrink, also with new engines). Stonecipher favored using risk-sharing partners rather than keeping work (and expensive investments) in-house.

Consideration of the 7E7 had been underway for some time. Before

9/11, Boeing floated the idea of an airplane that could cruise at Mach 0.97, just under the speed of sound. Dubbed the Sonic Cruiser, the airplane had a futuristic look that was nothing like the standard tube-and-wing jetliners flying the skies since 1952, beginning with the de Havilland Comet. Rather, the Sonic Cruiser had a strong resemblance to the Lockheed SR-71 Mach 3.0 spy plane. Since supersonic flight was banned from overland flying in the United States, Europe, and elsewhere, no SST had been built since the Concorde, whose success was killed by this very factor. Only twelve commercial versions of the Concorde were built, and service was confined to trans-Atlantic operations.[46] Mulally, by then the president of BCA and an accomplished aerospace engineer, had the enthusiasm of a true aviation geek when it came to the Sonic Cruiser. The airplane, he gushed, would shave hours off trans-Atlantic, trans-Pacific, and Singapore-to-London flights. It would cost no more than a 767 to operate, a feat worthy of note in those days when the 767 was considered one of the most efficient airplanes operated across the globe. Speed normally sucks fuel, and flying just below the speed of sound while not eating more fuel was a technological challenge.[47]

American Airlines CEO Don Carty loved the Sonic Cruiser. In a meeting with Boeing salesmen and his staff, Carty said he wanted to buy the first couple of years' worth of production. His staff groaned, seeing their negotiating position wither away. Agreeing would have replicated the United Airlines–Boeing 247 scenario described in Chapter 1.

But Singapore Airlines wasn't impressed. The plane was fast enough to shave hours off its flights to London, but arrival would now be at 2 a.m. local time, given the preferred departure time from Singapore. That meant a 4 a.m. departure from London, given the standard turn-around time. Who'd want to arrive and depart at those hours? Across the Atlantic, not enough time was saved to eliminate the use of relief pilots and flight at-

---

46. The Concorde carried only 100 passengers and barely had trans-Atlantic range, factors which also led to the airplane's demise. Entering service in the 1970s, when the environmental movement was gaining steam, the pollution emitted by the plane and the ear-splitting noise of its engines also hurt the Concorde.

47. The last commercial airliner designed to fly at Mach 0.97 was the 1962 Convair 990. The airplane was a joy to pilot and the airframe was like a tank. But it was a fuel guzzler that, even in those early days, had no peer. Only thirty-seven were built. American Airlines reduced its order of 990s from twenty-five to twenty when the airplane failed to meet its speed guarantees. The 990 was produced from 1961 to 1963. American began replacing them in 1965 and disposed of its last one in 1968.

tendants. Also, technical challenges of flying just below the speed of sound existed for the flight envelope and the engine design. The Sonic Cruiser also had to be able to traverse the speed of sound in the event of flight anomalies. There clearly were a lot of hurdles to overcome with the market for and the design of the plane.[48]

The Sonic Cruiser's technical and flight envelope challenges weren't inconsequential. But 9/11 killed the airplane. Airlines, facing billions of dollars in losses, were no longer interested in speed. They wanted airplanes that were a lot cheaper to operate. For Boeing, that meant not merely matching the 767's economics but surpassing them. Thus, Boeing shifted to the 7E7, which had already been conceived by engineers. (Boeing always has Plans A and B, and maybe even a Plan C, going in parallel.)

While salesmen showed the 7E7 concept to the market, consultants, Wall Street analysts, and even many customers doubted that Boeing would launch a new airplane under the influence of the McDonnell family and Stonecipher. Shareholder value was now deemed more important by Stonecipher than designing and building new airplanes, critics believed. Boeing's board of directors, on which John McDonnell and Stonecipher sat, with their large shareholdings, wielded inordinate influence at the company. While some point to the 757-300 and 767-400 models as examples of the MDC preference for derivatives versus new airplanes, development of each was underway before the Boeing-MDC merger was announced.

Boeing's previous all-new airplane was the 777-200. The program was launched in 1990; its entry-into-service (EIS) date was in 1994. The 777-300ER, which became the best-selling model of all variants, entered service in 2004. The 777-200LR followed in 2006, and the 777-200LRF in 2009. Critics of "McBoeing," as the company was sometimes derisively called at the time, pointed out that by 2003, it had been thirteen years since an entirely new airplane program was launched. These critics and skeptics doubted that the McDonnell-Stonecipher-dominated board would approve a new airplane.

To be sure, with billions of dollars at stake, any new airplane program is a risk. Derivatives tend to be where the profits come from. But the 757-300 and the 767-400 were poor sellers. Only fifty-five -300s and thirty-seven 767-400s were sold. Although each model has phenomenal cost-per-available-seat-mile numbers, the former was hampered by demand that dried up following 9/11, and the latter's operational performance was inferior to the 767-300ER and Airbus A330-300.

BCA CEO Alan Mulally and Mike Bair, who would become the program manager for the 7E7, were told by Stonecipher to spread the risk and in-

---

48. The Sonic Cruiser story is detailed in *Air Wars*.

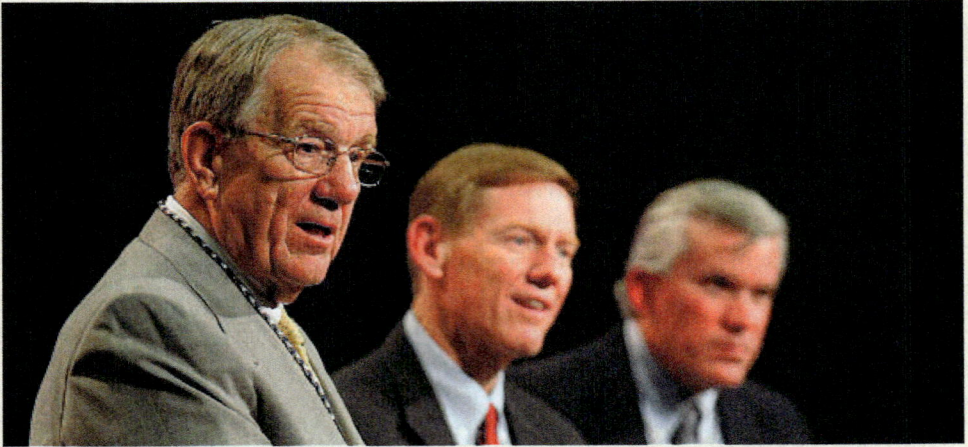

Figure 15. Harry Stonecipher, BCA CEO Alan Mulally, and 7E7 program head Mike Bair announcing that the airplane would be assembled in Everett, Washington. Getty photo.

vestment outside Boeing. This followed the strategy Stonecipher used at MDC, even though an internal white paper at Boeing by a former MDC engineer warned that the strategy was a recipe for chaos and losses.

In April 2003, *Wall Street Journal* reporter Lynn Lunsford reported that one Boeing board member, Jim McNerney (who was not identified in the article), warned that Boeing was placing too much emphasis on cost cutting and that doing so would wind up benefitting Airbus. McNerney at the time was CEO of 3M. Before becoming 3M's CEO, he had been at GE for decades, including at its GE Aviation subsidiary. He wasn't an engineer (something that would foster criticism during his ten-year tenure as Boeing CEO), but neither was he a neophyte to commercial aviation.

It was against this backdrop that Stonecipher became Boeing's CEO the following December. Thus, just about everyone was surprised when, a short time later, Stonecipher announced that Boeing would go ahead with the 7E7, now named the 787. Japan's All Nippon Airways (ANA) signed the first order on April 26, 2004, formally launching the program.

The 7E7 launch reinvigorated Boeing. The very concept of the 7E7 captured the imagination. The model had a shark-like tail and a pointy nose that gave it a sleekness that hadn't been seen in a plane since the Lockheed Constellation of the piston era. The plane would be a first for a commercial airliner: the fuselage, wings, and tail surfaces were to be made of composite. The weight savings versus a traditional metal fuselage contributed to fuel efficiency driven by a new generation of engines. The 7E7 was predicted to be at least 20 percent more fuel efficient than the 767s and Airbus A330s it was designed to replace.

Less than thrilling to the airline industry, because it didn't really care, but vitally important to Boeing's employees in the greater Seattle area was

Stonecipher's announcement that the 7E7 would be assembled locally. Washington state and local politicians were giddy. But another innovative element of the new program, an unprecedented amount of outsourcing, did *not* make IAM 751 happy. None of the fuselage would be produced in Seattle or be made by union members. The aft fuselage and tail would be made in Italy. Portions of the plane immediately forward of the aft fuselage and tail would be produced in South Carolina. The nose was to be outsourced to the Boeing Wichita (Kansas) plant. The wings and the center section would be produced in Japan. A fleet of 747-400s were to be converted to fly all these sections to Everett for assembly by a mere 850 IAM 751 members.

Boeing's other primary union, SPEEA, wasn't entirely happy, either. Some of the engineering work would be outsourced to (of all people) Russians and Ukrainians.

One of the legacy McDonnell Douglas engineers was especially unhappy. John Hart-Smith wrote a white paper warning Boeing that high degrees of outsourcing could lead to financial disaster.[49] He presented his findings during one of Boeing's annual conclaves in St. Louis (where MDC had been headquartered and which at the time served as the headquarters of Boeing's Defense division). Dominic Gates of the *Seattle Times* recounted the event in Hart-Smith's obituary in January 2025.[50]

> [Hart-Smith's white paper] scathingly critiqued the McDonnell Douglas strategy, now foisted on Boeing, of outsourcing work and divesting core design and manufacturing assets.
>
> He explained in clear, commonsense terms how this would ultimately increase costs, lower profits and jeopardize Boeing's ability to develop future airplanes.
>
> Hart-Smith learned afterward from colleagues in the room that after he'd finished and hung up, Boeing's then Chief Technical Officer Dave Swain stood up and spoke for a half-hour attempting to rebut Hart-Smith's arguments.
>
> "By the time he was through, there was no one in the room who didn't agree with me," Hart-Smith said dryly in 2019.

---

49. Dr. L. J. Hart-Smith, "Out-Sourced Profits–The Cornerstone of Successful Subcontracting," Boeing Paper MDC 00K0096 (2001), https://legacy.www. documentcloud.org/documents/69746-hart-smith-on-outsourcing/.

50. Dominic Gates, "Superstar Engineer John Hart-Smith Skewered Boeing's Strategy," Obituary (January 11, 2025), https://www.seattletimes.com/business/ boeing-aerospace/superstar-engineer-john-hart-smith-skewered-boeings -strategy-obituary/.

When Hart-Smith was done with his presentation, his conclusions were ridiculed by some superiors. The paper was basically buried until years later, when the 787 program's industrial plan fell apart. He was proved right on virtually every point he made.

Internally, not everybody was on board with the plan to use composites in building the plane. Within the engineering group, opinions were split. Some endorsed the composite construction. Another group, citing costs and risk, favored sticking with the tried-and-true metal fuselage, mating to composite wings, tail, and empennage method. Chicago (meaning company headquarters) favored the composites. Hart-Smith also criticized the plan to make the fuselage sections in one-piece barrels. Dominic Gates reported the opposition in the same obituary.

> In the mid-2000s, Hart-Smith fought another battle within Boeing, when he tried to warn that the plan to build the 787 Dreamliner was seriously flawed and would prove very costly.
>
> He first joined other engineers in recommending that it be made from metal, not carbon composites.
>
> In that period, Hart-Smith led a small research team that developed a new metal fuselage design that was cheaper to build and would last longer than previous metal fuselages. It was tested to five lifetimes without any fatigue cracks.
>
> When Boeing insisted on building the 787 from composites, Hart-Smith advised against the concept of fabricating the jet from single-piece composite barrels, each made by a different major subcontractor.
>
> He told them that perfectly joining these large fuselage sections would prove extremely costly. He wrote a report advocating a better approach: making the sections from curved, fuselage-length panels fastened together.
>
> Management again refused to listen. And once again, time proved Hart-Smith right.

Airbus chose to make its competing A350 using the panel method, a move ridiculed by Boeing in the inevitable public relations battle between the two companies.

Years later, when I toured the former Boeing Wichita plant, now operating independently as Spirit AeroSystems, I noted to the senior official walking me through the plant that the company made the 787 nose section here and panel sections for the A350 at its Kinston, North Carolina, facility. Which method was better, the barrel or panel approach? I asked. Without hesitation, the official said the panels. Still years later, a retired Boeing employee said that panels could be made more cheaply and layered into autoclaves for higher production rates than those resulting from the barrel method. And early into the 787's production, Scott Carson, then the CEO of BCA, told *Aviation Week* magazine that Boeing had to find a less-expensive way to produce composite airplanes than by use of huge autoclaves.[51]

Mulally's business model outsourced design and production of (among other things) the 787's wing, which previously had been a Boeing specialty. Many viewed wing design and production as one of Boeing's top advantages. Giving this away was akin to giving away Boeing's heritage.

IAM 751 and SPEEA warned that outsourcing efficiency and skills would fall short. But Stonecipher's focus on reducing risk and investment carried the day, despite a similar warning made by Hart-Smith in his white paper. It's unknown if Stonecipher ever read that paper.

While many feared that disaster lay in the 787's future, nobody could be certain. What was clear was that the plane's timeline from launch (officially April 2004) to EIS (May 2008) was extremely aggressive for a ground-breaking design of an all-composite airplane and was a radical departure from the way Boeing designed, produced, and assembled airplanes in the past.

Years later, one Wall Street analyst gave credit to Stonecipher for recognizing that emerging globalization meant that Boeing had to diversify its work. (Others would credit McNerney on this score.) But Stonecipher's focus on cost cutting, shareholder value, and profits was his mantra. Global vision was not something attributed to him at the time.

Still, Stonecipher's announcement in December 2003 that Boeing was (finally) going forward with the 7E7/787 energized employees, Wall Street, and aviation geekdom alike. It reassured customers that McBoeing maybe was Boeing after all.

ALAN MULALLY

Somewhere along the line, Mulally—who is revered by many within Boeing even today, nearly twenty years after he left to go to Ford—got on Stonecipher's bad side. The reasons for this aren't clear, though Stonecipher publicly complained about Mulally being a poor salesman and focusing too much on engineering rather than understanding finance. Some familiar with events at the time claim that Stonecipher said privately several times that he was on the verge of firing Mulally but didn't specify why. Perhaps the root of the animosity traces to the mid-1990s, not too long before

---

51. When Boeing was developing the new airplane for the middle-of-the-market sector, one airline was shown a concept in which the composite sections were produced laterally then mated together after installation of the wiring and monuments (gallies, lavatories, etc.).

Boeing and MDC merged. According to a retired Boeing official, Mulally interviewed with Stonecipher, when the latter was CEO of MDC, to become CEO of the company's Douglas Aircraft Company unit. Mulally didn't get, or take, the job. It isn't known whether this was Mulally's choice or whether Stonecipher didn't like him. Whatever the reason, Mulally stayed with Boeing, where he was crucial in the design and development of the 777, which ran badly over budget. For the cost-minded Stonecipher, the overruns probably didn't run in Mulally's favor when Stonecipher joined Boeing as president and COO in 1997.[52]

Mulally declined to comment about his interview with Stonecipher or about any other aspect of his long tenure at Boeing. But an ex-Boeing executive said that Stonecipher also told Mulally that unless he sold Boeing's production facility in Wichita, he would never get to be CEO of Boeing. The plant was sold in February 2005 to a private equity group named Spirit AeroSystems.

As it turned out, Mulally survived; it was Stonecipher who got the axe on March 7, 2005. Stonecipher was discovered to be having an affair with a Boeing vice president. He was married at the time. Coming only a few years after the company's tanker scandal, the board of directors decided that Harry had to go for violating Boeing's Code of Conduct.

Boeing didn't have a succession plan. Lew Platt, then lead director and chairman of the board, became the public face and leader on an interim basis. James Bell, Boeing's chief financial officer, was named interim president but was not considered for the job on a permanent basis. The board didn't look far. After only three months, it tapped board member Jim McNerney to become chairman, president, and CEO of Boeing.

---

52. John McDonnell tried to recruit John Leahy, at the time the head of sales for Airbus's Americas division. Leahy turned McDonnell down, unconvinced that MDC would resuscitate Douglas. Details of this episode are set out in *Air Wars*.

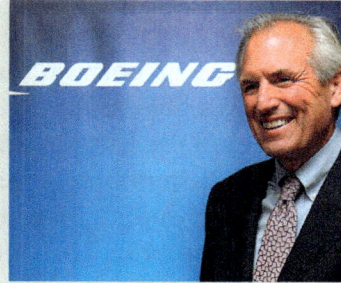

10

McNerney Faces Tough Choices, Labor Strikes

"The worst possible choice for Airbus."

—ANONYMOUS AIRBUS OFFICIAL.

WHEN JIM MCNERNEY WAS NAMED CHAIRMAN, president, and chief executive officer (CEO) of The Boeing Company, he was not the proverbial household name despite being a long-time executive within the GE engine and services units. McNerney was known to those who negotiated for GE engines. But because the limelight wasn't in his DNA, he was largely an enigma to many companies that existed within Boeing's circle. Certainly, Boeing's employees, and especially its unions, didn't know much about him.

One large aerospace company was so unfamiliar with McNerney that it commissioned a competitive intelligence (CI) report on him to not only figure out who he was, but also to predict what he would do. The CI report was prepared at the end of 2005, several months after McNerney was named CEO. Looking at the report twenty years later, the study proved largely prescient.

McNerney was 55 when Boeing's board of directors named him to succeed the disgraced Harry Stonecipher. He was familiar to board members, having served on that body since 2001. With ten years to go until McNerney reached Boeing's mandatory retirement age of 65, the board, Wall Street, and executives and employees throughout the company looked for stability after scandals cost Condit and Stonecipher their jobs.

PERSONAL PROFILE

McNerney was born on the East Coast but raised in the Chicago suburbs. He went to Yale and played baseball with George W. Bush, who in 2000 was elected the forty-third president of the United States. He credited his father with instilling in him values and personal drive. His parents and other family members were still in the Chicago area at the time of his appointment to Boeing. His father was ill with cancer and in a hospice in the area.

McNerney, in contrast with many if not most CEOs, shunned the limelight and made an effort to share credit. His personal style fostered leadership development, which was a critical part of his approach to corporate strategy. He avoided the press at GE, even as head of its Engines group. As CEO of 3M, he preferred letting his CFO deal with Wall Street, even on earnings calls. Whether his press shyness was strictly a personal trait,[53] a result of the corporate culture at GE, or a conscious 3M corporate strategy was unclear. However, a Boeing insider said that McNerney's view of press interviews was essentially, "What benefit is it to Boeing?" He regarded media interviews as taking time away from him running the business.

McNerney made corporate community involvement at 3M an important aspect of corporate citizenship. He served as a board member of community organizations and advocated corporate sponsorships of high-profile activities, such as United Way, natural-disaster relief funds, and environmental causes, which also reflected his tenure at 3M.

McNerney was considered personable yet forceful, with a dislike of "yes men." He listened to and was said to favor dissenting views, provided they were well-founded, prior to making decisions.

GE LEGACY

McNerney was employed by GE for eighteen years. Prior to joining GE, he was with McKinsey & Company, the giant and prestigious (but in some quarters, overrated) consulting company.

At GE, McNerney served in various senior and executive management positions, none of which exceeded three years in duration. He rapidly moved up the ranks, becoming president of GE's Asia-Pacific Operations in Hong Kong. Before he left GE in 2001 for 3M, he successfully inserted GE into China, significantly increasing the presence of GE's twelve busi-

---

53. Jack Welch noted that Jeffrey Immelt, whom Welch selected to succeed him as GE's CEO, was more comfortable in the limelight than McNerney, which apparently was a factor in his decision to pass over McNerney.

nesses in the region and going from zero to a $4 billion in business by 2004 and president and CEO of GE's Aircraft Engines division (GEAE) (later named GE Aviation and then GE Aerospace), where he successfully negotiated a deal with Boeing to become the sole-source supplier on the 777-200LR and 777-300ER projects. While McNerney was the head of GEAE (from 1997 to 2000), the unit became the second-most-profitable subsidiary of the entire GE corporation.

McNerney also served as an executive vice president and a director at GE's Capital Aviation Services (GECAS), at the time the world's largest lessor. His roles at GEAE and GECAS provided him with an intimate background in commercial aviation and production, and research and development (R&D).

McNerney was one of three people in the running to succeed Welch as chairman and CEO of GE. In November 2000, Welch chose Jeffrey Immelt, who was younger than both McNerney and the third candidate, Robert Nardelli. McNerney—who had previously said he would either become GE's chairman or leave the company—was immediately recruited to become the chairman and CEO of 3M. He was the first outsider to lead that firm.

3M PERFORMANCE

At the time of McNerney's appointment as 3M CEO on January 1, 2001, the company was described as stagnant; bogged down by flat revenues, flat earnings, and a flat stock price; and having plateaued in the area new products. 3M was characterized as a business that had gone adrift, with its research facilities turning out fewer and fewer commercial hits. Quarterly financial results were called "underwhelming." McNerney's charge was to reinvigorate the company, boost its profits, and expand its business.

When McNerney was named CEO, the market value of 3M shot up by $4 billion as Wall Street greeted the news favorably. McNerney also joined Boeing's board of directors in 2001. At 3M, McNerney demonstrated a keen interest in developing business in Asia, notably China; Eastern Europe (including Russia); and other Third World areas. Notoriously press shy, McNerney avoided the limelight, granting interviews only on occasion. For example, he was CEO of 3M for a year before he sat down for his first interview with a national magazine.

McNerney discovered that 3M was using what he termed a "menu" of quality-control procedures, including one called Six Sigma. Because Six Sigma was a sacred cow at GE, McNerney discontinued all other procedures at 3M, directing that Six Sigma be used exclusively. He credited Six Sigma for saving 3M $500 million in costs annually. The outsourcing of production and some R&D is credited with saving 3M several hundred million more each year (these measures also increased sales in the countries that received work from 3M).

R&D funding and undefined "related expenses" basically remained flat during McNerney's tenure at 3M. R&D and related expenses were $1.1 billion in 2000, before he became chairman, declining slightly to $1.08 billion in 2001. The number declined further in 2002 ($1.07 billion), the first full year after 9/11 and one that was part of a recessionary period, before rising slightly in 2003 ($1.1 billion) and again in 2004 ($1.14 billion). Researchers were reigned in from their previously free-wheeling ways to focus more on targeted projects likely to produce a return; 15 percent of their time was allocated for "free time" research.[54]

However, "New product development was the engine of 3M's growth[,] . . . fueled by . . . technical, marketing, sales, manufacturing and more working together to meet customer needs," according to the company's 2004 Annual Report. A Boston Consulting Group survey of more than 235 executives worldwide labeled 3M the most innovative company in the world.

3M established a company-wide, data-driven method of generating new products and bringing them to market. Called 2X/3X, it doubled the number of ideas and tripled the market success rate of these ideas. After a post-9/11 dip in sales in 2001/2002, 3M sales (revenues) and profits climbed by double-digit percentages through 2004 compared with 2000, the year before McNerney's appointment. Jobs were cut from 75,000 to 67,000. 3M's annual reports, as well media interviews with McNerney and others, credited Six Sigma more than any other initiative with bringing about 3M's resurgence.[55] By early 2004, one-third of 3M's 67,000 employees were "enrolled" in Six Sigma. Six Sigma focused on higher growth, productivity, and cash flow. During his three-year 3M tenure, McNerney cut nearly $1 billion in costs annually via Six Sigma and other initiatives. He also increased off-shore outsourcing and R&D (to China, e.g.) as a way of cutting costs.

McNerney's results earned him a spot on *Business Week's* 2003 "Best Managers" list and won him *Industry Week's* CEO of the Year title for 2003.

---

54. As described in 3M's 2004 federal Securities and Exchange Commission (SEC) 10K filing, "3M realigned its R&D efforts in 2003 . . . to develop technologies needed for the future, to more closely align technical resources with business priorities, and to shorten the distance between R&D and 3M's customers. 3M established a single global Corporate Research Laboratory . . . ."

55. The other corporate initiatives were named Global Sourcing Effectiveness, 3M Acceleration, eProductivity, and Global Business Processes.

MANAGEMENT STYLE

McNerney was described as blunt and probing in staff meetings. In keeping with his MBA degree, McNerney insisted on detailed financial data. Up until his future war with labor at Boeing, he also was known for being able to rally employees. He was described as attentive to key customers. Overall, McNerney was described as having a low-key management style.

Although McNerney was a product of "Neutron Jack" Welch's cost-cutting management style at GE, which included trimming the work force, he did not engage in slash and burn tactics at 3M or, initially, at Boeing. He brought GE management techniques and policies with him to both companies. At 3M, he worked with existing management, culling out officers over time. McNerney was a big believer in GE's leadership development[56] policies and techniques, which became one of the cornerstones of his leadership at 3M. When he arrived at Boeing, he publicly stated that leadership development "will be" 50 percent of his job at the company. His philosophy, oft repeated in interviews, was that as people grow and develop within an organization, the organization will also grow and develop.

McNerney preferred organic growth over growth from mergers and acquisitions. Upon his appointment at 3M, he generally avoided mergers, though he was open to rifle-shot acquisitions. When he began at Boeing, McNerney told analysts and reporters that he viewed some of the company's problems over the preceding several years as being the result of merger-integration issues.

SUCCESSES AND DISAPPOINTMENTS

McNerney's major achievement at GEAE was repositioning GE from a distant third-place supplier to the Boeing 777 program to the exclusive supplier of the company's 777-200LR/-300ER programs. The twenty-year contract he negotiated with Boeing was signed in 1999 and was valued at $25 billion. Revenues grew 71 percent and profits grew 103 percent during his tenure as GEAE's president. GEAE R&D accounted for the largest share of corporate R&D expenses, although no break-out was provided in GE's SEC filings. GEAE became GE's second-largest profit center after the General Electric Capital Corporation.

According to a 2004 *Bloomberg Businessweek* profile,[57] McNerney frequently traveled to Seattle to lobby Boeing to exclusively offer the GE

---

56. The GE Careers website describes the leadership programs offered by the company: https://jobs.gecareers.com/global/en/global-leadership-programs/.

57. "3M's Rising Star," *Bloomberg Businessweek* (April 12, 2004).

engine on its next generation of 777s. Boeing expressed concerns that airlines unfamiliar with GE engines would resist, so McNerney lobbied the heads of Singapore Airlines, Cathay Pacific Airways, and others with promises that GE would back and service the engines. GECAS was enlisted to promise to buy Boeing airplanes and lease them to airlines, and Jack Welch lobbied Phil Condit on the matter. Profit improvement at GEAE relative to revenue generation was attributed in GE's SEC filings to improved productivity and growth in product services.

For all the accolades sent McNerney's way during his tenure at 3M, a retrospective view of his time at the company shows a mixed picture. Revenues, profits, cash flow, and market share increased, often by substantial double-digit percentages, within business segments, exceeding overall corporate goals. Revenues in China went from $520 million to $1.3 billion in three years. Arguably, McNerney reinvigorated 3M and its work force and built a strong leadership program at the company.

But some analysts believe that McNerney was too conservative when it came to acquisitions, and his successor quickly announced that he planned to do more. The true success of Six Sigma remained to be seen at the time of McNerney's appointment as Boeing's CEO. News articles following that appointment questioned whether Six Sigma had become part of 3M's corporate culture. The program had generated an age discrimination lawsuit, with the powerful national organization the American Association of Retired Persons (AARP) as a co-plaintiff. According to the complaint, younger workers were favored as "black belts" (leaders) in Six Sigma to the detriment of older workers.

According to an article in the *St. Paul Pioneer Press*[58] following his appointment at Boeing, for all of McNerney's goals of organic growth for 3M, internal sales were lagging in 2005 when he left for Boeing. Profit increases appeared to come from cost-cutting and productivity-improvement measures, while organic sales increased 4 percent instead of the targeted 8 percent. Additionally, the cost cutting, plant closures, and layoffs instituted by McNerney in his three and a half years at 3M drew criticism, including from academics, who faulted him for not laying the groundwork for long-term success. (For all the effort McNerney put into leadership development, he never identified a successor at 3M. The company chose another outsider to replace him. In contrast to Wall Street's positive reaction to McNerney's appointment at 3M, the company's stock declined fractionally upon the announcement of his successor.)

In fairness, three and a half years was not enough time for McNerney to accomplish all the goals he set for 3M.

---

58. "James McNerney Largely Lived Up to his Advance Billing at 3M Co." *St. Paul Pioneer Press* (July 1, 2005).

MOVE TO BOEING

After a flurry of post-appointment interviews as Boeing's new CEO, McNerney largely avoided interviews with the mainstream media, instead using the in-house *Boeing Frontiers* magazine to convey messaging to employees.

Because McNerney had been on the Boeing board of directors since 2001, he was familiar with the company, its work, its policies, and its scandals. As a board member, he lived through the tanker dust up, the Lockheed Martin trade-secret theft incident, and Harry Stonecipher's "zippergate." McNerney famously was the board member who warned in April 2003 that too much focus on cost cutting (a Stonecipher trait) could lead to Airbus overtaking Boeing and harm Boeing's future. By the time McNerney became CEO on June 30, 2005, there was little to suggest that the company was on a path to industrial disaster. Nevertheless, McNerney did inherit some messes. Scandals had cost Boeing in terms of money (nearly $700 million in total fines), reputation, and executives. Employee morale, beaten down by the events and Stonecipher's open disdain for engineers and unions, was at a low point.[59]

His appointment at Boeing was greeted enthusiastically because of his long experience at GEAE and his membership on Boeing's board. He was perceived, on balance, to have had a stellar performance at 3M. An unidentified Airbus executive was quoted in the media as saying that McNerney was a good choice for Boeing and "the worst possible choice" for Airbus. In an interview with *Boeing Frontiers,* McNerney gave a nod to the company's recent scandals and ethical lapses. The article in the magazine's December 2005/January 2006 issue, presented in a question-and-answer format, focused exclusively on ethics and corporate compliance.

At Boeing, McNerney quickly reaffirmed his earlier-declared support for stock buybacks. His top priorities included the company's financial performance and how to enhance it; ethics and compliance; and playing "bigger" as a company and leveraging strengths across all areas of Boeing. The latter priority would emerge as McNerney's "One Boeing" campaign, in which divisions supported each other as needed rather than acting as standalone business entities. This approach would become more and more apparent as the 787 program sank into disarray.

"Playing bigger" meant driving improved growth and profitability; identifying and pursuing specific opportunities to gain more leverage in

---

59. An indicator of just how negatively Boeing employees now viewed management came in the form of a salacious story: The first time during McNerney's tenure that executives flew in a Boeing business jet to Renton, Washington, from Chicago, a second airplane full of mistresses was said to have landed right behind it.

sourcing, technology, and R&D; applying lean production principals more broadly; and establishing new performance targets in 2006. McNerney was quoted as saying the following: "Controlling our future has as much to do with advancing productivity year in and year out as having the right products, services and solutions for our customers." He also said that he would make leadership development a central focus for the company.

A growing complaint among customers involved "Boeing's arrogance." This arrogance on the part of Boeing was said to be a factor that helped Airbus make sales and win key customers. A 1992 sales campaign with United Airlines was Boeing's key wake-up call. United had at that time become an exclusive Boeing customer. But when the carrier's leadership opened a competition between Boeing's 737-400, a mediocre airplane in terms or range, power, and airport performance, and Airbus's A320, Boeing executives dismissed warnings from its salesman assigned to United that Airbus was in line to win the competition. When the executives refused to renegotiate the contract price for the 737-400, United ordered the A320. The loss led Boeing to develop the 737 NG, which, along with the 737-800 sub-type (essentially the successor to the 737-400), remains one of the best airplanes Boeing ever developed.

Boeing went on to lose other competitions for airline business, secure in the belief that the airlines involved would never leave Boeing. Two key U.S. competitions went to Airbus and the A320 instead of to Boeing. McNerney vowed to eliminate the arrogance that left Boeing out of touch with customers and the regulatory environment. It was expected that he would follow his 3M policies of outsourcing more R&D to suppliers and contractors.

McNerney's success rate at Boeing was mixed, as will be seen.

In a November 17, 2005, meeting with sell-side analysts (who focus on the issuing, selling, or trading of securities)—McNerney's first foray into Wall Street as Boeing's CEO—he told the analysts that his primary focus was margin expansion.[60] He said that he wanted Boeing to enter into the high-margin, profitable spare-parts business.[61] He emphasized his desire for productivity gains via lean manufacturing and procurement measures and the off-loading of greater amounts of development and sub-assembly work. At the time, McNerney said that Boeing's Integrated Defense Sys-

---

60. As reported in a November 18, 2005, Credit Suisse Research Report by Robert Spingarn and Brandon Woodard.

61. Credit Suisse wrote: "McNerney specifically talked about opportunities to become part of the life cycle supply chain for aircraft, participating in the lucrative spare parts stream that offers strong double digit margins to more of Boeing's suppliers."

tems (IDS) division was under market-based pressure and was likely to be slow-growth or flat for an indeterminate amount of time. He told the analysts that most of Boeing's risk had been absorbed in the company's space and satellite businesses. He said that he saw an extended selling cycle in commercial products based on the assumption that the U.S. market would recover as other world markets began to cool. Aircraft pricing and supply-chain capacities were constraints to growth, he said, citing Boeing's pricing vis-à-vis Airbus.

Finally, in talking with the analysts McNerney stressed the importance of Boeing being first to market with a new narrowbody airplane to replace its aging 737. R&D on this new airplane already had begun. But even though November 2005 was early in the 787 program, there may have been hints that all was not well. Officials said that Boeing was uncertain enough about the 787's technology and manufacturing techniques so as to delay proceeding with the project immediately, preferring instead to wait until those techniques were proved to be sound. The plan was to get the 787 into service (in May 2008) and then launch the replacement for the 737. Once the replacement was in service, or close to it, a program to replace the 777 was planned.

Research notes issued at the time outlined the following financial goals set by McNerney:

"Management outlined long-term goals of a 7% after-tax corporate margin and an unidentified double-digit Boeing Commercial Airplanes (BCA) group margin," wrote Byron Callan of Prudential Equity Group. "Prudential forecasts $4.50-$6.50 per share cash flow 2006-2009." In an unrelated December 8, 2005, report, Prudential forecast BCA R&D spending to decrease from $1.8 billion to $2 billion from 2006 through 2008 to $1.2 billion in 2009, expecting the amount to increase during 2012 as the R&D for the replacement for the 737 ramped up. In a Stock Equity Report dated October 19, 2005, Standard & Poor's predicted that Boeing's debt-adjusted return on equity would be between 15 and 17 percent and that free-cash-flow compound annual growth rates would be between 7.5 and 8.5 percent.

All these predictions, of course, were made long before the problems with the 787 emerged shortly before the July 8, 2007, roll out of the first airplane.

Although McNerney had been on Boeing's board of directors for four years when he became CEO, and even though he was well acquainted with the problems facing the company, becoming its leader thrust him into an entirely new role. The messes he inherited ranged from a need to clean up the ethics problems that put him there in the first place; to the 787 development, which by 2005 was beginning to show its first signs of strain after only eighteen months; to battles with labor unions and the World Trade Organization complaint mentioned earlier in this book. To say McNerney faced plenty of challenges is an understatement. But it's unlikely that he realized just how deep Boeing's problems were—or how deep they would become.

LABOR

McNerney was in office only two months and two days when the International Association of Machinists District 751 (IAM 751) union went on strike on September 2, 2005. Wages, health care costs, and pensions were the big issues, as was so often the case. Boeing was on the road to finally recovering from 9/11. Officials expected to sell more than 300 airliners that year. When IAM 751 members hit the picket lines, Airbus had sold 276 airplanes year-to-date. Alarmingly, analysts were talking about a strike that could last three months. The strike was forecast to cost Boeing $70 million a day.[62]

Labor negotiations had been underway for three months, beginning shortly before McNerney was named CEO. Boeing offered union workers a 5.5 percent raise and $66 a month in pension payments for every year of service. The union wanted $80 a month and parity for Boeing's Wichita workers, who were then covered by the company's contract with IAM 751. Boeing entered a contract with the Canadian equity firm Onex the preceding February to sell its Wichita facility and other facilities, but the deal hadn't closed yet. Onex wanted a five-year contract from the Wichita workers with give-backs on wages, benefits, and health care costs. The union rejected those demands by a vote of 57 percent to 43 percent despite Onex's threat to walk away from the deal. Unsurprisingly, IAM 751's president, Mark Blondin, denounced Boeing's offer as a strategy to break the union.

Under the campaign of "Do the Right Thing," Blondin and IAM 751 leadership rallied its members to strike. The membership voted on July 13, 2005, to strike. Around-the-clock negotiations began on August 15. *Aero Mechanic,* the union's newsletter, identified employee pensions as the top issue. A fully-funded pension for each worker was demanded.

Robert Spingarn, an aerospace analyst for Credit Suisse, was new to the investment bank at the time of the strike. He was in many ways still getting his grounding covering Boeing. Spingarn decided on a spur of the moment to fly to Seattle and go to the picket lines to talk with the strikers. He called Boeing's Investor Relations (IR) office to let them know. IR told

---

62. Leslie Wayne, "Boeing Output Halts as Machinists Strike," *New York Times* (September 3, 2005), https://www.nytimes.com/2005/09/03/business/boeing-output-halts-as-machinists-strike.html.

him that they weren't going to sanction his trip and that he wouldn't be allowed on Boeing property. But, the IR officer said, he'd be happy to hear what Spingarn found out.

"I hadn't been covering Boeing on my own for more than a couple of years, and I really didn't understand the whole labor situation," Spingarn recalled in 2022 in an interview for this book. "I just got it into my head very, very quickly, wouldn't it be a good idea to do some primary research on this and get on a plane and go out to Seattle and talk to people?" When he went to the picket lines, initially the reception was cool. In those days, suits were the common dress of the day. But the union members on the picket lines, of course, were in blue jeans and shirt sleeves, and many were unshaven. The members pegged the immaculately dressed Spingarn as a Boeing manager, executive, or surrogate.

"I started asking questions and they were very suspicious of me. Here's this guy in a suit asking questions about what is it you want in your contract? Why are you mad at the company? What would you settle for? Immediately I explained, I'm a securities analyst, which didn't resonate with anybody. They said, 'Look, you're in a suit asking these questions, we have to assume you're from Boeing.' I said I'm not from Boeing, and I showed my business card. Credit Suisse didn't mean a whole lot."

Spingarn went back to his hotel. The next morning, wearing jeans, he returned to the picket lines. "I got a very different response. People were less suspicious. I still had trouble explaining what my role was and why I was interested, but in addition to talking to all the folks on the picket line, I also linked up with Connie Kelliher." Kelliher was a long-time communications person for IAM 751 and an especially militant union member. She lined him up with IAM 751 president Mark Blondin, who explained the issues (wages and health and pension benefits). Spingarn returned to the picket lines and learned from his limited sampling that Boeing's demand that members share in their health care costs was the deal-breaking issue.

"The conclusion I came to, and this is the punchline on this whole thing, was there were two issues. One was health care, and they were very upset [about that]. The union folks were very upset that for the first time, Boeing was asking them to contribute to their health care plan cost out of their own pocket monthly.

"The numbers didn't seem that egregious to me since Boeing was still going to be paying the lion's share, but it was the first time they were not paying [the full cost]. It was the first time [union members would] pay more than zero, so for them it was a big deal. Then the other issue was something on the pension. When I did the math, and I'm going to use rough numbers that probably aren't accurate [this statement was made seventeen years after the fact, after all], the cost to Boeing of agreeing to their health care request was 1/10th the cost of agreeing to their pension request. While the union was pretty cognizant of what these two items were and how the math worked and that one was ten times the size of the other, I didn't get the sense that the average machinist was aware of this," Spingarn recalled. He then went home under the impression that if Boeing gave up on the health care demand, members would have voted "yes" even with Boeing's pension demand remaining on the table.

Within a few days, McNerney—still new to his job—agreed to labor's demands. Spingarn made the following recollection: "I got completely blindsided when McNerney shows up in Washington, DC, and strikes a deal with the head of the Machinist Union, the International IAM, and gives in on both [issues]. My thinking was, was he so out of touch with what the average machinist wanted? Why did he give in on the pension? He didn't have to. Rather than thinking maybe he just made a mistake, my feeling was these guys were out of touch. They didn't have any feelers on the ground. They didn't know what these folks wanted. I think it's an interesting observation.| Spingarn believed that McNerney may have been a bit naïve at the time.

He may have been right. As events unfolded during the next contract negotiations and following subsequent events, McNerney wouldn't make the same mistake twice.

But McNerney's next big challenge was the unfolding debacle of the 787.

11

The 787

"There were parts of the airplane that looked like they were made of wood."
—ROBERT SPINGARN, ANALYST FOR CREDIT SUISSE

ALTHOUGH OFFICIALS AT THE BOEING COMPANY kept up a good public façade that all was well and progressing nicely on the company's 787 program, internally it was a different story.

Key players even today are reluctant to point to a specific time when it became clear that the project was going south. The year 2004 was largely a get-started and ramp-up time for the project, so whether important problems and delays began to emerge this soon isn't clear. What is clear is that by 2005, bad signs were there. One former engineer who worked on the 787 program said that his group was stonewalled by another program group when the first group asked for important data it needed to carry out its work assignment. The first group couldn't get any explanation as to why information was not forthcoming, nor any details about when it would be. Additionally, the same engineer was told by a supplier that the 787 was never going to meet its target of a May 2008 entry into service (EIS).

What did the higher-ups at Boeing know and when did they know it? Those who were involved at the time said that the board of directors received briefings every time it met.

The board was inquisitive, but its knowledge was limited. Over the course of a year, Alan Mulally, then the CEO of Boeing's Commercial Airplanes division (BCA), and Mike Bair, the program manager for the 787 project, met with the board nine times for hour-long sessions. To the extent that a board member can be expected to be up to speed on matters based on nine hours of discussion within a year, plus whatever homework the member chose to do, board members did their best. They were interested, actively engaged, and asked good questions, according to a source with knowledge of the meetings.

"[The outsourcing] was what we had to do to do the airplane. It was the price of admission for us to get permission to do the airplane, and it was all about using other people's money in the product-development phase of the program," this source recalls. "In order to get the Japanese to pay for what we wanted them to pay for, they wanted to do engineering. They want-

Figure 16. Newly named Boeing CEO Harry Stonecipher launched the 7E7 program (later officially named the 787). The initial design concept captured the imagination of the airline industry. Stonecipher insisted on outsourcing work on the plane to lower the cost and risk to Boeing. Doing so proved to be one of Boeing's greatest strategic mistakes. Stonecipher's departure from the company under scandal left it up to Jim McNerney to deal with what was to come on the 787 project. Getty photo.

ed to do basically nose-to-tail over the parts that they were responsible for, as opposed to us doing the engineering and sending build-to-print plans . . . to the Japanese. You have to remember [that] back then, it wasn't just Boeing, ... [T]he industry all of sudden, large-scale systems engineering or whatever it was, [thought that this] was the way to go.

"The whole industry was headed down that path. There's no question that the 787 program was a huge step relative to a lot of other ones, but it wasn't just one company, one program. It was this large-scale systems-integration module that was going all throughout aerospace at the time. It had a lot of influence over the 787."

The industrial-model plan was not viewed as outrageous at BCA. But there wasn't enough margin for error built into the plan, and the plan's fatal flaw was that Boeing assumed that its industrial partners had the design and production experience to execute it. Boeing's failure to oversee its partners was so egregious that, by the time it was clear that things had spiraled out of control, it was way too late to recover on schedule or keep costs to minimal overrun.

Bair, the 787 program head, went to Boeing's Chicago headquarters monthly to update executives and the board of directors. But Mulally's departure from Boeing to become CEO of Ford was a major blow for the company. Mulally, an engineer, not only understood engineer-speak, he also famously created effective status boards with green, yellow, and red markers to identify progress, caution, or red alerts for any given issue. When Mulally left BCA in September 2006, he was succeeded by Scott Carson. Carson, who had been named head of sales by former corporate CEO Harry Stonecipher, was a finance and sales guy. Carson invigorated Boeing's lagging sales, especially on the 787. But he wasn't an engineer, and he didn't understand engineer-speak. Briefings and complaints often stopped when they hit Carson's door, say those who tried to warn him at the time of the growing problems within the 787 program.

"As you know, the schedule was the number one watch item from the start," recalled one Boeing officer from the period. "Things don't go bad suddenly (except in the case of a test failure like the side-of-body issue).[63] You watch schedule margins slowly start to evaporate. You also don't declare you're going to miss until it's either become a 'no way possible' or not redoing the schedule causes more harm than not. Once you say you're not going to make it, you guarantee that you won't because everybody resets. In the case of the 787, the first 'not going to make it' was the realization that we needed to let early customers know before they started to sell tickets on the plane."

Airlines typically open ticket sales about eight or nine months before a flight. With the 787's EIS planned for May 2008, eight months earlier would have been September 2007, the month of the plane's planned first flight.

With Bair going to Chicago, it can't be said that McNerney and the board weren't aware of the 787's issues. In fact, "Chicago was fully aware of the 787 schedule from the very beginning," said one ex-Boeing employee with knowledge of the situation. "[McNerney] became CEO in 2005, two years after we launched the program. But as a board member, he was up to speed on the program."

Signs were beginning to emerge that there was trouble. At the June 2007 Paris Air Show, word of a looming delay in the 787 was slipped to a group of aerospace analysts. The source was none other than Greg Hayes, now the chairman of RTX Corporation (formerly Raytheon Technologies Corporation) but at the time the chief financial officer of United Technologies, another predecessor of RTX. Credit Suisse analyst Robert Spingarn was present in the group.

Spingarn noted, "There was always a United Technologies cocktail event in Paris on the Sunday night at the show. There were people standing around, including Greg Hayes and a few Wall Street folks. Suddenly, Hayes let it slip that power-on [for the 787] was four months late." (Power-on is the process of turning all of a plane's electrical power on for the first time, a crucial step in the march to first flight.)

Joe Nadol, an aerospace analyst for JP Morgan, and David Strauss, then at UBS, were also present at the Paris event. Nadol was the one talking to Hayes when the latter let the 787 development snafu slip in casual conversation. Spingarn contacted Boeing's Investor Relations office (IR) to get details. IR "basically suggested that whatever I was hearing was either insignificant or it was mischaracterized or whatever," Spingarn recalled. Nadol

---

63. During static testing of the strength of the portion of the 787 where the wing mated to the side body, the structure failed before it was designed to.

went home and wrote up the news in one of his research notes. He later told me that IR went *tilt* with him and tried to discredit his note. (Nadol did not reveal in his note from whom he had heard the news about the 787.)

Jon Ostrower, at the time writing for his own online newsletter called *Flightblogger,* also began posting about possible 787 delays. Boeing's corporate communications office attempted to discredit him. The mainstream press was also on the scent of the 787 story. In June 2007, the *Seattle Times* reported that mating the plane's big barrels wasn't going well. A gap the size of a finger had occurred at some matings.[64] According to the *Times* article:

"It wasn't a perfect go-together the first time. There were a few challenges. We overcame them," the Times quoted Boeing spokesperson Mary Hanson as saying. "In general, [Boeing's engineers] are pleased with how all the joints are going," the Times reported.

"Hans Weber, an industry technical consultant and president of San Diego-based TECOP International, examined the entire sequence of photos and sees no cause for alarm," the Times wrote. "It doesn't strike me as all that unexpected," Weber said. "In the process of putting those splice plates on one side, they distorted the structure a bit. That's not unusual. The structure distorts fairly readily."

Spingarn said in his 2022 interview with me that he believed that BCA wasn't keeping the company's IR office fully informed about the 787.

When the 787 rolled out for its public debut on July 8, 2007 (7-8-7), airplane number one was nowhere near flight-ready status. In fact, it was an incomplete airplane. Temporary fasteners, wood doors and wing parts, and other cosmetic materials designed to hide the true status of the plane had been used. Even though the 787 wasn't remotely airworthy, McNerney claimed that the plane was on track to make its first flight in September, two months hence. Spingarn was among those present when these remarks were made.

Boeing threw a party the night before the 787 rollout. Aerospace analysts, customers, and others were invited to the black-tie affair. "This dinner reminded me of a high-end wedding in Manhattan. There were speeches. I don't remember the specifics about it, but it was very much like going to a wedding. There was music and very nice food. We were all wearing tuxedos. You can imagine what this looked like. The next day we all went to the hangar and opened the giant door. We were invited to walk around the plane. There were plenty of people who thought they were

---

64. Dominic Gates, "Boeing Finds 787 Pieces Aren't Quite a Perfect Fit," *Seattle Times* (June 28, 2007), https://www.seattletimes.com/business/boeing-finds-787-pieces-arent-quite-a-perfect-fit/.

looking at an airplane that wasn't finished, because there were parts of the airplane that looked like they were made of wood. Somebody noticed that things like trailing edges were made of wood and painted in some kind of electrostatic paint to disguise it," Spingarn recalled.

Soon, stories emerged in the press about the wooden parts on the 787 and just how incomplete the airplane was. Questions soon emerged, such as "How could McNerney claim that the first flight was slated for September when it was clear that this incomplete plane was never going to be ready?" Spingarn thinks that information simply wasn't flowing uphill to Boeing executives in Chicago. He opined that only those in the know had full information and that they weren't talking.

What was clear was that BCA was in the know. 787 program head Bair was on an airplane to Tokyo late the next month (or in early September 2007—memories are hazy on the exact date) to inform launch customer All Nippon Airways (ANA) that the 787 would be late. In September 2007, Boeing formally announced a three-month delay for the 787's first flight. On October 10, 2007, the company announced a six-month delay for the first deliveries of the plane.[65] By then, Boeing had orders for 710 787s from fifty customers. Boeing was still sticking with a robust delivery schedule in conversations with financial analysts, predicting that there would be 109 hand-overs through 2009, only three less than previously stated. Some analysts were skeptical.

These dates and numbers thrown out by Boeing were missed by wide margins. With one schedule slip after another, the first 787 flight eventually was planned for June 2009, concurrent with the Paris Air Show. BCA CEO Carson and Pat Shanahan, who had been assigned by McNerney to troubleshoot the 787 program and fix it, spoke to the international media on Monday at the air show, fully expecting the 787's first flight to occur the following day or the day after that. On Monday night, Boeing held its usual media cocktail reception. Carson was in good spirits. The evening was a social event with no on-the-record discussion about Boeing business. Indeed, the conversation Carson had with me at the reception was about his interests in restoring a Douglas A-26 twin-engine bomber and attack airplane designed and built in World War II and used in the Korean War. Carson worked on the airplane while he was in the military. He also spoke with envy about the restored Lockheed Constellation that made air show flybys. And, as an aside, Carson said that after the first flights of the 787 and 747-8, then also in development, he planned to retire. This was news, but Carson refused to release me from the off-the-record nature of the remark.

---

65. "Boeing Is Delaying Delivery of Its 787," *New York Times* (October 11, 2007), https://www.nytimes.com/2007/10/11/business/11boeing.html.

The good cheer didn't last. On Tuesday in Paris, neither Carson nor Shanahan were anywhere to be seen. News quickly emerged that test pilots had refused to fly the 787. A key structural test of the wing-to-body join had failed.

By the end of 2007, the 787 became a global story about failures of meeting schedule and supply-chain issues. *The Chicago Tribune's* recap on December 7 outlined how Boeing's troubles were trickling down the supply chain.[66]

WHAT WENT WRONG

One of the key elements of Boeing's industrial business model was farming out work to Italy's Alenia Aeronautica, America's Vought Aircraft, and a new joint venture between the two firms called Global Aeronautica. Each of the two companies and the joint venture were responsible for producing sections of the 787. Alenia built the tail section in Italy, and Vought built a major production facility in North Charleston, South Carolina, where Global Aeronautica also built a facility. The center and aft fuselage sections of the 787 were produced in Charleston and flown to Everett in Dreamlifters. After McNerney and the Boeing board of directors approved a second final assembly line in Charleston, work on these fuselage sections was split between Everett and Charleston. When the stretched 787 was launched, an assembled airplane could not fit into the Everett Line 1 final assembly line and, therefore, assembly of the 787-10 model was assigned exclusively to the South Carolina facility.

Vought was a long-time Boeing supplier. But in choosing Vought, Boeing looked at the money behind the supplier. As a former Vought official tells it, the outsourcing process included the after-effects of 9/11, when everyone was cash-crunched. Boeing was especially affected because U.S. airlines accounted for most of its orders. Neither the airlines nor Boeing had fully recovered by 2003, when Mulally, Bair, and officers at Boeing's corporate headquarters were debating whether or how to launch the 7E7.

Boeing approached strategic partners during this period. "Candidly, when they saw Vought, they saw the backing of the Carlyle Group," a huge private equity firm then and now, says the former Vought official. "They felt that Vought would be able to swing whatever cash was necessary, and to a certain extent, that was a realistic expectation."

---

66. David Griesing and Julie Johnsson, "Behind Boeing's 787 Delays," *Chicago Tribune* (December 8, 2007), https://www.chicagotribune.com/news/ct-xpm-2007-12-08-0712070870-story.html.

Vought was responsible for the aft third of the aircraft, basically designing, integrating, and building a barrel and manufacturing it. Alenia and the Japanese heavies (Fuji and Kawasaki) were responsible for the sections immediately ahead of the aft third. Spirit Aerosystems built Section 41, the nose section.

There was a lot of encouragement to involve as many suppliers as possible. By the time the dust settled, huge pieces of Vought's scope of work had been outsourced to other companies, and the design effort was outsourced as well. Vought had turned around and subcontracted to Boeing Winnipeg for structural components, design, and production.

Vought, like all lead contractors to Boeing, contracted with other suppliers. For example, Vought subcontracted all the floor structures to Israel Aerospace Industries (IAI). IAI, in turn, subbed these structures out to companies in the United States. The supply chain for the 787 became incredibly tangled and layered. "When you start injecting a lot of changes into a system that complex, you wind up with all sorts of second-order phenomena. You wind up with all kinds of sequential delays and backlogs. You can imagine the sort of ringing that takes place as changes cascade back up and down this thing, and there were thousands and thousands of changes," the Vought official said.

The real issue was that this complex system had been built that was multi-layered but that on the surface looked pretty simple. The scope of work was so great that a lot of parties were involved. Spirit Aerosystems had much the same problem. The Vought official explained, "We had been issued subcontractors, so we wound up being something of a master design integrator for the aft section. We were dependent on other companies' designs and production. Changes would flow from Boeing to us, would flow from us to IAI, would flow from IAI to their subs, and from their subs to their subs. I think that was a lot more complex the way it played out than anybody had anticipated."

Boeing initially chose not to embed its employees with its industrial partners. Assigning design and engineering to the partners, rather than using its historic build-to-print process, also turned out to be a mistake. The subcontracting by these industrial partners carried forward overarching mistakes. "There's virtually no way to execute that scope of work, because you weren't responsible for any of the piece parts. You were just responsible for integration and assembly, so your destiny was not in your own hands," the Vought official said. But he placed blame on the supply chain as much as on Boeing.

"I think it's the supply-chain guys that didn't foresee what really happened. You've got a bunch of people trying to get scope on this aircraft. The supply-chain guys had to create a hierarchy. At the end of the day, it's not just subbing out work. It's not subbing out just engineering and manufacturing. The problem was, [Boeing] subbed out things that are inherently OEM-ish [original equipment manufacturer], the overall integration. They went a bridge too far, I think inadvertently, by putting things out in the supply base, a layer of responsibility that they then couldn't honor," said the Vought official.

Vought, located in Dallas, had the legacy of having designed and built a lot of the composite structures for the B-2 when it was part of Northrop Grumman. It was a build-to-print shop in the way it was configured as Vought Aircraft after its various pieces had gone with different prime manufacturers. What remained was a shop with a really significant and unique structural composite capability. The aft pressure bulkhead conceived by Vought was a simple, carbon-fiber composite part. Had Vought been designing the 787, it would've looked clean and simple. That scope of supply was dedicated to Vought, but Boeing engineers jumped in and put titanium and other materials in the bulkhead. It wasn't strictly composite anymore.

The 787's floor beams were also designed as composites. Boeing engineers added brackets, stiffeners, and other components that added complexity. Boeing was still playing the part of an OEM, even though it subcontracted others to do OEM kinds of things. These subcontractors trying to do OEM kinds of things were disabled by Boeing's trying to make a fully integrated airplane. "Everyone's working with the best of intent, but the supply chain was designed wrong," one supplier said.

TIMELINE

As described in *Air Wars,* Boeing had an aggressive timeline laid out for the 787—four years from program launch to EIS. This was about the same timeline used for the world's first jumbo jet, the 747. Boeing's "Incredibles," led by Joe Sutter, met the 747's target date despite having to build an entirely new factory and delays from engine maker Pratt & Whitney. But planes had become much more complex since then, with advanced materials, advanced electronics, and the overall moonshot design of the 787. The industrial model was a radical departure from Boeing's past practices, in which the company retained much more design and production control over their products. One of the lead people on the 787 project said that the plane's timeline wasn't outrageously short—provided everything went according to plan. But it didn't, and this was apparent very early.

Suppliers weren't sanguine about the 787 timeline by any means. Privately, they expressed doubts about Boeing's plan and predicted that bringing the 787 into service would take seven years. (It took eight.) "It was really, really obvious that you couldn't get there from here," one supplier told me at the time. "There were some issues within Boeing being candid.

I suspect there were attempts at candor, but because this was an unconventionally complicated supply chain with an unforeseen, huge number of changes cascading down through that supply chain and approvals cascading back up, . . . there's no way to predict when the airplane could be built, effort notwithstanding."

By the second quarter of 2008, the 787 was mired in cost overruns and delays, with no end in sight for either. McNerney flew to Charleston for a tour of the Vought and Global Aeronautica factories. What he saw was a production still a long way from running smoothly. At one station, a Vought official pointed to a component on which work had stopped because the supplier hadn't delivered. McNerney wanted to know who the supplier was. "Let's get him on the phone," McNerney said. "It's Boeing Winnipeg, and they told us this morning [that] they don't know when we're going to get the parts," the Vought official said, adding, "[McNerney] says, 'Okay, I see what your problem is.'"

Issues like these were only a small part of the overall picture. The big fuselage barrels didn't mate properly. The wing-to-side body join didn't mate properly either. But these were the big issues that garnered headlines in the trade and mainstream press on a regular basis. Behind the scenes, one problem after another emerged, small and large. One example: the floor structure hadn't been designed yet when aircraft number one rolled out. Each problem took time to analyze, to come up with a solution—sometimes requiring a redesign—and to implement the fix.

"Structural fittings on that airplane have always been a problem from day one," one engineer from the development days told me. Boeing struggled, to put it mildly, with the early airplanes through unit nineteen. The first six aircraft were flight-test airplanes. The first three were so screwed up and subject to so much rework that they were unsellable. Two were donated to museums, one was scrapped, and three others were sold as VIP aircraft. Those with line numbers 11 through 19 were also reworked so many times that they were nicknamed the Terrible Teens. Eventually they were sold at steep discounts.

Despite going into production in 2006, which picked up after EIS in 2011, in 2020 Boeing found anomalies in production that caused eight 787s in service to be grounded, and delivery of planes was suspended. There were eventually 110 787s produced during the twenty-month delivery suspension that ended up being parked while Boeing designed a fix and obtained FAA approval to implement it.[67] It took five months to rework each airplane.

---

67. The delivery suspension began in October 2020, while the MAX was still grounded and Boeing was working with the FAA to recertify it. Recertification came in November 2020. The FAA yanked Boeing's authorization to certify each

The problem? Mating some of the fuselage sections didn't meet the tolerance requirements by the thickness of a hair or a piece of paper, depending on the locations. Also, an Italian supplier's supplier used unapproved parts, a move that wasn't caught until intense review of the 787 production occurred while deliveries were suspended.

In January 2013, a Japan Air Lines (JAL) 787 caught fire while parked on a Boston Logan Airport ramp shortly after incoming passengers and baggage were deplaned on a flight from Tokyo. A maintenance worker on board discovered smoke. By the time the fire department arrived, within minutes of the fire, the smoke was so thick that the source of the blaze had to be located using infrared instruments. It turned out to be the lithium-ion battery located in the hold of the airplane. It took firefighters an inordinate amount of time to put the fire out. A week later, an ANA 787 took off from Yamaguchi, Japan, for Tokyo. Eighteen minutes later, smoke was detected via instruments in the hold. The pilots made an emergency landing. The smoke was again traced to the battery. The FAA grounded the airplanes for what turned out to be three months. The root cause of the JAL and ANA incidents couldn't be found. Boeing designed a box in which to enclose the battery to contain any fire, and a pipe was added to vent smoke overboard.

An engineer told me years later that the best hypothesis about the cause of the fires was that condensation found its way into the batteries and shorted them out. Lithium-ion batteries are susceptible to thermal runaways and very hot fires, making them especially dangerous. A few months before the JAL fire, Airbus held one of its annual safety conferences. As it happened, an analysis of airborne fires was part of the agenda. Airbus's study concluded that an airborne fire could go out of control in eight minutes and that an affected plane would need to be on the ground in fifteen minutes. For the JAL flight, a disaster had been a very near thing. Had the fire occurred as the flight was transiting the Polar region or isolated areas of the Pacific or Canada instead of an isolated ramp at Logan Airport, the plane and all people on board would have been lost.

Investigators of the JAL and ANA incidents couldn't pinpoint the cause, though, and whether condensation was at fault will likely never be known. Condensation, after all, disappears in the heat of a fire.

In July 2013, only a few months after the 787 returned to service, an Ethiopian Airlines 787 caught fire at London's Heathrow Airport. Like the JAL airplane, it was empty. The fire was traced to the emergency locator

---

MAX as ready for delivery and also yanked Boeing's authority to certify 787s as ready for delivery. Having been burned badly by Boeing in the MAX crisis, the FAA was in no mood to be lenient, flexible, or overly cooperative with the company on the 787. It would take twenty months before the FAA approved the fix for the 787.

beacon in the top of the plane's aft fuselage. Pinched wires that eventually shorted out were identified as the likely cause. Even today some doubts remain because the fire melted the wires and the surrounding structure. There was no way to confirm whether pinched wires and arching were truly the cause of the London fire. But coming so soon after the JAL and ANA fires, plenty of eyebrows were raised in concern.

"The 787, for many reasons. is a very, very sick program," a former engineer from the program told me in 2022. "I think they would be lucky if one of the technical issues or any other manufacturing shortcomings don't come back to bite them in a 737 MAX 2.0 kind of a crisis, but much larger."

In 2024 and 2025, two 787s had uncommanded dives from cruising altitude. There were no injuries in the first event, which was traced to a flight attendant inadvertently hitting a pilot seat lock that allowed the seat to move forward, pushing the pilot into the flight controls. In the second incident, some passengers were injured by the unexpected dive. The event was under investigation at the time of this writing.

THE COST

The 787 program eventually became such an industrial nightmare, that by the time it was sorted out. it had accumulated more than $50 billion in deferred production and tooling costs. Losses associated with the first six test airplanes, including those that couldn't be sold, were charged to research and development. Customer compensation costs for the delays and the expenses related to failing to meet operating-cost guarantees were never revealed. Intangible costs for lost customer goodwill and for orders placed with Airbus for the A330 instead of with Boeing for the 787 are subject to WAGs, wild-ass guesses.

Scott Carson, BCA's CEO during some of the company's most troubling periods, is a glass-half-full rather than a glass-half-empty type of person. In my 2019 interview with him for *Air Wars,* Carson said that the lessons learned from the production debacles transformed how Boeing did things. "We didn't have any choice, to be honest," he admitted. "We learned a lot on the 787 and the production system. The success of the product, though, is, does

Type	Number sold		Type	Number sold
747 (All)	1,572	1	787	1,957
767 (All)*	1,430	2	777 Classic	1,822
777 Classic	1,822	3	747 (All)	1,572
777X	407	4	A330ceo*	1,479
787	1,957	5	767 (All)*	1,430
Sub Total	**7,188**	6	A350	1,344
A330ceo*	1,479	7	777X	407
A330neo	374	8	A340	377
A340	377	9	A330neo	374
A350	1,344	10	A380	251
A380	251		Sources: Airbus, Boeing	
Sub Total	**3,825**		Through 2024.	
Total	**11,013**			
Boeing Share	**65%**			
Airbus Share	**35%**			
*Including tankers.				

Figure 17. Boeing's long history of building twin-aisle airplanes beginning with the 747 gives it a commanding market share of this segment.

it retain economic value for your operator, and does it have a reasonable service life to it? There is a lot of cost that goes into operating an airplane that is not just the daily operating cost." Customers agreed. Through 2024, Boeing reported net sales of nearly 2,000 787s, making it the best-selling widebody aircraft of all time—outselling the previous record-holder, the 777 Classic family.

12

The Path to the 737 MAX

*"The MAX was created because it was the second choice of Boeing,
and it was the first choice of the operators."*

—A FORMER BOEING ENGINEER FROM THE 737 MAX PROGRAM

THE 787 WASN'T JIM MCNERNEY'S ONLY PRODUCT CHALLENGE. The Boeing Company launched its 747-8 model in November 2005, about eight months after McNerney became chief executive officer. He had been on the company's board of directors since 2001, so he was sufficiently versed in the history of the decision-making on, and in the business case for, the project to proceed with the next version of the iconic Queen of the Skies. Updating the plane had been the subject of great debate.

As described in *Air Wars*, doubts about continuing the 747 program dated to the launch of the 777-300ER in 2000. There was a group within Boeing that believed the -300 would supersede the 747 and that the 747 program should end with the -400. Others believed that there was still a future for the freighter. In the end, the latter argument was the driving force behind going forward with the 747-8. And if this justified forward motion on the 747, why not offer a passenger model as well to undermine the Airbus A380? The A380 program was launched in 2000, with entry into service (EIS) targeted for 2006. Boeing—and many others—thought that Airbus was nuts to launch the A380. The era of the Very Large Aircraft (VLA) had peaked long ago, and its future was limited. Airbus kept projecting a twenty-year market for up to 1,700 VLAs, often to the mirth of the A380's critics.[68] Boeing was right and Airbus was wrong when it came to the A380. But Boeing was wrong about the 747-8. Only 107 freighters and forty-eight passenger models were sold. A multi-billion-dollar forward loss was taken against the program, which ran nearly two years late.

The 747-8 ran into design and execution troubles, some due to the negative halo effect of the 787's issues. Engineers on the 747 program were

---

68. A lawsuit filed by Rolls-Royce against Pratt & Whitney, which was a partner in the A380 engine alliance powerplant provider, revealed that the true twenty-year market forecast was for 650 A380 sales.

diverted to the 787 project as troubles mounted. Engineering work was outsourced to Russia and India. When the results were delivered to Boeing, the work was determined to be flawed. The Society of Professional Engineering Employees in Aerospace union (SPEEA), which had objected to outsourcing in the first place, already overworked and stressed because of the 787, had to correct the flaws. Delays ensued and costs climbed. Flutter and vibrations were discovered in flight testing. More delays, more costs.

Then there was the U.S. Air Force tanker competition. Boeing's first contract with the government had been voided due to a leasing scandal. The second competition began under CEO Harry Stonecipher, as did a related World Trade Organization (WTO) trade fight. Stonecipher's successor, Jim McNerney, inherited both controversies. Executives and officers at Boeing headquarters in Chicago and in Seattle recognized that the days of the 737 were numbered. McNerney knew from his tenure on Boeing's board of directors that the 737—which entered service in 1968—had to be replaced.

Airbus launched the re-engined A320 family in December 2010, branded as the New Engine Option, or neo. Boeing, predictably, dismissed the viability of the neo program. Officials claimed that the neo would cost more than Airbus predicted and that, in any event, the improved economics only brought the Airbus family to par with the 737 NG's economics. It was wishful thinking at best and disingenuous at worst.

Jim Albaugh, the president of Boeing's Commercial Airplanes division (BCA), and Mike Bair, the head of the 737 program, wanted to launch a new airplane program to replace the 737. But as 2010 turned into 2011, and while Airbus began lining up customers for the neo, Boeing's hands were tied. The 787 hadn't been delivered yet (this finally occurred in October 2011). Cost overruns, unrecovered tooling costs, and customer compensation ran into the tens of billions of dollars. Write-offs approaching $2 billion were in store for the late 747-8. Engineering and financial resources were strained by these two BCA programs, with more stress being felt on the defense side. Investors, having suffered from a depressed stock price and absence of dividends during the 787/747 program developments, were itching for returns.

Importantly, airlines were skeptical of another new program, given the recent history of BCA missing delivery dates by years, not weeks or days. Internally, Boeing executives, salespeople, and engineers debated what to do next. Boeing always runs parallel studies to keep its options open. In this case, there was a new-airplane study of a twin-aisle, mid-size airplane, favored by Albaugh and Bair. There was also a single-aisle alternative that had its supporters. What materials would be used also was open to debate: composite, following the 787 example, or a metal fuselage with composite wings and empennage?

In 2011, Boeing was far from understanding how to build a composite airplane at the high production rates of the 737. High production rates were needed on their own merits. But it was also getting *to* the high rates that was a major concern. Ramping up production of a new airplane involved implementing the "learning curve," a key metric in efficient production. Rate breaks (the point when rates shift from one level to the next) had to be carefully planned. The supply chain had to be ready. So did Boeing's own production system and workforce. Rate breaks typically come in increments of five. In December 2010, when Airbus launched the neo, Boeing had delivered 376 737s that year, an average rate of 31 units per month. Boeing planned to dramatically increase rates in the coming years. Officials recognized that meeting the new rate targets and ramping them up would take years, something they feared would hurt market share if Airbus stuck with the A320neo (instead of building a new airplane). Airbus could deliver more current-model airplane units more quickly than Boeing could deliver more new-airplane units. A re-engined, versus a re-designed, 737, like the neo, would simply integrate into the existing final assembly line and the supply chain (except for the engines); it wouldn't have to retool or reinvent itself.

FUTURE SMALL AIRPLANE

There were those within Boeing who were adamant that the 737 replacement should be a single-aisle aircraft. The Product Development unit in Renton, Washington, was working on a single-aisle airplane. There was a separate Boeing group at the widebody plant in Everett, Washington, working on a twin-aisle aircraft.[69]

"At the time, there was an FSA, future single-aisle airplane, and that had been going on for a year and a half," said an engineer working in the Renton Product Development office. "The FSA was very, very serious. There was something like 800 people charging time

Figure 18. The Future Small Airplane concept was a three-member family replacing the 737 line. Under a proposed joint venture between Boeing and Embraer, the former would design and build twin-aisle aircraft and the latter would cover the single-aisle sector. Credit: Leeham Co.

---

69. In 2001, Boeing filed patents with the U.S. Patent and Trademark Office for twin-aisle airplanes that would seat fewer than 200 passengers (patent numbers US 6834833 and US 2010/0200697). The designs for these planes looked odd. The front two-thirds of each airplane was wide, and the aft one-third was narrower, a shape that prompted the nickname "Pollywog." These planes included a carbon-fiber fuselage-construction patent for non-round fuselages.

for it, so it was a big, big project. I went to the daily meetings on that, so I saw it very closely. The difficulty was that the performance of the FSA was simply never significantly better than the re-engine at the time."

This engineer said that the new airplane design only achieved 3 to 4 percent better fuel economics on a 715-nautical-mile mission over the re-engined airplane. "That's margin of error at that stage so they were essentially the same. They couldn't do a better airplane. That was the main reason Boeing chose the re-engine. If you actually ask people who were very, very closely married to the idea of launching that single-aisle airplane, what you're going to hear is that 'No, that airplane couldn't make production rates or the cost of the program was simply too high, et cetera, et cetera.'

"Those are trivialities. That is certainly the case, but any new airplane is like that. You don't expect that new airplane to cost as much as a minor derivative. You don't expect that airplane to start at 30 a month. It's not the case. All those are in the mix, and supposedly, they're going to be made up for by their performance, by their pricing, and ultimately owe it to the long-run grabbing of market share, but they couldn't. They simply could not design the FSA to have any sort of performance advantage over the MAX or RE at that time."

The FSA would have a profile like the 787 and a cross section competitive with the A320, allowing for containerized cargo. But it was a "me-too" airplane. Still, a new wing (the A320 family weak point once the NG wing was designed) would have given the FSA an advantage over the A320. Airbus officials were "terrified" (their word) that Boeing would launch a new airplane after Airbus placed its bet on the neo. If Boeing had done so, Airbus officials felt they would have been compelled to follow. Buried in A350 development costs and big loss-making programs with the A380 and A400m military aircraft, the last thing Airbus wanted was to be forced into another new airplane program, as it had been with the A350.[70]

The Renton-based engineer said that as the studies for a new airplane or a re-engined 737 evolved, the 787 experience had a negative effect on product development. There had been a conclusion that Boeing had overreached with technology, design, and production. Even Albaugh acknowledged in his interview for *Air Wars* that these things had not reached the maturity levels needed to apply to a new airplane, which is not surprising since the 787 hadn't entered service at the time. As the FSA studies

---

70. When the A350 was launched in response to the 787, Airbus tried a warmed-over A330 that quickly was rejected by the market as an insufficient response. Despite being embroiled in the WTO trade dispute, Airbus nevertheless went back to the till for government launch aid.

progressed, the engineer said that those working on the program were inhibited.

The Renton engineer said that "Some of it was mandated that you shall not use technology more advanced than X and Y. In the end, I don't think that people who were making the design decisions on that study really understood how this stuff actually works. I say that because I got to see what their actual understanding of these fundamentals were, and it was significantly lacking. That scared me and explained why they couldn't do the job back then. You can explain a part of that from the 787 experience, and say that, 'Yes, they went overboard with technology on that, and they were trying to overcompensate on the FSA.' I bet that's the case, but regardless, they still didn't do a good job on the FSA, which is why, ultimately, they had no leg to stand on.

"Towards the end, they got pretty bad. They started modifying the weight numbers that came from the weight group. Reducing them and then passing them on for performance evaluation. Essentially cheap, and then very quickly, it became clear that that's happening. They lost a lot of face and ultimately there was just nothing they could do about [it]. Then once the MAX got launched, all those studies, they all got shelved."

CHANGES TO THE NG (NEXT-GENERATION AIRCRAFT)

Boeing was still debating whether to go forward with a new airplane or not when its hand was forced in the summer of 2011, when Airbus was close to wrapping up a big order for its A319ceo, A321ceo, A319neo, and A321neo models with American Airlines. American had been an exclusive Boeing customer since 1996. The airline's CEO, Gerard Arpey, called McNerney to tell him that an Airbus deal was close. If Boeing wanted to compete with that, it had to come up with an offer. McNerney decided to go with a re-engined 737. American placed a sizable order for what became the 737-8, but Airbus clearly had pulled a coup.[71]

Having decided to re-engine the 737 instead of pursuing a new-airplane design, Boeing officials outlined some of the thinking behind the decision in a series of sessions known as Jim Albaugh's Excellence Hours. These were meetings that Albaugh held with employees from time-to-time. Occasionally, other executives joined in.

In one Excellence Hour held after Boeing launched the re-engined 737, Nicole Piasecki, vice president of Boeing's Business Development and Strategic Integration unit, joined Albaugh.

"The 737 MAX fuel efficiency improvement over the Next-Generation

---

71. Details of this feat are provided in *Air Wars.*

will be 10 to 12 percent. We already offer winglets on the plane that we have for the past ten years, and the fuel burn will be 4 percent better per seat than the competition," Piasecki said.

"Managing this program can be a task in itself, and while this is a very low-risk approach to what we're going to do with this airplane, this has to be managed very, very well and has to take into account all the lessons learned from all the programs we have done before," Albaugh told the gathered employees. "We believe very strongly that this is an airplane that will allow us not to just maintain market share, but . . . to grow our market share. We're going to call this 737 MAX, and we are going to designate the airplane the -7, -8, and 9 as opposed to the 737-800 and -900. We're going to call it MAX because we think the airplane will provide the MAX efficiency, the MAX capability, and also do the maximum job."

At this stage, Boeing knew the work scope that was needed to re-engine the MAX, but there were still some unknowns. Engineers were still working with CFM International on the plane's engine. Boeing was looking at two different sizes: the sixty-eight- and the sixty-six-inch fan blade. In either case, Albaugh said that Boeing was "very" confident that this was not going to require a lot of modifications to the landing gear. "Certainly, with the sixty-six inch, there's no modification. Even with the sixty-eight, there is a very low probability to have to touch the front gear." (Albaugh was wrong; Boeing had to lengthen the nose gear by eight inches.)

Boeing knew that the heavier engines meant that strengthening was needed for the wing and the side-of-body joint and that some localized stiffening of the airplane was called for.

"What we try to do with our decision on the engine is to maximize what this airplane can do. With a bigger engine, you get more efficiency because of the bypass ratio, but what you'll find with a bigger fan is you get more weight, and you get more drag," Albaugh said. Then, Albaugh hit on points that would come back to haunt Boeing eight years later.

"There are lots of things we could do with this airplane, but what we want to do is to limit the scope of work, and we're going to limit the scope of work to things associated with the engines. We're going to make this the simplest re-engine . . . possible. We're only going to touch parts of the airplane impacted by the engine and a couple of other clean-ups. There're a couple of things more fly-by-wire, but very minimal things, very minimal," Albaugh told the employees.

"On the cockpit, some people might say the cockpit is an old one. To us, it's state-of-the-art from a navigation standpoint and from a flight-control standpoint. We think it's what the customers want. One of the things that we do want to make sure we have with this airplane is compatibility with NG, compatibility with airplanes we've already delivered, and what our customers have told us is don't touch the cockpit, and our plan is not to do that.

"Recertification [questions], obviously, are some questions we have to work with the FAA [on.] Our expectation is there'll be a certification issue that has to do with the re-engine [but] nothing more. We don't believe the work scope on doing the final assembly of the MAX is going to be measurably different than the work scope for the NG."

One reason given to justify selecting a re-engined 737 over a new design was the challenge of meeting high-rate production demands and ramping up to the 737's rates. In 2011, the production rate was around thirty-one per month. Albaugh told employees at this Excellence Hour that Boeing was studying boosting the rate to forty-two per month by 2014, and even more after that. (By October 2018, when the first MAX accident happened, the rate was fifty-two per month. By the following March, when the second crash occurred and the MAX was then grounded, Boeing had planned to hit a rate of fifty-seven a month later in the year.)

WORRISOME TREND

The effort to keep the re-engining of the 737 "simple" was a subjective goal but, in and of itself, not an extraordinary one. The Douglas Aircraft Company had supported the re-engining of its DC-8-60 Series to the -70 Series using the early version of the CFM 56 engine. The 747 began with a sole-source Pratt & Whitney (P&W) powerplant and, over its lifetime, was re-engined with a different P&W engine, ones from GE and Rolls-Royce (RR), and, finally, the GEnx (used in the 747-8). The 707 model also began life with a sole-source P&W engine. Within a couple of years, Boeing sold the airplane with RR engines and bypass powerplants from P&W. McDonnell Douglas replaced early P&W engines with larger, quieter, and more fuel-efficient engines for its Super 80 and used International Aero Engines' (IAE) V2500 engine for its MD-90. Except for the 747-8 model, in most cases changes to the airplane itself were kept to a minimum for commonality, training, and certification requirements.

The 737 had undergone a re-engining from the P&W JT8D on the -100 and -200 models to the CFM 56 on the 300/400/500 models. Few other changes to the airplane were made. Having lost a critical United Airlines order to Airbus in 1992, Boeing realized that the 300/400/500 needed a revamp. A new, larger wing was designed to give the series more range and efficiency. An updated cockpit, where gauges were replaced with LED instrumentation (known as the "glass" cockpit) common to the 1990s and installed on the 767-400, 747-400, and 777 was adapted for the 737. But none of these changes was onerous, and none affected certification to the point that new certification would be required. There was nothing proposed for the MAX that raised concerns at the time about re-engining the plane. As the re-engining of the NG progressed through the design and program-launch phases, in those early days after the American Airlines order, nothing stood out to engineers as insurmountable or as red flags.

But there was a worrisome trend emerging within the engineering workforce that few at the working level recognized and of which mid-level management within BCA failed to take notice.

"When I first joined Boeing, I was very impressed with the culture," one former Boeing engineer recalled in 2022. "There were a number of clearly seasoned engineers on board, people who had been there for the original 737, original 747, and had worked on every subsequent program. They clearly had qualifications and a scientific understanding of the situation. [But by] 2010, 2011, some of the most capable individuals started departing Boeing, usually, [under the] guise of early retirement, occasionally unannounced, and some were fired. They start getting replaced by fairly junior people coming off programs, without experience in the aerospace industry [or] education for years in the space industry, but without any official engineering qualification, just basic degrees. Basically, the makeup of the teams started changing, and it just accelerated from there. It was like that throughout my career, and towards the end, obviously, the staff situation was quite terrifying."

This engineer also noted that the demographics of the company were becoming very old. People were retiring. "I didn't think much of it at the time, but quickly I started realizing that, no, the folks that are replacing those former guys, they don't know what it's about, they don't know the basics. They didn't seem very interested in the basics either. Basically, the realization that there's something ominous happening didn't really set in until I'd say late summer 2011, essentially around the same time as MAX got launched. At that point, all of a sudden, I realize that 'No, the situation is pretty bad,' or at least, clearly, there is a backward motion."

Presciently, Albaugh, an engineer himself, spotted the looming trend and warned about it in a 2011 speech to the Royal Aeronautical Society. The timing was ironic, coming a week before the June Paris Air Show and what would be little more than a month before the MAX program was launched. He noted that even then, about half of Boeing's engineers could retire in the next five years if they wanted to. (Boeing was not alone; Albaugh noted that Northrop Grumman and Lockheed Martin faced the same thing.) Albaugh also noted Boeing's dearth of new programs for the U.S. Defense Department.

"With no new starts going on in the Department of Defense, we are losing our capability to do detailed design. We are losing our capability to transition engineering into production. To me, that's the hardest thing you do when you work on these major programs. I know that this is an issue. We had the problem when we tried to do the 787 program at Boeing. We hadn't done a new-development program since the 777. We had really lost the ability to do development programs and lost the ability to transition detailed design into manufacturing."

Albaugh then hit the nail on the head.

"No matter what industry you're in, it really is about innovation and continuing to develop products that the market wants. That is really the key to survival. Today, we believe that we are a company that continues to innovate. To me, there are really five things that are required to foster innovation in a company. The first is, you have to have a passion to be the best, and you have to compete against the best in the world. Your goal has to be that you're not going to be a commodity play, you're going to have the best capability.

"The second thing is, you have to be a company that is willing to make the investment in research and development of technology, and you have to invest in your people as well. Another thing that's extremely important, I think, is to have a culture of openness where people feel comfortable coming forward with their ideas and schemes on how they might do things differently and better. We all have worked with a crazy engineer. Maybe there are a few of them in this room, the engineer that comes to you with ninety-nine crazy ideas, but he has the one that will set you apart from the competition.

"We['ve] got to make sure that we really encourage those crazy engineers and crazy ideas because you're going to find one, once in a while, that will change your company and change it forever. The other thing that you have to have is a skilled, adaptable workforce and a leadership culture that encourages innovation as a competitive advantage. You also have to have an awareness that the best ideas aren't necessarily within your company, the best ideas are not necessarily within your country. You have to take the best ideas from around the world. Boeing is not a low-cost manufacturer, we never will be.

"We have to differentiate ourselves in the marketplace, and we will do that. We're going to do that through innovation, and we're going to do that as we provide value to the customers. There have been some well-publicized challenges on the 787 program. We went into that program with some of the technologies not as mature as they should have been. We asked some of our partners to do tasks that they'd never done before, and we didn't provide the kind of oversight that they needed. We've learned from those mistakes, but still, our experience with the 787 can't drive us to be more conservative.

"We're an engineering company, and innovation is what we do. In my view, the times that the Boeing Company has got into trouble [were] when people other than engineers were driving many of the decisions. Bad decisions were made, not necessarily bad engineering. Some companies build an airplane and then they try to sell it, we sell an airplane and then we try to build it. There's a big difference in that. It puts a lot of pressure on our engineers to build that airplane that the customers want, but it does deliver the best and most capable airplane and the airplane that we can sell in the marketplace."

These remarks were made in June 2011. As events later proved, Boeing didn't get the message. And Albaugh would be gone sixteen months later. The crucial decision point for Boeing wasn't too far off. In fact, it was closer than the company acknowledged. The failure to recognize this fact was rooted in Boeing's arrogance.

As detailed in *Air Wars,* Barry Eccleston, the president of Airbus Americas, remained in constant touch with American Airlines' CEO, Gerard Arpey, and CFO, Tom Horton. In 1996, then-CEO of American Bob Crandall signed a twenty-year agreement with Boeing to be the sole supplier for the airline. It was a further nail in the coffin of the struggling MDC, which was down to a single-digit market share competing with Boeing and Airbus. The agreement was one of the rare times Boeing completely surprised Airbus super-salesman John Leahy. Arpey, American's CFO in 1996, called Leahy shortly before Crandall and Boeing announced the deal. Leahy was furious, and perplexed. Why would American agree to a deal that eliminates competition? He complained to Arpey.[72] Despite the exclusive nature of American's arrangement with Boeing, Eccleston would call on Arpey and Horton over the following years.[73]

By 2010, Airbus was closing in on launching what became known as the neo for the A320 family. Airbus had been running tests with the P&W geared turbo fan engine on the company-owned A340 test bed and knew the fuel savings achievable from the engine. P&W's rival, CFM, was developing the LEAP engine at the time. Airbus's Christian Scherer, a Leahy deputy, negotiated with CFM and P&W to install the engines on the entire A320 family. Airbus launched the neo program in December 2010.

Eccleston, now armed with hard economic data, ramped up his contacts with Arpey and Horton throughout the early months of 2011. Airbus took

---

72. The deal provided that American had Boeing's preferred Most Favored Customer status. Boeing pledged that no other airline would buy an airplane for a lower price than American paid. If Boeing sold a plane at a lower price, American would get a check for the difference. American never saw the numbers and had to take Boeing's word for it. American, and later, Southwest Airlines, Delta Air Lines, and Continental Airlines, cut similar deals. Boeing had to officially vitiate these exclusive deals to win approval of its merger with MDC, announced at about the same time as the American deal. But the four airlines nevertheless held Boeing to the terms and conditions of their deals.

73. Crandall retired in 1998.

great pains to keep the talks secret, meeting American Airlines officials in a downtown Dallas hotel and in Florida, where Eccleston arranged for a restaurant to remain closed to everyone else over lunch so that he could have a top-secret meeting with the airline officials.

But in May of that year, Horton had a golf game with Boeing's Ray Conner and told him about the Airbus talks. At the time, Conner was heading Boeing's supply-chain management operations, having rotated out of sales as part of Boeing's practice of giving its key people broad, across-the-board experience. Conner told Marlin Dailey, the salesman assigned to American, that Airbus was working hard on a deal with American. Comforted by Boeing's twenty-year exclusive agreement with the airline, Dailey, Conner later recalled, didn't heed the tip.

A week after Albaugh appeared before the Royal Aeronautical Society, the Paris Air Show began. In a press briefing at the show, Albaugh, Piasecki, Bair, and Pat Shanahan[74] assembled on a panel to pose and answer questions.

Albaugh was the presenter. His talk was standard Boeing messaging, with no new news. When the event shifted to a Q&A format, that's when new information emerged about airplane programs. Everyone knew Boeing was fast approaching a point where it had to decide about whether a new airplane would be built or whether a re-engined aircraft would be offered. If the decision was to go with a new airplane, would it be single-aisle, like the 737 the new airplane was intended to replace, or a New Lite Twin (NLT), which would be a major departure for this class of aircraft? A third choice was the one that few in Boeing really wanted, which was to follow Airbus down the path of re-engining an old airplane for the second time.

"I know that many of you probably came to hear an announcement today, and you're going to be disappointed [about] what we're going to do with the small airplanes," Albaugh told the assembled international press. "We have a very deliberate process for determining what we're going to do on the small airplane. One thing we know we're going to do is continue to improve the 737NG. Since 1998, when we delivered the first one, we've improved the economics of the airplane by about 6 percent. We will continue to do that for the foreseeable future.

"We are going to do either one of the next two [things]. We're either going to re-engine or we're going to develop a new airplane. Our customers know we're going to do one or the other. Our view is that the neo will just provide an airplane as capable as the current NG. We also think and know that if we re-engine, we can preserve the 8 percent operating-cost advantage that we have over the competition. We know we can do that by

---

74. Shanahan then was vice president of Aircraft Programs for Boeing.

mid-decade. In fact, we have the design pretty much on the shelf to be able to do the re-engine," Albaugh said.[75]

Albaugh said that customers preferred the new airplane (although later, he and others at Boeing would backtrack). "We believe the technology exists for a new airplane. We know that technology exists. As I mentioned, we've just done an airplane (the 787) that improves the economics [by] 20 percent, and we could enter this [new] airplane into service by the end of the decade. We really have two choices to make, and we're spending time with our customers, we're spending time understanding the market, and we're spending time making sure we understand what the technology is."

Albaugh said that customers were concerned about the price of fuel and the environment. Coupled with technology, Albaugh said that all three concerns were tied to the efficiency of the airplane. "We know that we can improve it. There's risk in trying to do a new airplane. On the re-engine, we know we can do it. It's a low-risk airplane, but the choice really comes down to, do we want to evolve an airplane that's very good and provide our customers with an incremental increase, or do we want to take more risk and design an airplane for the next fifty years?

"We'll be making that decision over the next several months," Albaugh said. "Doing a re-engine is a tactical thing to do. It's an expected thing to do. I think going with the new airplane certainly is a strategic one and would be one that would address the needs of our customer[s] even better."

Opening the event to questions, a reporter asked what the arguments were for a small twin-aisle airplane or a new single-aisle model. Albaugh passed the question to Bair, who was in charge of the 737 program at the time.

"There's a couple of things that we're looking at," Bair responded. "What you get with the twin aisle is obviously the ability to turn the airplane fast. If you look at some of the business models for low-cost operators getting people on and off the airplane very quickly, [the fact that] you can get another segment out of the airplane is very important. The trade is fuel burn. Twin aisles make the airplane fatter, make them weigh more, make the wetted area go up. There's an economic trade that we have to make as we go through a cross-section decision on a new airplane, if that's what we choose to do. That's part of the conversation that we're having with our customers, to look at the options, and in the end, they will give us their recommendations and we'll make [a] decision on cross section if we decide that a new airplane is the path to go down."

---

75. Boeing's view that the A320neo would only match the 737NG reflected the arrogance that existed in the company at the time. The neo would surpass the NG's economics, and that of the current generation A320, by a wide margin.

Bair said that depending on how "fat" the twin-aisle airplane is, the fuel burn penalty would be 2 to 3 percent. "You can make a fat twin aisle or a skinny twin aisle. There's a pretty big trade space that we're continuing to look at."

"Just think about turning the airplane faster, allowing you to have one more leg per day, per airplane," Albaugh interjected. "That's a huge deal for the customer. You've got to trade that against the fuel burn."

Albaugh wrapped up with typical Boeing confidence.

"We want to make the right decision for the next fifty years, and I don't think we want to be rushed into a decision. I think that the re-engine of the neo, again, it was tactical, and it was expected, and we're going to try to take a very long view at what we do"

Airbus used the Paris Air Show to announce more neo orders. Boeing, true to Albaugh's word, didn't announce anything on the new-product front.

A month later, Arpey called McNerney and alerted him to American Airlines' pending deal with Airbus. Unlike Arpey's call to Airbus's Leahy five years earlier about Boeing's exclusive deal with American, it wasn't too late this time for Boeing to act to get a part of the new, historic deal with American. McNerney and Albaugh had two days to decide what airplane to bring to the market. McNerney chose the re-engined 737, internally the least-favored option. But it was the quickest and, it was thought, the least risky.

After big orders (for more than 400 airplanes) from American were announced, splitting in Airbus's favor, Boeing officials altered the messaging advanced as late as the Paris Air Show. Now, officials said, as recounted in *Air Wars*, airlines preferred the re-engined solution as the fastest and least risky option, an important factor following the years-long saga of the 787 and 747-8 delays and risk factors. Albaugh said that the 787's technology wasn't mature enough to apply to another new airplane so soon. (Recall that the 787 was still months away from EIS at this time.) Furthermore, Boeing couldn't figure out how to build a composite airplane at high rates to match demand for the 737. Ramping up production quickly enough to deliver large quantities of airplanes to customers was another issue. Sticking with the 737 alleviated this concern. Finally, with the Everett and Renton factories full in 2011, Boeing probably would have to build a new production site somewhere else. Doing so presented its own problems, adding to the cost and calling for training of people new to the aviation industry.

These were all good reasons to choose the 737RE over a new airplane, and the decision was made rapidly once Arpey called McNerney. But the narrative that would emerge in 2019—that Boeing "rushed" the MAX, as the plane was branded, to market—was just plain wrong. The decision came within two days, yes. However, the airplane had already been engineered over several years. Detailed design was needed, to be sure, but with a projected EIS of 2017, six years hence, it just wasn't true that Boeing "rushed" either the basic design or the detailed design.

Launching the MAX was, to use Albaugh's words, a tactical decision. And despite the message that the MAX would be better than the neo, with an 8 percent per-seat economic advantage, this simply wasn't the case, either.

SECOND-BEST SOLUTION

Many of the factors that played into the decision on whether to proceed with a new airplane design or go with the (re-engined) 737RE model have already been laid out in these pages. What Boeing wound up with was what one former employee called the second-best solution from its perspective. But the 737RE was the preferred choice of operators. The new-technology problems, production woes, and industrial disaster of the 787 program, which negatively impacted the 747-8 development, hung over the prospect of a new 737 replacement.

"If the better airplane were to win, we would have never had a 737 MAX. We would have had a brand spanking new airplane that would have replaced the 737," the former employee said. "The MAX was created because it was the second choice of Boeing and it was the first choice of the operators. The new airplane was a much better airplane. None of the operators would buy it because they were happy with the margins they were making with their 737 fleet. They didn't want to upset the applecart and take on the extra risk of doing all of the changes to put a new design into service."

Although some engineers believed that the 737's new design didn't offer significantly better economics than the 737RE, those promoting the new airplane—Albaugh and Bair, in particular—believed that on paper, it was a fabulous airplane, much better than the MAX. But everybody passed on it. The A320neo forced Boeing into taking the second-place airplane to the operators who wanted a derivative instead of a newer airplane, and the second-place weaker choice airplane was built, said the former employee.

13

Production Choices

"There was not the stomach, or the bandwidth, and McNerney made the call to not go with a new assembly site."

—FORMER BOEING OFFICER

WHEN THE BOEING COMPANY LAUNCHED THE 737 MAX in July 2011, a prime message was that production challenges were a key consideration in the decision to go with the re-engined plane. The 787's production plan was a key factor in moving forward with the MAX program. Lessons learned from the 787's industrial and production FUBARs[76] were to be applied not only to existing 7-Series models, but also to the prospective New Midmarket Airplane (NMA) Boeing was working on. A corporate communications person once told me that the NMA was as much about production as it was about the airplane.

Production gets into the weeds for most people, but its importance to aircraft and engine manufacturers is as critical as the designs for an airplane and an engine. As we've seen, screwing up production not only threatens the business case of an airplane (the 787), it can affect safety (as it did with the MAX). Airbus faced a similar production mess with its A380 model in 2005. Entry into service (EIS) for that plane was planned for the next year, but when a wiring production miscue was discovered during final assembly, Airbus had to pause progress. It would take two years and a billion Euros before this production issue was fixed. The A380 entered service in 2008.

At that June 2011 Paris Air Show press conference detailed in Chapter 12, Jim Albaugh talked at a high level about production of Boeing's next airplane.

"One of the things that we have to do in order to make the decision on the new small airplane is to really understand what the production system's going to look like. We want to design the airplane and the production system together. In the past we've designed an airplane and then we figured out how to build it.

---

76. FUBAR: fucked up beyond all recognition.

Figure 19. The New Midmarket Airplane was conceived by Boeing to be "above the 737 and below the 787." This concept envisioned a three-member family. Credit: Leeham Co.

"This time we['ve] got to make sure that we design both the production system and the airplane together to make sure that we can build as many airplanes as we think we can sell. We think that number is sixty or seventy airplanes a month. We've never been at rates that approached that. In terms of global partners, we are going to have global partners. I mentioned that we put too much outside on 787, and we did. We will redraw those lines."

At this point, the 787 program was three years late and still four months from EIS. The industrial and production disaster that caused the program to be so late and billions of dollars over budget weighed heavily not only on that program, but on any future airplane development, including the 737 replacement. Bair took note of this point.

"We've liked what we learned on the 787. That's one of the intriguing things about a possible new airplane, is to be able to take advantage of all the lessons that we've learned on the 787. That includes the autoclave. Now, there are big parts in the 787 pressure bulkhead that are an out-of-autoclave part and we would like it if we had more. I don't think we're going to see wholesale change in technology. We want to harvest everything that we've learned so far on the 787 and do another generation of that airplane."

In an interview for this book, a retired Boeing production management employee who held key positions in the company detailed the production considerations in the months leading up to the MAX decision.

"I knew there was both a design for a single aisle and [a] twin aisle, both of which were viable and both [of] which were very good designs," this retired manager said. "Both also involved a different production method, and that ended up being, from my perspective, the real issue that people didn't really truly understand. If you think about that time, we were still trying to get Charleston up and running. That was a monstrous undertaking. Now we have three [production sites]. It was tough to get Everett and Renton to behave."

The manager said that the more variability between a company's major production sites, the more complexity it creates and the greater the likelihood that there will be cost issues and failures. "We had our hands full just figuring out how to get Charleston up and running. Yes, it was up and running, but by no means was it functioning at a level that didn't require a lot of engagement and [it] wasn't driving a lot of problems back into the rest of the production and supply chain that the other programs depended upon."

Airbus then had A320 and widebody production plants in Hamburg, Germany, and Toulouse, France. In addition to these two locations, A320s were also assembled in Tianjin, China, and, later, a production facility would be added at Mobile, Alabama.

There was no way that the production of a new airplane could basically be incorporated into any of Boeing's existing facilities because the new plane required a new production system. "The idea of building a new assembly site, whether it was in the Puget Sound or someplace else—there just wasn't the bandwidth for it. The money was there, perhaps, but there just weren't enough people that knew how to do that." the manager said.

Boeing was already looking at a different production system from the innovative one used on the 787. The very design of an aircraft was critical to its production. How Boeing would proceed on its next new airplane depended on that aircraft's design. The engineer made the following observation. "There was a lot of talk, a lot of studies that were done. You could join the airplane differently. You could have a top half and a bottom half, like the old days when you built model airplanes. On a smaller airplane, that's very doable. On a composite fuselage, it's doable. Whatever they settled on was not going to be the standard, basically, frame-and-stringer and skin-build. It was going to be something to get the cost down at higher rates. To do that, if you bring an all-new airplane in[,] . . . you can't slide it into the existing production system."

Boeing integrated the 737 NG into the 737 Classic's final assembly line. It upgraded the Classic line, incorporated it, slowly phased out the Classic, and then ramped up the NG. Boeing did the same thing with the MAX. "You couldn't do that with a new airplane. There was not the stomach, or the bandwidth, and McNerney made the call to not go with a new assembly site. It wouldn't work. That basically then limited your options on what to do with the Three Seven, which meant you had to find something that was a derivative that you could basically figure out how to integrate in," the manager said.

While McNerney's decision is described in the context of a new or a re-engined airplane decision, it can also be seen in another light, one that confirmed what many believed at the time, namely, that Boeing was using the production-site location decision as yet another form of blackmail to leverage the International Association of Machinists District 751 (IAM 751) union into another round of concessions on its contract. McNerney threatened the union with the possibility of locating the MAX assembly site outside Puget Sound. Doing so made no sense, but the union extended the contract and dropped a complaint it had filed with the National Labor Relations Board over Boeing's decision in 2009 to locate the second 787 assembly line in Charleston. The MAX assembly site remained in Renton, Washington.

In 2011, Boeing produced the 737 at a rate of thirty to thirty-five units a month. Forecasters already saw demand for a production rate of forty-two to fifty units a month. "That just blew everybody's mind in terms of how you're going to have to run the factory. The lean manufacturing work that was done, even in those days, . . . we couldn't see our way to how you get all that out of even the Renton site," the manager said. "I think there was a lot of changing factors at the time. You had options with production rates going to high rates. Do you build out and harvest some of the investment [on the 787] or do you jump in and do a whole new airplane and jeopardize your ability to capture the harvest piece of it? I think there were a lot of different dynamics that were going on. I don't think the Boeing team could sort out exactly what was the clear choice to go do. I think there was a fair amount of risk-avoidance given the situation that had happened with the 787."

The manager added that the more complex a production system becomes, the more likely it is to cost a lot of money. When it doesn't work, the harder it is to fix. "In the old days, when we used to do a lot of stuff internally, yes, cost [was] an issue and there are ways to get cost out. Engineering design is a big part of it. That was always one of my biggest beefs, especially, during the Partnering for Success [period]. I had a huge target. I had a $4 billion target. My counterparts in engineering did not have a target for getting cost out. That just used to piss me off beyond belief. The people that controlled 80 percent to 90 percent of my cost didn't have any skin in the game."

Partnering for Success, or PFS, became one of the most controversial policies pursued by McNerney, one that put some suppliers at risk of financial collapse and sent Boeing and some of its biggest suppliers into a face-off that often became bitter.

14

Boeing's Bank: Partnering for Success

*"Just because you want to get cost out and you think you can get your sup-
plier to do it, your supplier still has a vote, and they may say no."*
—BOEING SUPPLY-CHAIN OFFICIAL

THE PARTNERING FOR SUCCESS (PFS) APPROACH adopted by The Boeing
Company was straight out of the General Electric business model: Squeeze
pricing from suppliers to improve your own profit margin. Jim McNerney
took this tactic with him when he left GE for 3M, and he brought it with
him to Boeing.

During the 2000 decade, Boeing's Commercial Airplanes division (BCA)
was running single-digit profit margins (hurt in no small part by the 787
and 747-8 programs). Many of Boeing's suppliers were achieving double-digit profit margins. For some Boeing executives, hearing this was like
hearing fingernails scraping a blackboard. In fairness, since Boeing was
hemorrhaging money on the 787 and 747-8 programs, cost-cutting measures were needed. The business sector Boeing had the greatest leverage
over was its own supply chain. Boeing made it clear: Play ball and cut your
price or lose your work with us.

Understandably, Boeing's suppliers were less than thrilled with the ul-
timatum. "Preparing for sacrifice" and "preparing for poverty" were two
of the more-polite supplier descriptions of PFS. Some called the PFS approach blackmail. Others noted that they had to invest heavily in capital
expansion to meet Boeing's future supply demands. Smaller- and medium-sized suppliers complained that they didn't have the ability to cut
prices for Boeing without placing their own futures in jeopardy.

Some of the biggest suppliers, with their own broad-based business
foundations, simply pushed back. Some refused Boeing's demands. Across
the supply chain, some who didn't play ball were put on Boeing's own version of a No Fly List. One of Boeing's supply-chain managers explained,
"There were aspects of it that I very much welcomed. For the first time, the
finance people had to get in and actually see how to close a deal. That was
pretty eye-opening for some. Just because you want to get cost out and you
think you can get your supplier to do it, your supplier still has a vote, and
they may say no. Then what do you do? You can't just go beat up all the peo-

ple that don't have any leverage. That becomes all the small people when you're in your supply chain and those are the people that you absolutely depend upon. The whole production system's built on a pyramid."

Boeing, however, kicked out one of the industry's biggest suppliers, United Technologies Corporation (UTC), when it refused demands to cut costs on landing gear for the 777. A Canadian company, Héroux Devtek, got the work. "We switch suppliers all the time," the supply-chain manager said. "We did that for lots of different reasons. But the big spin was that when we switched the 777 landing gear, we took it away from UTC and it went to Héroux Devtek, that was a major shot over the bow. We did some other things that were major shots over the bow. We developed a second material that was comparable to Toray's material.[77] We had to demonstrate that we weren't going to be a captured fish. That was good, but I think the execution on the PFS was brutal. It became more about the numbers as opposed to about getting to some of the behaviors and opening up some of the options for doing business differently. The other thing that just was a failure on Boeing's part was [when] it said it would facilitate and help take cost out of the airplane and meet the suppliers halfway. Boeing didn't [do that]. Engineering ducked out and didn't do what they were supposed to do. They weren't accountable," the supply-chain manager said.

Boeing didn't stop there. A change in the way it handled accounts payable was implemented. At first, payables dates were extended from thirty days to sixty days, then to ninety days, and later from ninety to 120 days. In essence, Boeing began using the supply chain as its own bank. Nobody in the chain was happy, but small- and medium-sized suppliers faced serious cash-flow problems as a result. Some became insolvent, some were acquired, and others ultimately had to rely on Boeing to finance them because of their inability to get loans from banks and capital markets. The extent of Boeing's own financing program with suppliers was detailed in its third quarter 2024 10Q filing with the federal Securities and Exchange Commission, at a time when Boeing's own financial stability was very much under strain.

Supplier notes receivable for a nine-month period in 2024 tripled from the comparable 2023 period to $494 million. "At September 30, 2024, trade payables included $2.7 billion payable to suppliers who have elected to participate in supply chain financing programs compared with $2.9 billion at December 31, 2023. In future quarters, our suppliers' access to supply chain financing could be curtailed or more expensive if our credit ratings are further downgraded," Boeing reported in its 10Q.[78]

---

77. Toray Composite Materials America, Inc.

78. This was one of many reasons why Boeing was so adamant about

The stress on the supply chain from PFS and the changes to accounts payable procedures drew withering criticisms from consultants Kevin Michaels, Richard Aboulafia, and Michel Merluzeau, among others. Michaels was the principal owner of Aerodynamic Advisory, whose major client base was the supply chain. It also included, at times, Boeing. Aboulafia was a long-time employee of the Teal Group who joined Michaels' company in January 2022. Merluzeau owned his own consulting firm.

"It was well within Boeing's right as one of the key OEMs [original equipment manufacturers] to demand more of its supply chain in terms of productivity, accountability, and the like," Michaels said in a 2022 interview for this book. "After all, we're in a globalized world. You look at any other capital-goods industry, there's intense competition. Suppliers are on edge, always trying to improve. A lot of industries are cost down every year. For someone of Boeing stature at the time in 2011, when it launched PFS to do that, it was well within [its] right It was well within [its] right to question some of the decisions [it] made on the 787 supply chain in terms of whether [it] outsourced too much.

"The way they executed PFS, which rolled out in 2011, and then PFS 2.0 and subsequent variants, it's as if they looked at the profit pools in commercial aerospace and said, 'Hey, we're taking all the risks here. Why aren't we getting the rewards? Why are these suppliers always garnering 15 percent and 20 percent margins, sometimes more, when we're earning 8 percent, 9 percent, 7 percent at commercial?' It all became very adversarial. Not only adversarial, it was counterproductive. It destroyed the whole culture, and in many respects, really harmed the ecosystem that had been so successful for Boeing since the beginning of the jet age."

Merluzeau had a somewhat different take. "Basically, what PFS was designed to do was to manage the poor relationship with some of the suppliers. Manage and reboot the relationship as well, sometimes. The PFS goals were not just about financial margins. They were about rebooting toxic relationships and relationships that were not necessarily working. It was about setting the stage for supplier switches. The leadership of supply management at the time were telling me in no uncertain terms that they would not hesitate to switch suppliers in the middle of [a] program if alternatives and conditions were right." Merluzeau named the UTC 777 landing gear switch as an example.

"The UTC event was like the salvo that Boeing was willing to sacrifice. I remember I was shocked that Boeing was taking such a massive risk in going with a competent organization, Héroux Devtek, but fundamentally

---

maintaining its investment-grade credit rating throughout the long-running MAX crisis.

untested for such a large shipset on a critical product like the 777. Boeing had to invest considerable amounts of time and in human resources to get Héroux Devtek where they wanted them to be. Credit to Héroux Devtek leadership, they accepted that and they delivered, but it was not painless as you can imagine."

This switch resonated with other suppliers, Merluzeau said, who concluded that if Boeing dumped a big organization like UTC, then it would not hesitate to dump smaller suppliers. "Boeing to a degree was able to reboot its relationship with the supply chain for PFS at many different levels. Level one, financial, level two, sourcing, and level three, new relationships with suppliers of the future. I think [this] contaminated the relationship and trust with the established supply chain in particular, the legacy supply chain. I think the sentiment of partnership was eroded by those negotiations."

Aboulafia, along with Michaels and Merluzeau, often eviscerated Boeing and its supply-chain relationship at the annual conference of the Pacific Northwest Aerospace Alliance (PNAA) in suburban Seattle. Boeing, a sponsor of the PNAA, did not welcome the criticism, and relations between the supply-chain organization and Boeing deteriorated for several years. Boeing eventually suspended its sponsorship and speaking participation with the PNAA for two years, citing as the reason a sex discrimination lawsuit that had been filed against the organization and its director by a female employee. This was during the strongest days of the Me-Too era. But given Boeing's own history of discrimination lawsuits and the fact that the PNAA received a state grant in competition with a Boeing-backed organization, some believed that the discrimination lawsuit was just an excuse given the long, tense history between the PNAA and Boeing.

Boeing didn't stop with costs and payables. Michaels said that Boeing in some cases claimed ownership over intellectual property (IP). "There were aggressive attempts to take over intellectual property, to say that 'This now belongs to Boeing. You've been on my aircraft. You would not have a business without me. I own this IP.' There were huge attempts to grab aftermarket revenue and profits. That was tied in with IP. If I own the design IP, I have aftermarket pricing rights and this belongs to me." Michaels described a case in which there was a crucial component on one of Boeing's aircraft and the company decided that it wanted to bring in a supplier. "They would just do make-to-print, where Boeing would own the design. The supplier went to Chicago to meet with McNerney and was granted rights to make this component. They're not good. It was done, in this case, at the CEO level of Boeing to bring out an inferior supplier just so you could grab some more money. They made many mistakes."

PFS officially ended under Dennis Muilenburg, McNerney's successor as CEO (or so corporate communications claimed). At least the program name was ended. But continued emphasis on cost cutting was not—how could it, given Boeing's deteriorating financial condition in years to come? The effects of PFS, however, lived on long after the program's title was retired.

"The relationships that it broke and the behaviors that it changed are still coming back in ways that Boeing never appreciated it would," said a Boeing supply manager. "There were a lot of suppliers that were making way too much money. Boeing is the one that put up all the money to take the risk. It created the business stream, created the marketplace. Some suppliers basically just rode it. Quite frankly, a lot of suppliers made all that money because Boeing didn't do its job."

It must be noted that Boeing's policies toward the supply chain were not unique. Airbus likewise engaged in a multi-year cost-cutting drive. But suppliers common to both companies who complained bitterly about Boeing said that Airbus took a strong but much more collaborative approach. GE, like Boeing, adopted an accounts payables schedule over ninety to 120 days. It offered suppliers the ability to contractually accelerate payments—as long as they agreed to a 3 percent discount.

Boeing stepped up and gave financial support to key suppliers and offered billions of dollars in financing, as noted earlier in this book. Airbus did the same, in addition to purchasing a few suppliers outright. But PFS was, at its core, another bridge that Boeing burned in its decades-long descent into mediocrity. And when the IAM 751 union struck Boeing in 2024, idling many suppliers, Airbus swooped in, placing orders with suppliers for its A-Series airplanes to help fill the problems it was having with its supply chain. When the strike was settled in November 2024 after fifty-three days, Boeing wanted to resume and increase production rates. But some suppliers now were committed to Airbus and couldn't help Boeing.

The fallout of PFS will no doubt be an overhang at Boeing for years to come.

15

Falling Apart

"We're going to be sharks in Washington."

—FORMER BOEING LOBBYIST ON A SHIFT IN ITS APPROACH TO CONGRESS

THE 787 ROLLOUT was a masterful global public relations event. The aviation and financial industries were enthusiastic. After years of questions about whether The Boeing Company was truly committed to commercial aviation, the answer seemed to be an unequivocal yes.

By 2008, Boeing CEO Jim McNerney faced a growing set of problems. The 787 program's difficulties were spinning out of control. Its problems spilled over onto the 747-8. Profits and cash flow were squeezed. The company's board of directors suspended share buybacks and dividends—the all-important shareholder value. And Boeing's contract with the International Association of Machinists District 751 (IAM 751) union was expiring in September. The union, as usual, wanted to protect jobs, wages, benefits, and pensions. The issue of outsourcing was another rallying cry. IAM 751 members had been losing work for years. An illustration published in the union's house news magazine *AeroMechanic* early in the 787 program vividly told the story (see Figure 20).

Boeing also had been increasingly outsourcing engineering work, to the dismay of the Society of Professional Engineering Employees in Aerospace union (SPEEA), but there was no equivalent graphic from this union. The 787 was the crowning achievement of outsourcing at Boeing. The two unions were especially critical of the decision by Boeing to outsource the 787's wing design and production to Japan. Wings had always been considered one of Boeing's Secret Sauces.

The 747 sort of got a pass because it was so big. But the 767 was the first major example of how little a hand IAM 751 had in producing the aircraft, followed by the 777. The wings were still designed and produced in-house, and all the airplanes were assembled by IAM 751 members. The production contributions of IAM 751 members decreased even more on the 787.

Clearly, outsourcing at Boeing began in earnest in the 1980s with the 767—well before the McDonnell Douglas merger and the arrival of the ogre, Harry Stonecipher. McNerney became the target for labor's wrath as he moved not just touch labor work out of Washington state, but also en-

140

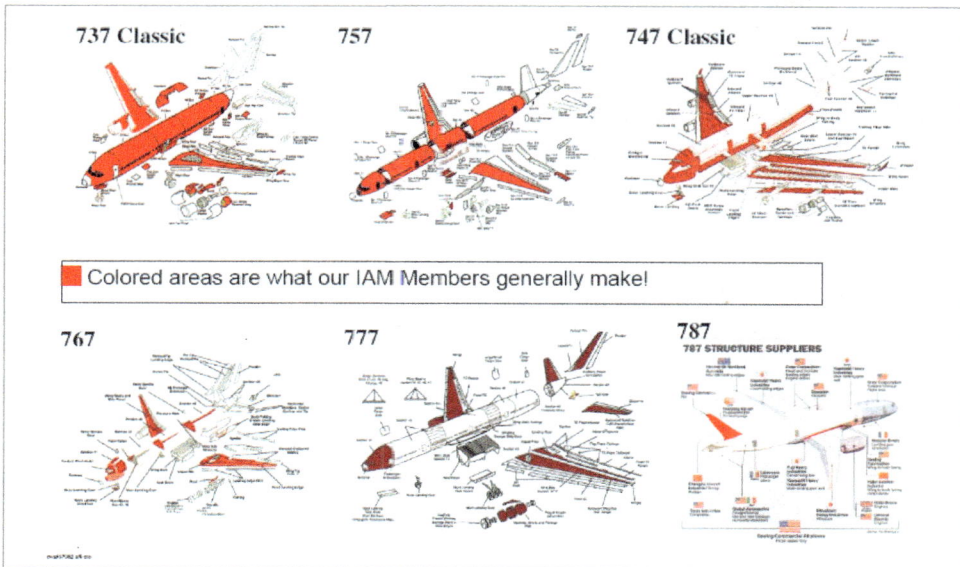

Figure 20. In 2008, this illustration appeared in *Aero Mechanic*, the union newsletter of IAM 751. It illustrates the progressive outsourcing of union jobs at Boeing. Credit: IAM 751.

gineering and technical work performed by SPEEA members. The unions complained that McNerney was anti-union, which he clearly was (another GE trait). But this was too simplistic a view.

World trade was changing, and so was the mix of Boeing's customers. McNerney, whose GE career included expanding the company's business in China, recognized that Boeing's approach to the new world order required a shift to a global perspective; the USA was no longer going to be the center of Boeing's commercial aviation ambitions. Boeing increasingly had to offer work in exchange for foreign sales, be it of airliners or defense products. This practice is called offsets. Offsets were considered under international trade rules to be illegal, so the practice was dressed up and called outsourcing. Heavens to Betsy, there was no such thing as locating business in a foreign country in exchange for orders (wink, wink). Airbus did it and so did McDonnell Douglas and Douglas Aircraft Company before its merger with McDonnell.

McNerney, however, elevated outsourcing and redefined it, at least as far as SPEEA and IAM 751 were concerned. In addition to international realities, McNerney simply moved union jobs in Washington and Oregon to non-union states like Texas, Oklahoma, Alabama, and the biggie, South Carolina. It's debatable which inflamed the unions more: shifting jobs overseas or shifting jobs to other states.

Either way, as contract negotiations got underway with IAM 751 for the 2008 contract, the union's membership was in no mood to give anything back.

Despite the increasingly contentious negotiations with Boeing, the union strongly backed the company's bid to win the second competition for the U.S. Air Force's aerial-refueling tanker. Boeing's entry was based once again on the 767-200ER. Winning the contract would mean providing union jobs in the coming decades. The union lobbied state and federal politicians on Boeing's behalf. It was the second time the union put all hands on war footing for Boeing. The first was after 9/11, when Boeing proposed a lease deal at a time when its Commercial Airplanes division (BCA) was in deep trouble because of the impact of the terror attacks on the U.S. airline industry, then Boeing's largest market.

"We worked hard," recalled Larry Brown, IAM 751's political expert, of the 2001 effort. "I personally worked hard on that tanker deal. I remember us having the announcement at the Everett [Washington] factory. A bunch of us were there to laud the accomplishment of the lease program that [U.S. Senator] Patty Murray really worked hard on." But after the win, Brown said, management, then led by Phil Condit and Harry Stonecipher, didn't seem interested in the union anymore. "It just was so disappointing that once we were done with that, it just seemed like now we're done with you. There just was no relationship."

After McNerney became CEO in 2005, antagonism toward the unions increased. Many attributed this to the Jack Welch–GE environment from which McNerney came.

"I just think that Boeing became so averse to having anyone else have any prerogative with respect to their business. McNerney was a disciple of Welch," Brown said.

As the 787 and 747-8 programs unraveled, IAM 751 and SPEEA stepped up to save the day. SPEEA had to work overtime to fix the engineering on the two planes and undertake rework of outsourced engineering. To pay for all the cost overruns on both programs, IAM 751 members suggested ways to improve efficiencies and increase production of the 737 and 777 Classic lines. Boeing desperately needed the profits and cash flows from these programs to cover the costs associated with the drastically over-budget 787 and the more modest overruns on the 747-8.

Nevertheless, it was against this backdrop that negotiations continued for the 2008 IAM 751 contract. The union was always militant—it had struck Boeing several times since World War II—and members were in no mood to be compliant.

In September 2008, the union walked out for what would be fifty-seven days. The next year, Boeing placed the second 787 assembly line at the fuselage plant in Charleston, South Carolina, after contentious renegotiations with IAM 751 to alter the 2008 contract. Boeing again wanted to terminate its defined pension plan and have union members contribute to health care costs, as well as extend the contract. As detailed in *Air Wars*, union leadership concluded that Boeing's negotiations to keep the second line in Everett in exchange for concessions were a charade. Boeing never intended to place the new assembly line in Everett, the union said after the company announced its decision to place the line in Charleston.

From the company's standpoint, it was a good decision. Privately, an IAM 751 spokesperson agreed, later telling me that doing so gave Boeing good leverage for future negotiations. Indeed, Boeing threatened in 2011 to put the 737 MAX assembly line someplace else other than Renton; in 2013, the company used the same tactic regarding the location of the new 777X assembly line. The union was skeptical of both threats but couldn't be sure because of the 787 experience.[79]

When McNerney launched the MAX in July 2011, BCA CEO Jim Albaugh said that the MAX would of course be built in Renton. McNerney, in a rare public rebuke to one of his officers, said not so fast. It may not be. In his interview for *Air Wars,* Albaugh dismissed the notion that there was a good-cop, bad-cop act. Ray Conner, at the time BCA's top salesman, laughed and said that Albaugh simply got ahead of things. Behind the scenes, however, Albaugh was known to be more sympathetic to labor than McNerney. It was reported that there had been some pretty strong disagreements between the two in front of other executives over union matters.

Regardless, IAM 751's Brown said that in 2011, Boeing wanted to talk about the existing contract, again seeking more concessions in return for keeping the MAX in Renton. But there was a bigger issue. After Boeing announced the siting of the second 787 line in Charleston, the union filed a lawsuit accusing Boeing of illegally retaliating against the union for the 2008 strike. Court discovery produced papers that gave the union a strong case. Boeing wanted the union to drop the lawsuit in addition to other contract changes.

"Boeing came to us maybe a month before we were going to court for the 787 second-line lawsuit," Brown said. "There was no explicit discussion about the lawsuit when we talked about the 737 MAX. They came in with a pretty difficult opening offer. They wanted to transfer a whole bunch of the health care costs to the membership, and it just wasn't a really good offer.

"We were like, 'If this is what your offer is, we're not interested in having a conversation.' They came in and bumped the pension and reduced the cost shift of health care, [offered] some decent general wage increases,

---

79. As will be seen in a later chapter, the union was correct about the MAX, a Boeing official confirmed for this book. As for the 777X, much later, the union came into possession of plans for construction of the Composite Wing Center for the 777X in Everett, and clearing for parking there began as well. Both threats by Boeing proved, in retrospect, to be just that.

and extended the contract, which would have expired in 2012 to 2016."

Brown said that Boeing got off its "bad" offer pretty quickly. "All the work that was being done in Renton then would be done on the 737 MAX in the future. That was guaranteed in that contract. I thought it was a good deal. What I probably didn't appreciate [was] how much of a choice did they have, and were we setting ourselves up for . . . future failure. As it turned out, that's exactly what we were doing."

The union's 787 lawsuit was dropped. As for "setting ourselves up for . . . future failure," Brown explained that not letting the contract expire was IAM 751's biggest mistake. "The only reason we did as well as we did with the MAX [was] because we had that lawsuit sitting there and they wanted to get out from underneath it. There was no explicit conversation of a quid pro quo, but at some level, I suspect Tom Buffenbarger and Jim McNerney had that conversation."

Buffenbarger was the president of IAM International, the "parent" to all the local districts, including 751. At the time, union bylaws gave the parent the right to overrule the districts and impose settlements or otherwise override local processes. This became critical two years later, in 2013, when the 777X vote arose. It was another maneuver by McNerney to extract more concessions from the union in exchange for locating the 777X final assembly line in Everett. IAM 751 members rejected Boeing's demand in a vote held shortly before Christmas 2013. In a sleight of hand, Boeing and Buffenbarger's International scheduled a second vote soon after New Year's, on January 3, when many workers were still on vacation. The timing was viewed as an early form of voter suppression. Union members had soundly rejected the contract's concessions the previous month. This time, the contract passed by 600 votes; a flip of 301 votes would have defeated the contract. About 8,000 members didn't vote this time because of the timing.

The president of IAM 751, Tom Wroblewski, was accused by some members of collusion with Buffenbarger. There's no definitive evidence of this, but it appeared that Wroblewski was broken; he resigned a short time later, citing health reasons. "I think Tom didn't have the vision or the courage or the hutzpah to oppose the international president. It's one of the saddest days in my career and in the labor movement," Brown said.

With this vote, the IAM 751 contract was extended until September 2024. McNerney succeeded in nearly breaking the union. He won that war, but the seeds were planted for the 2024 contract negotiations ten years hence that would essentially guarantee payback.[80]

---

80. More details of these labor votes appear in Chapter 32, "Payback."

WASHINGTON, DC

McNerney's management style also affected Boeing's lobbyists in Washington, DC. One of Phil Condit's goals in acquiring McDonnell Douglas was to improve Boeing's defense business. During his tenure, contracts with Boeing from the Pentagon were on the decline. MDC was also beginning to struggle with lower defense spending (it was still the Clinton Administration then) and consolidation within the defense industry, but it had better relations with the military than did Boeing. After the merger, Boeing's lobbying force—made up of the MDC crowd—began making progress. Defense spending also increased after 9/11 and under the Bush 43 presidency.

A lobbyist who came over with one of the Condit mergers saw first-hand the change in how McNerney used lobbyists compared with his predecessors. During the Clinton Administration, when Ron Brown was Commerce Secretary, there was close cooperation between Boeing, McDonnell Douglas, other aerospace companies, and the federal government. It was also the beginning of the era when Boeing was beginning to fend off Airbus at the government level.

"They gave Airbus a lot of credit back then that they were really well wired with their state departments and their ministries of foreign affairs. It was probably just more sort of organic. But at the same time, there was certainly a lot more official activity," the former Boeing lobbyist explained.

After McNerney arrived at Boeing and named federal Judge J. Michael Luttig as general counsel, the company established a law department in Washington. This department began making its presence increasingly known on Capitol Hill. McNerney's style was more "corporate" than other Boeing CEOs, this ex-employee described. "I don't want to say that it was more macho. But we were running fast. It was like we're not going to be tunas anymore. We're going to be sharks in Washington.

"I'm a tuna guy because I prided myself on my relationships. I got people to do way more stuff than you could just by my relationships. I got them to extend themselves and get their bosses to do stuff, just because I always provided them with a lot of data, satisfied all of their risks, and retired all their risks that they might have questions," the lobbyist said. "I thought, 'This is a relationship town.' It was dissonant to me, discordant" to take a more aggressive approach. "But he's the boss. He had his model. I was a company guy. So, let's go with it, and let's work it." The changing relationship with Congress would, like other policies, rear its ugly head in 2019 when Boeing needed friends on the Hill more than ever.

Boeing's desire to expand its defense business through mergers in the 1990s failed to pay off. It bought a company called Autometric that developed software to monitor the doors and windows of America's overseas posts. Eventually, Boeing proposed using this technology for a virtual fence program along the Southern U.S. border. The proposal was a colossal failure. Boeing also "squandered" its lead in manned space, the ex-employee said.

Under McNerney, Boeing began to "vilify" other companies for short-term gains, this lobbyist said. No better example can be pointed to than the second and third round U.S. Air Force refueling tanker competitions between, respectively, Boeing and Northrop Grumman/EADS, and Boeing and Airbus.

This lobbyist offered rare praise for Harry Stonecipher. "Something really nice about Stonecipher was he was very frank and you knew where he stood. McNerney was more aloof. McNerney was more of a telegenic, disconnected or distant CEO."

The Muilenburg Era

DENNIS MUILENBURG

Tenure at The Boeing Company: 1985–2015.
Titles: President, Boeing Defense, Space & Security
division, 2009–2015; President and Chief Operating
Officer, 2013–2015; Chairman, President, and CEO,
2015–2019. Muilenburg's legacy at Boeing is his
handling of the 737 MAX crisis. Getty image.

16

Changing of the Guard:
New CEOs at Corporate, BCA

"McNerney was actively hostile. Muilenburg was also hostile to labor."

—RAY GOFORTH, EXECUTIVE DIRECTOR OF SPEEA

JIM MCNERNEY INHERITED A MESS from Harry Stonecipher when he became CEO of The Boeing Company in 2005. It wasn't until 2013 that Boeing fundamentally began turning around. In January of that year, a fire traced to the lithium ion battery used for the first time on an airliner, in this case, the 787, caused a scare. A Japan Air Lines (JAL) Dreamliner completed a non-stop flight from Tokyo to Boston. All passengers were deplaned, and the aircraft had been towed to a parking area away from the terminal for its overnight stay. The fire filled the aircraft with so much smoke, a heat detector had to be used by firefighters to locate the blaze. A week later, the battery on an All Nippon Airways (ANA) 787 taking off in Japan began smoking. An emergency landing followed, and passengers evacuated safely. Each flight could have ended in tragedy had the timing of the battery mishaps been different.

McNerney and the FAA took decisive action to ground the 787 while investigations were underway. This reaction would sharply contrast with the handling of accidents six years later, when the second of two 737 MAXs crashed. In that situation, the FAA stalled and McNerney's successor, Dennis Muilenburg, called President Trump to ask that the MAX remain airborne.

The 787s remained grounded for three months following the battery incidents. Once they returned to service, Boeing began making money again. Shareholders began receiving dividends and stock buybacks resumed. McNerney was two years away from his ten-year anniversary at Boeing. Muilenburg was named president and chief operating officer in 2013. He became McNerney's successor in 2015.

Muilenburg was born in 1964 and raised on a farm in Iowa, the heart of the USA's Midwest region. He would repeatedly point to his origins during the MAX crisis as evidence that he was not an elitist and could relate to the families of the victims of Lion Air flight 610 and Ethiopian flight 302, the two MAX crashes occurring in October 2018 and March 2019, respectively.

Muilenburg earned a degree in aerospace engineering from Iowa State University. He served as an intern at Boeing in 1985 and later became a full-time employee. He spent the rest of his professional career at Boeing in various positions, including CEO of Boeing's defense unit, before being elevated to the corporate level in 2013.

A reserved individual, Muilenburg nevertheless stood in contrast to his executive predecessors. A health enthusiast and an avid bicyclist, he would ride with union members during his leadership roles at defense. He spent his entire career at the defense unit. His lack of experience at Boeing's Commercial Airplanes division (BCA) was a glaring hole in his resume that made him an enigma to airlines and lessors and would be a huge disconnect when the MAX crisis erupted after the Ethiopian crash.

But his credentials as an engineer were a welcome change from McNerney's MBA background. There was hope that he'd begin to return Boeing to its engineering legacy. This was further boosted when, in a surprise move, Boeing and the Society of Professional Engineering Employees in Aerospace union (SPEEA) announced a contract extension in January 2016, some seven months after Muilenburg succeeded McNerney, that had been negotiated in secret well before talks normally started. The current contract was to expire in October; talks normally begin closer to the expiration date. The new contract was for four years.

However, in an interview in 2021 for this book, SPEEA Executive Director Ray Goforth reflected that Muilenburg, while not as openly hostile as McNerney, was still no friend of the unions.

"McNerney was actively hostile. Muilenburg was also hostile to labor. I met him a couple of times and he was always charming as an individual. The attitude he brought was active hostility towards labor. Muilenburg was tense, maybe. A little bit of positives and a little bit of negatives," Goforth said.

The hope that an engineering emphasis would reassert itself under Muilenburg was never realized. Shareholder value (see Chapter 7), if anything, became even more important—and rewarding—under Muilenburg.

Boeing's stock price never hit $200 under McNerney; it would peak at $440 under Muilenburg shortly after the first MAX accident in October 2018 (which was at the time publicly shrugged off as probably as much the fault of historically safety-challenged Lion Air as it was about the airplane).[81]

Muilenburg benefitted from timing in his success. He became president and COO in 2013, shortly after the 787 returned to the air after a three-month grounding due to battery fires. The 747-8 was in service. Development of the 737 MAX was well underway. Development of the KC-46A was only two years into its cycle. By the time McNerney retired and Muilenburg added the chairman and CEO titles to his mandate in 2015, the 787 and 747-8 problems were in the past; the MAX was on schedule to be delivered in 2017; and as for the KC-46A—well, its problems had yet to become financial and technical black holes. Boeing returned to solid profitability. Muilenburg and CFO Greg Smith pledged to return 100 percent of free cash flow to investors.[82]

In 2016, Ray Conner, the CEO of BCA, announced his retirement. He would remain as a "consultant" for another year. Conner, then 61, was well short of the mandatory retirement age of 65. But he had spent his entire adult professional career at Boeing. He started on the factory floor and worked his way up through the ranks and various senior positions within BCA, including the top salesman under Jim Albaugh. Customers liked and respected Conner. He was in this position when, in 2013, the 787 battery fires on the JAL and ANA airplanes resulted in the FAA grounding the U.S. fleet for what turned out to be three months. Other regulators followed suit; all fifty 787s then in service worldwide were grounded until Boeing came up with a plan to contain (but not prevent) any future battery fire. Conner and his team flew to Japan to apologize to airline executives—an important element of the Japanese culture. Boeing then held a press conference at which more apologies were given to the Japanese public, another important gesture to the Japanese culture. Conner and Boeing were criticized for these actions by the National Transportation Safety Board (NTSB), which saw the statements as overstepping the rules for being a

---

81. At one point the European Union banned Lion Air from flying there, citing safety concerns.

82. After Muilenburg was fired in December 2019 and lead director David Calhoun succeeded him, Calhoun would criticize Muilenburg for his emphasis on stock buybacks and increasing dividends. Calhoun expressed puzzlement about why Muilenburg pursued these policies. It was a shameful abrogation of his own culpability. Calhoun had been on the Boeing Board of Directors since 2009 and had approved the policies, along with the rest of the board, and benefitted from the largesse the directors approved for themselves.

"party" to the formal investigation into the two incidents. However, the faux pas only resulted in a slap on the wrist and a warning to not speak out of turn again. But Conner's actions helped Boeing get through the crisis with minimal additional damage to its relationships with customers.

There was a question at the time as to whether Conner retired voluntarily or was pushed out. Boeing denied that he was forced out due to his criticism of president-elect Donald Trump's complaints that Boeing was opening a 737 finishing center in China. The company told Jon Talton, a business columnist for the *Seattle Times*, that Conner's departure planning had been underway for some time. Talton was direct: "Did Conner Walk the Plank?", he asked in a November 22, 2016, column.[83] Conner had been at Boeing for forty years, but had served only four years as CEO of BCA, with four remaining until he reached mandatory retirement age.

In an odd encounter I had in November 2024, in Munich, Germany, of all places, a former airline executive told me that Conner had been forced out. But an ex-Boeing executive familiar with the situation at the time told me a few months later that Conner and Muilenburg had a number of open disagreements in terms of direction and other issues and that this caused Conner to take his leave. In May 2016, Conner told Muilenburg that he had decided to retire. The two agreed that Conner would stay until June 2017 to help with the transition.

The full scope of the disagreements between Conner and Muilenburg may never be known. But Conner was a strong proponent of the argument that Boeing's next new airplane, once the re-engining process for the 737 was decided, should be a replacement for the 757. It was a position he still held when I was writing *Air Wars*. Muilenburg was persuaded to back a 767 replacement, albeit with somewhat less range. Probably the biggest difference between the two was Conner's belief that Muilenburg needed to spend significant time learning the commercial side of Boeing. It seemed folly to many—and probably to Conner, too—that the new president and COO of Boeing, who was also the heir to fleet up to chairman and CEO, didn't know or truly understand the company's commercial side. BCA, after all, was the largest business unit of the company. McNerney also worked the customers. But when the MAX was grounded, Southwest Airlines CEO Gary Kelly did *not* publicly offer any support for Muilenburg

---

83. Jon Talton, "Did Boeing Make Conner Walk the Plank Over Trump?", *Seattle Times* (November 22, 2016), https://www.seattletimes.com/business/economy/did-boeing-make-conner-walk-the-plank-over-trump/; Jon Talton, "Boeing's Conner Hits Back Against Trump on Trade, Jobs," *Seattle Times* (September 13, 2016), https://www.seattletimes.com/business/economy/boeings-conner-hits-back-against-trump-on-trade-jobs/.

in the wake of this disaster. Instead, the mild-mannered, gentlemanly Kelly praised Conner's successor, Kevin McAllister, during an appearance on the financial network CNBC for his hand-holding during the crisis. When asked about Muilenburg, Kelly dodged—and the dodge spoke volumes. By this time McAllister's contract hadn't been renewed, and he was the first executive to take the fall for the MAX crisis. Shortly after Kelly's clear message (sent by silence), Muilenburg was fired.

When Conner and Muilenburg agreed to part ways, Muilenburg reached outside Boeing to pick Conner's successor. He brought in McAllister from GE Aviation. McAllister joined GE Aviation in 1989 and went on to hold several engineering and sales positions with the company. He was CEO of GE Aviation Services when Muilenburg tapped him to lead BCA. His appointment was met favorably. McNerney and Muilenburg had set goals to grow Boeing Global Services (BGS) into a $50 billion company, and it was believed that McAllister's GE experiences could be valuable in helping Stan Deal, by now the CEO of BGS, accomplish this mission.

McAllister also brought a fresh outlook to BCA, which many viewed as too inbred, too stale, and set in its ways. The 787 and 747-8 industrial fiascos had upset BCA's plans to replace the 737 with an all-new airplane and to follow this with an all-new design to replace the 777. Both became another round of derivative products, enabling Airbus to further gain market share. Airbus's airplanes also had built-in growth capabilities to become even better competitors to the aging Boeing products. Re-engining the MAX took some creative engineering on this ancient pelican. The 777 could only match the A350-1000's seat-mile costs by adding around sixty seats, thrusting it into the category of the 747-400-size airplane—which was already too big for many markets.

McAllister, those in the know said, was brought in to shepherd Boeing's twin-aisle concept, the New Midmarket Airplane (NMA) designed for the Middle of the Market (MOM), into reality. The NMA, it will be recalled, was an outgrowth of the MOM concept that was originally based on replacing the 757 (which Ray Conner had urged). However, any move in this arena had to wait until Boeing recovered from the 787 and 747-8 financial disasters.

By the time McAllister showed up in November 2016, Boeing was well on its way toward this recovery. Both aircraft were in operation. The MAX was well into flight testing, with the first delivery expected in the first half of 2017 (it would be in May). Development of the 767-based KC-46A was well underway, albeit with some emerging problems (and write-offs). Development of the 777X was also underway.

Meanwhile, Muilenburg was basking in some fortuitous timing. McNerney never got Boeing's stock price up to the $200 target that was believed to have been set by the board of directors. Muilenburg not only blew through this target, under his tenure, the stock price peaked at around $440 a share.

Muilenburg and SPEEA quietly reached an early agreement for a new contract in 2016. But the leadership of SPEEA and the other union at Boeing, the International Association of Machinists District 751 (IAM 751), noted that except for some handshakes, Muilenburg failed to meet with either union, both during his time as president and his time as CEO. Still, the atmosphere between Muilenburg and labor seemed a sharp contrast to the open warfare between McNerney and the unions.

17

The Crisis Begins

"Safety is our Number 1 priority."
—NUMEROUS BOEING OFFICIALS

ON OCTOBER 24, 2018, The Boeing Company released its financial results for the third quarter and nine months ending on September 30. The results were outstanding. Nine-month revenues were up 5 percent year-over-year, with operating income up 6 percent and net income up a whopping 37 percent. Earnings per share—all important to shareholder value—were up 42 percent. Free cash flow, another shareholder value item and the metric most important to Wall Street analysts, was up 22 percent. Boeing delivered 568 airplanes during the nine-month period, an increase of only 3 percent over the same period in 2017. Most of these were 737s, around 240 of them MAXs.

Boeing's CEO Dennis Muilenburg and its CFO Greg Smith waxed optimistic going forward and reaffirmed a commitment to return 100 percent of free cash flow to shareholders. The company's stock opened that day at $349.74, higher than at any time under former CEO Jim McNerney and a high for Boeing.

Behind the scenes, Muilenburg was making headway to launch Boeing's next airplane, a twin-aisle aircraft dubbed the New Midmarket Airplane, or NMA. Studies had been underway since 2012. The NMA supplanted Ray Conner's push for a 757 replacement. Conner, in his role as CEO of Boeing's Commercial Airplanes division (BCA), had been the 757 replacement's strongest advocate. But he relinquished his position in November 2016 and left the company the following year after a series of disputes with Muilenburg. The NMA was now a 767 replacement to fill the Middle of the Market gap above the 737 and below the 787.

For Muilenburg, things couldn't be better.

But they were about to get worse.

On October 29, 2018, just five days after the rosy earnings call, a five-month-old Lion Air MAX 8 lifted off a runway in Tangerang, Indonesia, enroute to Pangkal Pinang, Indonesia. This was a short domestic flight, a milk run. The pilot was Captain Bhavye Suneja, 31, who had worked for Lion Air for seven years. He had 6,028 hours in the cockpit, including

5,176 hours on 737s. The first officer was named Harvino (Indonesians use only their last names; Suneja was an Indian national). Harvino, 41, had 5,174 hours of flight experience, including 4,286 on the 737. In view of the accusations that came later that the co-pilot was inexperienced, these number belie the smear.

Lion Air flight JT610 ("JT" being the two-letter code for the airline) had 181 passengers and crew on board. Within minutes of taking off, the virtually new MAX 8 began experiencing flight-control problems. The nose went into an uncommanded down attitude. Suneja pulled the nose up, but the plane pushed it down again. Suneja again pulled up, and again the nose went down. This cycle repeated itself over and over, again and again, for twelve minutes. While Suneja wrestled the airplane, Harvino used the aircraft's Quick Reference Handbook to try and understand what was happening and how to respond. After twelve futile minutes, Suneja decided to look at the handbook. Turning control of the airplane (such as it was) over to Harvino, Suneja physically took possession of the handbook. Unfortunately, while Suneja had managed to keep the MAX 8 flying despite the control problems, Harvino, who had no experience flying through this type of emergency for the last twelve minutes, lost control. The plane plunged into the Java Sea. Everybody was killed instantly upon impact.

Initially, fingers pointed to Lion Air as being at fault. Lion Air, a low-cost carrier, had a spotty safety record. The European Union once banned the airline from flying into its air space, citing safety concerns. A few Lion Air flights overshot or undershot runways, and a couple of flights wound up in shallow water as a result. Observers had no reason to consider a design flaw with the MAX at this stage.

But, as would be revealed much later, within a week of the crash, Boeing suspected that an obscure system called the Maneuvering Characteristics Augmentation System (MCAS for short) was a key—if not the triggering—factor behind the crash. MCAS is a system that kicks in when the angle of attack of the 737's nose is too high and approaching a stall. MCAS commands the airplane to push the nose down, avoiding a stall. Boeing repeatedly said that this wasn't an anti-stall device. However, this claim was refuted after an engineer involved in designing the software explained how the MCAS operated (see Chapter 18).

The crash was the first of a MAX. Boeing and the FAA issued a notice stating that any similar incident should be handled like a runaway trim incident. Every plane has trim tabs that counteract aerodynamic forces on control surfaces as the plane goes through the air. A runaway trim, while rare, can escalate into a dangerous event if pilots don't react quickly to shut down the runaway action. Potentially, a runaway trim can lead to the loss of control of the airplane and, possibly, the loss of the aircraft. Pilots receive training for runaway trims.

As the Lion Air investigation unfolded, the existence of the MCAS became known to pilots and the public. MCAS, it was revealed, repetitively brought the nose down to avoid a stall with such strength that it was impossible for a pilot to override its operation; MCAS had to be shut off, hence the idea of treating it like runaway trim. This was explained in the notice issued by Boeing and the FAA.

Thus, when, on March 10, 2019—five months after the Lion Air accident—Ethiopian Airlines flight ET302 taxied from the Addis Ababa, Ethiopia, airport terminal for a trip to Nairobi, Kenya, the pilots were aware of the existence of MCAS and the Boeing-FAA notice on how to respond to MCAS activation. This MAX 8 has 157 passengers and crew aboard. The pilot was Yared Getachew, 29, who had been flying for Ethiopian Airlines for nine years. He had 4,120 hours on the 737 and had been flying the MAX series since July 2018. The co-pilot was Ahmednur Mohammed, 25, who had 361 hours in the cockpit and 207 on the 737. The airplane was delivered to the airline in November 2018.

Just forty-four seconds after takeoff, the angle-of-attack sensor failed, possibly from a bird strike. MCAS read the failure as an indication that a stall was imminent and kicked in. The plane never got higher than 800 feet as the pilots fought the activation. Mohammed correctly assessed the situation as an MCAS activation. But, in a critical mistake, the engines were still in takeoff power mode, which overwhelmed the pilots' ability to manually trim the airplane. The pilots erred in other actions taken to correct the situation. The plane nosed over, diving into the ground at 500 m.p.h. All aboard died instantly. The entire event took about six minutes.

The radar profile from independent flight-tracking services looked similar to that of the Lion Air accident. China's regulator, the Civil Aviation Administration of China (CAAC), was the first to ground the MAX, doing so on the same day as the ET302 crash. It was widely reported that Muilenburg spoke with President Donald Trump urging him to *not* ground the MAX. Regulators in Europe (the European Aviation Safety Agency, or EASA) and Canada (Transport Canada) grounded the MAX within a day or two. The FAA dawdled, saying that it needed "hard facts" before it would do so. (Contrast this with the FAA's action to ground the 787 within hours of the second battery-fire incident in 2013.) Finally, on March 13, 2019, three days after the Ethiopian disaster, the FAA pulled the airworthiness certificate of the MAX. The remaining regulators around the world followed suit. Globally, 350 MAXs were now parked.

Two weeks later, Boeing held a press conference to explain the MCAS operation in detail and what the company was doing to fix it.[84] My book *Air Wars* details much of Boeing's presentation.

---

84. Dominic Gates, "Boeing details Its Fix for the 737 MAX, but Defends the Original Design," *Seattle Times* (March 27, 2019), https://www.seattletimes.com/

At the time, few thought the grounding would last very long. The 787 had been grounded for three months while a fix was being created from scratch. Boeing was already working on a software update, and had been since shortly after the Lion Air crash, when the Ethiopian flight went down. There was no reason to believe the MAX grounding would be much different than the 787's. Production of the MAX continued based on this belief.

But nobody died in the 787 incidents, compared with the 346 dead in the two MAX crashes. Among them was a niece to consumer advocate Ralph Nader, whose public profile dated to the 1960s, when he took on General Motors and the U.S. auto industry for building unsafe cars. The one-time third-party presidential candidate was also blamed by many for costing Vice President Al Gore the presidency in 2000 by siphoning off enough votes in Florida to throw the state, and the election, to George W. Bush. Nader criticized Boeing and the FAA after the MAX crashes, and his public profile added visibility to the outrage.

The delayed action by the FAA to ground the plane also came under withering criticism from the families of the victims of the two crashes, observers, and members of Congress. Boeing was in the center of multiple firestorms at the time. Muilenburg's call to Trump became known, and this didn't help matters. Very quickly, the CEO came under equally withering criticism. Muilenburg alternately accepted responsibility on behalf of Boeing for the crashes and pointed fingers at the pilots for being at fault. Unartfully, the point he was trying to make was that every crash has multiple factors underlying it. He was correct, but at the time, the actions of the Lion Air pilots on flight JT610 were unknown (the black boxes hadn't been analyzed yet), and those pilots didn't even know about MCAS. In any event, neither accident would have happened had Boeing not over-engineered the system or, perhaps, had the flight crews had simulator training. Muilenburg's initial acceptance of responsibility was refreshing and praised, but his backtracking a week later was roundly panned.

The timing of the MAX crisis was awkward in another way. Boeing's 2019 annual meeting was on April 29. By then, enough information had come out about the cause of the two accidents and about some of Boeing's actions in response to them, that a hot reception from shareholders was expected. The annual meeting itself was fairly benign. Shareholders rejected a motion to separate Muilenburg's chairman and president titles. The board of directors had recommended that the motion be rejected. Muilenburg was scheduled to meet the media for a thirty-minute press

business/boeing-aerospace/boeing-details-its-fix-for-the-737-max-but-defends
-the-original-design/.

conference following the meeting, his first since the accident. He got roasted by the gathered journalists. Muilenburg defended the MAX's design after a perfunctory expression of sorrow for the accidents and a vigorous defense of the 737.[85] He pointed fingers at the Lion Air and Ethiopian pilots for not following procedures. The media's questions were sharp and hostile. Muilenburg walked out after fifteen minutes. It was a disastrous appearance.

During the months that followed, the U.S. Department of Justice, the U.S. Department of Transportation, the U.S. House of Representatives, and the U.S. Senate opened inquiries into the MAX crisis. The National Transportation Safety Board (NTSB) was already a party to the Ethiopian and Lion Air crashes, and many lawsuits had been filed by relatives of the victims of both crashes. Federal grand juries were also empaneled to investigate the crisis. Boeing and the FAA were in the crosshairs of each investigation.

Multiple news media were also conducting their own investigative reporting, prominent among them the *New York Times, Washington Post, Wall Street Journal, Bloomberg News, Reuters*, and the *Seattle Times.* The latter's aerospace reporter, Dominic Gates, had a home-town advantage and local longevity in aerospace reporting on his side. Unhappy Boeing employees became regular sources of information, and Gates' reach into the aerospace community outshined any of his peers. He eventually would win a Pulitzer Prize, the gold standard of journalism honors, for his reporting.

On the broadcast media side, CBS News's U.S. newsmagazine *60 Minutes, 60 Minutes Australia,* PBS's *Frontline,* Amazon's movie production company, and movie producers Kathleen Kennedy and Ron Howard created long television segments or one-to-two-hour documentaries.

Between all these pieces, the sordid tale of Boeing's cost cutting, schedule pressures, and MCAS creation details emerged, as did often embarrassing and sometimes damaging internal Boeing emails. The relationship between Boeing and the FAA came under scrutiny, with special focus placed on how the FAA transferred much of its inspection authority to Boeing over decades. This fact, especially, became fodder for congressional hearings. Members of Congress considered this transfer a scandal. However, it was Congress, in prior years, that had adopted enabling legislation that permitted the transfers. The criticism about the transfer of authority also ignored the fact that the FAA simply didn't get the money it

---

85. Dominic Gates, "Facing Sharp Questions, Boeing CEO Refuses to Admit Flaws in MAX Design," *Seattle Times* (April 29, 2019), https://www.seattletimes.com/business/boeing-aerospace/facing-sharp-questions-boeing-ceo-refuses-to-admit-flaws-in-737-max-design/. This article contains a link to a sixteen-minute video of Muilenburg's press conference.

needed to do the work itself from prior Congresses. (It is worth noting that, at the time of the transfer controversy, other federal agencies designated company employees to represent them at the companies they oversaw.)[86]

In the months after the MAX grounding and running throughout the rest of 2019, Boeing officials parroted the message "Safety is our Number 1 priority" at every opportunity. Given the information that was coming out from the official and media investigations and from the civil lawsuits about how safety was compromised in the crashes, including the key factor that MCAS was linked to a single point of failure (the angle-of-attack sensor), in violation of every principle of aviation safety, the refrain rang hollow. At that disastrous press conference following Boeing's annual meeting, Muilenburg declared that after MCAS revisions were implemented, "the 737 MAX will be one of the safest airplanes ever to fly." From a public relations messaging viewpoint, there was so much wrong with this statement, not the least of which was why wasn't the MAX *already* one of the safest airplanes ever to fly?

On several occasions during the summer of 2019, and when congressional hearings were underway, Muilenburg mentioned that he was born, raised, and went to college in Iowa. These repeated references were clearly an effort to capitalize on his Midwestern roots (and, left unsaid, to demonstrate that he wasn't some elitist) in order to show that he was a common man. There's inherently nothing wrong with this, but he simply couldn't pull it off. Having been in the executive ranks at Boeing for years, with the compensation that comes with it, Muilenburg's own financial condition put him in a very different category than most of the victims and their families of both doomed flights. But more to the point, Muilenburg's personality simply didn't exude empathy. He's a stoic person. Even as he expressed sorrow for the loss of life at the press conference, it was clear that he was reading from a prepared statement. In this and other public appearances, he displayed little to no emotion. He did not appear to be visibly moved by the experience until he met with crash-victim families before a congressional hearing.

Throughout the MAX crisis, Muilenburg largely appeared to be a dispassionate engineer driven only by data. As the public face of the crisis, he did Boeing no favors.

Missing as another public face of the crisis was BCA CEO Kevin McAllister. Since BCA was the division in which the crisis was rooted, it would seem natural for McAllister to be front and center. But he wasn't, and he was barely mentioned in press releases.

---

86. *Air Wars* provides more detail on this aspect of the authority-transfer story.

McAllister became BCA's CEO when he joined Boeing in November 2016, when MAX flight testing was at an advanced stage. The plane entered service the following May, so McAllister didn't really have much history with the MAX's development, and he certainly had no history with MCAS. His predecessor, Ray Conner, said that he had never heard of MCAS until the accidents happened. Even so, McAllister's absence was noticeable—but it was also explainable.

Figure 21. Dennis Muilenburg, CEO of The Boeing Co., was visibly moved after meeting with families of the victims of two 737 MAX crashes before he testified at a congressional hearing. It was a rare moment of publicly displayed emotion. Getty photo.

When he was Boeing's CEO, Jim McNerney didn't like interacting with the press, and he often let BCA CEO Jim Albaugh, and later, BCA CEO Conner, be the front men on the infrequent occasions that Boeing allowed press access to its CEOs. Muilenburg, on the other hand, wanted to be the face of "one Boeing," so he was. He was confident in his ability to deal with the MAX crisis, though some wondered if the company's general counsel was calling the shots about what was said publicly to limit Boeing's liability from lawsuits. Some said yes, others said that Muilenburg was making the decisions. Muilenburg declined to be interviewed for this book (so did McAllister).

At the April 29, 2019, annual meeting, Boeing's board of directors and shareholders rejected a motion offered by some stockholders to separate the chairman's title from Muilenburg's CEO duties. But by October of that year, the board did just that. Boeing's public image continued to take a beating throughout the summer and fall. Muilenburg repeatedly suggested that recertification of the MAX was just around the corner, and in doing so, he irritated FAA Administrator Steven Dickson. The FAA was moving at its own pace and wasn't going to be rushed, especially following the revelations, and the ensuing criticism, that the agency had handed over so much responsibility for certification of the airplanes to Boeing.

When the MAX was grounded, Boeing continued production of the 737, first at full rate in the expectation that the length of the grounding would not exceed three months. It was a timeframe that was also expected by most analysts. When the grounding dragged on, Boeing lowered the 737's production rate modestly but kept rolling new aircraft out its Renton, Washington, factory's doors. The aprons at Renton, at nearby Boeing

Field, at the Moses Lakes airport in central Washington (often used for Boeing test flights), and at Boeing's facility in San Antonio, Texas, filled with new MAXs in colorful paint schemes of customers all over the world. The cost of this inventory ran into the multi-billions of dollars.

The board of directors stripped Muilenburg of the chairman's title on October 19, 2019. David Calhoun, who had been on Boeing's board since 2009 and who had become the body's lead director, was named chairman of Boeing. Calhoun had a long career at GE and, according to some, had been on the short list of possible successors to Jack Welch. After being passed over at GE, Calhoun left to go into the private equities sector, where he was when Jim McNerney tapped him to join the Boeing board.

In a press release, Boeing said the following: "The board said splitting the chairman and CEO roles will enable Muilenburg to focus full time on running the company as it works to return the 737 MAX safely to service, ensure full support to Boeing's customers around the world, and implement changes to sharpen Boeing's focus on product and services safety. This decision is the latest of several actions by the board of directors and Boeing senior leadership to strengthen the company's governance and safety management processes.

". . . The board has full confidence in Dennis as CEO and believes this division of labor will enable maximum focus on running the business with the board playing an active oversight role. The board also plans in the near term to name a new director with deep safety experience and expertise to serve on the board and its newly established Aerospace Safety Committee.

"'I am fully supportive of the board's action. Our entire team is laser-focused on returning the 737 MAX safely to service and delivering on the full breadth of our company's commitments,' said Muilenburg."

No matter how Boeing colored the move, it was a clear demotion for Muilenburg.

Kevin McAllister was ousted by the board on October 21, 2019. This move was disclosed by Boeing the next day. Stan Deal, a long-time Boeing executive and then the CEO of Boeing Global Services, was named CEO of BCA.

"We're grateful to Kevin for his dedicated and tireless service to Boeing, its customers and its communities during a challenging time, and for his commitment to support this transition," said Muilenburg in a press release announcing the change.

Although McAllister was the first top Boeing official to be fired in connection with the MAX crisis, this apparently wasn't the only reason for his ouster. "A senior Boeing executive with knowledge of the deliberations, who asked for anonymity because of the sensitivity of the issues, said McAllister was fired for a combination of negative developments 'on his watch,'" wrote Dominic Gates of the *Seattle Times*. "The major issue has been the grounding of the 737 MAX and the constant pushing out of its return to service as Boeing has struggled to meet the demands of international regulators. As a result, Boeing's stock has lost one-fifth of its value since the second MAX crash in March."

Gates continued, "The senior executive cited other issues, including the 777X engine problems that have pushed first flight into next year and the recent blowout of a door that happened during ground testing of that jet. Another factor, he said, was this month's discovery in older 737s of cracks in the so-called 'pickle fork' structure connecting the wings to the fuselage—although it's difficult to see how McAllister is responsible for faults in airplanes built long before he got there. And the shrinking backlog of the 787 Dreamliner is also a concern."

Despite clear signals from then FAA Administrator Dickson that there was no timeline in sight for recertifying the MAX, Muilenburg couldn't help giving hints that this was coming soon. By December 2019, it was all over for Muilenburg. He was fired and Calhoun was named president and CEO of The Boeing Company. Board member Larry Kellner was named non-executive chairman.

Upon being named chairman in October 2019, Calhoun said that the board had full confidence in Muilenburg. A few months later, after Muilenburg was gone and he was now president and CEO, Calhoun remarked that a board has confidence in its leaders until it doesn't. It was an observation that would come back to bite him four years later.

18

The 737's Troubled History

*"There is nothing more important to us
than the safety of the people who fly on our airplanes.
"The 737 MAX will be one of the safest airplanes ever to fly."*

—DENNIS MUILENBURG, CEO OF THE BOEING COMPANY, APRIL 29, 2019

FOLLOWING THE ETHIOPIAN AIRLINES MAX CRASH, investigations by the media, the U.S. Department of Justice, the U.S. Congress, and others revealed that Boeing's development of its Maneuvering Characteristics Augmentation System (MCAS) was at the heart of the crashes. Other mistakes were made, including by pilots, but the root cause was MCAS. The design and implementation of MCAS, and Boeing's internal actions related to MCAS, didn't just call into question the overall safety of the 737. Boeing's entire safety reputation came crashing down.

Although the safety of the MAX became a focus of investigations and critics alike, the history of Boeing's most ubiquitous and profitable airplane was, in fact, spotty. The MAX was the latest, and last, major upgrade of the 737. The original models, the -100 and -200, entered service in 1969, fifty years before the Ethiopian accident. The "original" 737 models (as the -100/200 unofficially became called) were powered by the first generation of jet engines, the Pratt & Whitney (P&W) JT8D. The 737-300/400/500 were re-engined with CFM International's CFM 56 product, with few other changes. This was followed by the Next Generation (Next Gen or NG) aircraft, the 737-600/700/800/900. The engines for these models were upgraded CFM 56s, but the airplane had a new wing—and other major improvements. The -300/400/500 was informally named the Classic to easily differentiate between the older CFM-equipped models and the NG aircraft. The MAX used CFM's LEAP engine and other modifications but otherwise was largely unchanged from the NG.

For the Classic through the MAX, Boeing obtained Amended Type Certificates (ATC) from the FAA (which allow an aircraft's design to be modified from its original design and approve not just the modification, but also its effects on the original design[87]). Much was made of the argument that pro-

---

87. U.S. Department of Transportation, Federal Aviation Administration,

duction on the MAX should have required an entirely new Type Certificate (TC) (which is time-limited and requires increased FAA involvement[88]). But the differences between the MAX and the NG weren't as drastic as between the NG and the Classic.

The 737-700 and -800 became excellent airplanes, with the -800 earning the honor of the family's sales leader. The -600 was a shrink intended to kill the ailing McDonnell Douglas's MD-95. It sold poorly, as did the competing Airbus A318, developed for the same reason and a double shrink. The initial 737-900 traded range for capacity, but it could only fly over two-thirds of the continental United States non-stop. Boeing added center fuel tankage to the plane, extending the range, but the -900 series compared poorly to the A321, which had its own deficiencies, and total sales paled in comparison to those of what became known as the A321ceo after the new-engine-option program was launched.

Although the Next Gen family of aircraft retained the name and looks of the 737 Classic, in reality it was a virtually new airplane.

"Boeing decided that they wanted to get more range, which is why the NG got the bigger wing," recalled an engineer who worked on the program. "They decided they wanted to be able to fly higher, so that meant higher delta pressure[89] across the fuselage and, therefore, basically the entire fuselage was gauged up. At the systems level, other than the flight deck going from the steam gauges to those little nine-inch screens, there was not a whole lot of significant change in systems architecture."

The NGs were designed to be able to fly as high as 41,000 feet versus 37,000 feet for the Classics. To achieve proper cabin altitude in the NG, the apparent altitude inside the cabin could not simply be increased by 4,000 feet. The skins of the NG's fuselage (and some underlying frames/stringers, etc.) had to withstand a greater pressure difference between outside and inside, along with the fatigue effects of essentially "inflating and deflating" the fuselage on every flight compared to their Classic and the Original forbears.

While the general structural design of the fuselage of the NG and the MAX is essentially the same as the Classic's, the details are all different, so there are new part numbers for the newer models relative to their predecessors. The NG still had the same two and a half hydraulic systems and

---

Amended Type Certificate (last updated June 7, 2024), https://www.faa.gov/aircraft/air_cert/design_approvals/amend_tc.

88. U.S. Department of Transportation, Federal Aviation Administration, *Production Certificates: Production Under Type Certificate*, "What Is Production Under Type Certificate?" (last updated April 3, 2025), https://www.faa.gov/aircraft/air_cert/production_approvals/prod_cert.

89. The pressure differential between the cabin and outside air.

pullies and cables making it work. The electrical system and the air conditioning systems were not significantly different.

"I was more interested more in how they physically fit together than the details. I knew more about those sorts of things later, but there were enough small changes that it was significantly different," the NG program engineer recalled.

Placement of certain cables along the fuselage became a point of criticism during the MAX crisis. A question about cable placement came up during development of the NG as well.

"The Joint Aviation Authorities in Europe was pushing back on the single rudder cable's loop that runs down the center of the airplane. The engineers had to put together a fly-through that showed them just exactly how there was not any place else to put the rudder cables in the floor than where they were. It was changed enough, but it was even then that those questions came up and we had to go through that same exercise, essentially, for the MAX. We did armor a couple of spots in the fuselage against rotor burst for that consideration as well."

When the NG was created, Boeing at one point promoted it as an 80 percent new airplane. Southwest Airlines, a launch customer, had operated nothing but 737s since it began operations in 1971. The Original model and the Classic had analog gauges in the cockpit. Southwest didn't want to introduce new systems that would require new training for the new cockpit on the NG, a philosophy that would be repeated with the MAX, which led to unfortunate consequences. Boeing arranged for its avionics supplier to program Southwest's NG's glass cockpit to look like the analog gauges of the Original and the Classic models. No extra training on this score was required.

With all the changes and the self-declaration that the NG was an 80 percent new airplane, how did Boeing persuade the FAA that an Amended Type Certificate was OK and that a new Type Certificate was not required?

"Great question," the engineer said. "It's an answer . . . which I honestly do not know." After the NG, the FAA adopted something called the Changed Product Rule, which dropped in early 2000s. "I think [that] was the FAA's answer to 'don't you ever do this again. You changed everything, but your change to your certificate basis is almost nothing. You cannot ever do that again.'"[90]

---

90. Despite the Changed Product Rule, when Boeing launched the 747-8, the company also called this an 80 percent new airplane. Airbus complained that the 747-8 bore little technical resemblance to the 747-100 that entered service in January 1970. Therefore, Airbus argued, the 747-8 should be required to obtain a new TC. Airbus got nowhere with the regulators with its campaign. Likewise, the

Boeing launched the MAX in 2011. "What a nightmare. In the end, the FAA allowed Amended Type Certificates but the hoops that we were required to jump through, and some of the things that we did on the MAX to satisfy the 'Don't change it beyond the currently defined definition,' were big. The door opening angles, and in the case of a collapsed gear, there were a bunch of things where we did silly things, or at least [silly-] sound[ing] things, in order to not go outside the boundaries of how the NG was certified so that we wouldn't have to open up another determination of whether it was a significant change or not. Still, they made up as they went along rules for how you dealt with it once you did that as a result of the Changed Product Rule," the NG engineer said.

"Under the Changed Product Rule, the basic requirement was that, instead of [how it was] prior to the Changed Product Rule, you could say that all you had to do was demonstrate that your change design met equivalent safety with the current design. You basically proved, from the point of view [of] the prior certification basis, that it was good enough."

Then the FAA, under the Changed Product Rule, said that Boeing would have to step up and follow all new rules unless it could demonstrate a compelling reason why a given change should not or could not meet new rules, the engineer explained. The grounds cited could be either technical or economic in nature. There were pages and pages explaining how and what Boeing had to do to make a determination.

The problem was that the MAX was the first Changed Product Rule airplane produced by Boeing, and so both Boeing's certification people and the people at the local FAA building had to sort through the new rules. "There was all this explanation of how to do it, but the actual process of going through it was being basically made up as we went, so it changed a lot. That led to much frustration and much back and forth that was unsatisfactory all the way around," said the NG engineer.

This engineer—who was not caught up in the crisis crash investigations—believes that the thesis that Boeing bullied and controlled the FAA is overstated but is not necessarily an unfounded characterization.

"I know that was the way that Boeing was used to operating. I know [that because] there was a lot of effort, . . . it felt like while they were trying

---

Boeing 777X is also a substantially new airplane. As with the 737 and 747-8, Boeing assumed that the 777X would receive an ATC. The MAX crisis and the controversies over the certification of the MAX upended all assumptions that the 777X would be able to slip in with an ATC. The original certification goal for the 777X was late 2019 or early 2020. With development delays, the negative halo effect of the MAX crisis, and the COVID pandemic, certification is now targeted for 2025 or 2026.

to collaborate with the FAA and figuring out how to just go through this whole Changed Product Rule thing and meet the spirit as well as the letter of the rules, I guess I should say that of course, Boeing would try to drive that situation.

"But I kind of push back on the public story that Boeing bullied the FAA or pushed them around or whatever. It certainly did not feel like that from where I was sitting. In fact, in some cases it felt like it was just the opposite, especially with ex-Boeing people that were working for the FAA. It felt like they had axes to grind and by golly, they were going to grind them. But at the overall level, I am not sure how to characterize it."

DEVELOPMENT OF MCAS

MCAS was put in the MAX to provide like handling characteristics with its predecessor airplane, the 737 NG. But this isn't the purpose for the system as described by engineers who worked on the MAX's development. As one engineer explained: FAA Certification Rules basically say that as a plane gets closer and closer to stall, it should take more and more force to pull its column back, so that basically the airplane is telling the pilot, "don't do this, idiot, you're going to stall." The design and placement of the huge engines on the wings were pushed up and forward in order to fit the bigger fans underneath the wings while using the same landing gear as was used in the predecessor aircraft.

The engineer continued: "They discovered that as you approach the stall, especially if you were doing a climbing turn, what they call a wind-up turn, that instead of the forces getting higher as you got closer to the stall, at some point those forces started to get lighter and so, it was a handling quality concern and then the solution. We elected to do several things, and they were some aerodynamic Band-Aid kind of things, turbulators and that sort of thing.

"Ultimately, Boeing wound up with this solution that was, OK, if you're climbing and you're in this climbing turn mode, we'll just have to down trim on the stabilizer and push the nose of the airplane down a little bit. How that was going to be done and what signals the computer sent was a question because on the 737, there is no central flight-control computer. It's got little boxes all over the place that do different things, and I don't remember where this function wound up . . . . Something that had to have the little program space. That was a chronic problem."

The implementation of these designs meant that when the angle of attack is high and the G-force is going up, the pilot would give the control a little bit of a tap. "The flight-control guys architected that. It seemed to be solving one small, handling-qualities problem, and it was in a situation that you almost never found yourself in, in applying the airplane on a regular basis. It was more of a thing that an FAA certification pilot was going to put the airplane in a wind-up turn to check for this one condition. Boeing wanted to make sure that the MAX passed this condition," the engineer explained.

Mating MCAS into the 737's system—which had been updated several times since the original 1960s design—was complicated. Explaining the challenge requires a techno-geek background with the ability to put concepts into layman's terms. Explains a former Boeing technical employee:

> When Boeing builds an airplane, they have a thing called the drawing tree, and the drawing tree starts out with what they call the top-level drawing. The top-level drawing will be something like, for a 747, a 65 B-something drawing. The 65 B was the program number. Then all of the numbers and letters that come after that are established by what they call a program item-number index. Program item numbers are a specific statement of work that the airplane has to have.
>
> All of the assemblies that go into the plane are listed, and each one of those is grouped. On the face of the drawing, it has a program item number, so all the windows are going to have a PIN number or a program item number. The PIN number list for the airplane . . . shows every assembly and everything that's needed to build the airplane. When Boeing wants to build a derivative, they say, 'We're going to build X like Y except we're going to add Z.' They take the program item-number list, the PIN number list from Y, and then they say, 'We have that program item-number list. We're going to take these PIN numbers out and [they] are going to be modified. There's a bunch of PIN numbers that won't be modified.'
>
> "Then those PIN numbers come out, and they have drawings and parts associated with them. The people in the engineering groups that own that PIN number then build a statement of work that is based on what they need to do to the existing drawing structure, to make a new drawing structure that will be the new product. After you do all of that, you have a bunch of engineers that do all of the drawings, and then you get a bunch of planners who write all of the work instructions and order all the parts and make all of that work. What happens is that's called the basic release because everything that's in the airplane happened right then."

When changes occur, Boeing has a process for cross-checking to ensure that there aren't unintended consequences. The technical expert continued:

"When you find that you have done stuff wrong, or when you find that you have forgotten to activate some PIN numbers because you missed something in the statement of work, then you have what they call a supplemental release. The supplemental engineering release says, 'Here's something we have to fix. What's involved?' Then it goes to a place called change management and change board. The change board captain gets a thing that comes to him that says, 'We f'ed this up, we need to fix this.' The change board guy will say, 'Well, when we fix that, we need to do this, that, and the other thing.'

"The change board guy, who's not an engineer, usually picks out all of the drawing's requirements that the statement of work looks like it needs. They activate those PINs and they send those out to get the statement of work from the engineers so they can estimate how many new engineering hours to get. Now, this is important, and it plays directly into how the MAX got fucked up. What happened was the MAX had a basic release. The airplane got built, it got into flight test, and they found out that at high angles of attack, the elevator didn't give enough feedback to the pilot to make the stick-force gradient be legal.

"That problem statement went to the engineers and to change board. The change board notified a bunch of engineering groups of what they needed to do. It was decided that they would modify the speed, the existing speed trim system, and they would write a subroutine in the computer program of the speed trim system to cause a down elevator trim input to be made if the airplane detected that it was flying in the zone where the stick-force gradient was insufficient. You get a couple of programmers, you write the subroutine, and everything's happy. The problem was that they missed something that an airplane guy would have caught in a heartbeat.

"That is that there are pitch vanes on the airplane. You have one on each side. The reason there's only one is that the pitch vanes up until that time were reference instruments. They were reference inputs. They were not command inputs. What was happening is the pitch sensors were telling the airplane things that were nice to know, but not crucial to flight. There was a thing on the instrument panel that said, 'Here's what your angle of attack is,' and they read that off the pitch vane. You don't need to know what your angle of attack is unless, of course, you're an ex-Navy pilot who uses units of pitch to feel comfortable about firming the airplane for an approach. That's why it was there.

"The reprogramming of the speed-trim system and the sub-routine that they called MCAS quietly used the pitch-vane input signal. It went from being referenced to being command. Nobody caught it because the change board guy didn't get flight-control dynamics people into the game because it looked really simple, like a little simple programming patch. It was insidious because this change from reference to a command input went right by everybody's nose. If there was an airplane guy in the room, they would have caught it. What that meant is that you now have established engineering that created a single point of failure.

"Nobody writing the engineering subroutine ever was smart enough to ask the question that says, 'Oh, what happens if my input signal is corrupt?' Because they don't care because nobody told them to protect for a corrupt input signal. It wasn't in the statement of work. That's how the 737 was killed. When they started using this command data, which was brand-new command data instead of reference data, they were getting it off of one pitch-vane sensor and they never considered what happens if they lose the fidelity of the data."

SIMULATOR TIME

When Boeing launched the MAX, one of its selling points to airlines and lessors, and its public relations messaging to everyone else, was that the transition from the NG to the MAX was a simple matter of "differences training" that could be done on an iPad in an hour. No simulator training was necessary. Southwest Airlines was adamant about this, including a provision in its purchase contract that if simulator training was required, Boeing would have to pay it $1 million per airplane. Whether there was a cap of the number of aircraft was included is not known, but this would make sense. At some point, the MAX will become the dominant airplane at Southwest as NGs are retired over the course of their twenty-five-year lifespans. Regardless, given the large number of MAXs that Southwest could be expected to order (444 at this writing, and counting), the payout would be huge.

Lion Air asked for simulator training; Boeing said it wasn't necessary. All references to MCAS were excluded from the MAX's operating manual, and the pilots were unaware of the system's existence.

When Boeing decided to go with the 737 re-engining, commonality with the 737 NG was a critical requirement and selling point, especially for pilots. Airlines didn't want to go through the time and expense of pulling pilots off the line and scheduling simulator training. Airbus didn't require simulator training for airlines upgrading from the A320ceo to the neo;

differences training is all that is necessary. Airbus, in fact, has essentially common cockpits across its entire family, precisely to minimize training requirements. Differences training for the sub-types within Airbus's family of airplanes generally involves computer- or, at most, classroom-based training. This training may be measured in hours or in a few days. Across family members, differences training is generally similar.

Boeing's differences training within family members likewise is measured in minimal time commitments. Cockpits between Boeing family members are more problematic, given the age of the original designs. Even so, the 737 cockpit began as an analog-based design common across the industry when the 737 first was designed in the 1960s. Cockpits for the 757 and 767 were more automated when designed in the late 1970s and early 1980s. These two aircraft had the same cockpit for commonality reasons, and differences training for them considered the fact that the 757 was a single-aisle airplane with one set of flying characteristics and the 767 was a twin-aisle airplane with considerably more weight, range, and characteristics. The 767-400, the largest model of the 767 family, has a "glass cockpit," while its sibling -200 and -300 were of an older design. The 777 was different still. The 787's cockpit was more advanced.

The 737NG has a glass cockpit, which Southwest didn't want, preferring instead the analog design in order to reduce training requirements. The MAX has a cockpit more closely aligned with the 787 and the forthcoming 777X.

Was simulator training for the MAX truly necessary? The retired Boeing technical expert, who wasn't a part of the MAX investigation, said that it wasn't.

"Let's talk about why MCAS was built the way it was and why simulator time wasn't needed," this former employee said. "The only reason simulator time became a reality later is because the lawyers got involved. Here's what happens. MCAS is a part of the flight-management computer. The flight-management computers do not have an off switch. You do not have a way to intervene. If the computer's bad, you can't turn it off. There's no off switch, so speed trim and Mach trim are on forever.

"If the speed trim starts screwing up, you'll see speed-trim fail. MCAS, being a subroutine of speed trim because it was attached to the speed trim program and speed trim, and not having an off switch, that means that there's no way for a crew to intervene if MCAS fails, because there's no path that they can take that would influence it. There's nothing the guy in the seat can do to change it," the retired employee said.

What happened, the employee explained, is that it became another mode of trim, a runaway, and trim runaways were already being taught. "They were already memory items, and it was a logical decision to not tell anybody that MCAS existed because you can't intervene on it. If you can't intervene, you can't train, and if you can't train, there's no reason to establish simulator time for it." The employee said that Boeing was correct in not requiring simulator time. It was also correct in not telling anybody it was in the airplane because you couldn't do shit about it anyway.

SCHEDULE AND COST PRESSURES

Boeing was severely criticized for cost and schedule pressures placed on the MAX program and for allegedly putting shareholder value, in the form of dividends and stock buybacks, over safety.

All manufacturers and all airplane development phases are under cost and schedule pressures. The MAX was no different. There were additional pressures because the 787 and 747-8 programs were already billions of dollars over budget and late by the time the MAX was launched in July 2011. The previous February, Boeing finally won a bitter competition over Airbus for a U.S. Air Force contract for the KC-X aerial-refueling tanker. Boeing's bid was 10 percent below Airbus's price, a figure officials of the European company could not understand. Boeing had to know that they bid a below-cost price on the contract. But they said that, over the life of the program, with services and foreign sales, it would be a money-maker.

Just how bad the tanker losses will be is an unknown. By 2025, Boeing wrote off more than $6 billion on an initial contract. Write-offs piled up one quarter after another. But as the MAX development moved from the drawing board (so to speak) through flight testing and entry into service (EIS), the enormity of the KC-X losses, now named the KC-46A, were still in the future. So were the delays that were to come.

But it's this context—cost and schedule pressure—into which the MAX was thrown. Boeing had to prove to stockholders, notably, the institutional shareholders, and to the airlines and lessors that with the MAX, Boeing actually could develop and deliver an airplane on time and on budget. In the end, Boeing delivered the MAX to the first operator two months early. Development costs, initially estimated at between $1 billion and $2 billion, came in at more than $3 billion. CFM, which provided the LEAP engine, shared the development costs.

Still, the cost pressure on the engineers within Boeing (as well as on the supply chain) was immense.

"We spent so much more money on the 787 and it was such an ongoing disaster," recalled one engineer on the MAX program. "That's why I talk about bad choices for how to break up the work. I'm so glad I didn't spend any time on the 787 program. I looked at it when they first started it and went, 'No way. I'm not going to get involved in this,' and that's it. That 747-8, sheesh, what a waste. Anyway, yes, lots of money. There wasn't a whole lot of money left to spend."

During the period when the 787 and 747-8 were eating up so much money and engineering resources, Product Development teams in Everett and Renton were trying to conjure up a new airplane to replace the 737 as well as the 737RE option.

"Cost and performance-wise, it turns out the [re-engining and, alternatively, the new airplane's designs] were pretty darn close, as we understood it, to whatever it was . . . the Everett contingent could conjure up. At one point we were told, 'OK, we're done spending time on the re-engine. Wrap up it, mothball it and put it away,'" this engineer said. "A few months later, along comes that American Airlines' neo order, and panic ensued. We got a call from somebody in sales. Instantly, we were pulling that stuff back out and flipping up the workaround charts of the re-engine. We took a couple of the more complicated things off of it and offer[ed] that as an alternative. That became the basis of the MAX 8."

Boeing put a new tail cone on the MAX, which was a drag reduction. A new display system was also installed, which surprised this engineer because doing so had nothing to do with improving economy.

The MAX was supposed to be minimum change for commonality, training, and controlling costs and schedule. Nothing new here, either. Derivatives—and Boeing viewed the MAX as a derivative—are intended to be minimum-change products. To be sure, design creep is always a threat. But the A320neo was, like the MAX, a minimum-change development. For a variety of reasons, not the least of which was that it was of a newer design than the 737 and was much taller off the tarmac, installing engines on the A320neo was a far less onerous task than on the Boeing plane.

The MAX, says an engineer from the program, was supposed to be minimum change and to require nothing more than level-B transition training. The guidance given to engineers was to achieve better fuel economy and to not do anything else that didn't have to be done.

"In the end, we did a few things that don't strictly fall in that bucket," the engineer said. "Putting [in] the 787 displays and switching flight-deck-display-system vendors was probably the biggest one. We did some drag-reduction things that had to buy their way on a tail cone and APU [auxiliary power unit] inlet." Other computerized upgrades were added, such as a maintenance monitoring and diagnostic system. (This upgrade, however, failed to match the one installed on the 787.) "That was one of those 'we're going to save the customer so much money in maintenance that it's worth putting on the airplane' [things]. By and large, it was 'stuff those big engines underneath the wing and do everything else . . . to make that work and no more.'"

RELIABLE AIRPLANE BUT PROBLEMS FROM THE START

The MAX was recertified by the FAA in November 2020. In the following eighteen months, with reentry into service globally slowed by the effects of the COVID pandemic, the MAX achieved 99.55 percent dispatch reliability during more than 1.5 million flight hours for more than 600,000 departures with more than 630 aircraft for 45 airlines. The performance was comparable with the performance of the NG.

More than 11,000 737s were built from EIS through 2024. The reliability of this workhorse is top notch. But the 737 also has been a problem child from its inception.

During the 1960s, Boeing's "A" teams were assigned to its Supersonic Transport (SST) program, the "B" team to the 747, and others to the 737. Sales for the 737 were so poor that, at one point, Boeing considered selling the entire program and its tooling to Japanese interests. The airplane was underpowered and its thrust reversers initially were ineffective. The basic 737-200 was an OK airplane (there were only thirty -100s built), but it wasn't until Boeing added more powerful engines and other changes to create the 737-200 Advanced (or 737-200A) that the airplane proved to be a success.

Nevertheless, the plane had inherent flaws. To save weight, thinner skin was used, and it wasn't robust. Skin cracks were common. Metal fatigue famously emerged as an issue for aging aircraft when, in 1988, an Aloha Airlines 737-200 enroute from Hilo to Honolulu, Hawaii, suffered an inflight failure of the top of the fuselage that was traced to metal fatigue and very high cycles (one takeoff and landing is one cycle) in a constant salt-air environment. The forward half of the fuselage from the floor line ripped off when metal fatigue caused the thin skin to fail, and the slipstream tore away the entire section. Passengers and cabin crew safely encapsuled a moment before were now flying exposed to the air at several hundred miles per hour. One flight attendant was pulled from the airplane and disappeared into the Pacific 20,000+ feet below. Passengers throughout the cabin were injured with flying debris. One engine ingested debris and failed. The two pilots had to learn on the spot how to fly the crippled airplane—no simulator training even remotely contemplated engine and system failures like this. The cockpit crew essentially became test pilots.

The problems facing the Aloha pilots were immense. The remaining engine was overheating. Aerodynamics were compromised. There was a slight downward bow in the fuselage forward of the wing. Doing a controllability check, the pilots found that flaps could only be slightly lowered for landing. Normal flap settings rendered the airplane unflyable. The landing speed was intentionally higher than normal, otherwise the airplane would begin to shake and vibrate with a potential for loss of control. The nose gear light didn't indicate a safe down condition, so the pilots didn't know if the gear would collapse on touchdown. They didn't know if the brakes would work. And they only had the one thrust reverser. There was little confidence that the airplane could stop in time on the 7,000-foot runway in Maui, where the pilots diverted the flight.

In what was dubbed a Miracle Landing, the pilots safely brought the airplane down. The accident led to the adoption of aging-aircraft inspections and remediations—not just for the 737 but for all other aircraft, too.[91] Unfortunately, it wasn't the first time fatigue from corrosion led to an explosive decompression on a 737-200. In 1981, a twelve-year-old Far Eastern Air Transport (Taiwan) 737-222 (ex-United) blew apart, killing all 110 on board. Just seventeen days before this fatal accident, the same airplane suffered a smaller decompression event. Repairs were made. On an earlier flight on the day of this minor decompression incident, the aircraft lost pressure ten minutes after takeoff. The flight returned to its point of origin for repairs. Taking off seventeen days later, the plane was fourteen minutes into its flight when the explosive decompression caused the plane to disintegrate.

In contrast to the Aloha incident, in which the top of the fuselage ripped away, the Far Eastern plane's fatigue broke floor beams and connecting frames. Control cables and wiring were severed, followed by a loss of power and control. One could argue that Far Eastern had plenty of warning—this seems obvious—and that, ultimately, the accident was the fault of the airline. But the aircraft's operation in the highly corrosive salt water environment should have been a wakeup call.

A rudder issue also emerged on the 737. In March 1991, a United 737-200 was on final approach to Colorado Springs when it suddenly and sharply nosed over, crashing. All twenty-five people aboard were killed. The National Transportation Safety Board (NTSB) was unable to determine the cause of the accident during its twenty-one-month investigation. Given that the airport involved is in the foothills of the Rocky Mountains, some thought that severe winds may have caused the upset. But the same airplane had some uncommanded rudder movement twice in the six days leading up to the accident.

Three and a half years later, on September 8, 1994, a US Air 737-300 was on final approach to Pittsburgh when it suddenly nosed over and dove into the ground. All 132 people on board were killed. The airplane had

---

91. The 747-100/200 was found to require major maintenance to Section 41, the far-forward fuselage, following implementation of the aging-aircraft inspections. Douglas Aircraft Company planes, which industry officials characterized as built like tanks, didn't require much in the way of fixes.

been following a 727, and there was some initial speculation that the 737 flew through the wake turbulence, upsetting the airplane. Boeing suggested that the pilots responded incorrectly and that they were to blame. But the event took only ten seconds from upset to crash.

Like the 1991 United crash, the NTSB's investigation on the US Air crash was extraordinarily long—more than four years. The breakthrough came when an Eastwind Airlines 737 at cruising altitude experienced a rudder hardover. Unlike on the other two flights, the pilots had time to recover. The power control units recovered from the Eastwind plane and, subsequently, from the US Air plane, were eventually determined to be susceptible to failure under certain conditions. It was discovered that the rudder could go in the opposite direction from input by the pilots in the cockpit. The NTSB concluded that the United 737 also was a victim of a rudder hardover event.

The 737 Classic had its own set of problems. No accident or even minor incident occurred with the plane, so little press about its issues resulted, and even when it did, it was in highly niched aviation circles. The Classic developed a long fatigue crack underneath its window line. Southwest Airlines flew the 737-300 on short segments, resulting in higher-than-average cycles and—along with the airline's high daily utilization—higher-than-average accumulated hours. A number of Southwest's planes had to undergo fixes. Because Southwest was the first and only operator of these particular airplanes, Boeing had to foot the bill under its sales contract with the airline.

The Classic had more fatigue issues. Once again, these occurred with high-time, high-cycle aircraft operated by Southwest. Incidents occurred a couple of years apart on two 737-300s with similar cycles and times. Each plane was cruising with portions of its fuselage roof ruptured, causing depressurization and an emergency descent. Both planes landed safely, with only minor injuries during the depressurization. A terrified passenger on one of the flights texted his wife, "Plane is going down, I love you."[92]

These incidents led to the beefing up of the fuselage on the NG. The NG didn't have similar fuselage issues, but something called the pickle fork emerged as a problem on the aircraft in December 2019, at a time when the MAX was grounded following the two MCAS-inspired accidents.

The pickle fork connects the wing to the landing-gear structure and fu-

---

92. Matt Molnar, "Southwest Airlines Scare: How the 737's Fuselage Weakness Went Undetected," *Popular Mechanics* (April 6, 2011), https://www.popularmechanics.com/flight/a6614/how-southwest-airlines-flight-812-737s-fuselage-weakness-went-undetected-5519864/.

selage. It's a structural piece that routes torque, stresses, and loads from the wing to the fuselage. Cracks developed in about 5 percent of the airplanes initially inspected. The fix was complex and costly, but safety was not believed to be compromised. Unfortunately, the cracks were showing up only one-third of the way through the plane's design life. Once more, Southwest planes (and those of other operators) were involved.[93]

Despite these serious and sometimes fatal issues, the 737 family, during its nearly seventy years of operation, has had a good safety record. The original 737s, the -100s and -200s, were designed as short-haul aircraft and built low to the ground for easy baggage loading and unloading. Some versions had "rough field" landing features. Some of Boeing's early sales were in the Third World, where airline maintenance and pilot skills are sometime spotty. These factors led to some accidents. Statistically, through 2023, the original 737-100/200 has a hull-loss accident rate (including fatal and non-fatal accidents) of 1.78 per million departures, according to Boeing's annual accident report covering all types of jets. The 737 Classic (the -300/400/500 models) has a hull-loss accident rate of 0.80 per million departures. The hull-loss accident rate for the 737 NG (the -700/800/900) is 0.17 per million departures.

In contrast, the Airbus A320 family, which entered service in 1988, overlapping the end of the Classic's production and competing against the NG and MAX, has a hull-loss accident rate of 0.17 for the ceo models and 0.08 for the neos. The MAX rate was 0.70 through 2023.

Thus, the MAX, by comparison, statistically had a significantly higher accident rate than its NG predecessor and the A320 family.

93. "Cracks Found on Boeing's 737 NG Pickle Forks," *Engineering.com* (December 9, 2019), https://www.engineering.com/story/ cracks-found-on-boeings-737-ng-pickle-forks.

DAVID CALHOUN

Tenure at The Boeing Company: 2009–2024.
Titles: President and CEO, January 2020–August 8,
2024; Member, Boeing Board of Directors,
2009–August 8, 2024. Getty photo.

19

Strategic Mistakes

"If you're plotting the downfall of Boeing,
those are some key milestones and bad decisions."

—KIRAN RAO, FORMER EXECUTIVE VICE PRESIDENT OF STRATEGY, AIRBUS

THE BOEING COMPANY'S LONG FALL from its engineering excellence and overwhelming dominance wasn't just about self-inflicted design, industrialization, and product-stagnation problems. A shift away from its engineering roots to a focus on appeasing Wall Street by prioritizing shareholder value led to flawed strategy and strategic mistakes.

Strategic (and tactical) mistakes predated Boeing's 1997 merger with McDonnell Douglas, an event which conventional wisdom points to as the catalyst for Boeing's decline. Boeing dismissed the threat that Airbus posed for two decades, and officials sniffed that Airbus airplanes were inferior to Boeing products. Based on the A300/A310 widebodies, this view wasn't entirely without merit. But dismissing the A320 was a major mistake. And after the merger, Boeing's miscalculations began coming with increasing frequency—and with major ramifications.

FIRST STRATEGIC MISTAKE

Napoleon Bonaparte, the infamous French Revolutionary general, said, "Never interrupt your enemy when he is making a mistake."

It's unclear whether Airbus, which made plenty of mistakes of its own, consciously followed Napolean's advice. But officials at the company certainly followed the principle. Kiran Rao, Airbus's chief strategist for many years, said that Boeing made five key strategic mistakes that allowed Airbus to overtake it and dominate the aircraft manufacturing industry.

The first was a 1992 order that Airbus won from United Airlines. Except for the McDonnell Douglas DC-10, ordered more than twenty years before, United had ordered nothing but Boeing jets beginning with the 720 in 1960. The 727, 737, 747, 757, and 767 followed. United considered buying Airbus's A340 model but went with the 777 instead. When United wanted a 150-seat twin jet, its choices were the 737-400 or the A320. (The MD-80 from McDonnell Douglas wasn't considered.) United operated the 126-seat 737-300 and the older 737-200. In fact, United was the launch customer of the -200. It also was a launch customer of the 727 and 747. Given strong incumbency and exclusive positioning for twenty years, Boeing was confident that United wouldn't buy from Airbus, which at the time was viewed by Boeing and others as little more than a European jobs program that catered to failing airlines and airlines that were poor credit risks.

Boeing took a hard line about the contract it had with United. When the 737-300 was ordered, United gave little thought to the possibility that it might want a higher-capacity model. The contract set the price of the 150-seat 737-400 based on a simple mathematical upscaling based on twenty-four more seats. Now, United officials wanted to renegotiate a price lower than the one that resulted from that formula. Boeing balked, saying a deal was a deal.

Airbus was winning market share around the globe but had made little headway in the United States. Officials knew what winning an order from United would mean, both as an endorsement of their A320 and because of the impact of flipping United from Boeing. The A320 was unquestionably a better airplane than the 737-400. The A320's technology was twenty years newer, passenger experience was better with its wider cabin and wider seats, it was more fuel-efficient and important to United, and it had transcontinental range (most of the time). The 737-400 fell short of range.

Hungry for the business, John Leahy, referred to in the industry as Airbus's "super-salesman," and Rao, who was assigned by Leahy to cover United at the time, were willing to deal.

"Up to that point into that decade, the Asian market was tiny," Rao recalled thirty years later. "There were no LCCs [low-cost carriers] in Asia, and if you sold a few little 320s here and a few 320s there in Asia, that was about it. Indian Airlines had its thirty-aircraft deal. The Middle East was hardly anything, especially for the 320 in those days. Europe, of course, had its big government-owned flag carriers, but the big market in those days was the United States. If you could crack the United States, then your airplane had a chance."

Airbus production rates in those days probably were about ten or twelve aircraft a month. Boeing out-produced Airbus by a wide margin with its broad family of airplanes. Orders were usually in the low double digits. Orders with big numbers were unheard of, Rao said. "You had to win at American [Airlines] or Delta [Air Lines] or Northwest [Airlines] or, to a certain extent, Air Canada. That's where you needed to make a difference. When United evaluated the 320 against the 737-400, I was there in the U.S. with John [Leahy]. We did loads of presentations, but we would come across a huge anti-Airbus, anti-[foreign] buying feeling. The 320 could stand its own against the 737-400. Airbus went ahead and won that deal. Boeing then had to quickly go from the regular 737-400 to the NG. When they went to the NG, it improved things a lot for them,"[94] Rao recounted.

Then Airbus made its own mistake. The 737 NG was a vast improvement over the 737-300/400/500, which informally became known as the Classic. Since the A320 was designed in the 1980s and entered service in 1988, Airbus had little incentive to make any changes. The NG entered service in December 1997.

Boeing designed a new wing for the NG and added a lot of incremental improvements. The 737-800 stretched the -400, providing twelve more seats than were offered in the A320 at the time. Essentially, all the shortcomings of the Classic, and especially the 737-400, were fixed. Much later, winglets were added[95] and there were all sorts of little aerodynamic improvements. "I remember we produced a very nice chart in Airbus which showed how the 320 had a good field-burn advantage against the 737-400. The NG closed that advantage down, and made it slightly better," Rao recalled. "Airbus stood still with the 320 development. Boeing then con-

---

94. The United Airlines campaign is described in detail in *Air Wars*.

95. Winglets were added, though many within Boeing did not initially support this improvement. In classic not-invented-here fashion, there was a feeling within Boeing that the NG didn't need the winglets. An independent company, Aviation Partners, Inc., invented the 737 winglet. Once the fuel-savings benefits of the winglets were recognized, however, Boeing embraced them and bought into the program. Aviation Partners Boeing, a joint partnership between Boeing and Aviation Partners went on to create winglets for the 757 and 767. Airbus, in the meantime, dismissed the benefit that winglets would bring to the A320. The airplane had wingtip devices called wingtip fences that gave the A320 some of its operating-cost advantage over the 737 Classic. Long after Boeing added winglets to the NG, Airbus finally added them to the A320 (calling them sharklets instead). Ironically, Airbus had initially worked with Aviation Partners on the sharklet but went on to development them internally. Aviation Partners sued for patent infringement. Airbus quietly settled.

tinued to innovate and innovate and innovate. Every three or four years, you'd get some small innovation which would improve the fuel burn by 1 percent, and then 2 percent, and 0.5 percent, whatever. By the time we got to the early 2000s, the 737 NG was actually pretty good in terms of its competitive fuel burn and all the other elements that make up the operating cost. It then had a very good . . . It had a significant advantage over the 320. It was almost the opposite of where we are today."

SECOND STRATEGIC MISTAKE

Then 9/11 happened. Rao said that this tragedy led to Boeing's next big mistake. Boeing slashed its production, whereas Airbus continued production at whatever small rate it was in those days.

"What that meant after 9/11 was all these major disruptions resulted in a dip in traffic. But it bounces back, and the market did bounce back. When the market bounced back, Boeing had dropped the production rate. Airbus had produced a lot of airplanes, and that's when the LCC global market started to pick up, not just in Europe. It started to pick up in Asia," Rao said. "In those days, 2002, 2003, 2004, and 2005, the Asian LCCs start to come alive. Boeing's production is taking time to get back into shape." Airbus was ready to deliver the A320. And Airbus was more than willing to take riskier bets than Boeing.

"Airplanes went to some very flaky customers," Rao said. "When the Asian LCCs came alive, I could offer an airplane in six months' time, whereas Boeing couldn't offer them an airplane. [You could close a deal] even if you had an airplane that didn't quite have the 189 seats (in the 737) against the (A320's) 180 seats in those days, which made a huge difference. [Normally, t]hat killed us all the time on campaigns because those nine seats kept on generating value. Even if you had a slight fuel-burn advantage, you couldn't overcome the nine-seat advantage of the 737-800."

Each seat in an LCC model was worth about $200,000 to $250,000 annually in revenue. Airbus figured that one seat over the life of an airplane, after considering load factors, would be worth millions of dollars.

The match between the A319 and 737-700 NG was about even. The A321 carried more passengers than the 737-900ER, a real plus for LCCs and charter airlines, but the -900ER had more range and, with its newer wing, could climb higher than the A321 on initial cruise.

The A320 and the 737-800 were in what Boeing called the "heart of the market," the segment where the most sales occurred. The smaller A319 and 737-700 sold well enough. The larger 737-900ER was Boeing's weakest sales member in the family, and the A321 had range limitations. Airbus finally started to undertake major innovations on the A320 family in 2010 when it launched a re-engining program called "new engine option," or neo. Major cabin upgrades increased seating on the A320 to be closer to the seating on the 737-800. A Flex Cabin option was added to the A321, boosting its capacity to a maximum of 240 passengers in a high-density configuration. While waiting for the neo to enter service in 2016, Airbus worked with its engine makers to improve operating economics in 1 percent increments. Boeing added similar improvements, so the 737-800 maintained a slight edge over the A320. Then, Airbus figured out how to add more seats in the A320 by adopting slim-line seating in coach and redesigning and relocating galleys and lavatories ("lavs") to reduce their footprints and add seats. Eventually, Airbus was able to jam 186 seats into the A320 in a high-density configuration, with a comfortable 160 seats in two classes. The latter was just two seats off the -800's usual 162 seats. The A320 became equally competitive with the 737-800.

Boeing didn't stand still. A few airlines followed the Airbus lead, adopting "space-saver" lavs. These lavs were a contortion-inducing space that, in its grossest terms, meant that it was difficult to sit and wipe at the same time. People of plus size could barely squeeze in. (Mile High opportunities collapsed, though this was hardly the motive for these torture features.) American Airlines jammed 172 seats into its 737-800s and, later, its MAX 8s. Not only did passengers object, so did flight attendants.

A key difference was that 737s were exit-limited while A320s had more flexibility before exit limitations were reached. This wasn't some far-reaching design planning on the part of Airbus. It was happenstance. Boeing had to add additional emergency exits for the high-density version of the MAX 8, which could seat 200 passengers—almost as many as the physically larger 737-10, which could seat, at a maximum, 210 passengers. The high-density MAX 8 was called the MAX 8200, for which Ryanair (which, in the view of some, doesn't care about passenger comfort) was the primary target customer.

Airbus made a quantum leap in 2010 with the launch of the re-engined A320, the neo. Seven months later, Boeing responded with the re-engined 737, the MAX.

THIRD STRATEGIC MISTAKE

The third strategic mistake Boeing made, from Airbus's perspective, came during the A380 struggles in 2005 and 2006.

"The A380 was dragging Airbus down," Rao recalled. "The 787 was now the 'Dreamliner' and the best thing since sliced bread. The A330 was almost finished. A340s were heaps of junk. The A380 couldn't get off that rocky start that it had. Fuel prices started to go up. At that point, Boeing had the chance, in 2005 and 2006, to redo the 737 and kill Airbus off completely because Airbus had no money, Airbus couldn't innovate, and Airbus had no plan. As I used to say in the meetings in those days, we were one step away from checkmate.

"Boeing never made that move. If they had moved in 2006, we'd be in a very different situation today. They made a couple of mistakes. They let the 320 into United. They dropped the production rate. They didn't take advantage of the fact that Airbus was on its knees." Leahy, when told in 2022 of this analysis by Rao, disagreed with his former lieutenant. Leahy rejected Rao's assessment that Boeing could have killed Airbus off in 2005–2006. Rather, Leahy conceded, Airbus would have lost share to perhaps 40 percent of the market.

Boeing at that time was beginning to run into production problems on the 787 and soon found itself in no position to replace the 737 with an aircraft clearly superior to the A320 family. But there is no dispute that, had Boeing delivered the 787 on time in May 2008 then replaced the 737 with a new design, then the 777, Airbus would have been set back decades, launch aid (which was then still a thing) or no launch aid. Not only was the A380 dragging Airbus down, so was the military unit's A400M—something that remains a financial drag to this day. Airbus's response to the 787 in 2005 was a re-engined, warmed-over A330 using the same GEnx engines as the 787. Market reaction was tepid at best. After a complete redesign, Airbus launched the A350 XWB composite airplane with new, more advanced Rolls-Royce (RR) Trent XWB engines. This program was announced in July 2006 at the Farnborough Air Show. Even then Airbus didn't get the product right. The smallest A350-800 was eventually dropped, and the largest A350-1000 needed an engine thrust bump and some wing modifications to meet performance targets. Rao admits that if he had it to do over, there would have been a four-member family: the -800 and slightly larger -900 with one set of engines and performance specifications, the larger -1000, and a fourth, even larger -2000 with another set of more powerful engines.[96]

Boeing, however, didn't launch a clean-sheet 737 replacement in 2005 or 2006, nor did it pursue a re-engined design. The company's Product Development unit (PD) continued research and development (R&D) efforts on both the 737 and 777 replacements, but Boeing was being crushed by cost overruns and delays on the 787. These negatively impacted the development of the 747-8, Boeing's response to the A380. The 747-8 had GEnx engines derived from the 787's engines, plus some wing modifications and a fuselage stretch. So, Boeing did nothing to take advantage of Airbus's weaknesses at the time.

---

96. The full details of the Boeing-Airbus twin-aisle battle between the 787, A330, and A350 is recounted in *Air Wars.*

FOURTH STRATEGIC MISTAKE

Rao said that the next mistake Boeing made was to be dismissive of the prospective re-engined A320. "They didn't believe in the 320neo. They were late coming into the 320neo," Rao said. CEO James McNerney; Jim Albaugh, CEO of Boeing's Commercial Airplanes division (BCA); marketing chief Randy Tinseth (the face of Boeing at most conferences other than investor conferences); and most salesmen sniffed that the re-engined A320 would merely "catch up" to the 737-800 in economics and performance. Airbus and some key analysts, plus *Leeham News*, concluded otherwise. Within PD at Boeing, and even within the sales division, the threat that the A320neo posed to the 737 NG was not laughed off. But the upper ranks weren't listening.[97]

Airbus finally launched the A320neo in December 2010. Within the next seven months, Airbus announced orders for about 1,000 neos. It was an enormous lead. Boeing still hadn't moved, dithering between a new airplane design and the re-engining of the 737. Albaugh and Mike Bair, the head of the 737 program at the time, favored a new airplane. A re-engining of the 737 was on the design shelf, deemed a Plan B if needed. In July 2011, Airbus forced Boeing's hand. On the cusp of winning a huge order from American Airlines, McNerney received a call from American's CEO Gerard Arpey, who told him that American was about to sign a deal. If Boeing wanted in, McNerney would have to act now. McNerney made the decision to offer the re-engined 737 and, within forty-eight hours, Boeing had a proposal before American, which split the deal between Boeing and Airbus, ordering hundreds of airplanes from each original equipment manufacturer (OEM).[98]

Airbus gambled that Boeing could be maneuvered into re-engining the 737 versus launching a new airplane design. In their words, they were "terrified" Boeing would choose the latter course. Airbus wasn't in a position, given its own turmoil and money-sucking programs, to respond with a new airplane design of its own. Airbus had done its own studies on the prospect of re-engining the 737 and concluded that Boeing would be challenged to do so. The Airbus engineers were right: the technical challenges of installing a bigger engine and tweaking the airframe to get solid double-digit economic gains were daunting. Yet Boeing figured it out. But

---

97. It's entirely possible that Boeing's leadership wasn't fooled, either. The public campaign could very well have been Boeing's strategy to raise doubts about the neo to stall orders while Boeing decided what to do. This form of disinformation was a common tactic used by both Boeing and Airbus.

98. The American Airlines deal is detailed in *Air Wars*.

initially there was no 737-10, and the 737-9 couldn't match the A321neo. The A320neo and the 737-8 were evenly matched, eliminating Boeing's inherent advantage. Despite Boeing's hubris, the market soon made its preferences known: Airbus captured about 60 percent of the A320-737 sector even before the MAX grounding in March 2019.

FIFTH STRATEGIC MISTAKE

Today, the single-aisle sector remains the heart of the aircraft market, even after the market up-gauged from around 160 seats to 190 or 200 seats (in other words, from the A320/737-800/8 size to the A321/737-10 size). Airbus, when launching its A321neo program, bet that the model would eventually outsell its A320neo, and it was right.

The fifth strategic mistake in Rao's view was Boeing's failure to launch an airplane for the so-called middle of the market, or "MOM," to use another acronym in the company's alphabet soup of acronyms. This is the sector Boeing defined in 2012 as larger than the 737-9 (at the time, the biggest 737—the MAX 10 had not yet been offered) and smaller than the 787-8. Boeing executives were constantly being pummeled for not having a viable competitor to the A321neo. Initially, as they so often did, Boeing executives pooh-poohed the competitive sector as too small to worry about—perhaps 1,200 airplanes, if that. Later, when interest within Boeing increased over the prospect of a new airplane for the MOM sector, Boeing reassessed and claimed that the market was about 2,500 airplanes. Still later, the number was restated as the "addressable" market of 4,500 aircraft. Basically, all A321s, 757s, 767s, and A330s (plus a few remaining A300s and A310s) fell within the "addressable" market. Internally, Boeing wasn't fooled by its own public rhetoric. Albaugh confirmed that all along, Boeing saw the New Midmarket Airplane (NMA) market as being about 2,100 airplanes.

The conceptual range of this new airplane, 4,500 to 5,000 nautical miles (nm), and its passenger capacity of 220 to 270 in typical two-class configuration overlapped the 787-8. A study by *Leeham News* of airline schedules showed that only 35 percent of the 787-8's flights were more than 5,000nm. These could easily be covered by the 787-9. A new Boeing airplane could cover most of the 787-8 routes. The plane would cost less to buy and, taking advantage of more advanced technologies, including a fourth generation (at the time) of the composite wings, would cost less to operate, too. Which was fine by Boeing. The 787-8, the first of the 787s, is a fine airplane operationally. But as the first of the family, it was the guinea pig for all the new design, production, and industrial outsourcing Boeing had adopted for the 787. The execution proved disastrous. By the time the 787-9 and 787-10 were introduced, production and design on these models were sufficiently different from the 787-8 that, from this perspective, the -8's commonality with the -9 and -10 was only about 40 percent. The production commonality rate between the -9 and the -10 was about 95 percent. The profit margin on the -8 was also much lower than on the -9 and -10. Boeing reached a point in the 2017–2018 period where it really didn't want to produce the -8 any longer. The business model foresaw producing only one 787-8 a month from 2020 onward.

Thus, a new airplane's overlap with the 787-8 wasn't a matter of great concern to the marketing people at Boeing. The company never publicly acknowledged declining interest in the -8, but in private conversation, the direction was clear.

Ray Conner, the top Boeing salesman of the Albaugh era, succeeded him as BCA's CEO in 2012 when Albaugh abruptly resigned. Albaugh told *Air Wars* that it was simply time for him to retire. Others said that Albaugh got in McNerney's crosshairs over the decision on whether to launch a new airplane or to re-engine the 737 and over his more accommodating messaging with labor unions, which contrasted with the more aggressive anti-union posture McNerney favored. In any case, Conner favored a new single-aisle airplane along the sizes of the 757-200 and 757-300. Mike Bair's team favored a 767-sized family of twin-aisle aircraft, arguing that dual aisles and bigger entry/exit main cabin doors allowed faster enplaning and deplaning. This would allow at least one more flight segment, and maybe two, per day, providing higher utilization and greater revenue potential than a single-aisle airplane. Lufthansa and Virgin Atlantic Airways liked the twin-aisle approach. So did many Asian carriers, though some had reservations about the elliptical shape of the proposed fuselage on this design, feeling that it inhibited full use of the lower deck for cargo.

Conner, who retired in 2017, said that the plane he envisioned instead evolved into the 767-size aircraft, which became the favored concept. PD at Boeing is set up in silos, with different teams working on different concepts. The Bair team (and that of his successor, after he retired) worked on the twin-aisle concept. A team in Renton, Washington, worked on the single-aisle concept. As is the case during development, the two teams competed rather than collaborated.

Bair and Albaugh favored the twin-aisle model, which seemed to gain favor within BCA and with Dennis Muilenburg, who succeeded McNerney as CEO when he retired in 2015. David Calhoun, then the lead director on Boeing's board, was said to oppose the twin-aisle. Chief financial officer Greg Smith was more succinct. Ron Spingarn, the Credit Suisse aerospace analyst, quoted Smith as saying, "I hate that fucking airplane" during a relaxed moment over drinks one night.

Regardless of the internal debates, Boeing dithered. The company began talking about the MOM sector airplane in 2012, months after the 737 MAX was launched with the American Airlines order in July 2011. And for the next seven years, Boeing was frozen by analysis paralysis. Leaders could not decide which design to pursue, whether to tie the business case to aftermarket services by Boeing Global Services (BGS), or how big the market was. They simply couldn't close the business case to their satisfaction.

Finally, all the stars seemed to be aligning for a twin-aisle airplane launch at the 2019 Paris Air Show. Then, in March of that year, a second MAX crashed in Ethiopia and the global fleet was grounded. By December, Muilenburg had been fired and Calhoun replaced him as CEO in January 2020. He killed all the R&D on the new airplane, by this time called the NMA. The MAX fleet was still grounded, and the recertification date for the plane was anybody's guess. In March 2020, the global COVID-19 pandemic broke out, and that was that.

Rao said that Boeing should have bitten the bullet and launched the NMA even while the 787 and 747-8 programs were in their in-service infancy. Although the forecasted numbers were small, Rao believes that Boeing would have created a broader market. Furthermore, he says an NMA response is something that Airbus would not have launched because it wouldn't have shot the A321XLR and A330-800 down. (Airbus officials claimed the A330-800 adequately covered the upper end of the MOM sector, but this was pure poppycock.)

"The NMA was like an arrow fired between an A321XLR and A330," Rao said. "If you look at the NMA's performance in economics against a 330, an NMA would've killed off the A330, even the 330neo. That same arrow that's fired between the two would have damaged the XLR. The NMA would have had the right economics to compete with the 321XLR. Airbus would've had to let the NMA go and make its market. It would have been what happened to the neo-MAX situation, where Boeing was reluctant to kill off their own NGs and so didn't fire the MAX bullet at the right time."

Airbus was known to have a concept airplane code-named the A321 Plus waiting on the sidelines. Also referred to as the A322, the airplane would have been about a twelve-seat stretch of the A321neo with a new composite wing and more powerful engines. Independent analysis concluded that this version would be economically competitive with the NMA, whether that plane was a single- or a twin-aisle model. But Rao said that going forward would have cost a lot of money and would have killed the XLR.

"You had gotten a situation where Airbus said, 'No, no, no. XLR can do the job. The 330 can do the job.' The NMA would have had such stunning economics against the 330," Rao recalled.

By the second half of 2022, PD was considering not just a twin-aisle NMA. It was also working on a single-aisle NMA.[99] As before, the twin-

---

99. With Calhoun having killed the NMA, Boeing's corporate communications team bristled at the use of this acronym by *Leeham News* through the summer and

aisle model was a 767-sized concept, and the single-aisle model was a 757-sized concept. The twin-aisle approach was different this time, however. Up until 2019, the focus was on a passenger airliner. The 2022 concept led with a freighter version to replace the aging 767-300ERF, which faced termination of production by the end of 2027 because of new, strict emissions regulations adopted by the International Civil Aviation Organization (ICAO) in 2017 and slated for adoption by the FAA in 2023. Boeing had already launched the 777-8F to succeed the aging 777-200LRF for this very reason. But without a new airplane, the company risked having no successor to the 767F. PD was also working on a freighter version of the 787. The airplane, especially the -9, is too big for a direct comparison with the 767F. There are also technical challenges in offering a 787F due to its barrel composite fuselage construction. (The A350F uses panel composites, an easier platform on which to develop a freighter.)

As usual, silo-contained PD teams at Boeing worked on the "NMA-F" and the 787F and the twin-aisle passenger MOM airplane versus a single-aisle aircraft. Then, on November 2, 2022, Boeing held its first Investor Day since 2018. During the event, Calhoun said that Boeing would not introduce a new airplane until the middle of the 2035 decade. All PD spending on airplane R&D was essentially terminated. R&D spending was to be focused on advanced design and production development and on supporting the WISK battery-powered unmanned air taxi–type vehicle (eVTOL) in which Boeing had invested jointly with another company. Calhoun said that this R&D was not so much about creating a viable urban air mobility (UAM) model (to fly at lower altitudes and operate in locations like cities or towns) as it was about learning how to certify an airplane for one-pilot or autonomous operation. Calhoun also said that there wouldn't be a step-change engine until 2035, which happens to be the target date set by CFM International for its Open Fan RISE engine.

Calhoun's comments were a bit disingenuous. The NMA's replacement target was the 757/767 and competing airplanes. An independent analysis by Leeham Company concluded that the NMA-F would be about 23 percent more efficient than the 767 and that the passenger model would have about the same economics as the 757-300, one of the most efficient aircraft flying on a seat-mile basis. The greater belly-freight capacity of the NMA, however, gave it the advantage over the 757-300.

The single-aisle NMA—the 757-sized concept—was envisioned to succeed the 737 MAX. Taken in isolation, Calhoun was probably right in saying that a new airplane would not offer a step-change advantage over the

---

fall of 2022. But the airplane under study, including the freighter, was based on the NMA, and Boeing hadn't invented a new acronym.

MAX with derivatives of the Pratt & Whitney (P&W) GTF or the CFM LEAP engines. And since all the criticism about Boeing's product line was largely focused on the MAX 10 being an inferior competitor to the A321neo, this was likely the context Calhoun was addressing. Boeing officials professed to be satisfied with the MAX 10's competitiveness. Only about 5 percent of routes require the longer range of the A321LR and A321XLR, so Boeing wasn't worried about filling this market segment.[100]

Rao calls this another strategic mistake for Boeing. "The last bad decision is the one they've just taken, which is, they will just live with what they've got for another ten years."

As one Boeing corporate communications person pointed out, there was a backlog of 4,800 737s. A new airplane wasn't needed, he said. But a skeptic observed, what if CFM can't successfully complete its RISE engine? This means that Boeing would have to stick with the 737 through the rest of the 2030 decade, giving Airbus the ability to achieve more market penetration.

Richard Aboulafia, an aviation industry consultant, eviscerated Calhoun in a commentary he wrote following the CEO's 2018 Investor Day comments. He predicted Calhoun would go down as one of Boeing's worst CEOs and that Boeing's single-aisle market share would shrink to 30 percent. Rao was more pessimistic: he predicted that Boeing's share of this sector could fall to between 20 and 30 percent. Stan Deal, then the CEO of BCA, told attendees at Investor Day that he was fine with Boeing having a 40 percent market share, the figure most often cited as 2022's market share (split between Boeing and Airbus). In fact, when the Commercial Aircraft Corporation of China's (COMAC) C919, Airbus's A220, Embraer's E190 and E195 E2 jets, and Russia's MC-21 are included in the global backlog, the MAX already was down to a 38 percent market share in the 100-to-240-seat single-aisle sector.

"If you're plotting the downfall of Boeing, those are some key milestones and bad decisions," Rao said.

---

100. This contrasts with Boeing's development of the 747SP, 777-200LR, and 777-8 passenger models. Each was developed for this 5 percent market segment.

20

Fixing Boeing

"It's become an extreme embarrassment. The [Boeing] board seems weirdly absentee. Investors seem weirdly complacent."

—**RICHARD ABOULAFIA** TO CNN, MARCH 14, 2024

THE BOEING COMPANY HAD A DEEP HOLE TO CLIMB OUT OF. Returning the MAX to service was the first step, beginning in November 2020, when the Federal Aviation Administration (FAA) recertified the airplane. But by then, the world was in the depths of the COVID pandemic, presenting a new challenge for Boeing. And global regulators didn't act in concert with the FAA, in which confidence had been lost. The FAA was no longer the gold standard of regulators. Transport Canada, the European Aviation Safety Agency (EASA), and Brazilian regulators followed quickly on the FAA's heels in recertifying the MAX. But other regulators—some 180 of them—were slow to do so. By the start of 2022, the Civil Aviation Administration of China (CAAC), the first regulator to ground the MAX, still hadn't granted recertification (though this had more to do with politics than with the airplane). Neither had regulators in Russia, which soon invaded Ukraine and had other things to worry about.

Also facing Boeing at the start of 2022: no new-build 787s were being delivered. There were still around 110 in inventory, and production was barely ticking over at one-half to one unit a month. As with the MAX, the FAA retained ticketing authority to certify the 787s for individual delivery. Boeing was resigned to the "new normal," however.

Certification progress on the 777X remained slow. Boeing in early 2022 stuck with its new certification target of late 2023, but Tim Clark, the president of Emirates Airline, which, by far held the largest order for the 777X, was skeptical. He was not alone. The consensus among customers, lessors (who had not ordered the airplane), aerospace analysts, and others was that certification would slip to 2024. Whether this meant waiting a few months, until the first quarter, or until later in the year was anyone's guess.

Still, as 2021 turned to 2022, MAX monthly production numbers were in the twenties. Boeing planned to hit thirty-one planes a month in February 2022, on its way to a pre-grounding number of fifty-two per month by

2024. The legacy inventory was slowly being chipped away. The company launched the 777-8F freighter with an order for thirty-four and options for sixteen from Akbar Al Baker, the mercurial CEO of Qatar Airways. However, twenty of these planes were swaps from the 777-9, so the net increase to Boeing was only fourteen 777Xs. Orders for the MAX were picking up, moving Boeing beyond the fire sale of white tails and customer compensation for the MAX grounding.

One of the reasons for the production-rate increase was the need to create production slots for future orders. Airbus had sold out on the A320 line well into 2027, so Boeing's ability to ramp up production helped win some sales that Airbus simply couldn't fill. For some of the new MAX orders, Boeing promised delivery as early as 2023. Company officials hoped to return MAX production to its pre-grounding level of fifty-two a month by 2024 and hit fifty-seven a month the next year. But Airbus hoped to take A320 production to seventy-five a month by 2025, amounting to a 57 percent production-market share. Boeing clearly was going to occupy a permanent number two position in the all-important single-aisle sector until it launched a new airplane.

THE MIDDLE OF THE MARKET (MOM) AIRPLANE

In 2012, Boeing began deeper internal discussions about the next Boeing airplane that would succeed the MAX. The A321neo, while better than what was then known as the A321ceo, still wasn't up to replacing the 757. In 2012, the top end of the MAX line was the MAX 9, which clearly wasn't the answer. Like its predecessor, the 737-900ER, the MAX 9 had less range than the A321neo, it needed more runway to take off, and it carried fewer passengers. Although the 757-300 wasn't a sales success, its operating seat-mile cost was the best in the single-aisle market, and winglets made the 757-200 a reasonable answer for thin routes of modest trans-Atlantic distances. The sector Ray Conner, the CEO of Boeing's Commercial Airplanes division (BCA), had in mind was above the MAX 9 and below the 787-8, which carried too many passengers for some thin routes and had a range of more than 7,200 nautical miles (nm), far more than needed. This sector became known as the middle of the market (MOM). The 757 replacement became known as the New Small Airplane, or New Single-Aisle Airplane, with the convenient initialism "NSA" representing either idea.

Mike Bair, who headed the 737 program and before it the 787 program, had a different vision: a family of twin-aisle airplanes seating between 180 and 250 passengers in two classes built with an elliptical fuselage, which in turn demanded a composite fuselage. Both were necessary to deliver a twin-aisle aircraft that, in its smallest version, had single-aisle operating costs. Twin aisles allowed faster enplaning and deplaning, reducing turn times at the gate. This in turn provided an extra trip or two a day for an airline. Or so the theory went. One critic maintained that there would still be a back-up at the door. Bair responded that it depended on the size of the door.

Bair retired in 2013, so his advocacy disappeared from the scene. Over the ensuing years, the internal debate at Boeing dragged on. A bit to Conner's chagrin, his vision of the 757 replacement evolved into a concept more closely aligned with replacing the passenger capacity of the 767-200ER/300ER with a two-member family. The range for Boeing's New Midmarket Airplane (NMA) was 5,000nm for the smaller NMA-6 and 4,500nm for the larger NMA-7. The passenger capacity now was identified as 225 to 270 passengers in two classes. Internally, Boeing debated whether the NMA would have a round fuselage for added below-floor cargo space, desired by many Asian airlines, or an elliptical composite fuselage with limited under-floor space that followed Bair's vision.

One of the biggest problems facing Boeing at the time was closing the business case for the twin-aisle NMA, whatever final form it took. By shifting from the 757 to the 767 replacement, Boeing also altered its competitive outlook. In a way, it had little choice. In October 2016, the 737-10 MAX was launched. The MAX 10, in seating capacity, now was squarely in the 757-200 space. Launching a single-aisle NSA would encroach on the MAX 10 before it got started. Conner retired from his CEO position at BCA in November 2016 and as an advisor to the Boeing Company at the end of 2017. His vision of a 757 replacement, from a practical viewpoint, no longer mattered.

Boeing concluded that the true market potential for the NMA was 2,100 airplanes. If one assumed that Airbus would respond with a plane that captured half of that total (an assumption Kiran Rao disputed), making the business case for the NMA was challenging indeed. The engine makers certainly wanted no part of being a dual-source supplier. Greg Hayes, the CEO of what was then United Technologies,[101] the parent company of Pratt & Whitney (P&W), told anyone who asked that there was no business case for two engine suppliers for the limited NMA market. But Boeing was trapped by its own MAX 10 decision. Officials could not say that they had plans to have a competing airplane. Internally, as always, there were two camps. One said that the plan was to develop the two-member NMA family followed by a single-aisle airplane that would replace the MAX 9 and MAX 10. This was called the two-tube strategy by aerospace analyst Robert Spingarn, then of Credit Suisse. It was the same strategy Boeing followed in creating the 757 and 767, the latter entering service before the former. Another camp, in a highly secret strategy, followed Bair's idea: a third family member starting

---

101. Later Raytheon Technologies Corporation, or RTX.

at about 180 seats with two classes. This would require smaller engines and a smaller wing, but the shorter fuselage would not be the classic "shrink" that almost always resulted in a bastardized airplane economically.

If the two-member family was projected to struggle with a market demand of 2,100 airplanes, resulting in a poor business case, a three-member family of planes ballooned the potential market to about 9,000. This is a market that Boeing could share with Airbus and still make money. For its part, Airbus sniffed that it had the MOM sector covered with the A321neo (as deficient as it still was) and the forthcoming A330-800neo. It was pure sophistry. Eventual development of the A321LR, with an advertised range of 4,100nm, and the A321XLR, with a 4,700nm range, solved most of the operational problems at the lower end of the market. But the A330-800 was way too much airplane, given its weight, size, and range of more than 8,200nm. An NMA-7 would beat the pants off it. Furthermore, the market universally rejected the airplane and, for a time, so did Airbus. At one point, its sales force didn't even try to market the A330-800. At its peak, there were fifteen orders for the plane. In 2024, Airbus announced that it would upgrade its multi-role tanker transport model (MRTT) to the A330-800 platform.

The longer Boeing fiddled around, the smaller its MOM airplane potential became. As Airbus improved the A321neo with the LR and XLR, and as Boeing dithered, more airlines turned to Airbus. Even United, whose current management favored Boeing airplanes, finally gave in and ordered seventy-five A321XLRs. It could no longer wait to replace its large, aging fleet of 757s.

As the years passed, Muilenburg and Kevin McAllister, who succeeded Conner as BCA CEO, enthused about the NMA. Lead Director David Calhoun and CFO Greg Smith didn't like the twin-aisle NMA. But by 2019, it appeared that Muilenburg was about to realize his goal of launching the NMA. Then, the second MAX crash, Ethiopian flight ET302, happened on March 10. By March 13, the global MAX fleet of some 350 airplanes was grounded. By the end of the year, Muilenburg was fired. Calhoun succeeded him in January 2020 and killed the NMA, and any plans for a new airplane, until the MAX returned to service. Then COVID happened, followed by a suspension of 787 deliveries and the addition of tens of billions of dollars in debt incurred to get through Boeing's several crises. Boeing was in survival mode.

THE NEXT BOEING AIRPLANE

Throughout its multiple crises, there was a $15 billion question hanging over the prospects for Boeing's future: What will the Next Boeing Airplane (NBA) be? Would the NMA make a comeback? Would Conner's 757 replacement vision be the preferred solution? Would it be something else? These questions became the cliche that the NBA "is a riddle, wrapped in a mystery, inside an enigma." Not even those inside Boeing had a clue. Calhoun slashed the company's research and development (R&D) budget, to much criticism from industry consultants Richard Aboulafia—a vociferous critic of Boeing's "low" R&D spending—Kevin Michaels, and others. However, Boeing was in survival mode, and with the pandemic, no airline or lessor was interested in buying airplanes anyway. Furthermore, a point seemingly overlooked by almost all critics and observers was that all the R&D spending on the NSA, NMA, or whatever you wanted to call it had already been spent on developing a new airplane. Most of it could be applied to the NBA, whatever that was going to be.

Additionally, Boeing had tens of billions of dollars in debt to pay down. It also had to restore MAX production to pre-grounding levels and get deliveries restarted on the 787, which would provide the cash flow needed to pay the final bills to develop the NBA. Boeing didn't see clearing its MAX inventory until perhaps early 2024.[102] Clearing the 787 inventory depended on restarting delivery; after this happened, it probably would take about two years to clear.[103] In 2022, this meant clearing the inventory by the end of 2024 or maybe into 2025. Even then, restoring 787 production to pre-pandemic levels of twelve to fourteen planes a month was wishful thinking. (Boeing nevertheless planned to expand its Charleston, South Carolina, plant to a production capacity of fourteen aircraft per month.) There was plenty of time.

Calhoun's focus was less on a new airplane for its own sake than on a major transformation in digital design and production advances. But even these goals changed in 2021 and early 2022. Setting aside the long-term effects of the Russian invasion of Ukraine, which wouldn't be known for some time, the green aviation movement picked up considerable speed in 2021. "EcoAviation" became a new catch phrase.

Also overlooked in early 2022, as Boeing took its knocks from the critics: Its Product Development unit (PD) was engaged in finishing up certification of the MAX 7 and MAX 10, the latter requiring some changes due to the MAX crisis; launching the new 777-8F; and increasing the gross weights on the 787-9 and 787-10.

It's likely that the 787-9 HGW (higher gross weight) will eventually emerge with a brand-new freighter version to ultimately replace the 767-

---

102. This date slipped to the end of 2025.

103. Boeing finished the last of the 787 rework in February 2025. Then it became a matter of delivering the airplanes to the long-suffering customers that had been waiting for them.

300ERF, which can't be produced after 2027 under new International Civil Aviation Organization (ICAO) emissions and noise standards.[104] With layoffs, early retirements, and natural retirements, Boeing faces an engineering resource challenge. A joint venture with Embraer was supposed to help fill the gap—but this went away when Calhoun killed it in April 2020 as the pandemic set in.

One final consideration: there are no engines ready to offer to Boeing. There's no point in developing an airplane without an engine.

So, when will Boeing make its move? The 2028 timeline suggested by Aboulafia, fellow industry consultant Michael Merluzeau, Leeham Company, and others still seems reasonable. Entry into service (EIS) would be in the 2035 timeframe. But Boeing risks being eclipsed by Airbus with a greener airplane (mostly via a more advanced engine) two to three years after Boeing's NBA enters service. It's a $15 billion bet Boeing can't afford to get wrong.

What does the NBA need to look like? Kiran Rao, the twenty-five-year veteran of Airbus sales and strategy and now an advisor to airlines on fleet selection, had clear ideas in 2019 when interviewed for *Air Wars*.

Looking at it from a customer's perspective, Rao said that Boeing had to get the 737 MAX right. "I don't think you can drop the 737 MAX to say, 'Let's just develop a new aeroplane.' It would take them too long to get there with a new aeroplane. Boeing has to get the 737 MAX back in the air, they have to get the aircraft flying, and they have to restore the balance between Airbus and Boeing, because otherwise from a customer point of view, it's a one-horse race. That's point number one."

"Then you need to run these two airplanes, MAXs and neos, into the 2020s," he said. "Not too far into the 2020s, but when the technology is right, they need to do a new airplane. Left without any pressure, MAXs and neos would probably run well into the 2030s. There's no pressure going to come from the Chinese or the Russians or anybody else in that period of time. Now that the Bombardier story is now an Airbus story, there's nothing coming to disturb that duopoly either."

Rao said that the MAX and neo will work side-by-side without anyone disturbing them. "But I think it would be a mistake for the world if those two airplanes go well into the 2030s without a replacement. You've got to get to the point where we were looking at minus 30 percent fuel relative to today's neo and MAX."

Thirty percent is a tall, tall order. Engine development has a goal of 10 percent by 2031 (P&W's GTF) and 20 percent by 2035 (CFM Internation-

104. Kelly Ortberg, after becoming Boeing's CEO on August 8, 2024, announced that 767 commercial production would end by December 31, 2027.

al's Open Fan). But this is before mating on an airframe, which results in some loss of efficiency because of the drag added by the pylon and (for a conventional engine) the nacelle. Calhoun was open when he said that the best number Boeing saw for a new engine was 10 percent by the turn of the decade. Undertaking a moonshot for digital design and advanced manufacturing and production was the prime cost-reduction method cited by Calhoun.

Rao agrees that an all-in 30 percent lower fuel burn is not going to come only through propulsion.

"It's not going to come through just the engines," he said. "A lot of technology has to go in, and single-pilot operation and all that stuff has to come into it. When all that is ready, we need to make the switch from the neos and MAXs into that new generation of aircraft. None of that technology stuff is ready. From an airline point of view, we have to put pressure on Airbus and Boeing to make sure that they continue to do that evolution in development. Pressure won't come from a third party."

The next Boeing airplane should be a single-aisle model, Rao believes. "Boeing needs to address the Middle of the Market with an NMA because [the] 737-10 isn't an airplane that can challenge the 321. It's a good airplane for doing 2,000-mile missions, but that's about it. It doesn't have a break-out performance, and it doesn't have the range. Boeing will lose a lot of campaigns going forward if it doesn't do the NMA. I would push Boeing to do the NMA before it launches a replacement of the MAX, but when the MAX is replaced, it and Airbus have to come out with a single pilot," Rao said. He added: "Boeing has to come out with a different technology on engines. It has to come out with a different technology on materials and all of that. And a lot more for ease of operation and maintenance, everything else, because you've got to bring that cost down dramatically to be able to pay for all that stuff. All that stuff has to happen if the aviation world is going to go into the 2030s and beyond, with technology evolutions rather than just patching up older airplanes." (John Leahy, Boeing's longtime nemesis, agrees.)

RESISTING CHANGE

Original equipment manufacturers (OEMs) are slow to make changes, and Boeing is no different. With billions of dollars at stake with each airplane development, hesitation is understandable. And OEMs, one and all, want to "harvest" the technology (in the words of Boeing's Scott Fancher, who came over from Boeing's defense division to fix the company's 787 program) and make their profits on derivatives. Then there is the topic that became a dirty word (beginning with the letter "C") in the wake of the MAX crashes and groundings.

"Big manufactures like Airbus and Boeing don't want to *change*, because of all the shareholder values and everything else," Rao said. "There is nobody else out there who is going to make change. That isn't the high-speed train, or a new manufacturer that's going to make that change. The only thing that can force that change early is what's gone wrong with the MAX. But if they force that change too early, then you won't get all the technology that's needed to really take the next generation of single-aisle [planes] into the next fifty years. The current situation on MAX is very interesting, but they need to get a grip of it, and if they don't get a grip of it, it could cause an early shift to a single-aisle, which is too early from a technology point of view," Rao said in 2019, when the MAX was grounded.

What should Airbus do to respond to Boeing? In 2019, Rao didn't think it would need to respond immediately. If Boeing proceeds with the larger NMA, the 767-sized airplane, he said, it will finally kill the A330, even in its neo form. And if Boeing does a three-member NMA, beginning at about 200 seats (the MAX 10/A321 size), the "NMA-5" will take a chunk out of the A321 markets, Rao said.

"The 321 market is big enough for the NMA to have its share, but if [Boeing doesn't] launch the NMA, then it will not have a share because the 737-10 does not have the capability to keep up with a 321XLR. The NMA will. It has to come there, otherwise it leaves the 321XLR unhindered basically well into the 2020s."

Rao, in his capacity as an advisor to airlines, received a presentation from Boeing on the NMA before the MAX crisis blew up. "I can't tell you what they presented to me, but I can tell you that I believe it's a good airplane."

In April 2025, the time of this writing, Airbus has been content to sit back and wait for Boeing to make a move. The A320 family, especially the A321, has been selling well. Between Airbus and Boeing, Airbus now has a 60 percent market share of the backlog between the A320 and 737 families. There is no reason for Airbus to move while Boeing checks its bet on the MAX instead of betting on a new successor design.

The A330neo has been ticking along, and the A350, boosted by the launch of the A350F, has been doing well. The 787 was stalled by its own quality-control issues, and the 777X has been caught in the negative halo effect of the MAX certification crisis. There has been no need to do anything on the widebody front, either. Instead, Airbus has been focused on R&D of hydrogen-powered aircraft. A target date for having a design ready to enter service is 2035.[105]

When Boeing launched the 777X program in 2013, the 777-9 concept

---

105. Airbus killed the effort in 2025.

nominally seated 425 passengers. The A350-1000, designed to compete with the 777-300ER, seated 365 passengers in its original form.[106] At the time, Airbus pondered whether to launch yet another version of the A350, larger than the -1000. The tentative name varied but largely came to be known as the A350-2000. Airbus decided not to proceed with this derivative. Boeing already captured the lion's share of the Middle East market (there are only four or five widebody operators anyway) with the 777X. Few other customers signed up for the 777X outside of the Middle East. Orders for the 777X remained stalled at between 300 and 350 for years. There were only eleven customers, including three from the Middle East and one unidentified, with no change for years.

But Rao and Leahy think that Airbus will get around to launching the A350-2000. "I think Airbus will eventually have to look at the 350-2000," Rao said. "The 777X will have its difficulties going into service. If you look at all the traffic growth and everything else, it will become the standard if Airbus does not [launch]. Because of the additional seats on the 777X, it will always have power over the 350-1000. Airbus is already losing that battle, and it needs to do something. It can just sit and wait, and then the market will come and the market will go, or it can do something. I don't think ten abreast is the answer."

---

106. By 2022, Airbus figured out how to cram thirty more seats into the -1000, going from nine abreast to ten abreast in coach. Airbus did this by shaving the cabin sidewalls and reducing seat width to allow for more seats. Airbus also found that by repositioning galleys and the aft bulkhead, a few more seats could be added. But by going from nine to ten abreast, passenger experience declined, "busting" decades of Airbus branding about a more comfortable cabin versus Boeing.

21

Where Would Calhoun Take Boeing?

"I'm going to focus on the programs we have right now."
—DAVE CALHOUN IN HIS FIRST PRESS CONFERENCE, JANUARY 13, 2020

WHEN DAVID CALHOUN BECAME CEO of The Boeing Company in January 2020, there was one thing on his plate that mattered more than anything else: getting the MAX back in the air. Calhoun later said repeatedly that when he took over, Boeing faced an existential threat because of the MAX crisis. The traveling public was beginning to avoid Boeing airplanes because of safety questions.

Calhoun's existential threat, however, became exponentially worse just two months later. That's when the COVID-19 pandemic erupted, nearly shutting down other deliveries from Boeing's Commercial Airplanes division (BCA) for an indefinite period. Then another crisis erupted in October, seven months later. Either Boeing or the Federal Aviation Administration (FAA) discovered production problems with the 787.[107] Tiny gaps in the mating of the plane's barrel sections, no bigger than the thickness of a piece of paper, were discovered. Boeing said that it wasn't a safety-of-flight issue, but regardless, the gaps weren't supposed to be there. Production was all but suspended for twenty months while Boeing engineered fixes. The FAA repeatedly sent Boeing back to the drawing board, dissatisfied with the company's proposals.

Deliveries were reduced to a trickle due to the pandemic, but an inventory had already been building before then. Boeing kept the production line alive at the reduced rate of just one-half airplane a month. This helped supplies stay "warm" during the pandemic, though the benefit was limited. Boeing eventually had 110 787s consigned to inventory. It was clear that a good portion of these were non-conforming and would require rework. The rework that would be required gave the Everett, Washington, 787 production line and its workers a lifeline.

Unsurprisingly, when the pandemic hit and the 787 was reduced to an

---

107. Calhoun claimed that Boeing discovered the issue. Others close to the situation say that the FAA discovered it.

initial rate of five per month from the ten to twelve pre-pandemic rate, Boeing announced that the Everett line would close and that all production would be done in Charleston, South Carolina. The 787-10 could only be assembled there. Charleston was still a non-union shop. Keeping the Everett line open just didn't seem to be in the cards.

But the 787 rework was going to be extensive. Calhoun said that it would take more time to do the rework than it did to build the airplanes in the first place. He didn't put a number on it, and Boeing never announced one publicly. But insiders said that a three-to-four-month process was required to, in essence, disassemble the airplane, install the required shims, and reassemble the aircraft. The old Everett line was going to remain operational for the next few years.

The MAX was recertified in November 2020. Deliveries resumed from inventory and from the restarted Renton, Washington, final assembly line. New production restarted from zero with thousands of new workers who faced a learning curve and an FAA that remained put off by having been dragged into Boeing's scandals in the first place. New production totaled just a fraction of the pre-grounding rate of fifty-two planes per month. Deliveries also resumed for the 787, and production of new airplanes began to slowly spool up.

There was no announcement on the matter, but in 2022, Boeing's Product Development unit (PD) was actively working on new airplane concepts. Some were pedantic: a new production freighter based on the 787, seen as an eventual replacement for the 767 freighter; a conventional tube-and-wing design with incremental advances over today's airplanes; and the radical Transonic Truss-Braced Wing (TTBW) concept, with either conventional engines or the Open Fan powerplant under development by long-time partner GE and France's Safran under the CFM International banner. Another faction in PD was working on the autonomous WISK eVTOL mentioned earlier in Chapter 19.

Calhoun was candid when discussing airliners. Despite strong opinions from consultants Richard Aboulafia and Kevin Michaels, aerospace analyst Ron Epstein (a former Boeing engineer), and a host of others that Boeing needed an airplane to compete with the runaway success of the A321neo, Calhoun disagreed. Doing an airplane to compete with the A321neo wasn't a good business case, he said. Boeing needed an airplane family. Not only that, a family that offered only 15 percent or so better economics than the MAX or neo was insufficient. Calhoun said that a gain of 25 to 30 percent was needed. This required dramatically new engines and advanced airframe designs, materials, and production, as well as lower capital costs for airlines. The critics groused that Calhoun was simply making excuses. But Calhoun wasn't wrong.

Furthermore, in 2022, Boeing was nowhere near being ready to proceed with a new airplane program and the costs associated with it.[108] At that time, there had barely been a dent in clearing the MAX and 787 inventories. Production rates were still very low because of the pandemic. Boeing wasn't yet profitable, and there was more than $50 billion in debt to repay. Skilled engineers and assembly line workers who were laid off, had retired, or had taken early buyouts hadn't been fully replaced. Those who were hired had years of experience to gain before becoming proficient. Institutional knowledge lost with the departures of the engineers and laborers had to somehow be passed on to the new hires. Boeing simply wasn't ready.

Perhaps more importantly, neither were the engine makers. GE and Safran were the only companies prepared to roll the dice on the radically different Open Fan technology. Pratt & Whitney (P&W) not only remained committed to its GTF engine, it was buried fixing technically deficient engines that would plague the company well into the 2020 decade. Rolls-Royce (RR) likewise was struggling to fix its Trent 1000 engines, which were used on the 787 and which formed the basis of the Trent 7000 model used on the A330neo. Development of the advanced UltraFan was slow and focused on the widebody market instead of the Middle of the Market and below.

Critics weren't mollified. At the time, Epstein wrote in his Bank of America research notes that the engines of the day could advance enough that, when combined with a new airframe, a 20 percent economic improvement over the MAX and neo could be achieved. Leeham Company's analysis yielded a number closer to 15 percent. Would airlines and lessors be satisfied with this improvement for the capital and integration costs of a new fleet type? Calhoun didn't think so.

Furthermore, in 2022, the airlines remained in recovery mode from the pandemic and from MAX and neo engine problems. When you combined this with delays on Airbus and Boeing widebodies, the carriers were left in

---

108. Calhoun said that a new airplane program would cost $50 billion, which seems like a ridiculous number on its face. Up to then, new airplane programs cost Boeing (and Airbus) $12 billion to $15 billion to $20 billion, assuming there were no program screw ups (a big assumption by then). Applying a 3 percent inflation rate to a 2022 new-airplane cost of $15 billion yields a $22.3 billion cost in 2035, the generally accepted target date for a new airplane's entry into service (EIS) following the production of a two-member family. Add a third member, and the cost goes up even more. But the real cost would come from ramping down and losing MAX sales, an inevitable market reality when a successor airplane is announced, and from ramping up to previous production rates in the new program. So, it's not impossible to get to a $50 billion figure.

no mood or financial position to commit to vague paper concepts of new airplanes. Additionally, there was a long way to go to phase out the 737NGs and A320ceos with MAXs and neos. The timing just wasn't right.

When this book was conceived, I was operating under several expectations. Boeing's recovery from the 2018–2019 MAX crisis and the COVID pandemic would be well underway. The MAX 7, MAX 10, and possibly the 777X would be certified in 2024. The MAX and 787 inventories would be well on their way to being cleared by the end of 2024. Production rates for the 737 and 787 would be well on their way to recovery. Relations with the FAA would be, if not repaired, then well on the way to normalization. And cash flow and profits would be returning, allowing Boeing to begin paying down some of the billions of dollars of debt the company took on during the two crises.

These expectations extended to problems at BCA. Boeing's Defense, Space & Security (BDS) unit was in many ways in equally bad shape. While BDS didn't have the FAA breathing down its neck and there weren't criminal charges against the company because of anything BDS did (at least in recent years), many of the division's programs were a mess. The T-7 Red Hawk, MQ-25, KC-46A, Air Force One, SLS Mars booster and, most embarrassingly, Starliner were and still are all late and way over budget. In the case of the Starliner space capsule, technical flaws stranded two astronauts on the International Space Station for months because the capsule couldn't be used to safely bring them home. NASA—which signed off on the maiden flight with the astronauts aboard—eventually decided to use Elon Musk's SpaceX capsule to bring them home.[109] On top of all this, mature fighter-airplane programs also slipped into loss positions.

Still, in 2022, Calhoun and CFO West assured Wall Street and stockholders on successive quarterly earnings reports that Boeing was well on its way to recovery. Every quarter, Calhoun boasted about how well progress in fixing BCA was going—until that January 5, 2024, door-plug blowout on Alaska Airlines flight 1282. Then all hell broke loose again. The FAA began a further crackdown and the Department of Justice pursued additional criminal action against Boeing. Development of the TTBW concept was suspended by Calhoun, dealing another blow to Boeing's future prospects.

Boeing officials had been confident by November 2022 that the company would be back on the right path. They made rosy predictions about the timeline to clear the 737 and 787 inventories (the end of 2024), about

---

109. NASA deemed it too risky to bring Starliner home with astronauts on board. After months of troubleshooting and remote fixes, Starliner successfully returned to Earth under automation. The astronauts returned on March 18, 2025, via SpaceX.

when production would be back to 2018 levels (the end of 2025), and about when there would be $10 billion in free cash flow (also around the end of 2025). Profits would return and debt-reduction would be underway by then, too. And studies were underway for the introduction of a new airplane by the mid-2030 decade.

22

Turnaround

"It's been a long twenty years."

—DAVID CALHOUN, REFLECTING ON HIS THIRD YEAR AS BOEING CEO

AS 2023 ENDED, FIVE YEARS AFTER THE LION AIR CRASH, The Boeing Company was still far from returning to its pre-grounding, pre-pandemic levels. Supply-chain shortages continued to hurt Boeing's ability to ramp up 737 production. Boeing's plan had been to produce 737s at a rate of around thirty-eight per month or even at a rate in the low forties. Instead, the company was hard-pressed to maintain a steady rate of thirty-one 737s per month, or even a figure in the twenties. CFM International was late delivering engines to Boeing for much the same reason: CFM's suppliers had their own difficulties getting parts. Labor shortages hurt everyone as well. Boeing openly blamed CFM for most of the slowdown in 737 production. But, to a degree, this was a red herring. Boeing had 140 MAXs in storage ordered by Chinese airlines; Beijing was failing to take delivery of these planes for reasons of its own (mainly political). GE urged Boeing to take the engines off these airplanes and to use them for new-production aircraft. The engine manufacturer had delivered more than seventy engines to Boeing, but they remained in storage, awaiting production of airframes and wings. In September 2023, Boeing finally yielded. With no end in sight to Beijing's intransigence, Boeing's CEO, David Calhoun, and its chief financial officer, Brian West, announced at different events on the same day that Boeing was going to remarket the Chinese airplanes.

Delivering 737s from the stored inventory, however, turned out to be more slow-going than expected. This was due to labor shortages, which continued to be a residual effect of the pandemic, and to the fact that full employment was shrinking worker pools, among other factors. Another reason for the delay was the difficulties connected with "waking up" the aircraft. Going into storage in 2019 meant that, by 2024, up to five years had passed.

Some planes had been stored at Boeing's facility in San Antonio, Texas; these had to undergo all the technical upgrades, systems checks and "waking up" that's been described earlier. A major portion of the 450 MAXs that were stored before Boeing suspended production in December

2019 were stored in Washington state—whose climate is hardly conducive to the long-term storage of airplanes filled with sensitive parts, components, and engines. The 737s stored at Renton Airport, Boeing Field, and Moses Lake in central Washington were all subjected to Washington's widely varied climate. Seattle, located on Puget Sound and known for its temperate summers, also has a rainy season, which officially runs from October through April and can run longer. From 2019 to 2023, the rains—sometimes heavy and prolonged—continued on as late as June. Seattle isn't supposed to get much in the way of snow. But the winters of 2019 to 2022 sometimes dumped up to two feet of snow, to the delight of children and skiers (especially in hilly Seattle), who took to the streets during the times when traffic was paralyzed. The weird weather added complications to the storage of Boeing's aircraft.

In central Washington, summers often hit temperatures of up to 110 degrees. Winters are often sub-zero, sometimes by wide margins, and snow is common. Boeing's workers had to deal with all the weather vagaries in bringing hundreds of MAXs out of hibernation. Then there was the fact that Boeing's authority to certify each airplane as airworthy before delivery could be made had been suspended by the Federal Aviation Administration (FAA). Agency inspectors now had to certify every airplane, and manpower at the FAA, as elsewhere, was an issue. The Maneuvering Characteristics Augmentation System (MCAS) and other systems on all of Boeing's 450 MAXs had to be updated as part of the company's required response to the MAX crisis (discussed in greater detail in the Introduction and in earlier chapters). Some of these systems had nothing to do with the accidents underlying the crisis, but flaws were uncovered during the ensuing intense scrutiny of the MAX program. Finally, as a matter of routine, any updates required as in-service operations revealed tweaks, fixes, or other issues that also had to be implemented.

Doing all this for each airplane, Calhoun said in September 2022, took as much or more time as assembling the airplane in the first place.[110]

CALHOUN'S FIRST THREE YEARS

By December 2023, Calhoun had been president and CEO of Boeing just shy of three years. Dealing with the MAX crisis had been more complicated than he expected. The COVID pandemic began three months after he

---

110. Calhoun made this remark during a press scrum following his appearance at the U.S. Chamber of Commerce Aerospace Summit in Washington, DC, in September 2022. Pre-grounding, Boeing was assembling a 737 every ten days at its Renton, Washington, plant.

became CEO. A new crisis was laid at Calhoun's feet on top of the MAX. Then, that fall, Boeing discovered production flaws in the 787. Further inspections revealed that an Italian supplier had sent faulty parts for assembly into the 787s. Defects around the plane's doors and cockpit also were discovered in the ensuing detailed inspections.

The MAX crisis had a negative halo effect on Boeing's 777X program. Calhoun said twice that certification and entry into service (EIS) were going to be delayed. He finally set a new target date of 2025—twelve years after the program was launched and five years from the original EIS target. Production of the 777X was reduced to one-half airplane a month, and about thirty of these aircraft ended up sitting around Paine Field and Boeing Field. With demand vanishing for the 777-300ER and the passenger version of the 777-200LR, cash flow also started to vanish. Only the 777LRF remained in production, at a rate of two per month.

When Calhoun appeared at the U.S. Chamber of Commerce Aerospace Summit in September 2022, he had been on Boeing's board of directors for thirteen years and had served as CEO for an intense, stress-filled thirty months. Suzanne Clark, the president and CEO of the Chamber, tried a little levity following her introduction.

"It's been a long ten years since you took the job, January 20th [2020]," she said. Calhoun one-upped her. "Yes, it's been a long twenty years."

Speaking at the summit, Calhoun recalled his last thirty months as CEO. "I never imagined exactly what was going to happen post-January of 2020. We had an issue to deal with. I refer to it as a bit of an existential crisis. Most people think that when I say that they use economic terms. Yes, they'll go and borrow a lot of money and they'll do this and do that. With no MAXs, how do we survive? For me the crisis was the confidence of [the] flying public. We went through a very rough period post-Ethiopia. A lot of changes, in significant ways, but the big question amongst investors and even in some of our own people was, will the flying public get back on the airplane?

"We were patient," Calhoun said. "I think we took the appropriate amount of time with our regulator to prepare our approach but to give them time to go through their own discovery. It would be unfair to keep pressing for a certification every next three months because that's what got us in trouble in the first place. We put a one-year timeline in place. We both worked diligently on getting from here to there, and since that time of roughly 450 parked airplanes, we returned more than half, and the only thing I thought about in that whole timeframe was that these airplanes need to go out."

Calhoun said that the MAXs needed to be accepted one airplane at a time and needed to be as perfect as they could be. The flying public had to love them. Then COVID happened. "While I know most people will talk about COVID as the big moment, we were already in the big moment, and then we have another one."

Boeing, and others, had little hard data from which to forecast a return to normalcy. The last global pandemic was the flu at the end of World War I. Airplanes had become a small part of the war, but no airlines existed. Forecasters, including those at Boeing, did the best they could. The impact of 9/11 and the Pacific-oriented SARS pandemic were analyzed. Some suggested a return to normalcy in 2024. It was as good a forecast as any other. Calhoun said that Boeing wondered if this was optimistic.

"It turns out it's come back much faster, and the reason is vaccine development. Never could we forecast the supply-chain issues that would become the constraint, and it is a constraint. I don't think there's a supplier, I don't think there's a company anywhere in our field, a customer that isn't feeling some of the impact and the constraint of workforce shortages, et cetera," Calhoun said.

CARGO HELPS BOEING GET THROUGH

With the MAX, 787, 777-300ER, and 777X all dead in the water, Boeing's one bright spot was cargo. Sales of the 767-300ERF and the 777LRF were robust. Demand for converting passenger aircraft into cargo airplanes, a solid business for Boeing Global Services (BGS), was strong. On an interim basis, many airlines stripped aircraft of their passenger interiors and installed tie downs for light cargo duty (focusing on volumetric-freighter, rather than heavy-cargo, capacity). Some airlines didn't even go this far. Rather, they figured out a way to load boxes on top of the passenger seats and, in some cases, into the overhead bins. These conversions were nicknamed Preighters. While these actions didn't help Boeing, they were indicative of the need for lift services to ship masks, goggles, testing kits, and, ultimately, vaccines around the globe.

With little 787 production to support, Boeing used its Dreamlifters (the oversized 747-400 freighters converted to ship big fuselage sections and wings for the 787 from Japan and Italy to the United States) to join the pandemic-related global cargo air lift. (Boeing was, however, slow to dedicate the Dreamlifters to the cause.)

Without question, the orders for new-production 767-300ERFs and 777LRFs helped Boeing get through its time of crisis. While the cash flow from these orders and deliveries was a pittance compared with the money coming in during pre-grounding, pre-pandemic days, every bit helped. (The U.S. Defense Department came to the rescue, too, handing Boeing one new contract after another at this time.)

By the time Calhoun appeared at the Chamber conference, U.S. and European passenger traffic was roaring back. China and the broader Asia-Pacific traffic was still down, while traffic to and through the Middle East was coming back nicely. Preighters were converted back to passenger use, and airlines operating dedicated freighters began to see some softening in demand. Overall, Calhoun remained optimistic.

"I don't think there'll be a give back," he told the Chamber audience. "For all the cargo development. I don't think the industry is going to give back to some other form of transportation. I think they're going to keep what they have. I don't think it can accelerate at the same pace it did, but even if it returned to its pre-COVID pace, that's going to be a very healthy, very robust market. Time-sensitive freight, time-sensitive packaging, and time-sensitive anything [that] relies on air and that part of the world is growing and growing."

Indeed, although the demand for the 777X passenger models had long stalled out, Boeing launched the 777-8F program in January 2022. Qatar Airways, then engaged in a bitter court battle with Airbus, was the launch customer for up to fifty airplanes (thirty-four of the orders were firm, sixteen were options).[111] Qatar Airways also ordered fifty MAX 10s, which was widely considered to be an "in-your-eye, Airbus," move. The airline had also been a target launch customer for the Airbus A350 freighter before things went south between the two companies.

PICKING UP ORDERS

During the first seven months of 2022, with MAX production back on track (if spotty) and Boeing on its way to clearing half the MAX inventory, the orders began to roll in. In addition to the Qatar Airways deal, Boeing won an order for 100 MAX 10s from Delta Air Lines, announced at the Farnborough Air Show in July, the first such event since the 2020 and 2021 Farnborough and Paris air shows had been canceled due to the pandemic. This was the first Boeing order from Delta in a decade, reversing at long last sour relations between the two companies that began when Delta started tilting toward Airbus for single- and twin-aisle aircraft.

Through September 2022, Boeing posted orders for 446 airplanes.

---

111. Qatar converted twenty orders from the 777X passenger model to the freighter, providing only a net increase of fourteen orders as listed on the Boeing website. Airbus eventually canceled all remaining A350 and all A321neo orders from Qatar, which hadn't even been delivered yet, as part of the dispute. Eventually, Airbus and Qatar settled their differences, and the orders were reinstated. Qatar Airways CEO Akbar Al Baker, who initiated the dispute, agreed to retire months later. It's unclear if his decision to step down was connected to the settlement.

(More commitments were announced, but until a firm contract was signed, these were not reported by Boeing.) Three hundred seventy-three, or 84 percent, of these orders were for MAXs. Of the remaining seventy-three orders, twenty-one were for 777-8Fs and the rest for 777LRFs.[112]

On the next to last day of September 2022, Canada's WestJet Airlines placed a big order for the MAX 10: forty-two firm and twenty-two options, bringing total orders to more than 900 for this variant.

Cash flow was slowly flowing in again, but Boeing still had fits and starts over the supply-chain shortages feeding into the MAX line. In the past, Boeing would have cranked out the 737s with the parts shortages (this practice is called traveled work) and installed the missing parts on the planes sitting around Renton Airport. Not this time. Calhoun said that Boeing would "pause" the production line and wait for the parts before finishing the airplanes. This created ups and downs in production and delivery rates, something that drove the aerospace analysts on Wall Street nuts. They like predictability, and Boeing couldn't reliably assure Wall Street that the production line was running at a consistent rate. Delays in completing the work on stored inventory airplanes also caused ups and downs in deliveries.

One thing that worked in Boeing's favor, however, was the very fact that it still had around 250 MAXs in storage, including the 140 that were intended to go to China. Beijing allowed the Chinese lessors to take delivery of MAXs as long as the lessees were not within Chinese boundaries, but this involved a relatively small number of planes.

With CFM running late on delivering engines, Calhoun said that Boeing would not produce gliders—that is, airplanes without engines. Airbus at the time had more than two dozen A320neos parked in France and Germany without engines. (CFM was late delivering to Airbus, too, as was Pratt & Whitney (P&W)). Neither country is an ideal location for storing airplanes. While Airbus didn't face the same level of work to "wake up" these aircraft (because they were in storage for months rather than years) that Boeing did, the situation was still an unwanted headache.

Calhoun's answer as to why he didn't see a need to build gliders was simple: engines would be taken from Boeing's stored airplanes and installed on its new-production models.

---

112. Lufthansa placed an order for seven of the 777XFs, which had the benefit of solidifying the airline's launch order for the 777-9. With the delays and the changing marketplace since the launch order in 2013, Lufthansa was known to be having second thoughts about the 777-9 order. Boeing also sold Lufthansa some 787-9s that had been destined for China, which, like 737s, had been frozen out by Beijing.

SUPPLY-CHAIN CHALLENGES

Boeing's path back to normalcy in 2022 was constrained by continued problems in the supply chain. Parts and labor shortages continued unabated. Suppliers of all sizes, especially smaller ones, had a hard time finding help.

At the same U.S. Chamber of Commerce event at which Calhoun appeared, executives from Spirit AeroSystems and Raytheon Technologies complained about how difficult it was to find help. Spirit built the entire fuselage for the 737 and the nose sections for the 747 (by that time, a terminated program), the 767/KC-46A, the 777, and the 787. Spirit also built panels for the A350 and wing components for the A320 family. Raytheon's P&W unit supplies engines; the Collins division supplies interiors, avionics, and other components; and the Hamilton Sundstrand unit supplies major components.

"I would say that the recovery has started for the supply chain, but we still have a long way to go," said Tom Gentile, then CEO of Spirit Aerosystems. "At the July Farnborough Air Show, there were few orders announced. The whole story was the supply chain. It's not a demand issue. There's plenty of demand. It's about [the] supply chain's ability to produce. The suppliers are stressed right now for a number of reasons. One is that during the pandemic, a lot of us had to take on additional debt because we had to get liquidity. The interest rates are higher. We're paying more interest expense, which means less to invest and grow the productivity. At the same time, the demand has not recovered back to where it was in 2019. For example, in 2019, we produced 606 737 MAX units. Last year, we only produced 162. This year, we've targeted 300. We're only about halfway back to where we were in 2019."

Gentile said that all suppliers were affected by inflation in labor, material, utilities, and logistics. Then there was a shortage of labor. "It's harder to hire people back right now." Spirit, which is headquartered in Wichita, Kansas, offered signing bonuses of $3,000 for some positions. Competitor Textron Aviation, which has a production plant nearby, offered a $4,000 bonus. "We're in a bit of an arms race, but that's the market," Gentile said.

Paolo Dal Cin, Senior Vice President, Operations, Supply Chain, Quality, Environmental, Health and Safety for Raytheon, said his company's suppliers needed to make investments similar to ones undertaken by Raytheon. The dynamics for workers and raw materials meant that Raytheon and its suppliers needed to be in step, he said.

"I think that we're going to have to go in steps and we need to find ways that make it easier," he said. "Even if you don't have the full suite of digital tools, you can still provide in a relatively simple way a manual input into where your status is."

MAX 7, 10

When Boeing's board of directors fired Dennis Muilenburg from his CEO post in 2019, one reason cited for the decision was the deterioration of the relationship between him and the FAA. Muilenburg irritated the FAA's staff and the administrator then in place, Steve Dickson, to no end with his repeated public suggestions that recertification of the MAX was months or weeks away. Dickson got so angry that he publicly released a letter that he had sent to FAA employees criticizing Boeing and saying that he had his staff's backs.

One of Calhoun's top missions was to repair this relationship. "It would be unfair to keep pressing for a certification every next three months because that's what got us in trouble in the first place. We put a one-year timeline in place," Calhoun said at the Chamber event.

In the press scrum after his Chamber appearance, however, Calhoun was optimistic. When asked about the certification timeline for the MAX 10, Calhoun replied, "I'll say what I always said. We have our heads down. The FAA has their heads down. We [Boeing and the FAA] are working to finish. There's a chance. There's also a chance it doesn't [work out]."

When asked about certification of the MAX 7, for which flight testing had been done for well over a year by that point, Calhoun responded, "What does that point to? This process is laborious. It's hard. It's a big documentation effort, which I get. We will support it every step of the way. The Dash 7 is a demonstration that it's the process as opposed to the product." Certification, Calhoun said, "is closer than the -10." He predicted that certification of the MAX 7 would happen by the end of the year. (A major supplier on the MAX program understood that certification of the MAX 7 would occur by mid-October.)

Thus, it was a major shock when, just four days later, the FAA sent a letter to Boeing's Mike Fleming, who was heading the effort to return the MAXs to service and shepherding certification through the FAA, telling him to "hold on."[113]

Calhoun told the Chamber conference that, in many ways, the supply chain was less commodity-oriented and material-oriented and more workforce-related. The aerospace industry has had a demographic problem for a long time, he said. For a lot of the big players, including Boeing, looming retirements was a bigger issue, he said. (There is no doubt that the industry lost a lot of very experienced people.) "Boeing's not excluded from that," Calhoun said. "When I talk to people and you go to the real

---

113. The letter didn't become public until the *Seattle Times* broke the story on September 29, 2022.

constraints, casting, forging, et cetera, where qualification times and cycles are long and they are very dependent on that expertise, it's in short supply. That's where I see that issue. In Boeing's case, we've actually been quite successful [on] the hiring front. We've probably exceeded our smaller targets already for the year but that doesn't displace the experience curve. I think that's going to be a challenge for us for years, honestly, and I don't see this getting resolved anytime soon."

Jim Albaugh, previously CEO of Boeing's defense unit and then of its Commercial Airplanes division (BCA), foresaw the brain-drain way back in 2011. Nevertheless, former CEOs James McNerney and Muilenburg aggressively shifted work from the experienced workforce in the Puget Sound region to green and less-experienced workers in South Carolina, Oklahoma, Texas, and elsewhere to cut costs and reliance on Washington State's heavily unionized workforce. The problem was that critical institutional knowledge went with the cuts and transfers.

As a former GE executive coming out of the Jack Welch school of slash and burn, Calhoun was on board with those policies. Remember, he joined the Boeing Board of Directors in 2009 and served for ten years before being named CEO. Calhoun claimed shortly after assuming his executive duties that he had only a front row seat in the movie house and wasn't an insider. While it's true that Boeing's board was known as a "get along, go along" board, Calhoun's claim rings hollow, even setting aside the Securities and Exchange Commission's posture that a director is the very essence of an insider. Unless Calhoun sat on the board in Maxwell Smart's Cone of Silence, he had to know what McNerney and Muilenburg were up to.

GOING FORWARD

"As you are aware, the FAA communicated that Boeing must turn in all remaining System Safety Assessments by mid-September if the company intends to meet its project plan of completing certification work (and receiving FAA approval for this airplane) by December 2022," wrote Liric Liu, executive director of Aviation Safety, Aircraft Certification Service, for the FAA, to Boeing in September 2022.

The letter continued: "As of September 15 [the very day Calhoun made his remarks in the press scrum], just under 10 percent of these documents are in various stages of review and revision. Most concerning, however, is that Boeing has yet to provide an initial submittal for six of the outstanding SSAs [System Safety Assessments]."

A System Safety Assessment is a detailed comprehensive assessment of an aircraft's architecture and design and of the installation of required systems to ensure that safety requirements are met.

Liu's letter noted that it would take the FAA "significant time" to review

U.S. Department
of Transportation
**Federal Aviation
Administration**

Aviation Safety
Aircraft Certification Service

800 Independence Ave., S.W.
Washington, D.C. 20591

September 19, 2022

Mr. Mike Fleming
737 Logan Ave N
Renton, Washington 98055

Dear Mr. Fleming:

As you are aware, the FAA communicated that Boeing must turn in all remaining System Safety Assessments (SSA) by mid-September if the company intends to meet its project plan of completing certification work (and receiving FAA approval for this airplane) by December 2022.

As of September 15, just under 10 percent of the SSAs have been accepted by the FAA and another 70 percent of these documents are in various stages of review and revision. Most concerning, however, is that Boeing has yet to provide an initial submittal for six of the outstanding SSAs. We expect many of these documents will take significant time to review due to their complexity and bearing on the overall safety of the new aircraft.

The FAA will continue to maintain sufficient staffing to complete the necessary safety reviews in a timely manner, but such work must be completed deliberately and in such a way that an arbitrary calendar date does not become the driving factor. We encourage continued coordination with the program office to facilitate the SSA reviews with the applicant and ODA.

I look forward to continuing our discussions about realistic timeframes for receiving the remaining documents.

Sincerely,

Lirio Liu
Executive Director
Aviation Safety
Aircraft Certification Service

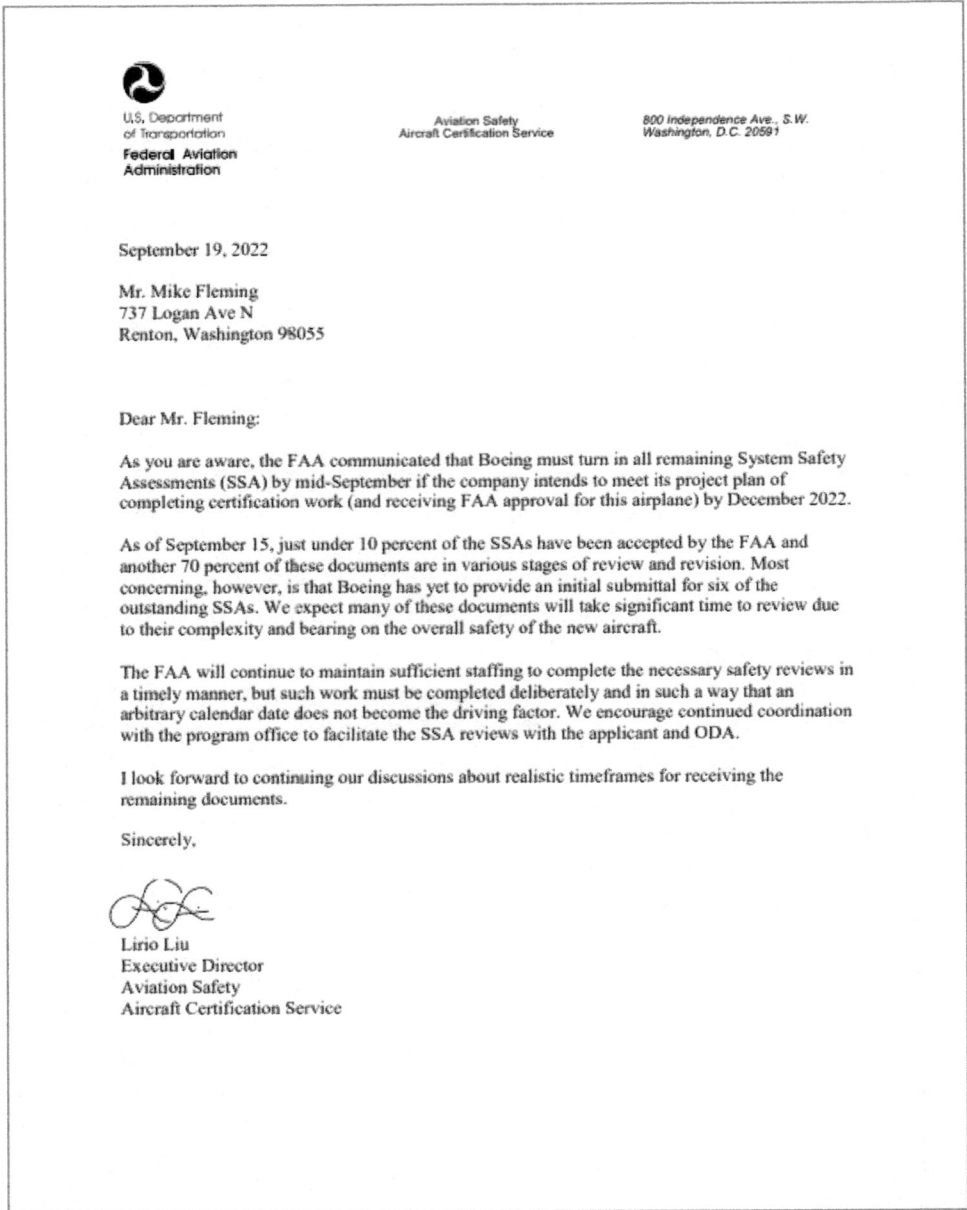

Figure 22. The Federal Aviation Administration wrote Boeing that it was still falling behind on meeting its information demands. Yet only days before, Boeing CEO David Calhoun told reporters certification of the 737-7 MAX was progressing

certification-related documents due to their complexities. "Such work must be completed deliberately and in such a way that an arbitrary calendar date does not become the driving factor." The letter did not name the MAX 10, or the MAX 7, so it's not unequivocal that Liu was referring to the certification of one model or the other, or to both. But it hardly mattered. Both models fell under the documentation overhang.

How Calhoun could wax optimistic on September 15 and not be aware that all was not well is a mystery. Granted, a lot goes on in the bowels of any large company that the CEO, in his or her inevitably rarified atmosphere, won't be aware of.[114] Still, it appeared on September 29 that Calhoun had fallen into the Muilenburg trap of predicting when certification would occur.

Simultaneously with the report of the FAA letter, it was revealed that an amendment had been attached to a congressional defense bill to extend the deadline for design compliance for certain cockpit alerting systems to September 30, 2023. The hope was that Boeing and the FAA would have the MAX 7 and MAX 10 certified by then.

PLOTTING FOR THE FUTURE

Ron Epstein, a Bank of America aerospace analyst and former Boeing engineer, is unusual in the analyst community. Most analysts treat Boeing with kid gloves, afraid of being frozen out of company earnings calls or meetings with executives and of losing Boeing's participation in client meetings. Boeing hasn't been shy about retaliating in such ways if an analyst is too blunt in his or her negative conclusions about the company or its products or if, God forbid, an analyst puts a "Sell" rating on Boeing stock. Epstein has been on the receiving end of some of these tactics. But he's nevertheless managed to slip in some blunt questions on Boeing earnings calls, and his research notes are often peppered with frank assessments. He's not shy about calling a spade a spade or making unsolicited recommendations. In a September 7, 2022, note entitled, "Where to now? How management can unlock value," Epstein pulled no punches.

"We believe that BA [the stock symbol for The Boeing Company] has become, in many ways, a fallen angel," he wrote. "We identify fourteen topics management could address to improve investor perceptions. These comprise capital deployment, engineering culture, emerging-tech strategy, customer relationships, industry partnerships, employee relationships, industry/regulatory perception, self-assessment, centralized leadership, product strategy, defense-program success, supply-chain relationships, objective prioritization, and performance-based compensation."

Since it merged with McDonnell Douglas in 1997, Boeing has been assailed by many for destroying the engineering culture that was a hallmark of The Boeing Company in favor of a financial-performance culture. Fail-

---

114. This supports the argument that Boeing should return to its roots and relocate its headquarters in Seattle. In 2022, perhaps unwisely, it relocated HQ from Chicago to the Washington, DC, area.

ure to strike a balance between the two extremes has been a major point of criticism. Despite throwing Muilenburg under the bus on stock price and dividends in a *New York Times* interview, Calhoun was very much a part of the prevailing policy at Boeing, having been a member of its board of directors since 2009. Coming out of the GE/Jack Welch culture and going into private equity, where shareholder return and profits are paramount, Calhoun's background cast suspicion over whether he was the right person to restore Boeing's greatness.

Below is an excerpt from Epstein's September 7 research note.

The first key to Boeing's success is culture change

Peter Drucker's phase, "Culture eats strategy for lunch," is apropos to BA's predicament. The key to BA's long-term success is culture change. Without it, management's strategy and operations would be impaired. We suggest that investors ask themselves, 'Can the current leadership successfully change the culture that led to the 737 Max tragedy, the 787 delivery halt, the loss of the right to certificate aircraft coming off the lines and the multitude of charges across the defense business?' It took the better part of 20 years to get to this point. Change won't happen overnight. But, turnaround stories can be good investments for the patient investor if the right leadership is in place, the right culture takes hold, and a good strategy is in place. Balancing short-term catalysts against long-term issues and challenges is the key to understanding BA's stock, in our view.

The two principal labor unions at Boeing, the Society of Professional Engineering Employees in Aerospace (SPEEA) and the International Association of Machinists District 751 (IAM 751), failed to see much difference between Calhoun and his predecessor. Representatives from each noted that they had neither seen nor talked with Calhoun during his first two years in office.

Calhoun came under withering criticism from industry consultant Richard Aboulafia, Epstein, and others for the pause in new-airplane development, which he announced at Boeing's November 2, 2022, Investor Day. Critics pointed to the free-cash-flow goal and said that the GE-bred (as was CFO West) Calhoun was once more placing shareholder value ahead of product investment. Certainly, product investment should play a large role in Boeing's long-term strategy. And whether Calhoun and West were prioritizing shareholder value over investment is a matter of debate. Objectively, though, it wasn't hard to see Calhoun's point given Boeing still had a long way to go with its recovery and technology simply wasn't ready for a new airplane.

In the meantime, Calhoun and Boeing were focusing on going more green and on their preferred solution for doing so: sustainable aviation fuel (SAF). Yet skeptics were beginning to realize that lofty goals for increasing SAF production and use by airlines in the coming years were not likely to be achieved.

Over at Airbus, Calhoun's pause of the new airplane program was greeted happily. Airbus production rates across its product lines were still below pre-pandemic levels. Orders had surged during the time Boeing was experiencing problems, and Airbus officials were studying increasing A320 production to a record seventy-five per month. Returning the A350 to a rate of ten produced per month and the A330 to four per month was also planned. And, in a mimic not especially welcomed by some, Airbus was under pressure to return greater value to shareholders. As with Boeing, Airbus was having its own challenges with the supply chain's health.

Boeing ended 2022 on the ascent, despite a rocky supply chain, production pauses, and loads of rework on the 737 and 787 yet to be done. Going into 2023, executives were optimistic. They had some reason to be. Although 737 production continued to be spotty, clearing the 737 and 787 inventories was going slower than expected, and certification of the MAX 7, MAX 10, and 777X was stalled, executives viewed 2023 as a major positive step toward normalcy.

23

What's the Next Airplane Going to Be?

"You have to be patient, you have to get ducks lined up, the technologies lined up and matured."

—DAVE CALHOUN, MAY 30, 2023

WHEN THE COVID PANDEMIC BEGAN IN MARCH 2020, The Boeing Company wasn't the only airplane manufacturer affected. Boeing's situation was exacerbated by the MAX grounding, of course, and by a series of subsequent self-inflicted wounds. But the pandemic's global impact was across all industries. Airbus, Embraer, turboprop original equipment manufacturer (OEM) ATR, engine manufacturers, and the entire aerospace supply chain was decimated.

In the U.S., the federal government offered billions of dollars to support industries and companies, including Boeing. The same was true in Europe. Airbus tapped hundreds of millions of Euros to help it through the crisis. Unlike with Boeing, no Airbus airplane was grounded. Production rates for the A320, A330, and A350 families were reduced but not suspended. Still, the money provided by the governments helped Airbus support its staff and reduced operations.

But France's contribution came at a price. As a condition to receiving its largesse, France required Airbus to up its research and development (R&D) in green aviation. This was the root of Airbus focusing on hydrogen fuel for the future.

Airbus created hydrogen-powered (H2) concepts. Boeing showed off its Transonic Truss-Braced Wing concept (TTBW). Embraer conceived the EVE urban air-mobility transport and announced another concept called Energia, a series of small aircraft of thirty seats or fewer that used batteries, hydrogen, or hybrid power. These are admirable projects, but they raise an important question: What are the engines for these concept aircraft going to look like? Without engines, none of the concepts are going anywhere.

Airbus said publicly that it saw a hydrogen-powered airplane as its vision for the future. Airbus used the money it received from the French government to launch a major research project on H2 airplanes.

Hydrogen comes in several forms, delineated by color. It's green hydrogen that's needed to reduce emissions. Without going into a tutorial about making H2, suffice it to say it's challenging, and the process itself offsets some of the benefits—just as making, charging, and recycling batteries is an offset to the "green" energy promoted by battery advocates. Producing hydrogen, delivering it on a widescale basis to airports, and fueling airplanes with it requires production capacity and infrastructure that doesn't currently exist and that requires billions and perhaps trillions of dollars to create at a rate sufficient to fulfill demand.

The Airbus jet concepts only support mid-range routes. Thirty-seven-hundred kilometers is 2,300 statute miles (sm). Shave 20 percent off a route's miles total for required holding times, travel to alternate airports, and winds, and you're down to 1,840sm—the distance between Chicago and Los Angeles, for example. Long-haul routes require a conventional airplane, powered by sustainable aviation fuel (SAF) or Jet A fuel (a kerosene-based aviation fuel). As discussed in an earlier chapter, SAF is expensive, developing the feedstock that underlies it is challenging, and production is virtually non-existent at the present time.

Technologically, H2-powered airplanes are achievable. But given market and technology realities, H2 airplanes will only be either demonstrators or niche aircraft. Widespread replacement jet airliners will have to be Jet A- or SAF-based aircraft.

The blended wing body (BWB) airplane design has been around since the McDonnell Douglas days. Boeing's lead product-development official, Mike Sinnett, once said that the trouble with a BWB is how do you stretch it for a family of airplanes? (Start-up Jet Zero, which is designing a BWB commercial mid-market airplane, believes it has an answer. This is discussed below.) Passenger comfort, the absence of windows for most passengers, and cabin tilt in even routine maneuvers are believed to be impediments for passenger acceptance. Airbus has a BWB concept, but insiders dismiss the prospect of going forward with the design for the next new airplane.

Airbus is closely watching Boeing's apparent favorite concept, the Transonic Truss-Braced Wing. Airbus's own futuristic concepts don't include a Truss-Braced Wing. The TTBW is a super-thin, extra-long wing design that helps lower operating costs and keeps the airplane within existing airport structures and that requires a brace when the folding wing is "up" instead of in flight mode. The braces add drag, however, so there is a trade-off. Boeing says that its concept aircraft featuring the TTBW and an advanced airframe design cuts between nine and 12 percent off fuel consumption. Coupled with an Open Fan engine, which GE says will shave at least 20 percent off fuel consumption after installation on the airplane, this gives the TTBW design the +/-30 percent fuel savings that former Boeing CEO David Calhoun said was necessary to justify the next new airlin-

Figure 23. During the COVID crisis, Airbus received hundreds of millions of dollars in government money from France. In return, Airbus pledged to invest in hydrogen power for "clean" future airplanes. In 2025, Airbus abandoned the goals as impractical. Airbus photo.

er. Leeham Company analyzed combining improved conventional engines with a TTBW design and arrived at a fuel savings number in the mid-20 percent range.

Airbus has talked for years about developing a heavily modified A321neo, variously called an A322 or an A321 Plus Plus. With two more rows of coach seats (for a total of twelve), an advanced folding wing but no truss to brace it, and advanced engines, Airbus thinks that the A322 could be the company's next step on its way toward a future airplane with radically better economics. The A322 might land in the 20 percent range; some believe it would be closer to 15 percent. But A322 sales would hurt sales of the A321XLR, and Airbus has no reason to launch the A322 given Boeing's impotence.

Leaders at Airbus have been fans of the Open Rotor engine for years. Christian Scherer, the CEO of the Airbus Commercial Aircraft unit in 2025, promoted an Open Rotor A320-size airplane before the company ultimately chose to re-engine the family with CFM International's LEAP engines and Pratt & Whitney's (P&W) GTF engines. Airbus has partnered with GE to put an Open Fan engine on an A380 test bed.

Boeing dismisses H2 as a feasible next step due to the fuel's production and infrastructure issues. It believes SAF is the most likely, most viable next-step fuel for reducing carbon emissions. As for concept airplanes, the TTBW was pretty much all Boeing talked about publicly. It's also what the company was showing at international air shows and to customers.

Perhaps significantly, Boeing's TTBW concepts all show a conventional engine—not an Open Fan. Within Boeing, there is a group that remains skeptical of the Open Fan. The doubts center around the prospect of the engine throwing a blade. Without a nacelle, the blade theoretically could penetrate the fuselage. But blades have been whirling next to fuselages since, well, forever. CFM's CEO told *Leeham News* in 2023 that, following advances in composite blades, millions of flight hours with LEAP engines, and technology borrowed from the giant GE9X engine, no blades had been thrown. Still, the energy from the high RPM of the Open Fan will require fuselage "armoring" adjacent to the fan, Stan Deal, the former CEO of Boeing's Commercial Airplanes division (BCA), once told *Leeham News*.

Figure 24. Illustrations from CFM International, the joint venture between GE Aerospace and France's Safran, depict potential positions of the firm's Open Fan RISE engine on aircraft. CFM concept renderings are not representative of any defined future aircraft configuration. Credit: CFM.

CFM's concepts for the Open Fan show three designs (Figure 24).

GE says that the blade-out issue discussed above has been resolved, along with the historical noise emanating from the Open Rotor, counter-rotating blades; maintenance concerns; and issues surrounding the ability to cruise at today's speeds (the Open Rotor concept was slower than the 737/A320/MD80 cruise speed). The Open Fan is quieter than the LEAP, GE says. There is no counter-rotating set of blades on the Open Fan. The second set of blades doesn't rotate but is able to move for maximum efficiency. However, real-world airborne trials are, at this writing, still a few years away. These tests will be key to the viability of the Open Fan on the next generation of airplanes, whatever form they may take.

What has enabled GE to make such big advances with the Open Fan compared with the Open Rotor? Access to a supercomputer, officials say.

Boeing remains divided about what engine design should be used for its next airplane.

While Boeing executives, staff in its Product Development unit (PD), its environmental group, and its salespeople have publicly promoted the TTBW design as the next best thing, behind the scenes, PD is also working on a conventional tube-and-wing design. Having two or more study groups working on different designs is standard operating procedure for Boeing. PD developed a re-engining design for the 737 and an entirely new design to replace the venerable airplane in parallel. The re-engining won out for competitive reasons. During the design process for what became the 787, composite and metal fuselage designs were created; composite won out. Boeing's New Midmarket Aircraft, which went by varying names, was either a single- or twin-aisle design with a range of 4,000 to 5,500 nautical miles (nm). It had an elliptical or constant-round fuselage. It was all composite or had a metal fuselage.

Boeing does multiple designs so that if one proves infeasible or fails to get sufficient backing from airlines (think the Sonic Cruiser, 747-500, and 747-600), there is another option. In this case, Boeing needs a conventional design concept to serve as a baseline against which the TTBW will be compared.

Boeing went one step further, however. As old-technology MD-90s (made by McDonnell Douglas) were retired, Boeing acquired two of them. One airplane would serve as a parts source, while the other would have its fuselage sections removed to "shrink" the airplane, a high wing would be installed with the truss brace, and P&W GTF engines would be used. NASA contracted with Boeing and is partially funding this big R&D project, now called X-66.

Boeing is continuing R&D on the production side, irrespective of what airplane design emerges as the winner. Going back to James McNerney, now three CEOs ago, the next new airplane was billed as being as much about production as it was about the airplane itself. Cutting design and production costs is a major objective for Boeing (and Airbus, and Embraer, and anyone else in the business).

Research also continues in the areas of advanced materials and processes. Whatever R&D is done in connection with the next new airplane can be applied to subsequent aircraft. So, it's not like all these costs *have* to be applied to the next airplane. The cost overruns for the 787 were so big that the executive director of the Society of Professional Engineering Employees in Aerospace union (SPEEA) suggested to Boeing that the 787 be considered one big R&D project. Boeing officials were not amused. But a comment by Scott Fancher, who came over from Boeing's defense division to fix the 787 program, during one pre-air-show media briefing provides perfectly illustrates the SPEEA official's point. The 787's advanced composite wing was considered at the time to be one of the airplane's best engineering achievements. (Ironically, work on this part was outsourced to one of the Japanese "heavies.") Fancher said over and over that the technology from the wing was to be "harvested" for the 747-8, the 777X, what would be the next new airplane (at the time, the New Midmarket Airplane, or NMA), and so on.

Composites require huge, costly-to-buy, and costly-to-operate autoclaves. Even during the 787's early production, Scott Carson, then the CEO of BCA, said that Boeing had to find a way to move on from autoclaves. At the time of this writing, Boeing has been, along with Kawaski (a Japanese heavy and major contractor on the 787), testing a process called pultrusion,[115] whereby a 100-foot fuselage section can be produced in one eight-hour shift with a handful of people. Windows and door openings would be

---

115. See *What Is the Pultrusion Manufacturing Process?* Chapter 1, "Introduction to Pultrusion" ("Pultrusion is a continuous manufacturing process used to produce composite materials with constant cross-sections and significantly long lengths. The term 'pultrusion' is derived from the words 'pull' and 'extrusion,' reflecting the unique nature of this process."), https://www.addcomposites.com/post/pultrusion.

cut once a given section emerges from production in a "next step" process. Multiple sections can then be mated. Different shapes are possible—round, elliptical, ovoid—and diameters can vary. In 2024, proof of concept was achieved. For all the advancement this process potentially offers, pultrusion is not new. The first patent for the concept was filed in 1944, but the first practical concept didn't occur until 1959.

Boeing's advanced design and production efforts will amount to another "moonshot," something McNerney said the company wouldn't do again following the 787 debacle. Calhoun's advocacy reversed McNerney's dim view, but ensuing accidents, quality-control issues, safety shortcomings, and three MAX accidents combined to blow up any progress Calhoun achieved—limited though it was.

Now that Kelly Ortberg has succeeded Calhoun as Boeing's CEO, development of a new airplane and the timing of such a project is more up in the air than ever. Ortberg has such a large mess on his hands that proceeding with a new airplane may be well down on his list of priorities.

With Boeing on the ropes and Airbus suffering from an embarrassment of riches, this means that there is an opportunity for a third company to enter the mainline jet business, provided barriers to entry can be overcome.

China's Commercial Aircraft Corporation (COMAC) wants to be this third company. But, as is recounted briefly below, the company's ARJ-21 (now called the C909) program was by any standard a *commercial* disaster, and its economics left a lot to be desired, too. Development of a second jetliner, the C919, has also been painful. The MA-700 turboprop, a product of the Aviation Industry Corporation of China's (AVIC) Xi'an Aircraft Industrial unit and about the size of the ATR-72, has been another failure. The C909 has had problems with systems integration, design, production, and delivery to airlines. The plane's reliability and economics are an open question, given China's general lack of transparency.[116] At this point, there has been no acceptance of the C909 or the C919 by airlines or lessors unaffiliated with Chinese ownership, and even these businesses can contain their enthusiasm.

COMAC announced development of a twin-aisle 250-passenger jet, the C929, as a joint venture with Russia. The latter's invasion of Ukraine blew up the joint venture, and development is already behind schedule. By the time the C929 enters service, probably well into the next decade, Airbus

---

116. With seven C919s in service by the 2024 Farnborough Air Show, COMAC had an opportunity to bring a flying example to the UK and to have its chalet/hospitality area and personnel make a splash. Instead, COMAC officials all but hid from the media and there was no airplane at the show.

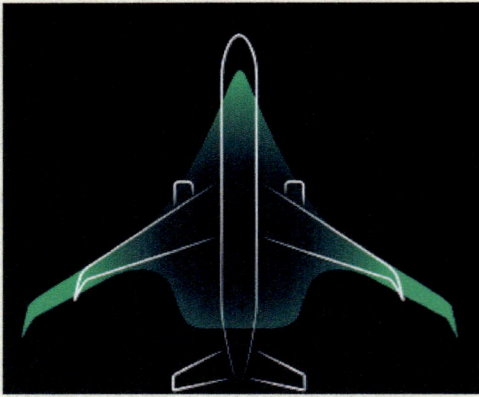

Figure 25. JetZero, a start-up company, is developing the first passenger Blended Wing Body airplane in parallel with a refueling tanker for the U.S. Air Force. The company has expert engineers, but only a fraction of the money needed to bring the BWB to market. Credit: JetZero.

Figure 26. JetZero's concept for a group of BWB aircraft. Credit: JetZero.

and Boeing will likely undertake major upgrades to the A350 and 787, respectively, relegating the C929 to a poor third.

Eventually, COMAC could become a viable third competitor, but this will likely take a generation or more.

With increasing frequency, the press has mentioned that Embraer, a regional airplane maker, has the potential to move up into the mainline jet business. Its CEO, Francisco Gomes Neto, told the *Financial Times* during the 2024 Farnborough Air Show that Embraer is studying the possibility. But officials are coy about what kind of airplane the company might be considering should it choose to pursue that path.

Technology and design being common across manufacturers, it's easy to guess that Embraer is considering a conventional tube-and-wing aircraft with either metal or advanced fuselage materials, a composite wing, and conventional or Open Fan engines. The heart of the market has shifted from 737-800/8- and A320-size models to something between these planes and the 737-10 and A321. By mid-next decade, this up-gauging will continue, and the A321/MAX 10 capacity may well be the heart of the market.

None of this stuff is secret. But Embraer's tiny size compared with Airbus and (a weakened) Boeing remains a major barrier to entry. However, unlike a start-up company, Embraer has a track record of success and international supplier partnerships from which it might be able to form an industrial partnership to give it the heft needed to compete against the duopoly. But the clock is ticking. Embraer must decide by 2026, 2027 or 2028 if it's going to take on Airbus and Boeing. A seven-year development timeline takes Embraer to 2033, 2034 or 2035; an eight-year development plan takes it to the following year. Embraer needs to be first to market with a more efficient airplane and must secure early delivery slots in order to break the duopoly.

There is a long-shot sleeper in the wings: JetZero, a start-up company in Long Beach, California. JetZero has proposed a middle-of-the-market 250-seat Blended Wing Body (BWB) aircraft. Staffed with retired McDonnell Douglas and Boeing engineers, the former group first undertook R&D on a BWB, and the latter continued the work. Company officials believe that their design will be 40 to 50 percent more efficient than the 767s and A330s (ceos) it's designed to replace.

While Boeing's Mike Sinnett rejected the BWB because of the inability to stretch the aircraft, JetZero says that more capacity can be added by widening the plane's center section. To address Boeing's objections that passengers won't have many windows, JetZero's concept has windows in the top of the airplane in addition to those on the side, forward of the wing.

JetZero landed a contract with the U.S. Air Force to develop a demonstrator, but officials expect a commercial airliner to come first, just after the turn of the decade.

But the Air Force contract is only a few hundred million dollars—a far cry from the billions needed for R&D, design, and bringing the airplane to production. Billions more will be needed to sustain production losses until the break-even point is reached. Historically, this milestone was about 400 aircraft, but in recent programs, it's been more than 1,000 due to cost overruns and other factors.

Aviation industry consultant Richard Aboulafia gushes about JetZero, but realities and his oft-repeated reminders about barriers to entry favor skepticism. Aboulafia, his fellow consultant Kevin Michaels, and aerospace analyst Ron Epstein believe that JetZero will be purchased by an established company for its intellectual property and that the buyer will be the one to bring the BWB to market.

24

Engines Are The Key

"The open-rotor of today is something that is very different than twenty years ago"."

—MIKE SINNETT, BOEING VP OF PRODUCT DEVELOPMENT

FORMER BOEING CEO DAVID CALHOUN'S DRUMBEAT about engines technology not being ready for a new airplane isn't a surprise. Engines are obviously the key to any airplane's development. Without a good engine, an airplane becomes a dud regardless of how innovative the airplane is.

During the propeller airliner era, Pratt & Whitney (P&W) and the Curtis Wright Corporation (CW) were the engine suppliers to Douglas Aircraft Company, Lockheed, Convair, and the Martin Company. Even CW's attempt at entering the airliner business, the CW-46, used P&W engines.

For its DC-3 and DC-4 models, Douglas used engines from both companies. Lockheed selected CW as the sole supplier for its entire Constellation series. Douglas used P&W exclusively on its DC-6 and CW exclusively on its DC-7. Martin and Convair chose the same engine used on the DC-6 for their Martin 202/404 and CV-240/340/440 twin-engine short-haul airliners. Boeing used the follow-on engines from the B-29 bomber for its airplane derivative, the Stratocruiser ("Strat").

In the UK, Rolls-Royce (RR) provided the engines for most of Britain's postwar piston airplanes, such as the Hastings, the Tudor, and other interim aircraft, and also provided engines to the even more temporary air transports converted from wartime Lancaster bombers. When Canada developed a piston airliner based on the DC-4 airframe with elements of the DC-6 thrown in, RR Merlin engines were selected because Canada was a UK Crown.

The track record of economy and reliability of these engines was mixed. P&W's engines proved to be the best engines overall. The PW2800, the most widely used engine after World War II on Martins, Convairs, and DC-6s, is considered the most reliable and economical piston engine ever produced for airliners. The huge, incredibly complex engine that P&W developed for the B-29 and its cousin, the Stratocruiser, was a maintenance nightmare, however. And it was not especially economical, either. It was prone to failure and fires, but, being the most powerful piston engine ever developed, it was what was needed for the B-29s and the only engine capable of supporting the heavy, fat, and ungainly Stratocruiser.

The U.S. Air Force had its share of disasters due to engine failures during this period, but it was wartime, and these things happened. For passenger airlines, however, the stakes were very different. Only fifty-six Stratocuisers were developed for Pan Am, United, American Overseas Airlines (AOA), Northwest Airlines, and British Overseas Airways Corporation (BOAC). The plane's spacious double-bubble fuselage and lower-deck lounge were perfect for the airlines' trans-ocean routes. In terms of passenger experience, the Strats were the epitome of air travel at the time. But failing propellers, failing engines, and engine fires caused an inordinate number of disasters, percentage-wise, within the in-service fleet. United was so unhappy with the airplane's operating costs and reliability that it sold its Strats to BOAC only a few years after putting them into service. American Airlines decided that it wanted out of the trans-Atlantic business and sold AOA to Pan Am, including AOA's fleet of Strats. Pan Am lost at least four Stratocruisers to engine failures. Northwest lost one or two, and in other incidents with the plane, emergency landings were required.

Lockheed chose CW to provide engines for its Constellations ("Connies") in part because P&W was so busy with wartime and post-war orders that it couldn't take on more work. CW's wartime engines were reliable, and the Connie first flew in 1943. It had been a pre-war project of TWA and Lockheed, and would have outclassed Douglas's DC-4, which used engines from both CW and P&W, but predominantly from P&W. Few Connies entered service during the war as transports, but after the war, Lockheed had the superior airplane until Douglas upgraded the DC-4 into the DC-6. CW's engines were sufficient for the early Connie models (the L-049 through the L-749). But the stretched, heavier L-1049 needed more powerful engines. CW added a turbocharger to boost power. It worked reasonably well but added complexity. Engine failures began to rise, and some pilots began calling the Connie the best three-engine aircraft they'd ever flown.

Lockheed's L-1049G long-range model slightly outclassed Douglas's DC-6B. American Airlines' CEO C. R. Smith asked Douglas to develop the DC-7 with more range than the DC-6Bs then used by the airline so as to compete with TWA's L-1049Gs. P&W didn't have an engine suitable for the heavier DC-7, so Douglas turned to CW for the same engine used on the L-1049. Like the Connie, the DC-7 had turbochargers. The largest version, the DC-7C, outclassed the L-1049 on trans-Atlantic routes. At TWA's behest, Lockheed responded with the L-1649, which had even more powerful engines. Also like the Connie, the DC-7's engines were prone to mechanical failure, fire, and high operating costs. When the jet age arrived in October 1958 with Boeing's 707, the L-1049s, L-1649s, and DC-7s were generally the first to be retired while the most reliable L-749s and DC-6s remained in service well into the 1960s.

Transitioning to jet engines wasn't a seamless process. Britain was far advanced over the United States in this area and had an easier time. The UK dabbled with jet-engine design before World War II. An engineer name Frank Whittle developed the concept and tried to get the Royal Air Force (RAF) interested, but the RAF was preoccupied with preparing for, and then was thrust into, combat in World War II when Germany invaded Poland on September 1, 1939. Britain and France declared war on Germany two days later. Demand for fighters and bombers, powered by piston engines, left little time to fool around with a revolutionary concept, and anyway, jet engines consumed prodigious amounts of fuel compared with pistons at a time when long range and time aloft would be needed.

Research and development (R&D) on jet engines continued in the UK, Germany, and the United States during this time. Germany was first to market. Its Messerschmidt Me-262 fighter saw combat in the last months of the war. Its deployment was too late to matter, but its design was eye-opening to the Allies' bomber and fighter pilots.

After the war, Britain largely skipped piston-airliner development, though its transitional airplanes had to use pistons. Vickers developed the Viscount airliner, the first to use jet engines, in this case hooked up to propellers. These "jet-props" proved highly reliable. In Europe, where distances were short, the higher fuel usage of these planes didn't matter as much, and it was offset by greater reliability and lower maintenance costs. Capital Airlines, which operated only in the Eastern part of the United States, placed an order for sixty Viscounts, an unprecedented order at the time. The Viscount was suitable for Capital's short- and medium-haul routes. Although Capital overextended its balance sheet in placing the order, the jet-powered Viscounts kept it competitive against American, Eastern, Delta, TWA, and United longer than would have been the case without them. On the brink of bankruptcy, Capital merged into United in 1960. United initially planned to return all the Viscounts to Vickers with the merger but turned out to like the airplanes so much, it kept forty-five of them until they had to be retired.

De Havilland took the bolder step of going straight to commercial jets with its Comet airliner, which used RR engines and dispensed with propellers. Passengers loved the vibration-free result. Operations began in 1954. The Comets were an instant hit. Tragically, de Havilland pushed technology beyond known science.

Just as the Comet was entering service in 1954, Boeing took to the skies with its 707 prototype. The myth built up in Boeing's history is that the CEO at the time, Bill Allen, bet the company on the $16 million development cost of the 707. The reality is far different. After the Allies won the war, Boeing's engineers were among the first to examine Germany's aerospace industry. The Luftwaffe's jet fighters and development program were of special interest. Among the concepts discovered was a flying wing developed by a small company called Horton. Boeing wasn't interested in this wing, but the Northrop Corporation was. In the post-war era, Northrop designed and developed a piston-powered and a jet-powered flying wing. Each took to the skies, but controllability was an issue that wouldn't be solved until the 1980s with the B-2 bomber.

Boeing was more interested in the swept-wing technology found in the German files.

Boeing's Stratocruiser was an outgrowth of its KC-97 aerial-refueling tanker, itself a refined design of the B-50. As such, this piston-powered airplane was fine for the B-50s and B-29s, but it flew too slowly and too low to efficiently refuel the B-47s and B-52s. A jet-refueling tanker was needed. Boeing designed one, ultimately called the KC-135, and the Air Force placed a large order. A derivative civilian model was developed, which became the 707. The cross-over wasn't identical to the KC-135; the latter's fuselage was slightly narrower. The Air Force turned down Boeing's request to use the 135's tooling for the 707.

Airlines wanted six-abreast seating, and the 135's fuselage could only accommodate five. So, some redesigns and additional costs were necessary, and these went toward the $16 million development cost of the 707. But there was another factor at play. Boeing faced excess profit taxes from its wartime work that coincidentally amounted to about $16 million. One way or another, this money was destined to go out the door. Why give it to the government when instead it could be used to develop an airliner that was based on a jet tanker designed for and ordered by the government? It was a brilliant move by CEO Allen and is a great example of Boeing benefitting from government largesse that decades later it would complain about concerning a European rival.

P&W developed jet engines for the B-47 and the B-52. As the development of the 707 and the rival Douglas DC-8 proceeded, these airplanes needed engines, too. The U.S. government eventually granted permission for P&W to offer civilian versions of the bomber engines to Boeing and Douglas. But the airlines faced issues that didn't matter as much to the Air Force. Prodigious fuel use was at the top of the list. Unlike the Air Force, the airlines couldn't do aerial refueling. Then there was the noise. Those early jet engines were very, very noisy. Ramp workers required sound-deadening ear plugs or ear covers to work around the jets, and take-offs were ear-splittingly noisy for anyone under the noise footprint. Compared with piston and jet-propeller planes, the pure jets were thunderous.

Early jet engines also spewed black smoke, in massive quantities, on take-off. Even well before the environmental movement, people complained about the air pollution coming out of jet tailpipes. Finally, early jet engines were a tad underpowered, requiring water injection on take-off from marginal runways (of which there were many in those days) or for heavy payloads. This added to the black smoke problem.

The first 707s and DC-8s didn't have trans-Atlantic range, so fueling stops (usually in Gander, Newfoundland) were necessary. Still, as with the de Havilland Comet, the speed, higher cruising altitudes, and vibration-free passenger cabins caused the flying public to rush to the new jets, surcharges on fares notwithstanding.

In Cincinnati, Ohio, GE developed the jet engine for Air Force fighters and the B-58 bomber. Like Boeing with its bombers and P&W with its engines, loud, smoky, and fuel-thirsty engines were tolerated at the time. When Convair decided to take the plunge away from its twin-engine short-range airliners and develop a medium-range passenger jet, it needed engines. P&W was busy, and, in any case, Convair needed differentiation. Its CV-880 and -990 models were designed to be faster than either the 707 or DC-8 and featured more powerful engines, capable of using more airports with shorter runways than could accommodate the Boeing and Douglas aircraft. Convair turned to GE.

Like P&W, GE had to get government permission for a civilian application of its military engines. The request was granted. Setting aside other factors that contributed to the failure of Convair's CV-series,[117] the engines on the planes were even noisier and thirstier, and emitted even more black smoke, than P&W engines.

P&W would improve those early jet engines quickly. By 1961, the first of the "fan" engines entered service. A somewhat larger fan replaced the one used in the original engines, allowing air to bypass the core and expel outside the casing. Called a bypass, this fan set the foundation for every engine to follow. It provided some additional thrust with no extra fuel usage, effectively lowering consumption. This, in turn, allowed enough range for non-stop flights across the Atlantic.

During this time period, Boeing added wingspan, creating the 707-320.

---

117. TWA, a launch customer of the CV-880, was owned by billionaire Howard Hughes. Even with his wealth and variety of other business ventures, however, Hughes was unable and unwilling to finance orders the airline had placed for 880s and for Boeing 707s. Improperly, he interfered with Convair's production line and refused to accept delivery. The disruption to Convair was immense. Convair was last to market with the 880, and Boeing and Douglas developed the 727 and DC-9, respectively, quicker than had been imagined. These planes were designed for the same routes the 880 was intended to serve. Airlines turned to these aircraft instead. GE engines proved costlier to maintain than P&W engines, and they were even thirstier. And there were design flaws in the 990 that cut its range and speed guarantees so severely that, combined with other elements, they destroyed the 880 and 990 programs. Convair sold only sixty-five 880s and thirty-seven -990s. It lost $250 million on the programs, an industrial record at the time.

Coupled with the P&W fan-jet JT3D, as the engine was called, the revisions were branded the 707-320B. Douglas essentially followed suit, using the same engine, and created the DC-8-50 brand. It later added more wing and stretched the DC-8 into the -60 series, the most efficient four-engine jets of the era.

Boeing developed the three-engine 727 (which entered service in 1964) and Douglas developed the twin-engine DC-9 (1965). P&W created a new engine for these smaller airplanes, based on the JT3D, called the JT8D. When Boeing developed the twin-engine 737, the JT8D was used on it, too. Douglas went on to create the super-stretched DC-9 Super 80 (1980) (later rebranded the MD-80), and P&W met the challenge with its JT8D-200 series engine.

The JT3Ds and JT8Ds proved to be superb engines. By today's standards, they were still noisy and thirsty, but by standards of the day, they were quieter than those first power plants (but hardly quiet), more economical, more reliable, and almost smokeless.

Boeing responded to the Super 80 with the 737-300/400/500 series (1984), which much later became unofficially known as the Classic when the 737 was further developed into the Next Generation, or NG (1994). The Classic replaced the JT8Ds with the CFM56, a larger, quieter, more economical engine developed in a 50-50 joint venture between GE and France's Snecma (now called Safran) called CFM International. The CFM56 is the most reliable engine ever to be put on an airliner. It can stay on wing for more than 25,000 cycles (each cycle is one landing and take-off) before it must be removed for a major overhaul. Today it powers more than half the Airbus A320 family fleet and, when coupled with the number of 737s using it, gives CFM a commanding two-thirds market share of the single-aisle airliner sector.

However, the CFM56 wasn't always a good engine. Early versions were mechanical nightmares. First used to re-engine the DC-8-60 series after production stopped with the introduction of the DC-10, the DC-8's successor, durability and reliability weren't great. But over the next fifty years, nothing could beat the CFM56.

What happened to P&W, which once dominated the jet market? It made one of the greatest bone-headed decisions in corporate history. Executives passed on the development of a successor to the JT8D when Boeing decided to upgrade the original 737 to the 737 Classic. Instead, P&W concluded that Boeing's new 757 was the future. Executives bet all their marbles on the successor to the 727. In doing so, P&W faced off with RR, which offered a new, smaller version of its RB211 engine first used on the Lockheed L-1011 TriStar (more on this later). Having created such a reliable engine for the 707, 727, 737, DC-8, and DC-9 models, one would think P&W would have no trouble doing so for the 757.

P&W's PW2030/2040 was the most economical engine for the 757, by a wide margin. But the reliability of this engine was much lower than that of the RB211. Maintenance costs are as important as fuel burn, if not more so, and the on-wing time for the RB211 was better than the time for the PW2000. By the time Boeing ceased production of the 757 in 2004, P&W and RR had roughly equal sales in the number of engines sold. But more customers chose RR over P&W, making the secondary market for RR much more attractive than the P&W-powered 757. P&W did as well as it did because of the large fleet orders by American, Delta, Northwest, TWA, United, and United Parcel Service. Eastern and Republic Airways chose RR, as did British Crown airlines and smaller operators around the world.

P&W executives completely misjudged the market. Boeing sold 1,049 757s. It sold more than 15,000 737s and will continue to do so into the 2030s, nearly seventy years after the program was launched.

The 757 wasn't the last of P&W's problems, however. When Airbus needed a small engine for its A318, P&W developed the PW6000. While the future market for the A318 was miniscule to begin with, the engine was so poorly designed that no one wanted it.

P&W's next effort was more successful but still created a disaster of epic proportions. The company spent more than twenty years developing a Geared Turbo Fan (GTF) engine for the single-aisle sector. Belatedly, executives realized that their bet on the 737-757 was wrong. The future was the single-aisle market. In any given year, this sector accounts for 85 percent or more of the orders in numbers. Values tend to skew the market value with widebody sales, but Airbus and Boeing twenty-year forecasts predict sales of more than 35,000 single-aisle aircraft versus around 8,000 twin-aisle aircraft.

A gearbox reduces the revolutions per minute of the fan at the front of an engine. If you can slow the fan down compared with the core of the engine, you save fuel—lots of it. If you put a big fan on the front of the engine, the bypass ratio goes way up, saving a lot more fuel (remember that JT3D described earlier).

A gear box is not a new piece of equipment. It's used on helicopters and propeller-driven aircraft, including jet-props. But putting a gear box on a big jet engine was new. Kinetic energy was one issue. Keeping the box lubricated for heavy use was another. A lot of people were skeptical about putting a gear box on the engine of a high-use passenger jet like the A320 or 737. GE, the CFM partner, was one. At the time, this may have been sour grapes from a competitor or genuine disbelief in the concept—it was impossible to tell from the outside—but the fact is, years after P&W successfully launched the GTF program, GE bought a company that makes gear boxes, and its proposed RISE Open Fan engine must use a gear box. RR also has a gear box in its proposed Ultra Fan widebody engine.

Finding a launch customer for the GTF proved challenging due to doubts over its durability and maintenance requirements and associated costs, which were anybody's guess. P&W's performance on the PW2000, its design of the PW6000, and the fact that it hadn't done a narrowbody engine on its own for decades for the A320-737-size airplane were all grounds for questions. So, the launch order for the program came from an entirely unexpected source.

Japan's Mitsubishi Heavy Industries (MHI) had been toying with the idea of developing a regional jet for decades. I was retained as a subcontractor to an MHI consultant in the 1990s to open some doors with U.S. regional airlines for a surveying tour, so the interest goes back at least that far. At the time, Bombardier and Embraer were the dominant jet providers, with, respectively, the cramped CRJ and ERJ aircraft. Mitsubishi's idea was to develop a better competitor.

But it wasn't until the early 2000s that MHI made its move. It became the first manufacturer to sign up for the GTF to put on what became known as the Mitsubishi Regional Jet, or MRJ. Mitsubishi proposed a seventy- and a ninety-seat model, the MRJ70 and the MRJ90. Embraer already had launched the E-Jet by then (2004), and Bombardier was floating a concept called the C Series. All three aircraft had two-by-two seating and overall similar design and operating specifications. Bombardier soon dropped the BRJ and returned later with the C Series we know today as the Airbus A220, which has a two-by-three seating plan and a range of up to 3,300 nautical miles (nm). It's a mainline jet rather than a regional aircraft.

Bombardier dropped the original C Series because there was no advanced engine available. But when MHI signed up for the GTF, Bombardier now had an engine. It signed up for the next size up and launched the larger C Series program.

Airbus had been watching the development of the GTF engine and decided to put one on an A340 four-engine jet for testing. Eventually, it signed up for a still-larger version of the GTF to re-engine its A320 family. Embraer, which had put its E-Jet into service in 2008 (the program was launched in 2004), in 2013 was backed into signing up for the GTFs planned for the MRJ and the C Series for a new line of E-Jets called the E2. From Embraer's standpoint, the timing couldn't have been worse. The original E-Jet wasn't that old and its costs hadn't yet been recovered. But on paper, the MRJ would squeeze the E-Jet from the bottom, and the C Series would squeeze it from the top. To remain competitive, Embraer had to re-engine its airplane.[118] P&W also won a commitment from Russia's Irkut

---

118. For a variety of reasons, Mitsubishi got cold feet and in 2020 killed its program. Doing so meant that P&W no longer had a business case for the small

Corporation to put the GTF on the MC-21 airliner, a competitor to the A320 and 737. P&W was back, big time, in the single-aisle business.[119]

Airbus all along was the prize. The A320 family, overall, was outclassed by the 737. The largest model, the A321, carried more passengers than the Boeing 737-900ER, but its range was shorter. It had won more orders, but the A321 needed improvements. The A320 carried slightly fewer passengers than the 737-800, which outsold it comfortably. The A319 sold better than the 737-700, but customers were up-gauging to the A320 and A321. The future for the A319 was bleak. The GTF was what Airbus needed to goose the 320 family. Coupled with a new winglet that it called the sharklet (a silly name to distinguish it from the winglets Boeing was putting on the 737), a new engine would give the A320 a serious economic and operational advantage over the 737.

Airbus also wanted CFM to provide an engine for the revamped A320. After all, Airbus had long offered an engine choice for the family: the CFM56 and the V2500 from a consortium called International Aero Engines (IAE), comprised of four international companies. IAE was led by P&W and RR.

IAE's entry into the market hadn't been smooth. It was formed to provide Airbus with an engine called the Super Fan, an early version of the GTF, for the A340. Had it gone forward, the four-engine A340's economics would have been superior to the twin-engine 777. But, as it turned out, the Super Fan wasn't ready for prime time, and P&W killed the engine. Airbus had no choice but to go scrounging for an engine. It turned to CFM, and the CFM56 was put on the airplane. Airbus never truly recovered from the blow; A340 sales trailed 777 sales by a wide margin.

IAE's V2500 was a perfect choice for the A320 in the 1990s versus the CFM56. IAE was late to the party, and CFM had been the A320's exclusive supplier up until IAE's entry on the scene. The first V2500 version, the A1, was beset by troubles, especially in hot environments like Phoenix. Reliability and durability were issues. P&W and RR, and their other partners, worked through all the problems and, by the time the A5 version emerged, the V2500 was a very good engine.

Airbus wanted the GTF offered through IAE, in part because of its good track record on the V2500, in part because of its horrible experience with

---

engine that was to power the MRJ and Embraer's E175-E2. With U.S. pilot unions refusing to alter their contracts to accommodate the heavier E2, Embraer "paused" this model and proceeded with the larger E190/195 E2s, which used an engine version similar to the C Series/A220. Embraer finally killed the 175-E2 in 2024.

119. Russia's invasion of Crimea and, later, Ukraine killed the MC-21 deal.

P&W on the PW6000, and in part because P&W hadn't been on its own in the single-aisle sector for decades. But in another boneheaded corporate move, RR withdrew from the IAE group over a legal dispute with P&W on the A380's engine. In a lawsuit, RR accused P&W of stealing technology from RR's Trent 900 engine for the GTF. The lawsuit was eventually settled, and one of the terms of the arrangement was RR's exit from IAE, evoking memories of P&W's withdrawal from the 737 Classic engine plan. RR now only offered engines for widebody airplanes.

Airbus's fears about P&W were well-founded. It wasn't the gearbox that was the problem, however. It was, figuratively speaking, everything else: the core, blades within the core, and, years after entry into service (EIS), the use of an inferior powder. The result: A320neos worldwide were grounded until fixes could be made and engines repaired. At its peak, 650 A320neos were parked for months at a time.

The problems weren't confined to the A320. The A220 also suffered similar problems, with airplanes parked awaiting repairs or new engines. Embraer, which shared the A220 engine, was least affected. Its largest airplane, the E195-E2, is 10 percent lighter than the A220-300, so there is less stress on the engine. Still, operators had to park some E2s awaiting repairs.

CFM, despite the fantastic durability and reliability of the CFM56, wasn't immune from new-engine problems. As noted, Airbus wanted CFM to provide a competing engine to the P&W GTF. Boeing *needed* an engine if the 737 was to be competitive with the re-engined A320. CFM came up with the LEAP. Instead of using a gear box, which during development it disdained, and before it bought a company making gearboxes, CFM used advanced composite materials and much hotter engine temperatures plus a bigger fan on the front of the engine to essentially match P&W's fuel-burn advances.

This approach came at a cost, however, quite literally. The durability (on-wing time) of the LEAP was far less than the stalwart CFM56. Maintenance costs proved to be triple that of the CFM56, according to an engine advisory firm. GE and Safran said that the LEAP was better than the CFM56 at the same point in its life in response to the complaints. But airlines, suffering from premature maintenance issues and shorter on-wing times, didn't care what the CFM56 was doing fifty or sixty years ago. They only cared about the schedule disruption and the added costs today.

In 2024, P&W said that it would be a few more years before things were fully sorted out on the GTF. The engine entered service with Airbus in late 2016. P&W's prediction meant that it would be ten years of trouble since EIS. Long term, the maintenance costs on the GTF are predicted by industry experts to be lower than the hotter-running LEAP, but in the near term, the LEAP proved to be the preferred choice for the A320 family.

Widebody engines fared no better than those for single-aisle airplanes. In the early 1960s, the U.S. Air Force sought designs for the first giant airplane that could transport tanks and other oversized cargo. Boeing, Douglas, and Lockheed submitted bids for the airframe. GE and P&W proffered designs for the big engines that were required for the airframe.

Lockheed won the contract for what would be named the C-5; GE won the engine contract. Boeing took what it learned from the competition to design the 747, the first of the passenger jumbo jets. Its iconic upper deck "hump" and twenty-foot-wide cabin earned the 747 the nickname Queen of the Skies. But it was a rocky road to get the airplane in the air.

Boeing's own cost overruns on the 747 and a concurrent recession nearly pushed the company into bankruptcy. P&W, having lost the C-5 engine contract, turned to developing the JT9D engine for the 747. Like with the airframe, engine development proved difficult. P&W was tardy in delivering engines to Boeing. As a result, there were 747s lined up on Boeing's Everett Paine Field airport with big yellow concrete blocks hanging off each of the four pylons to prevent the 747s from sitting on their tails while waiting for engines.

Even after delivery, the power plants proved problematic. They'd overheat during taxi. When Pan Am, the launch customer, scheduled its inaugural flight from New York to London, the carrier was ready with a back-up airplane. Sure enough, the engines on the flight overheated. The pilot went back to the gate and swapped planes. The second one got off OK. It took years for the big engines to achieve reliability. Western Airlines, which didn't order the plane, found itself out-performing Continental Airlines, which did, on Los Angeles-to-Honolulu flights with its reliable 707s versus Continental's temperamental 747s.

GE, which won the C-5 contract, developed a similar engine for the DC-10, the CF-6, which Airbus also used for its new A300B2/B4 twin-engine, twin-aisle, 250-passenger jumbo jet. The engine worked fine on the three-engine DC-10 but proved under-powered for the A300. Later, more powerful versions served the A300-600R well.

A few years after winning the C-5 contract, Lockheed decided to reenter commercial aviation with its L-1011 TriStar. Virtually identical to the DC-10 in size and performance, Lockheed chose RR as its engine supplier. RR developed new technology for the engine—but it didn't go well. Design, testing, and production issues arose that were so severe, the company with the storied name was forced into bankruptcy. Lockheed, already swimming in red ink over the C-5 program, now had an airplane with no engines. Lockheed avoided its own bankruptcy only because the U.S. Congress, in a highly controversial vote, approved a loan guarantee for the big defense contractor. The UK government bailed out RR, which delivered engines for the TriStar. After the inevitable teething issues, the RB211 proved to be a highly reliable engine. A smaller version was designed for the Boeing 757, offered against P&W's PW 2037. The PW2037 was more economical than the 757's RB 211, but the RR engine was significantly more reliable.

Engines on widebody airplanes thereafter proved to be solid derivatives. The brand-new engine for the 777, the GE90, had few problems, as did the RR Trent for the A330. But when the 787 was developed, the RR Trent 1000 and the GEnx initially fell short of fuel-usage guarantees. The GEnx had icing issues. But the Trent 1000 developed problems so severe after years in service that more than fifty 787s were grounded. RR couldn't repair or replace the engines fast enough, and some aircraft remained grounded for years. As late as 2025, RR continued to suffer fallout from the lack of maintenance, repair, and operations (MRO) shops for the Trent 1000s, which displaced normal MRO visits for the Trent 700 used on the A330ceo, the Trent 900 (A380), and later, the Trent XWB-97 used on the A350-1000. These engines lack durability in harsh environments like the hot, sandy Middle East or the salty environment of Hong Kong. Warranty costs all but destroyed RR's profit and loss numbers for years, causing a knock-on effect on its balance sheet.

The warranty costs for all the engine manufacturers led to a business model that worked for decades but that was, by 2020, clearly outmoded. When examined closely, the business model seems ludicrous on its face.

It's long been known that list prices for Airbus, Boeing, Embraer, Bombardier, McDonnell Douglas, and Lockheed airplanes (when these companies were in the commercial airliner business) bore no relationship to the price paid by airlines and lessors. Much as the ordinary consumer dickers with a dealership to buy a car, airlines and lessors dicker with airframe and engine manufacturers. Back in the day when GE, P&W, and RR had engines for most of the widebody offerings, the competition was nuts. P&W won the competition versus GE at Delta for the MD-11. P&W *gave* Delta the engines, for free, in return for a long-term maintenance contract. P&W and GE had a partnership called Engine Alliance to compete with RR for the A380 customer contracts. Discounts of 80 percent in return for MRO contracts were par for the course.

And that's the key to the engine business model: steep, steep discounts in return for MRO deals. Airbus and Boeing sold big orders to top-notch airlines for discounts of 50 to 60 percent and, on rare occasions, 65 percent, off list prices. After Christian Scherer became head of sales at Airbus, in 2018 he dropped publishing list prices because they were so meaningless. Boeing followed suit the next year. While aftermarket services became a part of many Airbus, Boeing, and Embraer sales campaigns, the companies still wanted to make money on aircraft sales. P&W once acknowledged that it didn't make money on engine sales for twenty years; profits were from its MRO business.

Airlines often entered into "power by the hour" (PBH) contracts with engine makers for routine and unexpected parts replacements, mid-life checks, and full overhauls. RR and CFM were loathe to grant any airline the right to maintain their own engines beyond normal requirements in the course of operations. And they were especially opposed to granting third-party MRO shops licenses to perform MROs on their engines. Airlines with their own shops, like Delta TechOps, Lufthansa Technik, and the Air France-KLM group, all but demanded the right to fully overhaul their own engines *and* to contract in work from other airlines. P&W was the most willing to grant the licenses. The others occasionally did so, mostly kicking and screaming. (Air France held off on ordering the A350 for months until RR finally granted it MRO licenses, for example.)

These elements were part of the standard business models the engine makers followed. Until the Trent 1000, GTF, and LEAP engines came on the scene.

Warranty work on the Trent 1000s was so great that RR had to restate its financial reporting and change the way it recognized future revenue. For a time during the COVID crisis, there were fears that RR was once more headed toward bankruptcy. There was even talk that Airbus would have to bail out RR to protect itself against the engine maker's exclusivity on the A330neo and A350. By 2024, these fears were gone, but a casualty was R&D. RR at one point was developing two engines, the Advance and the Ultra Fan. The Advance was dropped.

CFM's LEAP engine's economic efficiency relies on very hot temperatures and exotic composites. It begs comparison with the admirable on-wing record of the highly reliable CFM56. Unfortunately, the CFM56's bar is so high that any expectation that the LEAP could match the wing time and maintenance costs of the CFM 56 couldn't possibly be met. But CFM (GE, really) nevertheless made these comparisons and set these expectations. The result has been premature removal for shop visits. The cost to CFM's 50-50 owners, GE and Safran, has been huge. GE CEO Larry Culp was so irate that he virtually ceased offering PBH deals.

P&W's GTF problems began soon after the A320neo entered service in December 2016. As each problem was fixed, a new one emerged. P&W doesn't think that all of the engines will be fixed until 2025 or 2026. Fortunately for P&W, it's a unit of mega-company RTX, so the GTF costs—which could run into the billions—can be more easily absorbed.

The engine business model must change. But with GE pursuing the Open Fan and the history of recent engines failing to meet guarantees, will CEO Larry Culp have to grant PBHs for this new, radically different engine? Or is there something else GE can do to create maturity and satisfy customers with its reliability?

These are decisions involving tens of billions of dollars.

25

So Much for a Boring Year

"We're going to approach this, number one, acknowledging our mistake."
—DAVE CALHOUN AFTER THE ALASKA 1282 DOOR-PLUG BLOWOUT

On January 4, 2024, the trade publication *Leeham News* posted its 2024 outlook for The Boeing Company entitled, "Boeing needs a boring year in 2024." The next day, Alaska Airlines flight 1282, a MAX 9, took off from Portland, Oregon, for Ontario, California, at 4:30 p.m. Minutes later, as the flight was passing 14,800 feet, an emergency exit–door plug[120] aft of the wing on the port side blew off the airplane. A rapid decompression occurred, and the flight made an emergency return and landing at Portland. Fortunately, nobody was sitting next to the missing exit-door plug. A teenager sitting in the row ahead lost his shirt, ripped off in the event. No serious injuries were reported. Videos posted to social media showed oxygen masks deployed and passengers who, except for a few, remained calm for the return to Portland. The plane used for flight 1282, N704AL, had been delivered to Alaska Airlines a mere two months before the incident. It had only been in service for ten weeks.

Within hours, the airline grounded its sixty-five MAX 9s for inspection of the emergency exit. United Airlines followed suit, and the next day, the Federal Aviation Administration (FAA) grounded the MAX 9s until inspections and, if needed, fixes could be made. Alaska and United expected a short grounding. But the FAA declined to approve Boeing's first inspection instructions. In the end, it took three weeks for the FAA to approve the instructions. The grounding order was lifted after inspections and repairs were made.

So much for a boring year for Boeing.

---

120. A door plug on the Boeing 737-900ER and the 737-9 is installed in place of an emergency exit when these aircraft are configured for regular multi-class seating. Only when these aircraft are configured for all-coach, high-density seating is the emergency exit door installed. The plug is lighter, allowing a full row of seats at normal seat pitch to be installed. From a production standpoint, Boeing has a common fuselage on the assembly line, easing final assembly.

The affected exit, and its twin on the starboard side of the airplane, were inactive; given the passenger seating configuration used by Alaska, these two exits did not have to be "active" for emergencies and were permanently disabled. There were no markings inside or outside of the airplane showing that the doors existed. If a high-density passenger configuration were to be employed, such as those used by low-cost and ultra-low-cost airlines, the doors would be active for use in emergencies.[121]

The fuselages for all 737s were made by Spirit AeroSystems, the Wichita, Kansas–based company that was owned by Boeing (and known as Boeing Wichita) until 2005. This storied location built Boeing B-17s and B-29s during World War II and various military and commercial airplanes afterward.

Spirit installed the door plugs for operators like Alaska and United and emergency exits for the few carriers configuring the airplanes in high-density, all-coach seating. These door plugs were held in place by twelve flanges, six on each side, and four bolts that served in a fail-safe capacity. As long as even one of these bolts was installed, it prevented upward movement necessary to clear the flanges for plug removal. The plugs could be removed while the fuselage was on the Renton, Washington, final assembly line or, after the plans were delivered to an airline, for maintenance. The bolts are supposed to be reinstalled before final assembly is completed and an airplane is delivered to a customer.

Inside the cabin, the cabin wall is continuous over these inoperative exits; passengers wouldn't even know the exit doors were there. Outside, the door and exit outlines aren't applied. Rescue crews would also not necessarily know that a door exists.

Predictably, click-baiting headlines and the uninformed misrepresented what had happened. Some blared that a portion of the fuselage had been ripped away. Damage was confined to the missing door plug, with some ancillary damage to the door-surround. But no part of the fuselage was "ripped" away. Also predictably, because it was a MAX airplane, the crash-and-grounding history was brought up. Below is one example.

"Frightening Boeing Incident on a Boeing MAX Jet – Lead Aviation Attorneys Question Whether Officials Need to Examine if Certifying the Plane as Safe for Flying Was Hasty," screamed the headline of a press release issued by 9 a.m. Pacific time the following day.

"'This incident forces the aviation community, particularly

---

121. This practice dates back decades. Royal Dutch Airlines (KLM) "plugged" one of the doors on its Boeing 747-200 fleet, and the 737-900/900ER has plugged emergency exit doors in the same location as the MAX 9.

government regulators, to determine [whether] the Boeing MAX 8 was allowed to fly again too hastily [due to] Boeing's efforts to get those planes back in the air,' said Robert A. Clifford, founder and senior partner of Clifford Law Offices in Chicago. He is Lead Counsel in the litigation involving the tragic crash of a Boeing MAX 8 aircraft shortly after takeoff in March 2019 in Ethiopia that killed all 157 on board," the press release continued.

Setting aside the fact that a MAX 9, not a MAX 8, was involved in the current incident and that litigation over the Ethiopian accident continues, it took twenty-one months for the MAX 8 and 9 to be recertified, and the MAX 7 and 10 still had not been certified as 2023 turned into 2024 and 2024 turned into 2025. But this hyperbole and similar headlines and stories questioning the safety of the MAX were inevitable. The timing, perhaps, could not have been worse, however.

On the morning of January 5, 2024, less than eleven hours before the Alaska Airlines incident, the *Seattle Times* reported that Boeing sought an FAA exemption from certain safety requirements for the MAX 7 on the tortuous path toward *its* certification.[122] The controversial request was buried over the Christmas holiday, but the ever-alert journalist Dominic Gates nevertheless picked up on it. Some pilot groups objected to the exemption, as did safety expert John Cox, himself a retired 737 NG pilot.

The National Transportation Safety Board (NTSB) dispatched a team of investigators. Such probes usually take up to eighteen months, but this incident could take less time because everyone survived and the airplane was intact. A search for the missing door was launched, and it was found in some trees three days later by a school teacher who taught, of all things, physics. Needless to say, his students were unusually attentive the next day in class.

Leeham News was quick to label the accident a quality-control issue at either Boeing or Spirit or both, and not a "MAX issue." This turned out to be the case. Given that the bolts had to be in place to prevent the door plug from jumping the flanges, early speculation was that either the bolts failed—although it was unlikely that all four would fail at the same time—or that, for whatever reason, they weren't installed. When the door plug was found and turned over to the NTSB, its chair said that no bolts had been recovered. The plug was shipped to the NTSB's headquarters in Washington, DC, for microscopic inspection. Investigators hoped to tell whether

---

122. "Boeing Wants FAA to Exempt MAX 7 from Safety Rules to Get It in the Air," *Seattle Times* (January 5, 2024), https://www.seattletimes.com/business/boeing-aerospace/boeing-wants-faa-to-exempt-max-7-from-safety-rules-to-get-it-in-the-air/.

scratches in the bolt holes would reveal if the bolts were installed at the time of separation. Initial examination was inconclusive.

David Calhoun, Boeing's CEO at the time, told the financial news network CNBC that he wasn't going to point fingers. But he did just that, citing Spirit as the likely culprit. Calhoun said that ensuing quality was ultimately Boeing's responsibility. Still, in a customer call shortly after the accident, one of Boeing's customers reported that all the fingers on that call indeed pointed to Spirit as the responsible party. On January 8, three days after the accident, *Leeham News* published a detailed article about Boeing's inspection process.[123] The approved inspection procedures in place at the time involved up to four steps. Boeing said that final assembly did not call for the plug's removal to access the plane's interior. But there are times when "unplanned" removals occur, and a procedure is required to inspect the re-installation. *Leeham News* published a follow-up article on January 15 detailing the procedures for an "unplanned removal."[124] The next day, a reader identifying himself as a "current Boeing employee" posted a long two-part comment detailing that an unplanned removal occurred on the fuselage of the plane involved in the Alaska accident and that internal records showed that the required inspections were not completed. The employee's post is reprinted in the Appendix.

The FAA rejected Boeing's first Service Bulletin (SB) inspection procedure, issued within days of flight 1282, as inadequate. The second SB, issued Tuesday, January 9, apparently was more detailed (neither Boeing nor the FAA released the SB to the public), but by Thursday, January 11, United and Alaska said that they were still awaiting approved procedures. Alaska extended schedule cancellations through Saturday, January 13, and United wasn't far behind. The FAA wouldn't approve any procedure for nearly three weeks.

On Thursday, January 11, the FAA began to drop the hammer on Boeing. It sent a letter to Boeing stating that the company "may have failed to ensure its completed projects conformed to its approved design and were in a condition for safe operation . . . ." A formal investigation was opened. Since Boeing was the last to have its fingers on the airplane before delivery, whatever Spirit's role was, Boeing had the final responsibility.

On January 9, 2024, in a meeting with employees, an emotional Cal-

123. "737 Incidents Prompt New Scrutiny at Boeing," *Leeham News* (January 8, 2024), https://leehamnews. com/2024/01/08/737-incidents-prompt-new-scrutiny-at-boeing/.

124. "'Unplanned' Removal, Installation Inspection Procedure at Boeing," *Leeham News* (January 15, 2024), https://leehamnews.com/2024/01/15/ unplanned-removal-installation-inspection-procedure-at-boeing/.

houn told those gathered that Boeing had to own the mistake, which he did not identify in a short video clip that was posted to the Internet. "We're going to approach this, number one, acknowledging our mistake. We are going to approach it with 100 percent and complete transparency every step of the way. We're going to work with the NTSB, who is investigating the accident itself, to find out what the root cause is," he said.[125] Calhoun noted the gaping hole in the Alaska plane and the empty seats next to the hole. Invoking his own children and grandchildren, he said that his first thought when seeing the pictures was of who might have been sitting there. Nobody had been, but a teenage boy was in the window seat ahead of the hole. His shirt was ripped off and his mother, seated in the middle seat next to him, had to hold on to the teen as the decompression pulled at him. Had he not been seat-belted, the teen may well have been sucked out of the airplane, mom's grip notwithstanding.

The dark headlines and stories immediately took their toll on the MAX, on Boeing, and on Spirit. Stock prices plunged on Monday, the first trading day after the accident. Boeing's market value dropped by billions of dollars. Spirit's stock price also plunged. An informational, unscientific poll by Jon Ostrower on Twitter/X showed the drop in public confidence in the MAX.

Over the course of the next few weeks, Boeing undertook steps to calm angry customers. There was Alaska, of course, which operated the flight involved in the accident. Alaska's corporate culture presents a calm and friendly demeanor to passengers and stakeholders alike. Setting aside normal tension between management and labor, Alaska by and large succeeds in maintaining that calmness and friendliness. But in this case, CEO Ben Minicucci publicly castigated Boeing—a rare step culturally and for an airline that has "Proudly All Boeing" painted on the nose of its 737 fleet.[126] Minicucci publicly told everyone who would listen that he was more than frustrated, he was angry. What he told Boeing privately is unknown. Still, Minicucci vowed loyalty to Boeing in the future.

Scott Kirby, CEO of United Airlines, delivered a measured, mixed but pointed message to the people of United and to the public. Speaking with aerospace reporter Phil LeBeau on CNBC, Kirby expressed overall confidence in Boeing, but with the pat on the back came a kick in the pants.

---

125. Calhoun's emotionality contrasted with the stone-faced, dispassionate attitude shown by former CEO Dennis Muilenburg throughout most of the MAX grounding crisis. The only time Muilenburg's emotions showed was during a Congressional hearing where he met with crash-victims' families before testifying. The family meeting clearly affected him.

126. The fact that Horizon Air, a sister company to the mainline carrier that flies under the Alaska brand, operates Embraer E175 jets doesn't count in Alaska's universe.

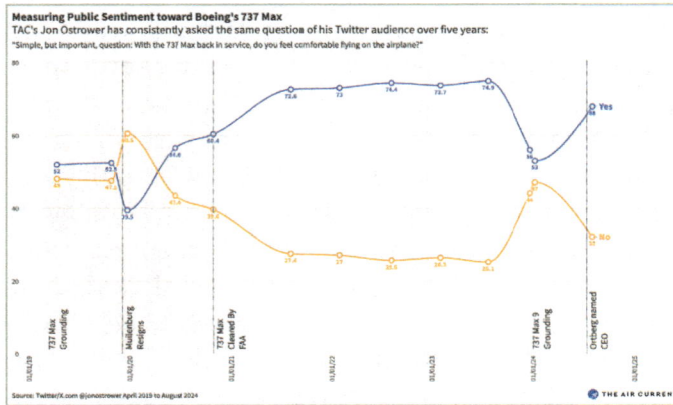

Figure 27. Jon Ostrower, editor of The Air Current (TAC), ran several polls on Twitter/X during the MAX crisis gauging the "avoidance" factor. While unscientific, the poll is illustrative. Credit: TAC.

"I have a lot of confidence in the people at Boeing," Kirby said. "There're great mechanics, great engineers, and [have] a great storied history. But they've been having these consistent manufacturing challenges, and they need to take action to get it [corrected]. That's the point to Dave and to anyone is that it needs to be real action. And when you tell Dave Calhoun this, what does he say? Well, he says yes. He doesn't disagree, of course. But I am a lot more interested in seeing the actions. But on the backside of this, what are the real actions to really get the manufacturing process back to the high levels of quality and consistency that historically existed at Boeing?"

If Calhoun and Boeing didn't get this message, Kirby was quick to deliver another swift kick to the rear end.

"We're now, best case, five years behind on the original delivery of the MAX 10. And as we've gone through the last year internally at United, we've grown increasingly to believe that, best case, the MAX 10 just gets pushed further and further to the right. So, we've already started working on alternative plans," Kirby said. "I think this is the straw—the MAX 9 grounding is probably the straw that broke the camel's back for us. We're going to at least build a plan that doesn't have the MAX 10 in it. Now, we'll hope that Boeing gets it certified at some point, but we're going to build an alternative plan that just doesn't have the MAX 10 in it.

"It probably means that we change the order books on alternative airplanes instead of MAX 10s, at least for the next few years, and it probably means we don't grow quite as fast as we were hoping," Kirby said. United Airlines later published its fleet plan in a federal Securities and Exchange Commission (SEC) filing, and it didn't include the MAX 10 until 2026.

Some thought that this meant Kirby would cancel United's orders for 227 MAX 10s (with options for 200 more). "Alternative airplanes" likely meant some MAX 10 orders would be swapped for MAX 8s or MAX 9s. He later said he wouldn't cancel the order. Nevertheless, word quickly leaked that Kirby made a side trip to Airbus's Toulouse headquarters to discuss obtaining more A321neos to fill the gap in the MAX 10 delivery schedule. Airbus, sold out until around 2030, was reportedly asking to buy back slots from lessors to accommodate United.

Boeing announced a one-day stand down and meeting at its Renton factory during which all production on the 737 stopped. The goal was to address safety and quality issues. Thousands of employees attended. Boeing later said that it received 1,000 suggestions and comments.

Calhoun also announced the appointment of a new, outside safety committee headed by retired Admiral Kirkland Donald, whose military career included work involving Navy nuclear submarines. "Donald and a team of outside experts will conduct a thorough assessment of Boeing's quality management system for commercial airplanes, including quality programs and practices in Boeing manufacturing facilities and its oversight of commercial supplier quality. His recommendations will be provided to Calhoun and to the Aerospace Safety Committee of Boeing's Board of Directors," said Calhoun.

It was the second time the Boeing CEO turned to a retired admiral to form a safety committee. In September 2019, then-CEO Muilenburg created a permanent Aerospace Safety Committee headed by retired Admiral Edmund Giambastiani, Jr., then a Boeing board member. Muilenburg announced a multi-level set of tasks for the committee to undertake. This admiral, like Donald, spent a career in the Navy, including on nuclear subs, and he was a former vice chairman of the Pentagon's Joint Chiefs of Staff. No public announcement of the outcome of this committee was ever made.

Skeptics could be forgiven for being skeptical. During the first twenty-one-month MAX grounding, Boeing officials parroted phrases like "safety is our number one priority" and "the goal is to safely return the MAX to service" so many times that they lost their meaning. For families of the victims of the Lion Air and Ethiopian crashes, the record of safety lapses that emerged from the various federal investigations and civil lawsuits rendered the statements meaningless.

The choice of a retired nuclear navy admiral in 2019 and again in 2024 to head an aviation-focused safety exercise was puzzling. Former Air Force generals might have been better choices, or perhaps key people from the likes of Lockheed Martin, Northrop Grumman, or even Airbus would have been preferable. The choices made by Muilenburg and Calhoun remain a mystery.

26

Safety Culture

"The FAA will hold Boeing accountable."
—FAA ADMINISTRATOR MICHAEL WHITAKER, SEPTEMBER 25, 2024

ACCORDING TO OBSERVERS—usually critics—The Boeing Company has two cultures: corporate and safety. The corporate culture of "legacy" Boeing (that is, the company that existed before Boeing's merger with the McDonnell Douglas) was considered to be a collegial, engineering-based culture. After the merger, the corporate culture shifted to combative toxicity, critics say. Before the merger, safety was considered to be paramount. Post-merger, critics allege, safety gave way to shareholder value.

Boeing's two largest unions, the International Association of Machinists District 751 (IAM 751) and the Society of Professional Engineering Employees in Aerospace (SPEEA), had been warning for years that company policies on outsourcing work, including engineering, and cutting safety inspectors from union payrolls were endangering safety. These complaints were largely dismissed by management in its drive to cut costs and reduce union influence. The unions were only trying to protect jobs, some would say. They are disgruntled employees, others said.

Joseph Heller, the author of the satirical book *Catch-22*, wrote, "Just because you're paranoid doesn't mean they aren't after you." There's truth in this. And just because the unions may have been trying to protect member jobs or employees were disgruntled doesn't mean their complaints weren't valid. In fact, the MAX crisis demonstrated all too clearly that Boeing's safety culture was broken. Despite publicized efforts after the MAX was grounded to fix the culture, the Alaska flight 1282 accident five years later proved that not only was the safety culture *not* fixed, but one could also be forgiven for concluding that all the steps taken in 2019 were little more than PR moves aimed at fixing Boeing's image and not substantive steps to fix the safety culture.[127]

Boeing's critics point to the MDC merger and the "GEntrification" of the

---

127. Scott Hamilton, "Boeing's Safety Improvement Since the 2018-19 MAX Crisis Needs More Work," *Leeham News* (February 27, 2024), https://leehamnews.

company as the turning points. The influence of these two events clearly shifted Boeing away from its engineering roots and culture, and a case
may be reasonably made that safety suffered—although a convincing argument that trading safety for profits and shareholder value was a deliberate strategy is harder to make. Costs were cut across the entire enterprise chasing profits; safety was not singled out.

The reality is that the foundations of today's culture at Boeing were in
place decades before the merger. A retired Boeing employee who worked
for the company in the 1980s reached out after the Alaska accident to tell
this story.[128]

"Back in the late 80s, FAA [Federal Aviation Administration] concerns
about quality at Boeing forced Boeing to answer with [the] creation of the
O&IR [Operations and Inspection Record, the paper trail of work done on
an airplane] improvement program. In a nutshell, the QA [Quality Assur-
ance] inspection planners on the team would audit build plans against
engineering drawings and Boeing specs. Only critical plans were audited,
but we found thousands of errors, most of which were drawing requirements . . . such as 'inspect-verify torque, and record.'

"Planning and the factory hated this program despite results, and as
management changed, the program slowly disappeared. I don't know if
the program was implemented in the supplier program, but my later experience in the Airworthiness Directive Compliance world made it clear
that supplier quality issues were unsatisfied."

This employee added that he would audit the particular job against the
engineering drawing. "My mission was to ensure that all engineering requirements were met before that job was sent to the mechanics. Missing
requirements were documented on a Planning Action Request form, telling the planners of the missing requirements."

He said that a planner was supposed to review and correct any discrep-
ancy and return the corrective action to the auditor. In theory, the auditor would then verify that the changes were made. The paper trail during
those years was all manual, so verification was hit and miss.

"My supervisor and lead planner were very supportive of the project,
but lack of manpower and an overwhelming workload meant that we
didn't really do everything that, it could be argued, should be done. This

---

com/2024/02/27/boeings-safety-improvement-since-the-2018-19-max-crisis
-needs-more-work/.

128. After the MAX disasters and the Alaska accident, many current and past
Boeing employees reached out to regulators, investigators, Congress, and the
media to tell stories about safety concerns and retaliations that occurred at
Boeing for decades. The U.S. Department of Justice also subpoenaed employees.

project also increased the workload on planners, mechanics, and inspectors. There was very little support, generally, for this program. The weak spot, in my opinion, was the planners who wrote, 'shop jobs missed a lot of requirements made by the drawings.' There was no way to document compliance."

This employee said that there were other forms of jobs categorized as Not Audited, such as Rapid Revisions, removal/OK to install, and work performed by Blueline or Greenline. Inspectors also wrote "pickups" and rejection tags.

A Blueline is a job that is out of sequence in nature. For example, a production job installs black box "X." A pre-delivery design change requires black box "Z." The Blueline in this case would bring the airframe into compliance with current design. Another example could be that a modified functions test is required or that an FAA or customer inspection is now required.

A Greenline identifies when a fault of some kind is discovered. For example, if an installed component, like a wire bundle, was determined by engineering to have a design or manufacturing fault, a Greenline would be issued against all affected aircraft (pre-delivery) directing repair or replacement. This action could also drive a service bulletin against affected but delivered aircraft.

On occasion, the corrective action specified may be dependent upon the opinions of the players involved.

The retiree quoted above was employed on the 767 and 777 lines in Everett, Washington.

There was a saying that Boeing's stock symbol, BA, also stood for Boeing Arrogance. The tension between Boeing and its regulators is not new. And in reality, there is often tension between regulators and the companies regulated. Nor is tension between management and unions unique.

But with Boeing, tension with regulators has often involved safety issues. The disputes between Boeing and the UK's regulator over the 707's and the 727's stability have already been recounted. While tension between management and unions is usually centered around contract negotiations, at Boeing, for its two principal unions—SPEEA and the IAM 751—safety has often been at the heart of some of the conflicts. Unfortunately, antagonism between unions and management over contracts and job security often resulted in dismissal of many union safety concerns.

In a 2016 survey of more than 500 Boeing employees, worker responses cited safety concerns, feelings of pressure, and other complaints.[129]

---

129. Leslie Josephs and Thomas Franck, "Boeing Survey Showed Employees Felt Pressure from Managers on Safety Approvals," *CNBC.com* (October 20,2019)

Before the two MAX crashes there was little said by Boeing about safety, whether in public statements, in the company's financial and proxy filings, or on its website. In 2018, safety was barely mentioned. The 2019 proxy statement, prepared for the 2018 financial year, mentioned safety once. (The Lion Air accident happened in October 2018, and the Ethiopian accident occurred on March 10, 2019; the proxy statement was prepared before the Ethiopian accident for an April shareholders meeting.)

The 2021 proxy statement, for the 2020 financial year, mentioned safety 145 times; some of these mentions dealt with the COVID-19 pandemic and other issues.

Boeing in 2018 adopted a set of safety policies outlined in a Safety Management System, or SMS.[130] This is discussed in further detail below.

POST-MAX CRISIS SAFETY CULTURE

Following the 2018–2019 MAX crisis, Boeing took several steps to improve its safety culture. In September 2019, then-CEO Dennis Muilenburg named a "permanent" board-level safety committee, the Aerospace Safety Committee. It was headed by Boeing board member and retired admiral Edmund Giambastiani, Jr., a former vice chairman of the Pentagon's Joint Chiefs of Staff and a career nuclear submariner. Other board members named to the committee were Lynn Good, chairman, president, and CEO, Duke Energy Corporation, and Lawrence Kellner, president, Emerald Creek Group and former chairman and CEO of Continental Airlines. Other members of the committee were Sean O'Keefe, former NASA administrator and head of the Columbia space-shuttle accident investigation and CEO of EADS North America, at the time the parent company of Airbus North America; Richard Stanley, a retired engineer and vice president of GE Aviation; John Tracey, retired senior vice president chief engineer for Boeing; retired admiral Kirk Donald, director of the Navy nuclear propulsion program; Skip Bowman, another nuclear program expert, who participated in the BP safety review panel after the Deep Water Horizon oil rig disaster; and David Dunaway, former commander of Naval Air Systems procurement, testing, and evaluation. Airbus had originally been named to the committee, but it dropped off without explanation (probably due to the fact that Boeing's proprietary information would be revealed).

---

https://www.cnbc.com/2019/10/20/boeing-survey-shows-safety-workers-felt-pressure-from-managers-report.html.

130. Boeing, "Boeing Safety Management System Policy" (rev. September 2024), https://www.boeing.com/content/dam/boeing/boeingdotcom/principles/safety/SMS_Policy.pdf.

The Boeing Board of Directors also recommended the following:

- Realignment of the Engineering division and a new Product and Services Safety group whose members would report directly to the company's chief engineer, who now would report to Boeing's CEO.
- Enhancement of the Continued Operation Safety Program.
- Re-examination of the company's flight-deck design and operation. This was the result of the revelation that pilot training and expertise in certain parts of the world were not up to standards in the United States, Europe, and Eastern Asia.[131]
- Expansion of the role and reach of Boeing's Safety Promotion Center.

A week later, Muilenburg announced additional organization changes that would build on the elements listed immediately above.

Despite the rhetoric and policies, IAM 751 employees at Boeing continued to complain about the culture, which they said suppressed the willingness to bring safety concerns to the forefront. The *Wall Street Journal* reported in August 2022—more than two years after the Ethiopian accident—about an internal survey at Boeing that concluded that about 14 percent of those reporting to the FAA under the Organization Designation Authorization (ODA) program "perceived interference in their work on aircraft development and safety matters." This was an improvement over 2019 survey results, when 40 percent reported feeling pressure, the newspaper reported.[132]

While the atmosphere at Boeing improved between 2019, following the Ethiopian crash, and 2022, 24 percent of those surveyed in 2022 still felt

---

131. Recall that Lion Air had asked for simulator training on the MAX and was told by Boeing that it wasn't needed. Additionally, a former executive at Boeing's Commercial Airplanes division (BCA) told this author that when it came to certain parts of the world, he'd prefer being a passenger on the A320, with its computerized flight envelope protection against lesser-skilled pilots, than on a 737.

132. Andrew Tangel, "Boeing Employees Working on FAA's Behalf Report Less Interference," *Wall Street Journal* (August 25, 2022), https://www.wsj.com/articles/boeing-employees-working-on-faas-behalf-report-less-interference-11661432400. See also "What Is an ODA and Why Is It Critical to Understand It," *Leeham News* (February 14, 2024) ("The ODA program is how the FAA grants compartmentalized designee authority to organizations or companies for specific types of work. . . . The ODA designation means that you are allowed to be the FAA on their behalf and do their work on your items. This is a huge responsibility, and it is not lightly granted."), https://leehamnews.com/2024/02/14/what-is-an-oda-and-why-is-it-critical-to-understand-it/.

Boeing Top 5 Primary Offense Types

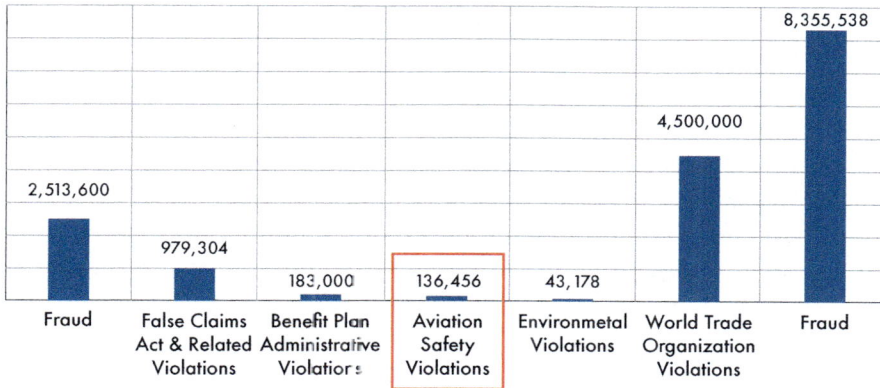

Figure 28. From 2000 through 2023, Boeing had thirty-three safety violations, the fines for which totaled $136.5 million. For a company the size of Boeing, these fines were merely the cost of doing business. Sources: FAA, WTO, ViolationTracker.com.

that retaliation was a concern (down from 37 percent in 2019). About 700 of the 1,000 ODA representatives responded to the survey, which was conducted on Boeing's behalf by the consulting firm Integrity Lab.

In April 2021, a tracking service recording Boeing fines from 2000 through 2020 revealed that the company paid more than $136 million in penalties for thirty-three safety violations. Among them, in 2015, were fines for failing to adhere to a previous safety-related settlement agreement. When viewed over a twenty-year span, this amounted to $6.8 million per year, which was pocket change to Boeing; at one point, the company reported more than $100 billion in revenues. During the same period, Boeing paid $2.5 billion in fraud penalties and another $979 million in false claims penalties to the U.S. government. The $136 million in fines imposed by the FAA was simply the cost of doing business. Just these three categories of fines (safety violations, fraud, false claims) total more than $3.66 billion—money that could have gone into product development at BCA and Boeing's Defense, Space & Security unit (BDS), employees' pockets, or shareholder value.

Aerospace analysts didn't seem to care about the fines, or even the huge program forward losses and charges. When Bank of America analyst Ron Epstein was asked once about this at an aviation conference in Lynnwood, Washington, the candid Epstein waved off the question, replying that analysts only cared about what's ahead, not what's behind.

One of the fines imposed on Boeing was related to the company's adoption of a voluntary Safety Management System (SMS).

Another now-retired Boeing employee, whose career included helping to create and implement the company's SMS and Quality Management System (QMS), told me that the FAA publicly stated that Boeing's voluntary

SMS would be made mandatory following the 2018–2019 MAX accidents. But the FAA did not mandate adoption of the system until after the 2024 Alaska accident.

"Boeing got a Level of Acceptance, as the FAA termed it, for their SMS," the former employee said. This "Level of Acceptance" meant that Boeing had systems in place to address how risks are brought to the attention of the FAA. "They have knowledge of it in complete transparency," but the system wasn't even completely in place in 2024, much less earlier.

"If you go to Boeing's public website [in February 2024], go see if they have anything in there about safety. If you go to Airbus's website, they have a huge, huge piece on, 'Here's what we do for safety.' You don't see that on the Boeing website. I pointed that out to my bosses years ago, 'How come Boeing doesn't have something about that?' Nobody responded to me about that. I'm not saying they don't care about safety. I'm not saying that. It's just like, 'Maybe you should stress that on the public website.'"

In 2020, Boeing announced that it found paper-thin gaps between fuselage sections on its 787. Deliveries would be suspended for twenty months while a fix was engineered, and, after repeated submissions to the FAA, approval was received. Then-CEO David Calhoun repeatedly claimed that Boeing had discovered the gap problem. The retired Boeing employee quoted above said that the FAA discovered the gaps during an audit.

A Boeing employee who left during one of the company's early buyouts went to work for a U.S. airline that operated A320s and 737s. He represented the airline during deliveries of both airplanes. His opinion: the A320 was the better airplane—quite the statement from a former long-time Boeing employee. The 737, including the MAX, does not include the sophisticated computerization found on the Airbus A320. Whereas the Airbus family of airplanes uses computers to prevent the pilots from exceeding a variety of flight scenarios within the flight envelop, the 737 gives more control to the pilot over some perilous flight conditions. Boeing touted this level of pilot control as a virtue. But the 737's roots dating all the way back to the original model led to a lot of issues with the MAX (or "Mad Max," as the former employee called the last 737 version; John Leahy, Airbus's super-salesman, also called the latest version the Mad Max, but for very different reasons.) "I just think the A320 is a much better airplane," the ex-Boeing employee said.

Boeing's installation of the Maneuvering Characteristics Augmentation System (MCAS) on the 737 MAX was intended as an automated flight-control system to push the nose of the plane down if a stall was deemed imminent. But the second version of the system went too far, and Boeing's decision to keep pilots in the dark about MCAS's existence was perhaps the fatal error.

"Just take a look at what's going on with the 787," the ex-employee said in 2023. "Here's a program that's twenty years old now. It was launched twenty years ago, 2003. They haven't delivered an airplane now in over a year, for crying out loud," due to the paper-thin gaps between fuselage sections.

"It goes back with the design philosophy," this employee continued. "I'm not saying it's a bad design. It's just the way Boeing designed the barrel sections and how they make, and they take up, the gaps from the imperfect manufacturing because there are going to be flaws. That's the whole issue with why they're having the gaps on the mating of the barrels. The gaps are exceeding the design drawing tolerances. It wasn't Boeing that discovered it, it was the FAA. Of course, the FAA's saying, 'Boeing, you're not going to deliver these airplanes until you get this squared away.'"

The FAA started raising these questions with Boeing, he said. The company acknowledged there was a problem. The FAA asked, "Well, what are you going to do about it?" and Boeing replied, "Well, I guess we're going to stop delivering until we figure this out."

At the time of this recounting in 2022, three years had passed since the second MAX crash, two years and five months had passed since Muilenburg and the board of directors announced safety changes, and two years and two months had passed since Calhoun succeeded Muilenburg as CEO. "They have a lot of work to do on their safety," a former Boeing safety official said.

Remarkably, Boeing still didn't seem to get the message. Following the Alaska flight 1282 non-fatal accident on a ten-week-old MAX 9, the safety culture issue again reared its head at Boeing. The same former Boeing employee interviewed in 2022 and quoted above, who maintained contact with former co-workers, lamented, "Boeing set up these processes for people to report any time there's a problem that they feel is going on without impunity, and I don't think it's working very well. Sadly, they have this direction of reducing the quality buybacks. It's all about leaning out the process. So many of us said 'You're going in the wrong direction.' There are different ways you can go to lean out the process and not do that. Here's a classic example of what happened on Alaska 1282, because you don't do that.

"This is systemic throughout the company. This isn't [just] in the 737 factory. It's in the 787 line in South Carolina. It's up in Everett. It's in St. Louis," the ex-employee said. Current employees remained afraid to identify problems through the company's Speak Up program, he said.

Boeing's Starliner space crew capsule has been troubled from the start. It was plagued with technical issues and was billions of dollars over budget and years late. Finally, in 2024, Boeing and NASA approved the maiden flight with two astronauts for what amounted to a giant test flight to the International Space Station (ISS). En route, some of the capsule's guidance rockets malfunctioned. NASA and Boeing wouldn't approve a manned return flight. As 2024 evolved into 2025, the two astronauts remained marooned at the ISS while the capsule successfully returned to earth after repairs to the rockets (nobody had confidence that the repairs would hold). In 2019, a Boeing employee at the Huntsville, Alabama, space facility raised concerns about the development of Starliner. His concerns fell on deaf ears. The astronauts didn't return home until well into 2025, using a SpaceX capsule for the return, and not Boeing's Starliner.

On January 5, 2023, the FAA named an independent group to review Boeing's commercial safety culture. The membership included people from the Massachusetts Institute of Technology, airlines, Boeing's unions, and other aerospace interests. Exactly one year later, the group was in the final stages of preparing a report when, ironically, the Alaska flight 1282 mishap occurred. The group extended its work while members debated whether to include a discussion of the Alaska accident. The report was finally issued on February 26, 2024, and it was blistering.[133] In its Executive Summary, the group (referred to as the Expert Panel) wrote the following:

- The Expert Panel observed a disconnect between Boeing's senior management and other members of the organization on safety culture. Interviewees, including ODA Unit Members (UM), also questioned whether Boeing's safety reporting systems would function in a way that ensures open communication and non-retaliation. The Expert Panel also observed inadequate and confusing implementation of the five components of a positive safety culture (Reporting Culture, Just Culture, Flexible Culture, Learning Culture, and Informed Culture).

- The Expert Panel found Boeing's SMS procedures reflect the International Civil Aviation Organization (ICAO) and the FAA SMS frameworks. However, the Boeing SMS procedures are not structured in a way that ensures all employees understand their role in the company's SMS. The procedures and training are complex and in a constant state of change, creating employee confusion especially among different work sites and employee groups. The Expert Panel also found a lack of awareness of safety-related metrics at all levels of the organization; employees had difficulty distinguishing the differences among various measuring methods, their purpose, and outcomes.

- Boeing's restructuring of the management of the ODA unit decreased opportunities for interference and retaliation against UMs, and provides effective organizational messaging regarding independence of

---

133. "Section103 Organization Designation Authorizations (ODA) for Transport Airplanes Expert Panel Review Report," https://www.faa.gov/sites/faa.gov/files/Sec103_ExpertPanelReview_Report_Final.pdf.

UMs. However, the restructuring, while better, still allows opportunities for retaliation to occur, particularly with regards to salary and furlough ranking. This influences the ability of UMs to execute their delegated functions effectively.

- The Expert Panel also found additional issues at Boeing that affect aviation safety, which include inadequate human factors consideration commensurate to its importance to aviation safety and lack of pilot input in aircraft design and operation.

The Expert Panel's reference to the much-maligned ODA program caused *Leeham News* to report that Boeing previously had been fined for violating an agreement over the ODA program.[134] On February 29, 2024, the FAA gave Boeing ninety days to come up with a new, actionable ODA process.

FAA Administrator Mike Whitaker was blunt: "Boeing must commit to real and profound improvements. Making foundational change will require a sustained effort from Boeing's leadership, and we are going to hold them accountable every step of the way, with mutually understood milestones and expectations." The nuclear option the FAA held in reserve was suspending Boeing's production certificate. This extreme action was unlikely, but at a press conference on March 11, 2024, Whitaker raised the possibility.[135]

Boeing had pledged full cooperation with the Expert Panel. But deep within its report, the Panel wrote that Boeing lawyers pre-interviewed at least some of those who were going to appear before the Panel. One can't help but conclude that these briefings had an intimidating effect on the employees or at the very least resulted in inhibiting cooperation.

"Each interview with Boeing employees started with an opening statement that the Expert Panel was 'very interested in hearing your perspective on each topic.' However, it appeared to some Expert Panel members that Boeing employees viewed the Expert Panel's work as an audit; not an opportunity to collaborate. Interviewees asked minimal questions of the experts. Some interviewees mentioned a briefing was provided by Boeing legal prior to the interviews," the report said.

---

134. Scott Hamilton, "Pontifications: Boeing Violated Previous FAA ODA, SMS Demands—Been There, Done That," *Leeham News* (March 5, 2024), https://leehamnews.com/2024/03/05/pontifications-boeing-violating-previous-faa-oda-sms-demands-been-there-done-that/.

135. "'If Something Requires Us to Cease Production, We Will Do That': FAA," *Leeham News* (March 13, 2024), https://leehamnews.com/2024/03/13/if-something-requires-us-to-cease-production-we-will-do-that-faa/.

Within a few weeks of the Alaska 1282 incident, I asked Boeing about the results of the Giambastiani Aerospace Safety Committee's work. The Corporate Communications team responded with a long list of things Boeing had done. But information regarding implementation and accomplishments, along with data supporting the claimed improvements, was absent.[136]

After Alaska flight 1282 and the revelations that Boeing's safety culture was far from fixed, the FAA clamped down on the company even more. Calhoun in January 2024 announced a new panel to conduct a safety review, this time from the outside and once again headed by a retired admiral from the nuclear submarine navy.[137] As of May 2025, no report has been publicly issued.

---

136. "Boeing Board Aerospace Safety Committee Recommends Realignment, Enhancement of Procedures," *Leeham News* (September 25, 2019), https://leehamnews.com/2019/09/25/boeing-board-aerospace-safety-committee-recommends-realignment-enhancement-of-procedures/.

137. "Pontifications: Boeing Turns to US Navy Admiral for Second Time in Max Crises (January 23, 2024), https://leehamnews.com/2024/01/23/pontifications-boeing-turns-to-us-navy-admiral-for-second-time-in-max-crises/.

27

"It Ain't Over Till It's Over"

—YOGI BERRA, MANAGER, NEW YORK METS, 1973

THE BOEING COMPANY HOPED that the Deferred Prosecution Agreement (DPA) imposed upon it by the U.S. Department of Justice (DOJ) as a result of the MAX crashes put to rest those liabilities. But some families of the victims relentlessly pushed for the federal court in Texas that approved the agreement to reverse itself.

Yogi Berra was a famous catcher and, later, manager of the New York Yankees and a manager of the crosstown team the New York Mets. He was one of baseball's great players. He also became known for his life observations and philosophical sayings, such as, "when you come to a fork in the road, take it." Another had to do with a pennant race in which his team was trailing. In another take on life, Berra replied, "It ain't over till it's over."

Boeing was about to experience this principle in spades.

After the January 2024 Alaska Airlines accident—which occurred just days before the expiration of the DPA would have let Boeing off the hook—the DOJ opened a new inquiry into whether Boeing had lived up to the terms of the DPA. As recounted in more detail below, grand jury investigations were opened in Los Angeles and Seattle. The DOJ concluded that Boeing failed to live up to the terms of the DPA. Boeing, as a company, was criminally charged again. Unlike the first time, however, no individuals were charged, a decision that once more came under criticism from victims' families.

As with the first case, the DOJ once again entered into a DPA.[138] Boeing pled guilty and was to pay a criminal fine of $244 million, the same amount as under the first DPA. Boeing also agreed to spend at least $455 million on safety protocols. The DOJ, which had been savagely criticized the first time around for the amount of the total fines it imposed ($688 million), made a point of saying that the fine was the maximum amount allowable under law.

---

138. U.S. Department of Justice, Criminal Division, United States v. The Boeing Company, Deferred Prosecution Agreement (DPA) (December 2024), https://www.justice.gov/criminal/criminal-fraud/case/united-states-v-boeing-company. See also United States v. The Boeing Company, Docket No. 4:21-cr-00005-O, Government Status Report and Proposed Plea Agreement (N.D. Tex. July 24, 2024), https://www.justice.gov/criminal/media/1361546/dl?inline.

The victims' families weren't satisfied with the new DPA or with the fact that no individuals were held accountable. Lawyers filed motions in Texas federal court to overturn this latest DPA.

Among the provisions in the second DPA was an agreement between Boeing and the DOJ that a special Independent Compliance Monitor of Boeing would be created and deployed. "The Government will select and oversee the Independent Compliance Monitor. With respect to selection, the Government will post on its public website a request for proposals from potential monitor candidates, and, with feedback from Boeing, select a candidate that meets the specific qualifications articulated in the public posting and the general qualifications articulated in the Criminal Division's Revised Memorandum on Selection of Monitors in Criminal Division Matters," the DOJ wrote in its court filing.

The families objected to one step in the process of the Monitor's selection: the application of Diversity, Equity, and Inclusion (DEI) policies in the selection of the Monitor. They also objected to a provision in the agreement stating that the Monitor would not report to the court but, rather, to the DOJ. (There were other objections, but these were the two key ones.)

On December 5, 2024, the U.S. District Court for the Northern District of Texas rejected the DPA.[139] "Among the Court's priorities at this point is to ensure Boeing adheres to an ethics and anti-fraud compliance program overseen by an independent monitor during Boeing's probation. As explained below, the plea agreement requires the parties to consider race when hiring the independent monitor. Additionally, the plea agreement marginalizes the Court in the selection and monitoring of the independent monitor. These provisions are inappropriate and against the public interest," wrote Judge Reed O'Conner at the beginning of his order rejecting the DPA.

"The plea agreement prohibits imposing as a condition of probation a requirement for Boeing to comply with the monitor's anti-fraud recommendations. Additionally, the independent monitor is selected by and reports to the Government, not the Court. Moreover, Boeing will have the opportunity to prevent the hiring of one of the six monitor candidates chosen by the Government. And finally, the Government will select the independent monitor 'in keeping with the Department's commitment to diversity and inclusion,'" O'Conner continued.

The judge recounted a history of the practices used by Boeing and the DOJ in following DEI goals and policies before concluding, "In a case of this magnitude, it is in the utmost interest of justice that the public is confident this monitor selection is done based solely on competency.

---

139. United States v. The Boeing Company, Docket No. 4:21-CR-5-O, Order (N.D. Tex. December 5, 2024), https://www.justice.gov/criminal/media/1379296/dl?inline.

The parties' DEI efforts only serve to undermine this confidence in the Government and Boeing's ethics and anti-fraud efforts. Accordingly, the diversity-and-inclusion provision renders the plea agreement against the public interest."[140]

He also objected to the "marginalization of the Court."

"The plea agreement's process for selecting the anti-fraud monitor, including prohibiting the Court from considering violations of the monitor's anti-fraud recommendations, improperly marginalizes the Court. The Government has monitored Boeing for three years now," O'Conner wrote. "Boeing hints that it may have legitimate arguments in opposition to the Government's determination of breach. Regardless, taken as true that Boeing breached the DPA, it is fair to say the Government's attempt to ensure compliance has failed. At this point, the public interest requires the Court to step in."

The timing of the court's rejection of the DPA was inconvenient, to say the least. With the reelection of Donald Trump, a Trump Administration DOJ was left with following through on the court order. It was the first Trump DOJ that entered into the first DPA and pursued criminal charges against one mid-level Boeing employee who was widely viewed as a scapegoat by critics. That defendant was ultimately acquitted in a federal trial in Texas.

It was unclear what would happen next. The DOJ could appeal the ruling, drop the case, modify conditions to comply with the court, or prosecute Boeing in a trial. (In May 2025, Trump's DOJ abandoned the DPA and entered into a non-prosecution agreement with the same penalties but no criminal plea. The judge accepted this.)

The stakes were high for Boeing, on paper at least. The biggest threat to the company was that it could be eliminated from bidding on future government work. Boeing is one of the nation's largest defense contractors, so elimination would be a big deal for Boeing and for the Pentagon.[141] In reality, it seems unlikely that the Pentagon will implement this penalty; it hadn't done so following the tanker scandal (see Chapter 4 for more details) and after trade-secret theft cases involving Lockheed Martin.[142]

This is another of the messes that incoming Boeing CEO Kelly Ortberg would inherit and be faced with cleaning up.

---

140. After he took office on January 20, 2025, President Donald Trump purged the federal government of all DEI policies and requirements.

141. Given Boeing's recent history of poor program performance and billions of dollars in write-offs, one cynic noted that the Pentagon and shareholders might be better off if Boeing were eliminated from future contract bids.

142. Boeing dodged this bullet when, in March 2025, it won a $20 billion contract for the sixth-generation fighter, the F-47. See Chapter 34.

28

Monday Morning Massacre

"[Boeing has shown] a complete abdication of leadership."
—CONSULTANT RICHARD ABOULAFIA AT A CONFERENCE IN 2023

ON MONDAY, MARCH 25, 2024, at 5 a.m. Pacific time (8 a.m. Eastern), The Boeing Company dropped a bombshell. Stan Deal, the CEO of Boeing's Commercial Airplanes division (BCA), was "retiring." Larry Kellner, non-executive chairman of the company's board of directors, would not stand for reelection. David Calhoun, Boeing's CEO, would retire at the end of the year. Stephanie Pope, who had been named the preceding December as executive vice president (EVP) and chief operating officer and had assumed office in January, became Deal's successor in addition to her role as corporate COO. The day has been described as Boeing's "Monday Morning Massacre."

Changes were sorely needed, but these were met with mixed feelings. Kellner would remain on the board until the May 17 shareholders meeting as a lame duck. Steven Mollenkopf, who became a director in 2020, was named chairman. When he joined the board, some believed that he would be a contender to become CEO when Calhoun eventually retired. Some believed that he still wanted Calhoun's job as a new search began for the CEO's successor.

As for Calhoun, some believed that he should have been canned immediately instead of remaining CEO until the end of the year. After all, Calhoun failed to deliver on most of the mandates given to him by the board when he was named CEO in January 2020. Richard Aboulafia, an industry consultant, nominated Calhoun as the worst CEO Boeing ever had. Calhoun said that he would be around to help the board pick his successor. When Pope moved from CEO of Boeing Global Services (BGS) to EVP and COO of the corporation, it was widely assumed that she was being anointed by Calhoun as his successor. This was reinforced on April 24, 2024, when Calhoun appeared on the financial news network CNBC following the release of Boeing's first quarter numbers. Calhoun praised Pope and later, in the company's formal earnings call, told analysts that there was an internal candidate (whom he did not name at the time) who he thought was well qualified to succeed him.

Pope's appointment, first as COO of the corporation and then, additionally, as CEO of BCA succeeding Deal, was met with widespread skepticism. She came to Boeing from McDonnell Douglas (MDC) when the two firms merged, a strike against her in the minds of some—but that was twenty-seven years earlier and, by 2024, it could be argued that she was a "Boeing" person. More to the point was that Pope was another MBA, not an engineer, who spent her entire career at Boeing in finance until being named CEO of BGS, where she succeeded Deal. Deal, who also came to Boeing at the time of the MDC merger, was considered by some to be Pope's mentor. A few pointed out that BGS's profits increased under Pope. But when Pope became BGS's CEO after Deal moved to BCA in October 2019 after Kevin McAllister was fired and when the MAX was in its seventh month of grounding, BGS revenues and profits were down. After the COVID pandemic erupted in March 2020, airlines needed even fewer services from BGS. But once the pandemic was over, the grounding was lifted, airlines recovered, and profits and revenues at BGS had nowhere to go but up. Deal's successor at BGS was in a position to shine regardless of who took over from him.

Pope didn't have any program, production, or hands-on experience that qualified her to succeed Deal at BCA, nor, for that matter, to become CEO of Boeing. The last thing, under the circumstances, that the company and its BCA division needed was another MDC financial type who, it was assumed and feared, was another shareholder-value advocate. What the two organizations needed, many suggested, was someone along the lines of Alan Mulally (BCA's CEO from 1998 to 2006), Pat Shanahan (who served in several leadership positions at Boeing between 1986 and 2017), or Ray Conner (who served in several leadership positions at Boeing between 1977 and 2017).

Within six weeks of Pope's appointment as CEO of BCA, word began to emerge that she was spending time on the production floor talking to line workers. She was initially compared favorably to Deal, who, it was reported, didn't really resonate with line workers. (The labor unions' leadership complained that they saw little of Deal after he became BCA's CEO.) As time went on, however, Pope was tagged with the unflattering nickname, Stephanie Hopeless.

As the weeks rolled by, the most common chatter among analysts, consultants, and observers was that Shanahan should succeed Calhoun and Pope should succeed Brian West as CFO of the corporation. There was no obvious name to become CEO of BCA, but there was general agreement that it should not be Ihssane Mounir, whose leadership style as the top salesman at BCA was often criticized inside and outside of the company. Elizabeth Lund, who was a respected manager of several programs at Boeing and was named by Calhoun to lead the safety crisis rehabilitation effort after the Alaska Airlines accident, was an obvious choice. But, according to one source, Lund wanted to retire before the COVID pandemic and had to be talked into staying. This made it unlikely that she would agree to become BCA's CEO if offered the job. She would retire after the new corporate CEO Kelly Ortberg assumed office in August 2024.

Calhoun, in addition to announcing that he would stay on as CEO through 2024, also stood for reelection to the company's board of directors. Boeing's board is structured with one-year terms for members, so if Calhoun were to serve his entire term, that would take him to the spring of 2025. His staying on as CEO drew criticism in many quarters. His announced intention to contribute to the efforts to choose his successor was derided because his tenure as CEO was now considered a failure. As for staying on the board—one shareholder advocate group urged that his reelection be rejected by shareholders.

Calhoun's 2023 compensation package of $34 million also drew widespread complaints. By the time Calhoun announced he would leave his post at the end of 2024, he had been CEO for fifty months. (As it turned out, Calhoun left his CEO position on August 7, 2024. Kelly Ortberg succeeded him the next day. Calhoun's 2024 compensation was $15 million.) Initially viewed as a badly needed breath of fresh air following former CEO Dennis Muilenburg's disastrous handling of the MAX crisis, Calhoun quickly proved to have his own foibles. As recounted earlier, he quickly stumbled in his very first press briefing upon taking office on January 13, 2020. This incident was compounded by other embarrassing foot-in-mouth statements.

Almost every executive at some point makes major a faux pas. Former Boeing CEO James McNerney famously said that he'd be around for employees to "cower" at his leadership. He had to apologize for this, because the ill-advised attempt at levity backfired spectacularly. Calhoun pulled back on media interviews after his missteps, giving them to only the most friendly of forums thereafter. What mattered more was how his leadership affected Boeing's recovery. And on this score, it can be argued that Calhoun fell short.

The safety failures at BCA have been widely reported. Since the 2018–2019 MAX crisis, fixing the company's problems had been laid at the feet of Calhoun. He became CEO in January 2020. But he was lead director before that and chairman of Boeing's board from October through December 2019. Members of any board of directors are, by their very nature, dependent upon information provided by the executive team of the company they serve. Directors are supposed to look out for shareholders and provide oversight. During Calhoun's time, Boeing's board had a history of, some would say, rubber stamping executive actions, preferring shareholder value over strategic importance, and failing to adequately oversee or recognize Boeing's long descent into mediocrity.

In one two-week period beginning in April 2024, Boeing's engineers' union, the Society of Professional Engineering Employees in Aerospace (SPEEA), alleged that the company retaliated against two employees who were serving as Federal Aviation Administration (FAA) representatives[143] and who raised production issues. Whistleblowers came forward questioning the production safety of the 777 and 787[144] and of production patterns in general.[145] SPEEA and Boeing reached an impasse over how a new proposed safety program would be crafted.[146]

CALHOUN'S OTHER PERFORMANCE ISSUES

Calhoun took over the CEO position at a time when Boeing was in crisis. The MAX had been grounded for nine months, and there was no indication as to when the grounding would end. (The grounding eventually consumed twenty-one months' time.) Two months after he became CEO, the global COVID-19 pandemic hit. Governments around the world locked down societies. Commercial aviation travel grounded to near-zero levels. Airlines and lessors deferred aircraft deliveries.

Boeing's cash flow, already under stress because of the MAX grounding, worsened. Then, in October 2020, Boeing suspended deliveries of the 787 for what turned out to be nearly twenty-one months because of production-quality failures.

At the peak, Boeing had 450 737s and 110 787s assembled and stored, tying up billions of dollars in production costs and resulting in a loss of cash flow and profits.

The lingering effects of the pandemic shutdown continue to this day. Suppliers (to both Boeing and Airbus) at all levels still have labor shortages. Quality control remains an issue with many of them.

---

143. SPEEA, "Labor Complaint to Secure More Information, SPEEA Alleges Retaliation in Boeing ODA Case" (April 23, 2024), https://speea.org/Communications/PressReleases/Press_Releases_2024/ODA%20ULP%20press%20release_4_23_24.pdf.

144. Dominic Gates, "Boeing Whistleblowers Describe 'Criminal Cover-Up," Safety Risks to Senate," *Seattle Times* (April 17, 2024), https://www.seattletimes.com/business/boeing-aerospace/boeing-hid-safety-risks-in-criminal-cover-up-whistleblowers-tell-senate/.

145. Niraj Chokshi, "Former Boeing Manager Says Workers Mishandled Parts to Meet Deadlines," *New York Times* (April 24, 2024), https://www.nytimes.com/2024/04/24/business/boeing-airlines-plane-issues.html

146. https://leehamnews.com/2024/04/23/speea-boeing-at-impasse-over-safety-program-union-says/.

Boeing's defense unit programs were in bad shape, too. The T-7 Red Hawk trainer, the unmanned MQ-25 aerial-refueling tanker, the KC-46A manned aerial-refueling tanker, the SLS space booster, the Starliner space capsule, and the Air Force One 747-8 programs were all late and over budget, most by billions of dollars. Even legacy jet-fighter programs were losing money. Many of these programs were entered into under fixed-price contracts, some dating to the McNerney administration and others to Muilenburg's. Billions of dollars in cost overruns had to be absorbed by Boeing.

Calhoun bemoaned these fixed-price contracts Boeing was awarded as the root cause of many of the company's losses. He has, on occasion, laid the blame on his predecessor, Dennis Muilenburg. But Calhoun's position on the board of directors meant, ultimately, that he shared the responsibility for approving these contracts.

And, in March 2024, Boeing had more than $40 billion in net debt to pay down.

In addition to all this, Calhoun's mission was also to restore Boeing's tattered relationship with the FAA. But as 2023 ended, the FAA still retained ticketing authority for the 737 and 787 (meaning the agency revoked Boeing's ability to certify its planes as airworthy) and exercised detailed control over a wide variety of processes. Then, after the Alaska flight 1282 accident, the FAA upped its scrutiny even more. The FAA "capped" Boeing's 737 production rate at thirty-eight per month and flooded its factory with inspectors. The cap was really symbolic. Boeing hadn't produced at this rate since before the grounding. New production hovered plus-or-minus twenty a month, for several reasons. The supply chain was still running behind, having never fully recovered from the layoffs during the pandemic. Boeing's own production workforce, trimmed by the thousands during the grounding and the pandemic, was replaced by new hires who had to be trained. The learning curve was still immature. Spirit AeroSystems was delivering flawed fuselages (and nose sections for the 787), requiring assembly-line slow-downs and rework along various stages of production.

On February 26, 2024, the FAA released an overdue safety report (see Chapter 26 for more details) by an Expert Panel it had appointed on January 5, 2023—exactly one year to the day before the Alaska accident.[147] The FAA's displeasure was apparent. Three days later, on February 29, the agency gave Boeing ninety days to come up with a plan to fix the safety concerns outlined in the report.

---

147. "Breaking News: Congressionally-Mandated Safety Study Finds Flaws at Boeing (Updated with Boeing Content)," *Leeham News* (February 26, 2024), https://leehamnews.com/2024/02/26/ breaking-news-congressionally-mandate-safety-study-finds-flaws-at-boeing/.

There was more to come. On May 6, 2024, stories broke that some records on the 787 production line had been falsified. It turned out that in April of that year, an employee spotted discrepancies in production records at the company's Charleston, South Carolina, plant. He notified his manager, who alerted executives, who told the FAA. Boeing issued a media statement praising the reporting employee for raising a flag, citing this as an example of how its Speaking Up program was supposed to work. The statement was a nice punt, but, as *Aviation Week* noted, record falsification is about as bad as it gets.[148] More black headlines were generated.

INVESTIGATIONS

Within days of the Alaska Airlines accident, the FBI issued subpoenas for a criminal investigation. Grand juries were empaneled in Los Angeles and Seattle—though why the FBI's office in L.A., where Boeing had only an ancillary presence, was involved was not known. The involvement of the FBI in Seattle, and the location of a grand jury there, made sense; BCA's headquarters was located there, and Boeing's 737 factory is in suburban Seattle in Renton, both in King County.

The L.A. subpoenas were issued within three weeks of the Alaska accident. The paperwork indicated that a criminal probe was underway, but why this was and what it covered what was not detailed. The information requested related to Alaska flight 1282, but the nature of the criminal investigation was not included in the FBI letter accompanying the subpoenas.

Bloomberg News reported on March 15, 2024, that Spirit AeroSystems had also been subpoenaed.[149] The news agency revealed that the criminal probe was not only looking at the Alaska accident, but also at whether Boeing had failed to live up to all the terms of its January 2021 Deferred Prosecution Agreement (DPA) with the U.S. Department of Justice (DOJ), approved in the waning days of the first Trump Administration. The DPA expired two days after the Alaska accident, contingent upon Boeing living up to the terms of the agreement, which mandated certain safety and reporting procedures. If the investigation were to conclude that Boeing failed

---

148. Sean Broderick, "Some 787 Production Test Records Were Falsified, Boeing Says," *Aviation Week* (May 6, 2024), https://aviationweek.com/air-transport/some-787-production-test-records-were-falsified-boeing-says.

149. Chris Strohm, Julie Johnsson, and Greg Farrell, "Boeing Criminal Probe Widens with Seattle Grand Jury Subpoena," *Bloomberg.com* (March 15, 2024), https://www.bloomberg.com/news/articles/2024-03-15/boeing-criminal-probe-widens-with-seattle-grand-jury-subpoena.

to follow through on the terms, DOJ—by now under the Biden Administration—could pursue criminal charges.

The FBI later wrote to passengers who had been on flight 1282, informing them that they may have been victims of a crime. Once more, no details were included in those notices. But local news outlets were told that it was possible that records related to the door-plug work on the ill-fated aircraft may have been deleted from Boeing's records. Nothing was ever confirmed on this score; Boeing told the National Transportation Safety Board (NTSB) only that the records didn't exist. But of all the records that Boeing generates, for these to be missing was suspicious at best.

With the DOJ, FBI, and grand jury investigations underway, in addition to the NTSB and FAA probes, the U.S. House and Senate announced their own congressional hearings.

It was déjà vu all over again, invoking memories of the 2019–2020 investigations into the two MAX accidents. (Then, the U.S. Department of Transportation's Inspector General also opened an investigation.)

By May 2024, the federal Securities and Exchange Commission (SEC) announced that it had opened a probe into whether Boeing had made misleading statements about its safety practices that could have misled investors. The company's stock was off nearly a third since January 5 of that year, closing on May 10 at $178.79. (The low year-to-date figure was $164.33.) Boeing was one of the worst performing stocks on the Dow Jones.

It had been just over two weeks since Boeing reported its first-quarter financial results—encompassing the first period following the Alaska accident. The numbers were ugly, especially for what was supposed to be a year of continued recovery. Corporate revenues were down 8 percent compared with the same period in 2023, from $17.9 to $16.6 billion. Boeing actually reported a narrower operating loss ($86 million to $149 million), but this was on lower one-time year-over-year charges, and a profit—finally—for its defense unit and continued healthy results for BGS. BCA, however, had a whopping 24.6 percent negative margin due to lower 737 deliveries and the MAX 9 grounding.

Operating cash flow was a stunning negative $3.36 billion compared with a negative $318 million in 2023. After other cash usage, the company's net negative cash flow was more than $3.9 billion in the first quarter of 2024 compared with a negative $786 million the year before.

Boeing ended the quarter with $7.5 billion in cash and marketable securities, compared with $16 billion on December 31. A good portion of the cash reduction was due to paying down debt. There was $47.9 billion in debt on March 31 compared with $52.3 billion on December 31. But the cash and debt figures were a little bit misleading, albeit not materially so under accounting rules. To bolster its cash position and avoid adding to its debt, Boeing quietly struck a deal with at least one customer, and possibly more, to generate enough cash to pay compensation to Alaska and United, the two airlines most adversely affected by the MAX grounding. Structured as a big deposit for airplane orders not yet placed or for progress payments not yet received, Boeing could bury these transactions in "deposits" or "advance payments" and keep the cash advances off the debt line on the balance sheet. In an unusual move, Boeing agreed to pay interest to the customers for the cash advances.

These moves were a variation of what some called accounting tricks that Boeing had used for years. To meet free-cash-flow objectives set by executives and guided toward aerospace analysts, Boeing frequently agreed with customers to advance progress payments early from one quarter to the preceding quarter to meet its numbers. Until *Leeham News* revealed this trick, analysts didn't have a clue. But once the maneuver became known, analysts were on the lookout for repetitive advances. Even though this became commonplace, analysts didn't seem to care, and investors only looked at how Boeing met, exceeded, or perhaps fell short of guidance. Shifting progress payments from one quarter to the preceding quarter was, of course, a form of robbing Peter to pay Paul.

Boeing's financial performance in the first quarter of 2024 was a disaster. And the 737 line was a disaster. The 737 production rate, which was supposed to be thirty-eight per month, rarely came anywhere close to this. Even before 2023 became 2024, Boeing couldn't meet its target production rates on either the 737 or 787. In fact, rates of new-airplane production commonly ran in the low-to-mid-twenties and occasionally even in the high teens. The 787 production rate was supposed to be at five per month by the end of 2023. In reality, three was the more common number.

As with the cash data, Boeing executives were less than forthcoming over the true production rates. Analysts, however, were on to Boeing. Using publicly available data and an established history of Boeing's own numbers, analysts figured that of any given month's reported deliveries, "X" number (usually between eight and ten but potentially lower) came from the inventory of MAXs parked throughout Washington state and elsewhere. Simple math concluded that new-production airplanes numbered between seventeen and twenty-five in any given month. The same method was used to calculate 787 production rates.

On the first-quarter earnings call on April 24, 2024, officials fessed up to the true rates.

ANOTHER DAY, ANOTHER BLACK HEADLINE

Bad news kept on coming. Like a bad coin constantly rejected by a vending machine, it seemed that each day brought another black headline for Boeing. Unfairly, a string of airline incidents on Boeing airplanes generated headlines that a "Boeing" airplane did this or that. A Delta 757 lost a nose-wheel tire on takeoff. So did a United 777. A United 737-8 MAX went off a taxiway at Houston's George Bush Intercontinental Airport. An older 737-800 Next-Gen airplane left a runway on landing—and so on. None of these incidents had anything to do with Boeing per se. They all were airline-related. But because the name of the airplane was "Boeing," Boeing got the headline. And it would be weeks or months before the mainstream media would tumble into the fact that Airbus airplanes were similarly involved in like incidents. Nevertheless, Boeing's thumping continued.

But there were substantive incidents that were, in fact, Boeing's fault. The Starliner manned space capsule, already seven years late, had last gone to space in 2019 on the watch of CEO Dennis Muilenburg. Embarrassingly for Muilenburg, under fire for his handling of the two MAX crashes and for problems at Boeing's defense division, the Starliner flight failed to achieve orbit due to a simple software-programming issue that never should have happened. Five *years* later, Starliner was ready to return to test flights, this time with test-pilot astronauts. Once more, failure happened. The launch was scrubbed when a valve didn't work.

The T-7 Red Hawk trainer and the MQ-25 unmanned aircraft added more delays and more costs to these already troubled programs at Boeing. Converting two 747-8Is from a commercial design to the presidential fleet as Air Force One continued to be a costly mess, with more delays and more write-offs. The KC-46A tanker racked up more losses. New flaws in the 787 were discovered as new whistleblowers came forward. Then, in May 2024, as mentioned above, news broke that employees at the 787 Charleston plant had falsified records in assembling the airplane. In April of that year, one employee discovered some suspicious-looking records. He brought them to the attention of his manager, who alerted executives. Boeing alerted the FAA and released an email from a 787 program executive to employees praising the reporting employee and touting the new atmosphere in which employees were encouraged to come forward with reports.

This was all well and good, but it came after yet another whistleblower had come forward, first to the media and then to Congress in a hearing, claiming retaliation. He charged that production of the 777 Classic and 787 was so flawed that Boeing was delivering unsafe airplanes and stated that the in-service fleets of the planes should be grounded. In damage-control mode, Boeing hastily arranged a press gig in Charleston with Internet access for reporters who couldn't pick up and go to the 787 plant on short notice. The whistleblower was inaccurate, Boeing responded. The whistleblower, within a few weeks, filed a formal complaint with the federal government claiming that he was being subjected to continuing retaliation. Other whistleblowers came forward, citing other complaints.

All this, predictably, generated one black headline after another.

"FANTASY LAND"

While all this was going on, Boeing's stock price continued to fall. Between January 2, 2024, the first trading day of the year, and April 24, the price tanked by 29 percent. Except for March 20, 2020, when the pandemic shut down the world and Boeing's stock price hit a low of $95.01, and September 30, 2022, when the stock price was $120.70, the April 24 price was at its low point under Calhoun. The stock was $329.92 on January 10, 2020, the Friday before the Monday Calhoun became CEO. On May 17, 2024, the date of Boeing's last annual shareholders' meeting under Calhoun, the stock price was $184.95, down 44 percent from the day he took office.

Since its 1997 merger with MDC, Boeing wrote off more than $70 billion in charges, forward losses, and government fines. Among the latter: nearly $164 million for thirty-six safety violations, according to the website Violation Tracker.[150] Boeing had more fines by dollar volume ($4.2 billion, boosted by the MAX DPA) than any other aerospace company doing business in the United States. The number of fines, 122, ranked third, after General Dynamics (161) and RTX Corporation (130).

Under Calhoun's four-year CEO tenure, through 2023, Boeing wrote off $31.5 billion. Under Muilenburg (who served for three years), the figure was $21.98 billion. Both regimes were affected by the MAX crisis. McNerney (ten years) wrote off $11.66 billion. Harry Stonecipher, CEO for a mere two years, wrote off $3.3 billion. Phil Condit (four years) wrote off $4.7 billion.

By division, BCA cost the company more than $44.66 billion in charges, forward losses, and write-offs since the MDC merger—61 percent of total charges. (Another $2.3 billion was written off by Boeing Capital Corporation (BCC), Boeing's commercial airplanes leasing arm until it was disbanded in 2023. BCC was the new name for the McDonnell Douglas Finance Corporation, inherited by Boeing in the MDC merger.) The KC-46A tanker and its predecessor, the KC-767 tanker, accumulated $7.87 billion in charges through 2023.

Performance issues at BCA that led to charges involved the 737 NG and MAX, the 747-8, the 777X, and the 787; a minor charge for the end of production of the 757 and a small-end-of production charge on the 717

---

150. Scott Hamilton, "Pontifications: Boeing Violated Previous FAA ODA, SMS Demands—Been There, Done That," *Leeham News* (March 5, 2024), https://leehamnews.com/2024/03/05/ pontifications-boeing-violating-previous-faa-oda-sms-demands-been-there-done-that/.

(nee MD-95) were also incurred. The charges involving the company's KC-46A/767 tankers, based on the commercial 767, are in this analysis considered defense program charges.

Given Boeing's performance on its commercial MAX, 747-8, 787, and 777X programs, a systemic problem appeared obvious. But to the company's executives and board of directors, shareholder value and executive and board compensation appeared to be more important. For a company whose board of directors placed so much emphasis on shareholder value, the write-offs and charges logged by Boeing—which amounted to more than $73 billion from 1997 through 2023—was a stunning number that could have gone to shareholder value and new airplane programs. Another $4 billion went out the door for fines.

To be fair, write-offs, charges, and fines are part of doing business. But Boeing's executives—and its boards of directors—seemed oblivious to the systemic waste. For comparison, Airbus wrote off 33 billion euros (€) between 1999 and 2023 (about half that of Boeing during the same period). The military A400M Atlas (or "Albatross" to others) accounted for nearly one third of Airbus's write-offs. The A380 accounted for €3.7 billion in write-offs.[151]

It was now clear to most that Boeing's November 2022 Investor Day outlook of a production rate of fifty per month for the 737, ten per month for the 787, and $10 billion in free cash flow was in jeopardy. Analyst Seth Seifman of JP Morgan opined that Boeing's ability to meet those production rates would be set back by about two years and that the company's free cash flow would move to the right accordingly. But Boeing executives told a different story. On earnings calls for the year 2023 and for the first quarter of 2024, Calhoun and CFO Brian West still painted a rosy picture for 2025/2026 target dates.

Robert Stallard, an aerospace analyst with Vertical Research, perhaps summed it up best in his note about the first-quarter earnings release.

> **"Fantasy Land** – If there has been one thing that has been consistent about Boeing over our many years of covering the company it has been its hopelessly optimistic timetables for improvement. We think this will again be the case with what has been set out today, with management seemingly nonchalant about the regulatory, political, legal, contractual, customer,

---

151. "Airbus Charges and Write-Offs Since 1999: More Than €33bn," *Leeham News*, https://leehamnews.com/2024/04/08/airbus-charges-and-write-offs-since-1999-more-than-e33bn/.

competitive, supply chain, and internal employee pressures that it faces. Hopefully, a new management team will rebase expectations realistically, with a more humble view of the challenges Boeing faces," he wrote.

The note was titled "Seven hundred and thirty seven problems."

29

Calhoun's Legacy

"Dave Calhoun is perhaps the worst CEO ever of any company ever created on this planet."

—AVIATION INDUSTRY CONSULTANT RICHARD ABOULAFIA,
AT THE PACIFIC NORTHWEST AEROSPACE ALLIANCE (PNAA) CONFERENCE,
FEBRUARY 2025

DAVID CALHOUN WAS CEO OF THE BOEING COMPANY from January 13, 2020, to August 8, 2024. In 2023, I asked the Corporate Communications (Corp Com) office several times for an interview with Calhoun for this book. I knew the request was unlikely to be granted, and it wasn't. I also asked if Corp Com would pose these questions to Calhoun: What does he want his legacy to be? Does he want to be known as the man who saved Boeing? Or as the man who saved Boeing and launched the next new airplane? I never got any answers, and I don't know if the questions were even posed. But Calhoun will not be known for either achievement.

Calhoun is viewed by many as having failed in his job as Boeing's CEO. He was named to this position to fix the company, and he didn't. The list of things to do when Kelly Ortberg assumed office on August 8, 2024, was long and damning of Calhoun's failures (see Chapter 31 for a bullet list of items high on Ortberg's to-do list upon assuming office).

Calhoun received $33 million for his 2023 compensation. Unfortunately for optics, this figure was revealed in the 2024 Proxy statement (for 2023) shortly after Boeing's Monday Morning Massacre (see Chapter 28). By all appearances, it looked like this was his golden parachute. It wasn't until the 2025 Proxy statement was issued in April (for 2024) that it was revealed that Calhoun was given $15 million for his 2024 service. Stan Deal received a $6+ million exit package for 2024 and $12 million for 2023. The 2023 compensation packages did not go unnoticed by the International Association of Machinists District 751 (IAM 751) union. These figures may well have had an impact on the union contract vote that was yet to come.

Calhoun and his hand-picked CFO Brian West came under harsh criticism for their work-from-home arrangements and their absenteeism from Boeing's operations and even from company headquarters, first in Chicago and later in Arlington, Virginia. In September 2023, a *Wall Street Journal* article (which was picked up elsewhere) detailed the two men's remote-work habits, which continued long after lower-level employees returned to onsite work following the end of the pandemic.[152] Calhoun's primary residence was in New Hampshire. He bought a condominium in Chicago, but he didn't relocate to Boeing's corporate headquarters there. This is understandable. Taking office in January 2020, the pandemic broke out two months later and office workers across the globe, up and down all companies, began working remotely. But after the pandemic was over and Boeing relocated its corporate headquarters from Chicago to Arlington, Calhoun continued to work remotely despite the closer proximity of Arlington versus Chicago. Calhoun flew from New Hampshire and from a second home in South Carolina on "Air Boeing," one of the company's corporate jets. West worked from his homes and from a new, special office established near his Connecticut residence.

Calhoun's seemingly hands-off approach to day-to-day events at the company and his failure to meet with top labor union leaders at Boeing's Commercial Airplanes division (BCA) also drew criticism. Visits to BCA's troubled factories were few and far between, according to flight records the *Wall Street Journal* examined.

After Calhoun left Boeing, some management employees were candid in their assessments of him. Speaking on condition of anonymity, they said that Calhoun was "disengaged" from daily operations. (One person also criticized former CEOs Dennis Muilenburg and James McNerney who, it was said, used the company as an ATM.) One aerospace analyst who met with Calhoun on occasion said that he simply wasn't up to the task of fixing Boeing. While this analyst believed that Calhoun genuinely cared about the company and wanted his legacy to be as the man who saved Boeing, he simply was the wrong person to deal with all the problems Boeing had—and which got worse. However, these views are not universally shared. One person who has known Calhoun for decades called him one of the smartest executives he knew.

Still, it's hard to see how Calhoun's performance can be seen as anything but a failure or an incomplete tenure. Certainly, he inherited a massive mess that just kept getting worse and worse, beginning with the pandemic. But the long list of items he was supposed to fix remained outstanding four years after he assumed office, when the Alaska Airlines flight 1282 accident brought everything tumbling down—again.

The Boeing Board of Directors, as usual within the company, was slow to

---

152. Andrew Tangel and Mark Maremont, "Private Jets and Pop-Up Workspaces: Boeing Eases Return to Office for Top Brass," *Wall Street Journal* (September 11, 2023), https://www.wsj.com/business/airlines/boeing-ceo-private-jets-return-to-office-9bee2035.

act. Aerospace analysts with connections to the board said that as a group, it still had confidence in Calhoun. It was only after key U.S. airline customers demanded a meeting, without Calhoun, that the board responded.

Another Calhoun critic pointed to metrics not specifically mentioned in the list above. Boeing missed its earnings guidance in twelve of thirteen consecutive quarters. For a board of directors obsessed with financial performance, this, too, should have been at the top of the list of Calhoun's failures. Calhoun punched out as CEO for the last time just days after the release of the company's 2024 first-half financial results. A final accounting of what losses were taken as charges and write-offs during his tenure is presented below.

Yearly totals, in millions

Year	Charges
2023	$3,112
2022	6,620
2021	6,944
2020	14,829
Total	**$31,505**

Source: Boeing data.

Charges Added during Calhoun's Final Six Months at Boeing, First-Half 2024, in millions of dollars

Program and Description	Charges
787 abnormal production costs	$157
737 earnings charge	443
VC-25B reach forward loss	250
KC-46A reach forward loss	391
T-7A reach forward loss	278
Commercial Crew	125
Total	**$1,644**

Source: Boeing financial report for first-half 2024.

A total of $33.149 billion was written off during the stewardship of David Calhoun. In fairness, much of these losses related to programs undertaken before he became CEO. But he joined Boeing's board of directors in 2009 and by 2019 had become the lead director. Nearly all programs began after 2009, when he had a vote on fixed-price contracts with the U.S. Defense Department.

Boeing Write-Offs and Charges, by CEO and Year, in millions of dollars

CEO	Year	Write-Offs and Charges	Adjusted
David Calhoun	2024	$33,149	$33,149
Dennis Muilenberg	2016	21,984	29,153
James McNerney	2005	11,662	19,213
Harry Stonecipher	2003	3,278	5,668
Phillip M. Condit	1996	4,709	9,582

Source: *Leeham News and Analysis*, Boeing Charges by CEO.

Note: The data presented in this table was compiled using a Consumer Price Index (CPI) calculator, and the CEO charge amounts listed have been brought forward into 2024 dollars.

In order to be as generous as possible to Calhoun, each of the other CEOs listed in the table above had his total amount of charges calculated from the first year of his tenure. Dennis Muilenburg finishes strongly in second place, while the bronze medal goes to James McNerney, who cost the company almost $20 billion (adjusted). David Calhoun tops the podium with over $33 billion in write-offs and charges.

Newly minted Boeing president and CEO Kelly Ortberg will have a lot of cleaning up to do on Calhoun's behalf, as he was left substantial balances in deferred production charges sitting in the company's inventory asset account.

Boeing Expenses Incurred by the Time Ortberg Became CEO, in millions of dollars

Program	Deferred Production Costs	Unamortized Tooling	Customer Compensation	Total
737	$7,638	$880.00		
777X	2,612	4,218		
787	12,336	1,441		
			4,546	
Subtotal	**$22,586**	**$6,539**	**$4,546**	**$33,671**

Source: Boeing data.

The $33.7 billion in expenses must eventually fall onto Boeing's income statement, which bloats the company's inventory account. This is in addition to Calhoun expensing $10 billion in reach-forward losses on the 777X program in 2020 ($6.5 billion) and the 787 program in 2021 ($3.5 billion).

More than 45 percent of the inventory of Boeing's commercial aircraft programs noted on the company's balance sheet are attributable to either expenses, tooling, or customer compensation.

Excerpt, Boeing's 2024 Second-Quarter Report, in millions of dollars

Note 6–Inventories		
Inventories consisted of the following:	June30, 2024	December 31, 2023
Commercial aircraft programs	$4,544	$68,683
Long-term contracts in progress	370	686
Capitalized precontract costs´	941	946
Commercial spare parts, used aircraft, general stock materials and other	9,806	9,426
Total	$85,661	$79,741

1. Capitalized precontract costs at December 31, 2024 and 2023, includes amounts related to Commercial Crew, T-7A Red Hawk Production Options, and KC-46A Tanker.

Source: Boeing quarterly report for second-quarter 2024.

The Boeing Company and Subsidiaries
Consolidated Statements of Financial Position (Dollars in Millions)

	December 31, 2019	June 30, 2024	Change
Assets			
Cash and cash equivalents	$9,485.00	$10,894.00	$1,409
Short-term and other investments	545	1,727	1,182
Accounts receivable, net	3,266	3,155	(111)
Unbilled receivables, net	9,043	9,660	617
Current portion of customer financing, net	162	60	(102)
Inventories	76,622	85,661	9,039
Other current assets	3,106	3,282	176
Total current assets	**102,229**	**114,439**	**12,210**
Customer financing, net	2,136		
Financing receivables and operating lease equipment, net		785	
Property, plant and equipment, net	12,502	10,976	(1,526)
Goodwill	8,060	8,108	48
Acquired intangible assets, net	3,338	2,067	(1,271)
Deferred income taxes	683		(683)
Investments	1,092	1,026	(66)
Other assets, net	3,585	5,319	1,734
Total assets	**$133,625**	**$142,720**	**$9,095**

Table continues →

BALANCE SHEET COMPARISON

Boeing's balance sheet at the end of 2019 was still in good shape (above). Even though the MAX had been grounded since March of that year, the pandemic hadn't yet begun and 787 deliveries were proceeding nicely. BCA's losses were manageable. By the time Calhoun left in August 2024, the picture had changed.

Four items leap off the page when comparing the starting and ending balance sheets of the Calhoun era:

- a $9 billion increase in inventory,
- a $6.6 billion increase in deposits from customers,
- a $33 billion increase in long-term debt (LTD), and
- a $6 billion decrease in Treasury stock, at cost.

Holding inventory is never a good thing, especially in the case of the

The Boeing Company and Subsidiaries
Consolidated Statements of Financial Position (Dollars in Millions), cont'd.

	December 31, 2019	June 30, 2024	Change
Liabilities and equity			
Accounts payable	15,553	11,864	(3,689)
Accrued liabilities	22,868	21,850	(1,018)
Advances and progress billings	51,551	58,151	6,600
Short-term debt and current portion of long-term debt	7,340	4,765	(2,575)
Total current liabilities	**97,312**	**96,630**	**(682)**
Deferred income taxes	413	291	(122)
Accrued retiree health care	4,540	2,159	(2,381)
Accrued pension plan liability, net	16,276	6,248	(10,028)
Other long-term liabilities	3,422	2,212	(1,210)
Long-term debt	19,962	53,162	33,200
Total liabilities	**$141,925**	**$160,702**	**$18,777**
Shareholders' equity			
Common stock	5,061	5,061	0
Additional paid-in capital	6,745	10,727	3,982
Treasury stock, at cost	(54,914)	(48,841)	6,073
Retained earnings	50,644	25,469	(25,175)
Accumulated other comprehensive loss	(16,153)	(10,392)	5,761
Total shareholders' equity	**(8,617)**	**(17,976)**	**(9,359)**
Noncontrolling interests	317	(6)	(323)
Total equity	**(8,300)**	**(17,982)**	**(9,682)**
Total liabilities and equity	**$133,625**	**$142,720**	**$9,095**

Source: June 30, 2024, Boeing Quarterly Report.

airline industry, where machinery needs constant attention and maintenance. What makes the data from Calhoun's tenure doubly shocking is that $10 billion was written off and taken out of the company's inventory account in 2020–2021, and yet the balance was still up by $9 billion.

Deposits from customers is a liability item, also know as unearned revenue. While not normally a problem for most companies, it was for Boeing, because when the company returned aircraft to customers, it did so at negative margins—to the tune of $26 billion during the Calhoun years, costing the company even more.

The biggest elephant in the room during Calhoun's time as Boeing's CEO was, and still is today, the company's debt load. Consolidated debts were

$58 billion as Calhoun left, with long-term debt up over $33 billion. Just to get back to the point they were at when Calhoun took the reins would require paying off more than $27 billion in borrowings or dedicating almost three full years of $10 billion free cash flow exclusively to debt. In fact, an analysis by *Leeham News* in December 2024 concluded that Boeing could deliver all of the nearly 5,000 jets in its backlog and there still would not be enough money to return the company's debt to its pre-MAX crisis, 2018 level. Total liabilities also rose by about $19 billion over the same period.

Boeing also used stock to fund pension plans in 2020.

"In the fourth quarter of 2020, we contributed $3 billion of our common stock to our pension fund. In the fourth quarter of 2020, we also began using our common stock in lieu of cash to fund Company contributions to our 401(k) plans for the foreseeable future, which we estimate will conserve approximately $1 billion of cash over the next 12 months," the company reported in a federal Securities and Exchange Commission (SEC) filing.

Using previously recovered shares that were purchased in stock buy-back plans (to the tune of $43 billion during the 2013–2019 period) was a wise decision by the company. Additionally, during Calhoun's first year as CEO, the workforce declined by about 20,000 employees, from 161,000 to 141,000. Over this same period, IAM 751 lost 2 percent of its members (going from a total of 22 percent of Boeing's workforce to a total of 20 percent), while Boeing's engineering union, the Society of Professional Engineering Employees in Aerospace (SPEEA) lost 1 percent of its members (going from 11 percent to 10 percent of the workforce).

Reports at the time indicated that in addition to issues related to the pandemic, Boeing was eager to reduce the financial burden that the company's top hourly-wage earners represented; notably, these workers also happened to be Boeing's most senior and experienced staff.

Decline in Boeing's Accrued Pension-Plan and Health Care Liabilities, 2019–2024

Period	Accrued Pension Plan Liability (in millions)	Accrued Retiree Health Care Liability (in millions)
2019	$16,276	$4,540
2020	14,408	4,137
2021	9,104	3,528
2022	6,141	2,503
2023	6,516	2,233
1H2024	6,248	2,159
Total (2019 to 2024)	**$10,028**	**$2,381**

Source: Boeing.

Boeing Commercial Aircraft (BCA) Numbers during the Calhoun Years

Period	BCA Deliveries	Revenues	BCA Earnings
2024	2024	$33,149	$33,149
2023	2016	21,984	29,153
2022	2005	11,662	19,213
2021	2003	3,278	5,668
2020	1996	4,709	9,582

Source: 2020–2024 Boeing earnings release.

Note: Revenues and earnings are expressed as dollars in millions.

During the Calhoun years at Boeing, $10 billion was shaved from the company's pension account, almost exclusively during the CEO's first two years. Share buybacks were suspended during this time, and there was no indication of when the financial benefits of layoffs would be realized. The pension account subsequently stabilized in 2022 at around the $6 billion mark. About $2.4 billion in retiree health care liabilities also evaporated during Calhoun's tenure. But the effects on the labor force of his decisions will be felt for a long time to come, as less-experienced employees struggle with a very sharp learning curve.

During the first quarter of Calhoun's stewardship of Boeing, the company reported that there were approximately 450 737 MAXs in inventory, produced and waiting to be delivered to customers. As of June 30, 2024, that number had been reduced to approximately ninety 737-8s and thirty-five 737-7s and 737-10s, according to Boeing's 2024 first-quarter earnings release.

Calhoun was unable to turn those inventoried 737 MAX aircraft into meaningful profits, as the product, historically a cash cow, contributed to a $26.2 billion loss from operations. Deliveries averaged 373 planes per year, less than half of the 800 delivered in 2018.

Some industry observers concluded early on that Calhoun was not the person to fix Boeing, especially after he negotiated a $7 million payment for himself if he were to successfully get the MAX past regulators and back into service. From moving Boeing's headquarters to Virginia to remaining home-based in his New England boating community residence while other employees returned to the office, it was evident to some that Calhoun lacked enthusiasm and a desire to make necessary changes.

A chart of the stock performance of CEOs since Phil Condit tells a stark story.

Exhibit 2 - Previous Boeing CEOs (since 1986)

Previous Boeing CEOs	CEO Tenure	BA Stock Performance Throughout Tenure	Notable Developments During Tenure	Education
David L. Calhoun	Jan 2020 - Present	(48.0%)	• Stepping down at the end of 2024 amid BA's production quality and execution issues • Struggled to increase and stabilize production rates on key commercial programs, significant defense charges, Alaska Airlines' 737 MAX-9 door blowout	BS: Accounting, Virginia Tech
Dennis A. Muilenburg	July 2015 - Dec 2019	159.0%	• Resigned in the aftermath of the two 737 MAX crashes • Stock surged on $46B capital return to shareholders while CEO (~$30B for buybacks)	MS: Aeronautics and Astronautics, University of Washington BS: Aerospace Engineering, Iowa State University
W. James McNerney Jr.	July 2005 - July 2015	145.7%	• Oversaw development of the 737 MAX, 787 entry into service • Helped recapture the lead in commercial airplane deliveries • Executed steady airplane production increases and maintained strong position in defense markets	MBA: Harvard BA: Yale
Harry C. Stonecipher	Dec 2003 - March 2005	56.0%	• CEO of McDonnell Douglas from 1994-1997, helped negotiate the merger with Boeing • Oversaw launch of 787 Dreamliner • Initiated sale of BA's Wichita manufacturing facility (present-day Spirit AeroSystems)	BS: Physics, Tennessee Polytechnic Institute
Philip M. Condit	April 1996 - Dec 2003	0.7%	• Acquisition of Rockwell Aerospace, merger with McDonnell Douglas, and the addition of Hughes Space & Communications • Aggressively pursued defense contracts • Lost market share to Airbus during tenure	Doctorate: Engineering, Science University of Tokyo MS: Management, MIT MS: Aeronautical Engineering, Princeton BS: Mechanical Engineering, UC Berkeley
Frank A. Shrontz	April 1986 - April 1996	275.9%	• Led BA to be a leading US exporter • Launched the 777 and the 737 NG • Expanded BA's presence in the space industry	MBA: Harvard Law Degree: University of Idaho

Source: FactSet and company reports

30

Airbus Wasn't Standing Still

"I am not happy with the problems of my competitor."
—GUILLAUME FAURY, CEO OF AIRBUS, AT EUROPE 2024 CONFERENCE

WHILE THE BOEING COMPANY WAS STUMBLING from one crisis to the next, its prime competitor, Airbus, wasn't sitting still.

Boeing's weaknesses only strengthened Airbus, whose market share in the single-aisle arena grew to +/-60 percent, largely on the basis of the A321neo. The MAX 10, a good aircraft for what it does, simply doesn't do enough to be fully competitive with the A321. Sales of the MAX 10 stalled for lack of certification and production, contributing to an A321 backlog in 2024 that was roughly five times that of the MAX 10. Boeing still led with widebody sales, on the success of the 787, but at long last, by 2024 sales of the 777X began to pick up slightly after a long, long sales drought. Airbus's widebody offerings aren't as broad as Boeing's, and sales of the A330neo are driven in part by delivery positions that are earlier than those available on the A350. Sales of the A350-1000 remained sluggish in part due to durability issues of the Rolls-Royce (RR) Trent XWB-97 engine in the harsh Middle East environment.

Airbus's ability to deliver a knockout punch to Boeing was muted in part because its suppliers, notably engine makers but others as well, couldn't keep up with current production rates let alone future targets. The A220 was sold out through 2027 due to an inability to increase production rates to fourteen per month until then. Airbus wanted to hit this mark in 2025. The A320 family was sold out into the 2030 decade. Delivery positions for the A330 and A350 were filled for years to come.

Airlines and aircraft lessors, frustrated by delivery delays from the duopoly and Boeing's self-inflicted wounds in particular, expressed, perhaps wistfully, a desire for a third supplier. But everyone recognized that there was no option in sight.

To be sure, the pandemic had hurt Airbus. Boeing tapped the bond market to raise $25 billion instead of letting the federal government into its knickers through the Coronavirus Aid, Relief, and Economic Security (CARES) Act. Long used to having the French and German governments sharing its bed, Airbus had no qualms about letting France pony up billions of euros to help it through the global meltdown. The French government required Airbus to dedicate some of the money to green aviation, in keeping with Europe's drive to reduce aviation carbon emissions. Airbus focused its research and development (R&D) efforts on a hydrogen-powered (H2) airplane. Boeing sniffed that H2 would not be an eco-aviation solution any time soon (it was right) and instead focused its attention on Sustainable Aviation Fuel (SAF), believing it to be the best near-term advance toward reducing emissions. There were lots of issues with this approach, but that is a discussion for another time.

Airbus, of course, didn't have a grounding to contend with like Boeing did. Boeing was slow in shutting down its factories after COVID broke out in a Kirkland, Washington, retirement home located less than twenty miles from the company's Renton factory and about twenty-five miles from its Everett plant. Unlike Boeing, Airbus quickly paused production at its French and German facilities. Airbus thoroughly cleaned the factories and quickly adopted safety protocols. However, while production resumed relatively quickly, it was at lower rates than before the pandemic. The A320 production rate was reduced to around forty-two a month across Europe, the United States, and China. Europe's labor laws made furloughs problematic, in contrast to the United States, where layoffs could begin after a ninety day "WARN" notice was issued. In any event, Boeing had already laid off workers because of the MAX grounding.

The differences helped the Airbus supply chain stay working and, in the long run, provided a more stable, albeit imperfect, ability to ramp production back up. Nevertheless, because Airbus relied on a large number of U.S. suppliers, many of whom were shared by Boeing and had been hit hard by the MAX grounding and compounded by the pandemic, supply-chain issues took a long-term toll on Airbus as well.

Setting all this aside, Airbus was building and delivering airplanes. Boeing was not. If Airbus could get its suppliers ramped back up quickly, it could proverbially kick the dog while it was down. Airbus was helped immensely by the fact that Boeing's product strategy was flawed even before the first of the many crises it was hit with following the back-to-back MAX disasters. The MAX 9 was an in-between airplane, sized between the MAX 8 and the A321neo, that simply didn't fit well into the market. Its predecessor, the 737-900/900ER, sold only 557 units, or a mere 7.8 percent of the 7,112 civil and military models of Boeing's Next Generation (NG) series. Belatedly, Boeing stretched the MAX 9 into the A321-sized MAX 10. This model fared better than its "tweener" sibling: 17 percent of the net orders of the MAX family were for the 10. Seven percent were for the MAX 9. In contrast, the A321ceo represented 24 percent of ceo family sales, and the A321neo accounted for 64 percent of neo family sales. The A321neo outsold the MAX 10 by a ratio of 6:1 through November 2024. Even taking into account the fact that the A321neo was launched in December 2010 and the MAX 10 didn't come along until 2017, customers spoke loudly and clearly: the A321neo was the preferred airplane in its class. Airbus offered a long-range version (LR) and an extra-long-range model (XLR) that on paper boosted the range to a maximum of 4,700 nautical miles (nm) versus the MAX 10's anemic 3,100nm. The A321neo has better runway performance, especially in hot-and-high environments.

Overall, Airbus had gross orders for the neo family of 10,969 through 2024 compared with Boeing's gross orders of 8,218 for the same period. This is a 57 percent market share for Airbus. When the A220-300, Embraer E195-E2, and COMAC C919 (produced by the Commercial Aircraft Corporation of China) competing airplanes are factored into calculations, Boeing's share of the single-aisle sector drops by another percentage point or two.

Boeing continued to show better strength among widebody airplanes. Its market share was boosted by the long-running, successful 767-300ER and 777-200LR freighters and by a broader line of passenger aircraft as compared with Airbus. The latter's forays into freighters never matched Boeing's success. On the passenger side, Boeing offered a three-member family of 787s (though the smallest model, the 787-8, was by 2020 essentially an afterthought among airlines) and a three-member family of the struggling 777X (the passenger -8 and -9 and the -8 freighter). Airbus offered the A330-900neo (the -800 was and is a non-factor), the popular A350-900, and the A350-1000 model, which has generated so-so sales.

Airbus officials naturally saw a golden opportunity during Boeing's prolonged series of crises to capture more A320neo orders and to provide a boost to the slow-selling A330-900 and to the A350 twins. Indeed, Airbus landed hundreds of orders at Boeing's expense, especially for the A321neo and the LR/XLR versions. But it became an embarrassment of riches when the supply chain, notably, engine and interiors companies, couldn't keep up, either for the A320neo family or for the interiors for the A350s. Airbus quickly sold out its A320 production line into the 2030 decade. The A350 wasn't far behind. The A330-900 began picking up orders, largely because of its earlier availability. Airbus had ambitious production ramp-up plans to meet the demand but, due to supply-chain difficulties, the target dates kept moving to the right.

This helped Boeing once deliveries of the 737 and 787 resumed. With Airbus sold out, customers had no choice but to turn to Boeing for earlier delivery positions. But with its own propensity to shoot itself in both feet time and again, Boeing couldn't ramp up its production to keep up with demand, supply-chain difficulties notwithstanding.

When it came to new-product development, Airbus was content to sit back and wait. Officials wanted to see what Boeing would do about its next new airplane. In November 2022, at an Investor Day conference discussed further in earlier chapters, Calhoun provided an answer: Boeing would not introduce a new airplane until the middle of the next decade. Calhoun was hot to trot on the Transonic Truss-Braced Wing (TTBW) concept. GE and France's Safran, through their CFM International joint venture, were focused on their radical new engine design, the RISE Open Fan. Pratt & Whitney (P&W) and Rolls-Royce (RR) were convinced that evolutionary advances of conventional turbofan engines were the answer for a future airplane. As noted above, Airbus was publicly focused on a hydrogen-fueled (H2) airplane. What was going on was a classic case of three-dimensional chess. Airbus was raking in profits on the A320 family and doing OK on the A330-900 and the A350. (The A220 was still a money loser, in part because its production ramp-up to fourteen planes per month was stalled by supplier issues.)

Within Airbus, there was a belief that the hydrogen airplane was infeasible and that all the R&D was going on just because French government financial COVID aid required it. This money was set to run out in 2027, which prompted some within Airbus to believe that R&D efforts on the H2 program would come to a halt when funding ended. In fact, Airbus pulled the plug on the project in February 2025. The eventual replacement for the A320 will be a conventionally-fueled, SAF-capable airplane, most likely of standard tube-and-wing design (albeit with folding wings and not a TTBW). The big question will be what kind of engines it will have: conventional or the Open Fan? When the new plane will debut remains a question, too.

Airbus CEO Guillaume Faury said in 2024 that he didn't see Airbus proceeding with a new airplane until between 2035 and 2040, potentially meaning that a launch might not come until 2030 or even later. Some within Airbus don't think that engine technology sufficient to justify a new airplane will be ready until 2040 or later. GE, at the time of this writing, is sticking with its goal of having the RISE ready for entry into service (EIS) in 2035. The first engine isn't targeted for flight testing until 2027. Some observers already believe that the RISE won't be ready until maybe 2037.

There could be a lot of life left in the A320neo and 737 MAX families.

Airbus has had other problems to contend with besides the supply chain and the imbalance of supply and demand. Boeing has a well-deserved reputation for arrogance, followed by an over-emphasis on shareholder value. As Boeing dealt with its successive crises, airlines and lessors began to increasingly complain that Airbus had also become arrogant, refusing to negotiate prices and showing indifference to supplier-induced delivery delays. Airbus also was regularly buying back shares of its stock for employee-retirement funds and for equity-based executive compensation.

The complaint that Airbus wasn't negotiating about prices was spurious.

Of course, customers want to negotiate price. Who doesn't? But production lines were sold out for years and Boeing was in tatters. Why should Airbus cut prices further, or at all, under these circumstances? As for delays, there were reports that top Airbus officials pointed to the supply chain, notably, the engine makers and interior providers, then essentially threw up their hands and said "What can we do?" These same customers noted a contrast with previously arrogant Boeing salesmen, who now were humble, apologetic, and ready to talk about compensation.

Airbus's share-buyback program pales in comparison to Boeing's past program, and the purposes of each are somewhat different. Boeing's program focused on shareholder value and compensation tied to stock price for executives and the company's board of directors. Some stock also went into Boeing's 401(k) pension plan. While Airbus's publicly stated reason for its program was its employee-retirement program and executive compensation, buying back shares also helped its broader stockholders, too. And, according to information obtained by *Leeham News,* institutional shareholders were complaining that Airbus wasn't benefiting enough from Boeing's woes. The company's profits and stock price weren't where these shareholders thought they should be, and they also thought that Airbus should be selling more airplanes. These complaints ignored the realities of Airbus's inability to aggressively ramp up production when it wanted to, a problem that all comes back to the supply chain. Profits were also hurt by Airbus's decision to hire thousands of workers and to train them to meet desired production goals. When these goals didn't materialize, the company was stuck (under European labor laws) with a surplus of employees, which drove up costs.

There was also a notable culture shift at Airbus from the Tom Enders administration (2012 to 2019) to the Guillaume Faury era (2019 to the present). Airbus hasn't been as open internally or with the media as it had been under Enders, and relations with customers have taken on a harder edge under Faury. Much of this may simply be the difference between Enders, the German, and Faury, the Frenchman. They are two different personalities, each with its pluses and minuses.

Still, when Akbar Al Baker, then the volatile CEO of Qatar Airways, grounded a number of A350s over flaking paint jobs that appeared to cause damage to the composite fuselages, Faury played hardball. Qatar sued Airbus in a London court, and Airbus counter-sued. Airbus cancelled a large order for the A320 family that Qatar had placed, an action that as far as could be remembered had never happened before in the annals of customer relations. Airbus quietly floated the theory that Al Baker had grounded the airplanes to reduce surplus capacity, induced from over-ordering aircraft, and that the paint damage happened because a Qatar vendor had been engaged to strip paint in order to repaint the aircraft in a special livery for the World Cup and had used compounds not recommended by Airbus for use on composites.

Eventually the lawsuit was settled, with Airbus paying Qatar an undisclosed sum. (The airline sued for over $1 billion.) In 2024, long after the lawsuit, Airbus and Qatar restored the original A320 order.

China's COMAC designed its C919 to be a direct competitor to the A320 and 737. But its gestation has been long and painfully slow. The first aircraft wasn't delivered until December 2023, eight years late. Only nine had been delivered by the end of 2024. Commercial sanctions imposed on China, first by President Donald Trump in 2017 and then by President Joe Biden after China's covert support of Russia's invasion of Ukraine became overt, have stymied the C919's potential. A large portion of its parts and suppliers, including LEAP engines from CFM, come from the U.S. and Europe. The future of the C919 rests almost entirely on China developing a massive domestic aerospace sector, which will take years, and ramping up production from its dismal one-a-month rate.

As for Russia's once promising MC-21, also a direct competitor to the A320 and 737, Vladimir Putin's seizure of Crimea and adjacent areas in 2014, and then his 2022 full-scale invasion of Ukraine, have all but killed this airplane.

Boeing's long-running crisis-to-crisis-to-crisis situation, beginning in 2019 with the grounding of the MAX, has potentially opened the door for Embraer to make the leap from regional jets to the mainline sector, as discussed in Chapter 23.

PART 3

THE WAY BACK

31

Kelly Ortberg Joins the Company Rebuilding Not Quite from Scratch, but Close to It

"The extremely welcome appointment of Kelly Ortberg as CEO shows that Boeing's board can always be trusted to do the right thing, after they've exhausted all other possibilities."

—RICHARD ABOULAFIA, AVIATION INDUSTRY CONSULTANT, AUGUST 2, 2024

THE BOEING COMPANY HAS SO MANY PROBLEMS, such big losses, so many programs in bad shape, such massive debt, and strained relationships with just about everyone, that rebuilding it would require starting from scratch. Or, one could argue, close to scratch.

At the start of 2024, Boeing said that it hoped to produce thirty-eight new 737s a month later in the year. It was supposed to hit this rate by the end of 2023, but it missed this target—as it had with every rate target since its recovery began in 2022 with the end of the pandemic. Boeing, as did Airbus with its rate targets, overestimated the pace of recovery of the supply chain. All it takes is one widget needed at one critical place in the production process to muck up the works. Engines from CFM International, needed for the 737 and the A320, or from Pratt & Whitney (P&W), needed for the A320, were consistently running late. Whole interiors were late for widebody airplanes, at both OEMs (original equipment manufacturers).

But Boeing's plethora of problems were, and are, so widespread and so embedded that it will take years to reverse course. These have been

287

discussed in detail in several chapters of this book. On July 31, 2024, the Boeing Board of Directors announced that Kelly Ortberg, the former CEO of Rockwell Collins, was picked to succeed David Calhoun as president and CEO of Boeing effective August 8. In no particular order, these were Ortberg's immediate problems to solve:

- Boeing's union contract with the International Association of Machinists District 751 (IAM 751) union was in negotiations and set to expire in September 2024
- Quality-control (QC) issues existed at all Boeing Commercial Airplanes (BCA) and Boeing Defense, Space & Security (BDS) factories
- Losses at BDS had to be stemmed
- BCA production needed to be brought back up to normal rates (fifty+ planes per month for the 737, ten to twelve for the 787)
- The MAX 7, MAX 10, and 777X had to get certified
- Boeing had to regain the confidence of the Federal Aviation Administration (FAA), the European Aviation Safety Agency (EASA), and other regulators and had to regain authority from the FAA to oversee its operations and ticket its airplanes
- The balance sheet was in need of repair
- Spirit AeroSystems had to be integrated into Boeing
- BCA needed to be returned to profitability
- A new airplane had to be launched to replace the 737
- Boeing needed to regain global market share to bring itself closer to parity with Airbus
- Supply-chain relations were in need of repair
- A new contract had to be negotiated with the engineers union, the Society of Professional Engineering Employees in Aerospace (SPEEA), in 2026
- Relations with the airlines and with aircraft lessors were in need of repair
- Relations with IAM 751 and SPEEA were in need of repair

At age 64, Ortberg was older than Boeing's usual picks—the board of directors historically favored candidates in their 50s who could serve for at least ten years. But Harry Stonecipher was 67 when he was chosen to be CEO following the resignation of Phil Condit, and Calhoun was 63 when he became CEO after Dennis Muilenburg was fired. Ortberg was a career aerospace employee, beginning as an engineer with Texas Instruments before joining Rockwell and working his way up to CEO. His experience is in the supply chain and not with airframe manufacturers, he doesn't have a GE background (like Stonecipher, Calhoun, and James McNerney), and he doesn't come from private equity (like Calhoun). The board agreed to waive the mandatory retirement age of 65 for Ortberg through 2031 but in a federal filing noted that Ortberg didn't have a contract with Boeing through 2031.

Ortberg and his chief financial officer must fix Boeing's balance sheet. As set out above, this means clearing inventories; getting production of the 737 and 787 back to normal and certifying the MAX 7, MAX 10, and 777X; eliminating losses at BDS; and finding money for a new airplane to refresh Boeing's product line.

Labor peace was also going to be a key issue facing Ortberg. The IAM 751 contract was already in negotiations and was set to expire just a month after Ortberg's appointment. The union had long been saying that it wanted to claw back concessions given to McNerney during his war on Boeing's unions. Leadership also wanted a guarantee that the next new airplane, whatever it was, was going to be built in the Seattle area. And the union wanted a seat on the board as well as a 40 percent wage hike over the life of the contract, which it proposed to be four years.

Labor relations had simmered along during the long-term contract and extensions negotiated at gunpoint under McNerney. The MAX grounding and pandemic decimated union ranks through naturally occurring retirements, early retirement packages offered by Boeing as a way to cut costs during two crises faced by the company (detailed in earlier chapters), and outright layoffs. The loss of institutional knowledge and experience was devastating. This contributed to quality-control issues at two Seattle factories, complementing existing QC issues at Boeing's non-union Charleston 787 plant. The new Washington state hires in Everett, and especially in Renton, who replaced experienced workers face a long learning curve before they will become proficient.

How Ortberg and his new executive team dealt with all the challenges, including the IAM 751 contract, would make or break Boeing's recovery, which had stalled and, arguably, gone backwards in Calhoun's last year.

The 737 was sold out through 2027, with positions allocated well beyond then. The 777's entry into service (EIS) was increasingly looking like 2026 instead of 2025 (which itself was five years later than the original plan). Few 787 delivery slots remained available in the last half of the 2020 decade.

NEW COMPETITORS

For years, aviation consultant Richard Aboulafia was the key speaker at the Pacific Northwest Aerospace Alliance (PNAA) conference in a Seattle suburb. His role, year after year, was to give an overview of the commercial, military, and business jet sectors. Discussing the commercial market, Aboulafia went back decades with charts and graphs to show how the Douglas Aircraft Company (later McDonnell Douglas) was overtaken by Boeing; Lockheed (later Lockheed Martin) reentered and exited the mainline jet market; Bombardier and Embraer became the largest players in the regional airliner sector; and Airbus overtook not only MDC but also Boeing.

BOMBARDIER

Aboulafia was a pessimist about Bombardier's attempt to enter the mainline market with its C Series. However, he shot at the wrong target, criticizing the airplane, which was not only a good design but was also much more advanced than the 737-700 and A319(ceo) it was created to replace. It took years for Aboulafia to adjust his thinking about the C Series and to focus instead on the company, which he correctly began noting was incompetently run and financially incapable of taking on Airbus and Boeing. It is this latter point that Aboulafia homed in on in future presentations: financial capabilities.

The barriers to entry for a company to challenge Airbus and Boeing are immense, Aboulafia noted. It takes billions of dollars to design a new airplane and bring it to production. It takes billions more to ramp up production and deliver enough airplanes to reach a break-even point financially. A global product-support system is needed. A supply chain, already feeding Airbus and Boeing, is needed to feed a new competitor. An airline that has been reliant on the duopoly for decades must be convinced to switch manufacturers altogether or add a new entrant's airplane type to its fleet. Integrating a new fleet type affects training, stocks, reservations programming, and on and on and on.

Very few companies have the financial depth to address all these known issues, not to mention unknown issues. Bombardier certainly didn't, and the C Series' development—running concurrently with the development of two new corporate jets, poor sales of the Q400 and CRJ, and a money-losing train division—nearly bankrupted the company. Even though Bombardier had global product-support systems for the CRJ and Q400, this advantage didn't fully offset the investment required to add the C Series to the mix.

Just getting the funding for design, development, and production is a huge task for any company. Airbus infamously received billions of dollars from its member states, principally France and Germany but also Spain and, to a lesser extent, the UK (for the Broughton wings plant). Some of the money took the form of tax breaks and grants for facilities construction. Other aid was directly invested in airplane development. Airbus called it launch aid, later rebranding it as Reimbursable Launch Investment (RLI) after the United States filed a complaint with the World Trade Organization (WTO) over unfair subsidies in 2004. RLI was repayable after sales of a given aircraft reached the break-even point. If this didn't happen, no repayment was required. It was this latter feature that ate at Boeing's craw, since it didn't have an equivalent funding program. (Boeing, however, was masterful at extracting, and sometimes extorting, tax breaks and grants from states and governments.)

The European Union filed a counter-complaint against the United States for its aid to Boeing. After more than a decade, the WTO found both parties guilty of violating WTO rules, though Airbus was more guilty than Boeing. After more years of appeals and maneuvering, the U.S. and the EU agreed to put any penalties on hold and turned their attention to the state aid China was giving to its new aerospace industry. But no formal complaints were filed as of this writing.

Bombardier had once before gone through a WTO complaint process. Brazil, the home of Embraer, and Canada, the home of Bombardier, previously filed complaints against each other alleging illegal export-financing programs. Each was found guilty and enforcement actions were pursued. Since these involved regional aircraft, few really cared, but the violations were on the record.

When Bombardier, with its weak balance sheet and sub-investment-grade credit rating, plotted about how to finance its C Series—this was in the 2005–2008 period, early in the WTO process between Airbus, Boeing, the EU and the U.S.—officials structured launch aid along the RLI model, capping it at 30 percent of estimated costs. This cap was in keeping with a previous international trade agreement called the General Agreement on Tariffs and Trade (GATT) in which parties agreed that 30 percent was a reasonable amount for government participation. This cap would be vitiated in the WTO complaints against Airbus and Boeing, but at the time Bombardier tried to avoid new complaints. The Quebec Province, home to Bombardier's C Series production plant at Montreal-Mirabel International Airport (Mirabel); a Quebec pension fund; and the UK ponied up substantial funding. The UK's interest was tied to the Bombardier aerospace plant in Belfast, Northern Ireland, where high-paying jobs were historically scarce and unemployment was high. Bombardier bought the plant when it acquired Shorts Brothers, designer and builder of the Shorts 330 and 360.[153] Bombardier selected this plant to build the new, composite wings

---

153. When Bombardier began selling off assets to avoid bankruptcy as its financial position worsened during the C Series/business jet development programs, Canada's Longview Aviation bought the Twin Otter, the Q400, two firefighting aerial tankers, the Beaver programs, and the assets of the defunct Shorts programs. In 2024, Longview, having adopted the historic de Havilland Canada (DHC) branding that Bombardier dropped when it acquired DHC, announced that it may restart production of a modernized Shorts 360 military

for the C Series. Despite such financing efforts, Bombardier officials still got it wrong.

Development of the C Series ran a few years behind but somewhat parallel to Boeing's development of the 787. Bombardier was a sub-contractor to a 787 supplier. Having witnessed the delays and cost overruns on the 787, Bombardier officials were confident that they could learn from the experience and avoid or mitigate delays and overruns on the C Series. The program ran $3 billion over budget, a big number for a small company.

In the end, Bombardier sold the C Series program to Airbus for a nominal $1, also agreeing to cover the first $700 million in program losses and to fund construction of a U.S. assembly plant next to the Airbus A320 final assembly plant in Mobile, Alabama. Even shed of the remaining developments costs, Bombardier was unable to keep its end of the bargain. It sold its remaining 25 percent interest in the C Series to Airbus (though the Quebec pension fund still owns a piece). Airbus, having rebranded the C Series as the A220, paid for the new plant, covered the losses, invested huge sums of money, and absorbed losses even as sales picked up. Through 2024, 905 orders were placed for the C Series/A220, more than 600 having been sold by Airbus. The company is still losing money on the program and hopes to cross the break-even point around 2026.[154]

MHI

Mitsubishi Heavy Industries (MHI) is a major supplier to Boeing on its 7 Series programs. Notably, MHI, Kawasaki, and what is now Subaru's aerospace unit are big suppliers of the 787. The Japanese government advanced billions of dollars to MHI to buy participation on the 787, which was at a level unprecedented compared with previous Boeing contracts. Neither the United States nor the European Union included this largesse in its WTO complaints over illegal subsidies for the 787. Boeing's decades-long relationship with the Japanese heavy industry and near-monopolistic sales to Japan's major airlines was at stake. Airbus, being fully aware of Japanese government subsidies, opposed any inclusion of them in its WTO complaint against Boeing.

MHI for years had ambitions to build a commercial airliner. Japan's only such project had been the YS-11 sixty-passenger turboprop of the 1960s.

---

version called the Sherpa. Production, if pursued, will be at a new DHC plant outside Calgary, Alberta, Canada.

154. A Bombardier salesman once told me that the company estimated the break-even point at 1,200 airplanes, given the cost overruns and early program sales losses. The COVID pandemic, subsequent supply-chain disruptions, and a new labor contract at Mirabel may move this big figure to the right.

In the 1980s, MHI toured U.S. regional airlines to gauge what airplane they might like to see. Bombardier and Embraer were the principal providers then, with the CRJ produced by the former and the ERJ by the latter. Nothing came of the MHI effort. But in the early 2000 decade, MHI created the Mitsubishi Aircraft Corporation (MITAC) to develop seventy- and ninety-seat regional jets, the MRJ70 and MRJ90. These would compete with the Embraer E-Jet, with similar size, capacity, and dimensions. MHI assigned some of the aerospace experts and engineers who gained experience on Boeing programs to MITAC, and Boeing agreed to lend technical and potentially sales support. An aerospace engineering firm in Seattle, whose employees included some ex-Boeing engineers, received a contract to work on the MRJ models. Even with these advantages, the novices at MITAC's design center in Nagoya, Japan, didn't have the experience to design a complete jet that met the exacting requirements needed for a durable, safe jet, nor did Japan's regulator have the experience to oversee and certify a home-grown airplane. The MRJ prototypes revealed technical design defects that required costly and time-consuming redesign. The regulator simply didn't know what it was doing. Processing progressive paperwork toward certification was excruciatingly slow. The program was repeatedly delayed, and costs piled up.

MITAC retained an outside consulting company to assess the MRJ program from an engineering standpoint. The company made a host of recommendations, which resulted in the adaptations of many redesigns into a revamped airplane based on the MRJ70. The M100 SpaceJet was the result.[155] The consultants, knowing that a global product-support system would be necessary and recognizing that building one from scratch would be costly, time-consuming, and viewed by the industry with a skepticism associated with any start-up, recommended that MHI buy Bombardier's CRJ program. The CRJ was already on its last program legs, but the real asset to be purchased was the global CRJ product-support system. MHI agreed to purchase everything for $550 million. The price was inflated over the analyzed value of the assets because MHI assumed a portion of the residual value guarantees Bombardier gave in connection with some of its CRJ sales.

By this time, it was 2019. MITAC's program was seven years behind schedule. Costs had ballooned to $8.5 billion, and program leaders estimated another $3.5 billion would be needed to bring the airplane to market. There were 500 orders under memorandums of understanding (MOUs), including from the big U.S. carriers. But MOUs are not firm orders, so few deposits had been paid.

---

155. The name SpaceJet referred to the redesigned interior that added overhead bin space and more seats.

At about the same time, MHI changed CEOs, as it did every five years as a matter of policy. The new CEO didn't know, like, or understand the commercial aircraft business. As far as he was concerned, the MRJ/SpaceJet program was a money suck (he wasn't wrong) and had no future (he was wrong). With Bombardier leaving the regional airliner business, SpaceJet would become the only alternative to Embraer's E-Jet, and airlines like having choices. The SpaceJet's economics, which were much better than those of the MRJ, were competitive with those of the E-Jet E2 and certainly better than the economics of the E175-E1 used by U.S. airlines. The M100 was Scope-compliant, and MITAC already had visions of a 130-seat M130. But the new CEO of MHI had had enough. Quietly, in the way of the Japanese, MHI began closing down the SpaceJet program while denying this was the case (Japanese "saving face" and all that). When the COVID pandemic began in March 2020, MHI shut down MITAC publicly. A few months later, officials announced the formal closing of the entire project.

COMAC

The examples provided above are exactly why Aboulafia talked about barriers to entry. But the Chinese are determined to make the Commercial Aircraft Corporation of China (COMAC) a viable commercial airliner designer and producer. The company's C909 (ARJ-21) is by all accounts a thoroughly uneconomical airplane. It's a shrunk version of the MDC MD-80 once assembled at a Shanghai plant. Shrinks are almost always disadvantaged airplanes. The C909's engines are ancient GE CF34s, used on the earliest versions of the E-Jet and the improved E1 (the E2 uses entirely different engines). The C909 is a seventy-passenger airplane, which, given its MD-80 antecedents, looks like the MD-80 and *its* antecedent, the DC-9. One wag remarked that the Chinese had reinvented the DC-9-10, the earliest version of the long-running DC-9 series that carried seventy passengers and entered service in 1965. The C909 was about eight years late entering service; its certification was difficult to obtain; it had no product-support system outside China, except in Indonesia where an airline partly owned by a Chinese lessor accepted the airplane for regional routes; and Western airlines and lessors want nothing to do with it.

The COMAC C919 is a direct competitor to the A320 and the 737. Since Airbus has an A320 final assembly line in Tianjin, China, just like MDC had in Shanghai for the MD-80, it's also unsurprising that the C919 looks an awful lot like the A320. But like the C909, design, development, and production of the C919 was slow. It's years late—also about eight years from its intended EIS. The first one was delivered to China Eastern Airlines in December 2023, but it didn't enter service until the follow spring. By mid-2024, only five had been delivered. COMAC officials say they will produce

150 C919s a year in five years, but this is a pipedream given the realities of production learning curves and the molasses-like pace of the program. The government mandated that orders be placed by domestic airlines and lessors, so ostensibly there are 1,000 orders in backlog as of this writing. Except for orders placed by Indonesia and five by the aircraft lessor Aer-Cap, which inherited the orders through its acquisition of the U.S. lessor GE Capital Aviation Services (GECAS, which ordered the planes only because its sister company, GE Aviation, is supplying engines for the C919), none of the orders are from outside China.

COMAC doesn't have a global product-support system for either the C909 nor the C919, and it's questionable just how widespread its domestic product-support system is. When first conceived, the C919 was facing the 737-800 and the A320(ceo). Equipped with the new CFM LEAP-1C engine and a lower capital cost, the C919 would have been economically superior to the duopoly's airplanes. But production delays allowed Airbus and Boeing to develop the A320neo and the 737-8 MAX. The heavier C919 now is, by outside analysis, slightly worse economically than its two competitors. The plane's lower capital cost, however, is a major advantage.

COMAC announced development of a twin-aisle C929, about the size of the 787 and the A330neo, intended as a joint venture with Russia. But Russia's invasion of Ukraine blew up this partnership, and China's own slow aerospace-industry development already puts the C929 years behind the target EIS date announced when the program began. EIS might be in the mid-2030 decade, but don't count on it.

China's government takes the long view of virtually everything it does, and it's willing to spend whatever it takes to achieve its goals. Some day, China's commercial aerospace industry is likely to be a viable competitor to Airbus and the weakened Boeing The government doesn't give a damn about WTO rules, so the money will be forthcoming as needed. Nor does the government care about protecting intellectual property (IP), so resorting to IP theft to achieve its goals is also an option.

Anyone who thinks China won't someday have a commercially competitive family of airliners ignores these factors. If China can go to the moon and potentially Mars, if it can build a credibly threatening Blue Water Navy and more electric vehicles than any other country, developing successful commercial airliners is a given. It may take a generation or two—it took Airbus twenty-five years to overtake Boeing—but it will happen.

EMBRAER

But what about nearer term?

Embraer is the only nearer-term potential alternative to the duopoly. Even so, Aboulafia, who likes the company and its airplanes, sees the financial barrier for Embraer to move up to the mainline and challenge Airbus and Boeing as significant. In 2023 and 2024, multiple news articles appeared in trade and financial press that Embraer was considering moving up to the mainline jet sector held by Airbus and Boeing. Company CEO Francisco Gomes Neto acknowledged that this was the case in the *Financial Times* in an interview during the 2024 Farnborough Air Show.

Embraer has a global support system for its E-Jet that can be adapted to mainline jets. Sales of the regional airliner not only have been to traditional regional carriers but often to major airlines, which have assigned them to regional subsidiaries or regional partners. Embraer knows many of the major airlines and, importantly, they know Embraer. Unlike Airbus and Boeing, Embraer produced its new E2 jets on time and on budget and delivered them on time. Unlike Boeing, Embraer has a good relationship with its regulator, which helps immensely when it comes to certification. Embraer's engineers are among the best in the business. And, contrary to the image of the company as a small airplane builder, the E195-E2 dimensionally is the size of the 737-800/8 (the cabin width is only wide enough for four seats versus six). The C-390 military airplane's dimensions are about the same as the A320, but its fuselage width is about the same as the Boeing 767. The downside is that Embraer doesn't build a lot of these airplanes every month. It will be a huge effort to boost production rates to the point where it can capture a solid share of the mainline market.

The company also has to convince airlines and, by extension, lessors, that adding an entirely new fleet type and manufacturer on top of or in place of its decades-long reliance on Airbus and Boeing is a good move.

Embraer may have little choice but to move up into the mainline sector. The twenty-year market demand for regional jets is shrinking. Airplanes are getting larger because of demand, pilot shortages, and limited airport capacity. If Embraer is to have a long-term future in commercial aviation that goes beyond being a niche player, moving up is the only move.

But there's that financial barrier of entry again. As healthy as Embraer is—it's in much better shape than Bombardier was, for example, and in 2024, Embraer's balance sheet looks much better than Boeing's—the company is dinky compared with Airbus and Boeing. In 2024, Boeing, even in its reduced state, recorded revenues of $66.5 billion. Airbus had revenues of $79.7 billion. Embraer reported revenue of $6.4 billion. Airbus revenues were 12.4 times greater; Boeing's were ten times greater. Embraer in 2024 set a goal to grow to $10 billion in revenue by 2030. But this is still a fraction of the revenues of Airbus and Boeing. One doesn't have to turn to Aboulafia to conclude that the financial barrier for Embraer is nothing but daunting. If Embraer is to take on Airbus and Boeing, it almost certainly must take on a giant, healthy, deep-pocket industrial partner.

For Embraer, one of the big questions (of many) it must deal with is what kind of airplane should it propose? It's a question that's common to Airbus and Boeing as well.

RELATIONSHIPS

For more than two decades, beginning with Jim McNerney's Partnering for Success (PFS) initiative, Boeing's relationship with its supply chain remained strained, both financially and personally. The inability to provide suppliers with a reliable production stream, or even reliable information, makes it impossible for them to plan. In some cases, the very survival of small-to-medium-sized suppliers was threatened. Battered first by the MAX grounding beginning on March 13, 2019, most believed that the disruption at Boeing would be measured in weeks or perhaps three months. Then-CEO Muilenburg repeatedly tried to reassure all stakeholders that recertification was a short-term target. Production initially continued at a reduced rate with this anticipated return to service timeline in mind.

By December 2019, it became clear that there was no end in sight for the lifting of the FAA's grounding order. Boeing suspended all production of the MAX. Suppliers had been able to weather the reduced rate pretty well. But now, they had no idea how long to plan for production suspension. Adding to the uncertainty, Steve Dickson, the FAA administrator, felt compelled to issue a public rebuke of Muilenburg's repeated public comments about an imminent recertification date. By Christmas, Muilenburg had been fired. Calhoun replaced him on January 13, 2020. He made it clear that he wasn't going to predict any return-to-service date. Suppliers were totally in the dark—their Boeing contacts had no idea when the situation would improve, so all they could do when asked was shrug.

Suppliers were no sooner dealing with the cessation of MAX production when the global COVID-19 pandemic began in March 2020. Nearly all of Boeing's remaining production, of 777Fs and 787s, ground to a virtual halt; only one-half of one airplane a month continued in order to keep the lines, and the supply chain, "warm." (Airbus cut its A320 production rate to the low 40s a month and reduced production of the widebody A330 and A350; drastic drops to be sure, but at least the bottom didn't fall out of its supply chain—as it did at Boeing.) As if the MAX grounding and COVID pandemic weren't enough, in October 2020 Boeing suspended deliveries of the 787 for what turned out to be twenty months, further battering the supply chain.

The 777X program also became a headache for suppliers. Originally planned to enter service in the first quarter of 2020 (with hopes of delivery in December 2019), flight testing was halted when a technical problem with the giant GE9X engines was discovered. The engines had to be removed and sent back to GE for a fix. By the time they were returned, some nine months later, certification of the airplane was caught in the negative halo effect of the MAX certification controversies. Even after the MAX grounding was lifted and 787 deliveries resumed, flight testing of the 777X remained stalled. Finally resumed in 2024, progress was slow. Boeing set a new target for certification and delivery in 2025, more than five years late. But Tim Clark, president of Emirates Airline (which had more orders for the airplane than any other airline), and officials at Lufthansa (the very first customer) said they didn't expect the airplane until 2026.

Flight testing of the 777X revealed a flaw in a strut under the cowling of the plane's giant engines, affecting all four flight-test aircraft. More delays ensued. More vexing, however, was the need to rewrite some of the aircraft's flight-control software. Flight testing revealed a tendency for the aircraft to pitch down, uncommanded. The horizontal tail planes, according to some, are a little small for the bigger size of the 777X, and the giant engines might disrupt some airflow inboard along the wings. The process of analyzing the software was slow and meticulous, adding more delays.

Overhanging all of this was the PFS program instituted by McNerney and carried on by Muilenburg to put the squeeze on suppliers to lower costs. It was one blow after another, after another, after another that brought some of the suppliers to the brink.

All of this turmoil in every program at BCA except the 767F and KC-46A programs further strained the supply chain. Small and medium suppliers were hit hard. Some had undertaken major expansions associated with one Boeing program or another, and their new facilities or spaces, following in some cases millions of dollars in capital outlay, were idle. These suppliers teetered on financial ruin.

Boeing, even in its weakened financial condition, advanced money to some of its suppliers. In some cases, Boeing embedded its own employees at suppliers' companies. In one case, a decades-old supplier wasn't able to survive independently. A foreign company bought the firm.

It wasn't until 2024, after the Alaska flight 1282 accident, that Boeing at long last began repairing relationships with the supply chain. With the FAA blocking expansion of the 737 production lines to add a fourth one at the widebody plant in Everett, capping production at thirty-eight per month (a symbolic gesture because Boeing was barely at rate twenty) and breathing down the company's neck at the Renton 737 plant, suppliers took yet another hit.

A month after the Alaska accident, Ihssane Mounir, who had been named head of BCA's supply-chain department, spoke at the annual PNAA suppliers conference. Mounir, whose reputation was that of a hard ass, was uncharacteristically humbled—and by extension, so was Boeing—in the aftermath of the accident. Furthermore, during the remainder of 2024, PNAA, which Boeing had boycotted for two years (see Chapter 14), facilitated meetings between certain suppliers and Boeing. When Mounir again appeared at the conference in February 2025, the humility was still evident, Boeing had worked with suppliers to get through the latest crisis, and all was forgiven with PNAA.

Boeing's relationships with customers—airlines and lessors—was often battered as well. With the official grounding of the MAX and suspension of deliveries of the 787, fleet planners and schedulers faced repeated needs to revamp delivery dates and schedules. Plans to retire aging aircraft were put off over and over. Emirates Airline, which liked to flip its fleet every twelve years, was forced to put off selling 777-300ERs scheduled to be replaced by the 777X. Some were sold to freighter-conversion companies on spec and others to lessors that planned to convert them to freighters. Emirates, Qatar Airways, and Etihad Airways—the Big Three Middle Eastern airlines that accounted for 63 percent of the 481 777Xs on order in late 2024—all held onto their mid-life -300ERs.[156] Emirates, frustrated by the repeated and seemingly endless delays in getting its airplanes, committed hundreds of millions of dollars to refurbish -300ERs, including those it sold anticipating phasing them out of its fleet.

Michael O'Leary, the outspoken CEO of Ryanair, was beside himself over his inability to get his airplanes. Never shy about negotiating in the press or criticizing Boeing, he was perhaps the most vocal 737 customer expressing frustration over the repeated delays. The always-polite executives at Alaska Airlines blew up in public after Boeing's sloppy assembly practices almost blew up flight 1282, a new MAX 9 that Alaska had in service for only ten weeks.

On various quarterly or annual earnings calls, airline CEO after CEO complained about Boeing. Scott Kirby, the candid CEO of United Airlines, was one who also took his complaints public, both to the financial news network CNBC and to selected print media. Frustrated, Kirby's United placed large orders for the Airbus A321neo and the 321XLR—straying from United's almost inviolate policy of buying only Boeing jets.

The complaints went on around the world.

If relations with suppliers and customers were bad, Boeing's relationships with its two largest unions were worse—if that was possible.

When Kelly Ortberg took over from Calhoun as CEO on August 8, 2024, he stepped into an impossible position vis-à-vis Boeing's largest union, IAM 751. Contract negotiations were already underway, with the current contract set to expire on September 12. Union members had sixteen years'

---

156. Etihad had twenty-five 777Xs officially on order at the end of 2024 but had long before decided that it no longer wanted the airplanes. Emirates had 205 on order, 43 percent of the backlog.

worth of resentment built up over their first open contract negotiations since 2008. Although Boeing offered what it said was the best, most generous contract it had ever created, IAM 751 members rejected the offer by a 94.6 percent vote and authorized a strike by a 96 percent vote. These margins stunned everyone. Boeing was probably expecting a narrow rejection and a failure to reach the required two-thirds majority needed to OK a walkout. Failure to get a super-majority would mean that the contract would have to be imposed, under "parent" IAM International's rules, despite a rejection. The near-unanimity of the votes stunned everyone.

Ortberg's early outreach to labor drew plaudits. He visited assembly-line floors and met personally with union president Jon Holden shortly after taking over from Calhoun—who never met with Holden (neither Muilenberg nor McNerney had met with Holden's predecessor). Ortberg said that he wanted to "reset" labor relations. The union votes were stunning rebukes.

But negotiations began under Calhoun and were well underway when Ortberg stepped into the CEO role. He might be forgiven by less-militant union members for the unacceptable contract offer, given that he was new on the job. But what happened next blew up any remaining good will for Ortberg. On the Monday following the Thursday night walk-out by the union, Boeing issued what it called its Best and Final Offer (BAFO). The wage increase was boosted to 30 percent from 24 percent, the signing bonus was doubled from $3,000 to $6,000, modifications were made to sweeten the 401(k) pension contribution by Boeing, and a year-end bonus that was eliminated from the rejected tentative agreement was restored.

Boeing prepared the BAFO without negotiating with IAM 751's team. The *Seattle Times* reported that it was delivered to Holden minutes before it was released to the press and that the offer was sent directly to IAM 751 members. Boeing told me that it had been delivered to Holden "hours" before it was released to the press and to union members. Either way, the BAFO was immediately met with disdain. Union members wanted a 40 percent wage hike and wanted their defined pension plan back. Union leadership was irate that the negotiating team was bypassed, and so were members. Boeing set a Friday night deadline for union members to accept the BAFO.

Holden refused to put the offer up to a membership vote. A survey gauging members' reaction to the BAFO and whether they wanted to vote on it skewed heavily in Holden's favor, the union said (it never released the results). Federally overseen mediation talks failed to achieve any movement. Boeing and the union filed competing unfair labor practices complaints, and the company withdrew its BAFO.

32

Payback

*"That's not OK, to take away that reasonable benefit
that was hard fought for."*

—JON HOLDEN, PRESIDENT OF BOEING'S TOUCH-LABOR UNION,
THE INTERNATIONAL ASSOCIATION OF MACHINISTS DISTRICT 751 (IAM 751),
IN ADVANCE OF 2024 CONTRACT NEGOTIATIONS

THE MEMBERS of The Boeing Company's largest and most militant union, IAM 751, had been seething since a 2009 decision by the company's then–chief executive officer Jim McNerney to locate the second 787 final assembly line at a non-union plant in North Charleston, South Carolina.

Tensions continued to rise after a 2011 threat to locate Boeing's 737 MAX production somewhere other than Renton, Washington (a threat that made no sense). McNerney's threats and tactics in 2013 to force a union vote to kill a defined-benefit pension plan and add medical co-pays further enraged IAM 751 members.

The union's labor contract, having been amended twice and extended to 2024 by a vote in 2008 meant that wage increases failed to keep up with inflation. Housing and fuel costs in the Puget Sound area were especially high, causing a knock-on effect on food prices. Newly hired blue collar workers at Boeing didn't earn a livable wage for the expensive Seattle area. Voluntary employee and matching company contributions to Boeing's 401(k) retirement plan, which replaced a defined-pension plan, weren't of much use to the young workers who struggled to pay rent and put food on the table (if you can't afford to contribute anything, an employer match doesn't mean much).

Jon Holden succeeded Tom Wroblewski as president of IAM 751. As early as 2020, the union put its members on notice: start saving for a strike fund for when the current contract expires in September 2024. The notice's timing was unfortunate: it was issued just as the COVID-19 pandemic broke out. Boeing already was suffering financially because of the MAX grounding, now into its first full year. In October 2020, with no end in sight for either the MAX grounding or the impacts of the pandemic, Boeing suspended deliveries of the 787 (such as they were during the pandemic) after production flaws were discovered. The suspension ultimately lasted twenty months. Only a trickle of 777 and 767 freighters and KC-46A tankers were being delivered out of Puget Sound factories. Boeing was bleeding cash.

By October 2022, 787 and 737 deliveries resumed, but at low rates. The pandemic was over, although the aerospace sector was in tatters, from the original equipment manufacturers (OEMs) to the supply chain. Still, Boeing executives were optimistic that the worst was over. In November of that year, the company held its first Investor Day since 2018. Then-CEO Dave Calhoun and CFO Brian West (still in this post as of this writing) gave optimistic projections that, essentially, Boeing would be in full recovery by the end of 2025 or early 2026. For the gathered aerospace analysts and stockholders, they forecasted free cash flow of $10 billion (with the unstated implication that dividends and stock buybacks would resume around then). Calhoun also said that there would be no new airplane "introduced" until the middle of the 2030 decade. This was music to the ears of analysts and institutional investors, who disliked the diversion of cash flow into research and development.[157]

In a 2022 interview for this book, Holden outlined his thought process for contract negotiations that would begin two years hence. With the IAM 751 contract up in 2024, Boeing would still be in recovery mode, with billions of dollars of additional debt incurred during its crisis year still to be repaid. Full production would not have resumed by then, so Boeing's financial picture would be, if not weak, then certainly weaker than it was on March 9, 2019. How could the union hope to recapture givebacks and obtain huge wage increases if Boeing's financial picture was still under pressure?

The union's 2020 message about saving for a strike fund was about preparing for success in negotiations. "Our members have to be financially secure. It's important that they save for contract exploration. There's a whole lot of great things that happen when a family can save a little bit of money and be prepared and stand on principle. When you're making a decision on whether you should give up reasonable things that a company is overreaching to take away, your financial stability at that time is very critical. Our goal is to reach a contract without having to strike. It is not our goal to be on strike. The livelihoods of 28,000 to 29,000 families are in the balance at that time and in a strike," Holden explained.

---

157. Never mind that delaying new-product development was taking Boeing down the same path followed by the McDonnell Douglas Corporation (MDC) that eventually led to its merger into Boeing in 1997 with a commercial aviation market share of an embarrassing 7 percent. The death of the Douglas Aircraft Company was a particularly ignominious end.

"It's our job to prepare people to be secure. Our members make it through strikes and they're proud of the stance they take. No one is ever ashamed of standing up to power and saying, 'That's not good enough. I'm not going to accept that.' Sometimes it's the only opportunity [you get] to stand up and say no in any aspect of your life. You get to negotiate the things that are important to you. You get to say, 'That's not OK, to take away that reasonable benefit that was hard fought for.'"

Holden said that Boeing would hope that union members wouldn't be prepared to weather a strike. "They hope our members aren't prepared because they'll roll right over the top of us if they could." This certainly may have been true under former CEO McNerney. But by 2024, Boeing was hardly in a position to withstand a strike, let alone a long one.

Holden recounted some history when asked about the impact of the pandemic on Boeing's current financial condition, but he didn't really address the realities of the current situation.

"[Boeing] would have made it through the pandemic much better had they not made other decisions," he said. "How do we navigate the issues that you kind of laid out there? Is the reality being we're asking for reasonable things? We will be asking for reasonable things. Job security is not something that costs the company. It doesn't put them in debt, putting airplane programs here and offering the programs that the carriers need and will buy are what brings success to the company.

"Stability of the workforce is what brings the company out of those things. It's what it does to pay off that debt. It's what helps you increase the rates on the 737 and any other program that they need to in order to be more profitable. The reasonable things that we're asking for will bring stability. Asking for more concessions on top of an overreach from 2014 doesn't bring stability. If that's the direction they go, then I know that it's going to be a rough patch, rougher than it already is."

One uncertain element hanging over the inevitable union vote was the fact that the demographics of IAM 751 had shifted dramatically in recent years. As far back as 2009, *Leeham News* analyzed the demos of IAM 751 and the engineering union at Boeing, the Society of Professional Engineering Employees in Aerospace (SPEEA). Within a five-year period, each of the unions experienced a turnover of about 5,000 members due to retirements. Increasing retirement eligibility followed every year thereafter. When the MAX was grounded, Boeing—initially thinking that the grounding would be short lived, as with the 787 in 2013—kept all employees, especially those in IAM 751, who assembled the 737 in Renton. But when the pandemic all but shut down Boeing's Commercial Airplanes division (BCA), drastic action was required to stem the cash bleeding, already at an unacceptably high rate. Boeing offered early-retirement buyouts to thousands of employees across the company, including to IAM 751 and

SPEEA members. Boeing also resorted to involuntarily layoffs. On top of continued natural retirements and attrition, thousands more workers left Boeing—and with them, institutional knowledge and line experience that would be critical to restarting production after the MAX grounding was lifted and the pandemic was over. The trade was losing this knowledge over the long term to keep the company alive in the short term. Boeing commendably tried to ease the pain, but in the end, officials had no choice. The company's very survival was at stake.

After the "ungrounding" of the MAX and the end of pandemic, Boeing hired thousands of new people who were inexperienced in the ways of building highly complex and technologically designed airplanes. The company also hired thousands of additional people, engineers and assembly line personnel, in anticipation of ramping up production and designing a new airplane. IAM 751's membership increased from 28,000 to 29,000 in 2022, according to Holden, and rose to 33,000 in 2024. Boeing bragged that it hired 10,000 new engineers, a number that on its face seemed inflated given the nationwide labor shortage. Whether this figure was inflated is beside the point. What was undeniable was that all the new hires for line assembly created a huge training demand and created a big learning curve. Several years are required for assembly line workers to become proficient. On the engineering side, the new hires were largely new to the aerospace sector. Both employee sectors lost institutional knowledge and experience critical to efficiently designing and building airplanes. Oversight by remaining, experienced professionals was vitally important to Boeing. It's easy to see how overwhelmed everyone could, and would, become. All this converged for everyone to see with the January 5, 2024, Alaska Airlines flight 1282 accident.

According to a person familiar with the situation, Boeing entered contract negotiations thinking that the union would not strike, an assumption that no doubt colored its approach with IAM 751 negotiators. Calhoun also was unconcerned about the provision in the proposed contract stating that Boeing would commit to building its next new airplane in Everett for the duration of the contract (through September 2028). He had no plans to launch a new airplane program during the contract period.

In 2024, about half of IAM 751's 33,000 members had around six years of employment at Boeing as the members headed into the contract vote. About half of these workers had been employed by Boeing for two years or less. These members didn't have bitter memories of the 2008 strike, the 2009 relocation of the second 787 final assembly line to Charleston after a bitter contract negotiation in which IAM 751 leadership and key politicians thought they had been sandbagged by Boeing, the 2011 MAX threat, or the 2013 777X threat and contentious contract-amendment votes. These members didn't have a defined-benefit pension plan yanked away from them and had only experienced health benefit co-pays. Given that they struggled to pay for rent, food, gas, and other living expenses in Puget Sound's high-cost environment, was a pension plan of any kind high on their list of priorities, or was a higher wage the most important consideration? Nobody knew how half the membership would rank priorities that were so important to the older members who had lived through all the McNerney wars on the unions.

An indicator of the vote outcome was evident when more than 20,000 union members rallied at the Seattle Mariners baseball stadium in July 2024. In a near-unanimous result, 99.9 percent favored a strike in an informal vote. Some dismissed the meaning of this vote since this was a rah-rah rally, but in retrospect, dismissing the sentiment was a perilous act.

Boeing and the negotiating teams for both of its unions reached a tentative agreement (TA) that included, among other things, a 25 percent raise (well short of the 40 percent ask) and a commitment during the life of the contract to build the next airplane in Puget Sound. IAM 751 issued a press release and posted a statement on its website praising the TA and calling it the best agreement ever negotiated. The union's negotiating team and leadership endorsed the TA and recommended adoption. Boeing issued its own statement praising the agreement.

What happened next is a matter of dispute. One version comes from Holden. The other comes from within the company.

Within twenty-four hours of the TA, the pushback on social media and within the union was overwhelmingly negative. Holden and the leadership at IAM 751 backtracked their support of the TA. Holden later said that Boeing had essentially forced the union's negotiating team into a corner, demanding endorsement of the TA in exchange for the 25 percent wage hike and the commitment to build the next airplane in Puget Sound, the two key elements of the agreement. When union members voted on Thursday, September 12, they overwhelmingly rejected the agreement (94 percent) and authorized a walkout (96 percent). It was a stunning result. Boeing certainly didn't expect it.

Neither did the media awaiting the results at IAM 751's headquarters in South Seattle. Members in the union hall also didn't expect the overwhelming margin but were elated. While awaiting the systemwide tally, it was clear that members at the union's HQ who counted the onsite vote results knew that the contract had been rejected and that a strike vote had passed. They were only waiting for vote counts from outlying areas to be reported to HQ and for the final results to be announced.

A key reason for the contract rejection and the strike: the TA did not restore the defined-benefit pension plan which thousands of union members regarded as the line in the sand. Boeing was never going to agree to restoring the plan. Everyone except the membership seemed to acknowledge this. But the 2013 vote and underhanded tactics of Boeing (in the minds of members) were not forgotten. Members were solidly in payback mode.

Going into the vote, Boeing claims that it had no reason to expect rejection of the contract despite social media chatter. It had been endorsed by union leadership. The company felt somewhat sandbagged by the reversal. It was reminiscent of what happened at Spirit AeroSystems the previous June. Spirit's primary workers were represented by a different district of the IAM. In those contract negotiations, an agreement was reached and union leadership recommended approval. But the membership rejected the contract and authorized a walkout. Spirit's executives felt double-crossed by the union. Spirit, also in dire financial condition, quickly reached a new agreement, and this strike was over in a week.

At Boeing, when the TA was reached on September 8, 2024, there was a joint celebration between company and union negotiators at a downtown Seattle hotel where talks had been underway for six months, according to a company official, adding to the expectation that the contract would be approved. According to Boeing, Holden and his team believed that the 25 percent pay hike and a commitment to build the next airplane in Puget Sound—a commitment Boeing never had before given in advance of a program launch—were key wins for the union.

Critics viewed the commitment as an empty promise. Boeing was in no position to launch a new airplane program during the next three years of the life of the contract, they correctly pointed out. A Boeing official acknowledged to *Leeham News* that this was the case but countered that the following contract that would run from 2027 to 2030 would have to be negotiated during a period when a program launch was possible. The union, this official said, would fight any effort to remove this commitment from the next contract. Left unsaid was the probability that a strike would happen if Boeing insisted on removing this provision from the next contract.

Holden stuck to his story that the union's negotiating team and leaders had been maneuvered into endorsing the contract. Boeing claims that Holden had to change his tune when initial member reaction was so negative.

Within a week, Boeing returned with a Best and Final Offer (BAFO). The wage hike was increased, as was the signing bonus figure and the 401(k) contribution, and some other modifications were made, but all other elements of the original contract offer remained in place—including the commitment to build the next airplane in Puget Sound. There are two stories about this, too.

Holden complained that he was informed about the BAFO after Boeing released the offer to the media. Boeing says that Holden got the BAFO before the public release. Both sides agreed that the union's negotiating team hadn't been involved in reaching the BAFO, and this prompted resentment over Boeing's "disrespect" for the union. And whether Holden got the offer before or after it was released to the media, a span of minutes was involved rather than a collaborative process. It was a colossal, tone-deaf blunder by Boeing. Predictably, opposition from members was so great that IAM 751 leadership didn't even put the BAFO up for a vote by members. Equally predictably, Boeing and the union filed complaints with the National Labor Relations Board (NRLB) over unfair practices.

Finally, Boeing and IAM 751 negotiated a third contract offer. The wage increase was boosted again so that, when compounded over the life of the contract, it equaled 43 percent, slightly more than the original ask. Sweeteners were added to the signing bonus and the 401(k) plan. The airplane-build-site commitment was retained. But there was still no return to a defined-benefit pension plan. The *Seattle Times* reported that CEO Kelly Ortberg threatened to come back with an inferior offer if the union rejected the contract this time and didn't end the strike. This time, 60 percent of the members voted Yes, fifty-three days after the walk out. Some members began returning to work within days; all had to be back on the line by November 12. Refresher training across Puget Sound assembly lines was required, delaying production re-starts. Then, with the holidays, Boeing couldn't truly get back to work until the new year.

A company insider says that Ortberg didn't "threaten" the union. Rather, he conveyed that Boeing had reached the limit of its ability to give more, considering that it was going through cash at the rate of $1 billion a month during the strike on top of the negative cash flow already in existence. The cash position was so dire that Boeing went to the equity and debt markets while the strike was underway to raise $24 billion to carry it through the continued negative cash flow in the coming months and to service billions of dollars of debt coming due in 2025. Officials previously said several times that they didn't want to go to the equity markets to raise money. Doing so diluted existing shareholders, and equity is considered an "expensive" way to raise money. But in the intervening time, real concern emerged that Boeing could face bankruptcy because there was no indication as to when normalcy would return, and the strike could tip the balance. In the end, dilution was the best bad decision facing the company and its shareholders.

When the company's 2024 annual financial results were announced, it became clear that Boeing had nearly burned through its entire cash and short-term investment balance by early October. Only an untapped credit line of $10 billion remained. Boeing had had no choice but to go to the markets for a new cash infusion.

After the union adopted the contract, there were many media stories that Ortberg's honeymoon with the unions was over almost before it began. Only time will tell how quickly, if at all, Ortberg can reset labor relations. More than twenty years of poor relations had been embedded as a result of the GEntrification of The Boeing Company. It would take years to reverse this.

After the IAM 751 contract was approved, Ortberg turned his attention to other pressing matters. It wasn't until February 7, 2025, that he finally met with the leadership of SPEEA. Its contract was up for negotiations in 2026. There were also other labor contracts to be negotiated in 2025 and 2026.

- April 2025: Boeing drivers (Teamsters Local 174) in Puget Sound. They haul wing components from Auburn and Frederickson north to Renton and Everett. A strike there would seriously impact Boeing production.
- July 2025: IAM assembly workers in St. Louis. They build T-7s, F-15s and F-18s.
- October 2025: Boeing welders in Puget Sound. They are a small group—a few hundred people—represented by the International Union of Operating Engineers Local 302. There's a pretty serious shortage of welders both nationwide and regionally, so they have more leverage than their numbers would indicate. They are needed more for plant operations than for production.
- January 2026: SPEEA Wichita Technical and Professional Unit. They number about 1,600 people now working for Spirit.
- October 2026: SPEEA Northwest Professional Unit and Technical Unit. This group is made up of slightly more than 17,000 workers in Washington, Oregon, California, and Utah who are covered by two separate but connected bargaining agreements.

Ortberg has his work cut out for him.

The ruinous Jack Welch legacy, it seems, will live on for an indefinite period.

33

Who's Responsible?

"[Boeing] will have to do more to make sure the board is trusted to lead the company into the future."

—CORPORATE BOARD MEMBER MAGAZINE, MARCH 2024

THERE IS NO SIMPLE, ONE-LINE ANSWER to the question, how did The Boeing Company fall so far?

When an airliner crashes, investigators point out that there are always a series of events that led to the accident. The National Transportation Safety Board (NTSB), and before it, the Civil Aeronautics Board, and investigating agencies of countries other than the United States all follow the path to an accident in the same way. There are many contributing factors.

Then-CEO Dennis Muilenburg initially seemed to acknowledge that Boeing bore some responsibility for the MAX crashes of Ethiopian Airlines and Lion Air flights. It was a seminal moment in the company's long history of blaming pilots for accidents. But a short time later, Muilenburg appeared to backtrack when he said that every accident has a chain of events. He seemed to be pointing a finger at the pilots after all, which in the view of many returned Boeing to its habit of not accepting blame for its own shortcomings. In reality, he wasn't wrong. It was argued in some corners, including among some U.S. pilots, that the Ethiopian and Lion Air pilots weren't well trained and that the co-pilots were inexperienced, leading them all to make mistakes.

This view ignored Lion Air's ignorance of the Maneuvering Characteristics Augmentation System (MCAS) on the MAX because Boeing had removed references to it in the plane's operating manual. Critics pointed out that, on the last flight of the MAX operated by Lion Air the day before the crash, pilots had successfully recovered from flight anomalies. The pilots didn't know it at the time, but MCAS was kicking in. Luckily, those pilots successfully flew through the event and safely landed the airplane. There was a third pilot in the cockpit on that earlier flight who had helped sort out the problem. On flight JT610, the deadly flight, there were only two pilots, and the experienced captain wrestled the airplane for ten minutes at an altitude at which there was room to maneuver, while the less-experienced co-pilot scoured the Quick Reference Handbook looking for a solution. The captain decided to have a look for himself and turned control over to the co-pilot, who—with no experience wrestling with the airplane as the pilot had just done—lost control of the plane and dived into the sea.

The MCAS on the Ethiopian flight engaged immediately after takeoff. The plane never got higher than about 800 feet—about the height of an 80-story building—before nosing over into the earth.[158] The Ethiopian pilots had no room to maneuver. They were aware of the existence of MCAS due to the earlier Lion Air crash and had been briefed on the procedure to use in the event of a failure. The ensuing investigation indicated that the pilots did not follow the procedure precisely. Some critics claim that this procedural failure, along with the actions of the Lion Air co-pilot, were at fault for the crashes.

One can argue about this conclusion, but what's clear is that if pilot error contributed to these accidents, the root cause of those errors went straight back to Boeing. Muilenburg was right about the chain-of-events concept. But it was a cheap shot that sullied the pilots.

When all is said and done, who is responsible for Boeing's decline?

As with any corporate story, whether it's about success or failure, the answer rests not with any one individual. Most heritage Boeing employees and critics blame Harry Stonecipher and Boeing's merger with McDonnell Douglas as the turning points that changed Boeing from an engineering company to one focused on shareholder value. But this is too convenient. It was former CEO Phil Condit who, after his own conversations with GE's Jack Welch, introduced a shareholder-value ethos into Boeing. It was Condit who pursued the MDC merger to diversify Boeing's reliance on commercial aviation and to regain Pentagon business that Boeing once dominated with its heavy bombers and aerial-refueling tankers. (He was not wrong in this strategy.) After the merger, it was Condit who took the view that a company's chairman and CEO (in this case, him) should concentrate on long-term vision and strategy while its president and chief operating officer (Stonecipher, who would succeed Condit as CEO) should run the day-to-day business. In theory, there's a lot to be said for this approach. In practice, and in hindsight, one can credibly argue that Condit's hands-off approach to day-to-day operations went too far.

Certainly, Stonecipher's cold-hearted outlook of Boeing's heritage was a huge mistake. He sent a clear, face-slapping message to thousands of engineers that their work, experience, and expertise wasn't valued, and this attitude infected the entire company. Shareholder value is something that executive suites and boards of directors of public companies must consider—but there is a trade-off that must be built in for the long-term health of

---

158. This was roughly the height of the two airplanes flown into the North and South Towers of the World Trade Center on 9/11.

a company. Is it really a good strategy to return 100 percent of free cash flow to shareholders at the expense of research and development (R&D) and the introduction of new products? Critics of Stonecipher's leadership approach raised warning flags early on; history proved just how disastrous the foundation laid by Stonecipher had become.

Stonecipher's short tenure as CEO of MDC saw the final decline of its Douglas Aircraft Company division, but this process had been underway from the moment the McDonnell Corporation acquired Douglas in 1967. The McDonnell family never understood the commercial side of the business and weren't particularly interested in learning about or investing in it. The company's DC-10 was already a Douglas project when the merger took place. It was the last all-new airplane that Douglas would ever introduce. MDC outsourced key components of their DC-9, MD-80/90/95, DC-10, and MD-11 models. John Hart-Smith, a Douglas engineer who migrated to Boeing with the merger, wrote a white paper in 2001 that became famous within Boeing and within the aviation industry generally warning about the consequences of overdoing outsourcing. It's unknown whether Stonecipher ever read the paper, but if he did, it's pretty clear that he disregarded its conclusions. Coming at a time when Boeing was designing the 787, the lessons contained in the white paper should have been required reading. But Condit (who was still CEO at the time), Stonecipher, and the board of directors had already shifted the company's focus toward shareholder value and away from engineering and financial risk management. The 777, the last airplane program Condit oversaw before becoming Boeing's CEO, had gone more than twice over its $5 billion budget.[159] As a result, Stonecipher and the board wanted to keep Boeing's share of the 787 development to $5 billion. Boeing outsourced that plane's industrial design and production at levels never before undertaken.

Ironically, it was another GE alumnus, Jim McNerney, who warned the board about overdoing cost cutting as they weighed whether to proceed with the 787. Lynn Lunsford in 2003 was the aerospace reporter for the *Wall Street Journal.* In April of that year, he reported that McNerney warned the board that cost cutting could go too far and that rival Airbus would benefit if Boeing overdid it. It turned out that McNerney would be proved right. But after he became CEO following Stonecipher's firing in 2005, McNerney didn't follow his own advice. He went on a cost-cutting binge over the ten years of his leadership that did incalculable damage to the company and to labor relations.

To a large degree, McNerney was forced into his cost-cutting binge. The

---

159. Outside the company, the final figure never was revealed. But it's generally accepted to have been between $11 billion and $12 billion, or more than $23 billion in 2024 dollars.

outsourcing of engineering, design, industrialization, and production on the 787 became such a financial disaster that, in 2025, Boeing still hasn't recouped its program costs. This program disaster led to a diversion of engineers from the 747-8 program, resulting in loads of engineering re-work by Boeing's engineering union, the Society of Professional Engineering Employees in Aerospace (SPEEA), of outsourced work done in India. The 747-8 ran billions over budget and was nearly two years late. It's never made money for Boeing.

After winning a contract to lease 100 KC-767s to the U.S. Air Force after 9/11—a highly unusual arrangement that ended in scandal, two Boeing executives going to jail, and a canceled contract—Boeing lost the next contract round to Northrop Grumman but won a third round after the second contract was canceled due to procurement irregularities by the Air Force. But to win that third round, Boeing bid 10 percent less than Airbus (then called the European Aeronautic Defence and Space Company, or EADS), a money-losing proposition. Boeing didn't say outright that it had bid below costs, but in Boeing-speak, McNerney said that long-term, the company would make money on the program.[160] No wonder he had to squeeze every penny out of the company's cost structure.

This is where life-long GE exposure kicked into high gear. "Neutron Jack" Welch, GE's long-time chairman and CEO, was ruthless in slashing labor costs and taking on GE's unions. McNerney proved to be no different. Soon after he took over from Stonecipher, in 2005, the International Association of Machinists District 751 (IAM 751) union walked out and went on strike for two months. It was an inauspicious way for McNerney to begin his tenure, and it had a lasting effect. Three years later, the union struck again, this time for another two months. McNerney retaliated the next year by locating the 787's second assembly line in South Carolina. The state is a right-to-work state, essentially meaning that unions weren't required. The Charleston facility was represented by a different IAM union district than the one operating in Puget Sound; employees eventually voted IAM out, and the Charleston facility became a non-union shop. South Carolina state and local governments ponied up nearly $1 billion in incentives, and the combination won the second assembly line. In all likelihood, McNerney would have put the line there anyway out of spite and retaliation. As previously discussed, IAM 751 filed a complaint with the National Labor Relations Board over the company's conduct.

---

160. Through 2024, thirteen years after winning the contract, Boeing not only hadn't made a dime from it, it wrote off more than $6 billion in losses with no end in sight.

McNerney's war on labor continued in addition to his other overall cost-cutting measures. First, there was the threat of relocating 737 production away from Renton, Washington, for the new re-engined model, the MAX. IAM 751 granted concessions and extended its contract with Boeing in return for a guarantee that MAX assembly work would stay in Puget Sound. Boeing got labor stability and also demanded that IAM 751 withdraw its NLRB complaint, which it did. Even then, McNerney's war on labor wasn't over. Next up was the threat of moving 777X production elsewhere. The controversial union vote involving more contract concessions and another concession was recounted earlier. It was then, at last, that McNerney declared victory with his infamous "cowering" crack.[161] He resumed the emphasis on shareholder value, even though Boeing hadn't fully come out of the debacles of the 787, the 747-8, and the KC-46A tanker. His ten-year contract-expiration date was coming up—and so was his mandatory retirement age of 65—and the reins of leadership would be handed to Muilenburg in 2015.

McNerney had been Boeing's longest-serving CEO since Frank Shrontz. In retrospect, as a result, his tenure following Shrontz was the most consequential—and perhaps the most damaging to Boeing's heritage.

The hand-off to Muilenburg, a "lifer" Boeing engineer, didn't result in a return to the company's legacy culture. It's fair to conclude that Muilenburg had been GEntrified through his tenure as CEO of Boeing's defense unit and as president and COO of the corporation. By 2015, the 787's problems were behind it. Production between Everett and Charleston was on its way to 14 per month (seven at each plant). Losses on the 747-8 were largely in the past, having been written off. Production of the 737 was humming along. The 777 Classic was still being produced at a hefty rate. Profits and cash flow were becoming abundant. Even the 787 program, in 2015, became cash-flow positive. Muilenburg and CFO Greg Smith (who by this time had also been fully GEntrified) boasted to Wall Street that Boeing was going to return 100 percent of free cash flow to shareholders. After all, they had suffered through all the turmoil during the bad times and should be rewarded in the good.

McNerney was never able to boost Boeing's share price to $200. Muilenburg and Smith, with the board of directors' blessing, aggressively pursued stock buybacks and dividends. By 2019, the stock peaked at $420

---

161. In an attempt to be humorous on an earnings call in response to a question about this relationship with the unions, McNerney noted that he would be 65 soon and perhaps could stay beyond Boeing's mandatory retirement age. It was then that he added that he would be around for employees to "cower" at his leadership.

per share. Profits were aided by Muilenburg's cost cutting (his nickname in some circles was Dennis the Knife). How much impact this had on the safety culture at Boeing can only be a matter of conjecture. Engineering design of the MAX had been underway while Muilenburg was still CEO of the defense unit. Muilenburg became president and COO of the company in December 2013, and chairman and CEO in July 2015. The MAX's first flight was in January 2016, a mere six months after Muilenburg became CEO. The term "Maneuvering Characteristics Augmentation System," or "MCAS," was likely something he had never heard before.

This raises the overarching question of just how far down in Boeing's ranks GEntrification had permeated. It's a matter of record following the MAX investigations that Boeing faced a $1-million-per-airplane penalty from Southwest Airlines if flight-simulator training was deemed necessary for pilots moving from the 737 NG to the MAX. From the get-go, Boeing promoted the MAX as a plane that only required a type of training that could be done on a laptop in a matter of hours. There is no question that the MAX was under cost and schedule pressures, especially coming after the other program debacles then dominating Boeing. But any program at any original equipment manufacturer (OEM) is under cost and schedule pressures, and in this respect, there was nothing at all different about the MAX.

Still, when engineering decisions were made to tie MCAS to a single angle-of-attack (AOA) sensor to avoid simulator training, and when a decision was made to not inform pilots of MCAS's existence, how much of this was tied to cutting costs? Or how much of this was the result of complacency, arrogance, and bad assumptions on the part of engineers and laboratory test pilots? As with all aircraft accidents, and as demonstrated throughout this book, a series of factors combined to lead to disaster. Cost cutting, complacency, arrogance, and bad assumptions are all to blame for problems with the MAX programs.

Even taking into account all the factors relayed above and discussed throughout this book, there are still more parties at whom fingers can be pointed for Boeing's decline over nearly three decades. Several boards of directors at Boeing bear responsibility. The boards signed off on the company emphasizing shareholder value. The boards also signed off on tying executive compensation (and their own) to Boeing's stock price. The feckless boards failed to exercise detailed oversight of the company's corporate, or "C," suites until the tanker, Stonecipher, 787, 747-8, KC-46, and MAX crises became so pervasive that they could no longer be ignored.

The GEntrification of Boeing began when Jack Welch had his shareholder-value conversation with Phil Condit. Over the following twenty-two years (from 1996 to 2018, when the Lion Air crash happened), shareholder value, cost cutting, and beating Wall Street consensus ruled from Boeing's boards down to the budgets of its program managers. Welch was GE's CEO from 1981 to 2001, and he died in 2020. But his legacy at Boeing lives on to this day.[162] It will take Kelly Ortberg years to reverse the Gentrification at Boeing.

There are still others who share responsibility for Boeing's plight. The Federal Aviation Administration (FAA) clearly failed in its oversight of Boeing, delegating too much responsibility to Boeing employee-representatives and failing to back them up against company pressure. The FAA came under withering criticism for this. But critics ignored important realities, the first of which is that few, if any, federal agencies are funded or staffed enough to *not* designate company employees to represent the overseeing agency. This is true for the Food and Drug Administration, the Nuclear Regulatory Commission, and the FAA, among others.

In fact, the FAA was formed in 1959 because its predecessor, the Civil Aeronautics Authority (CAA), failed in its oversight duties. Despite federal regulations clearly stating that airliner designs had to be created so as prevent faults, three post–World War II airliners were grounded precisely because design faults had made their way onto airliners. The twin-engine Martin 202, from the Martin Aircraft Company, the first post-war airplane intended to replace the pre-war (and venerable) DC-3, used metals in its wing spars that were prematurely subject to fatigue. Northwest Airlines (NWA) lost two Martins when the wings separated from the airplanes. When the metal fatigue was discovered on the relatively young aircraft, inspections discovered cracks in other NWA Martins. The fleet was grounded.

The Douglas DC-6 was grounded after two aircraft, one from American Airlines and one from United, caught fire mid-flight. American's DC-6 crashed, killing all aboard. United's airplane made an emergency landing. The ensuing investigations discovered that a cabin-heater air scoop was placed behind a wing-tank gasoline-overflow valve. When transferring fuel, the pilot of a DC-6 had to be sure to turn off the transfer before the wing tank filled. If he didn't, fuel exited the overflow. The fuel then

---

162. Welch's legacy is well documented in the books *The Man Who Destroyed Capitalism* and *Lights Out*. His choice to be his successor at GE, Jeffrey Immelt, failed spectacularly (though he inherited what turned out to be Welch's mess, which Larry Culp, the current CEO of GE, finally sorted out throughout 2023 and 2024). Robert Nardelli, who also trained at GE under Welch, left the company after being passed over and became CEO at Home Depot, where his record was mixed. After serving under Welch at GE, McNerney first went to 3M, where his tenure was cut short when he was tapped to run Boeing. At 3M, McNerney was criticized for too much cost cutting and for reducing R&D. By and large, few at 3M were sorry to see him leave.

streamed into the air intake and into the cabin heater, which ignited the fuel. The DC-6s were grounded until the scoop's location was changed.

After an in-flight fire occurred on a pilot-training flight of Lockheed's Constellation, the airplane crashed landed. An investigation revealed a through stud containing electrical wires could arch, starting a blaze. The aircraft was grounded as a result.

The CAA was under-funded and relied on employees at the companies it regulated to perform some of its required oversight duties. Which brings us to Congress.

During the MAX crisis, and a few years later following the Alaska Airlines flight 1282 accident, Congress held hearings to investigate the three accidents and the roles of Boeing and the FAA in those accidents. Some members of Congress were sincere in their investigative roles, while others seemed more interested in their fifteen minutes in the spotlight. Whatever the motives, Boeing and the FAA caught the blame for the aircraft crashes. But it was Congress that, dating back to the CAA days, consistently refused to fund the CAA/FAA properly so that the agency, and not Boeing, could do its job. Indeed, the budget process for the FAA (called Authorization) usually became a political football for members who used it as leverage for something else. It was also Congress that passed legislation, often at the behest of lobbyists from Boeing and other U.S. aerospace companies, to loosen and "streamline" aviation regulations and oversight in the name of deregulation (this loosening began under President Ronald Reagan).

Of course, few if any members of Congress would own up to the institution's culpability, let alone acknowledge that individual members were responsible for advocating and voting for budgets or for regulatory "reform."

Even today, frustrated Boeing employees, retired or not, and critics point to the MDC merger as the primary cause of Boeing's decline. This ignores one key fact: Jim McNerney did not come to Boeing from MDC. He came via 3M from GE. Following the fired, scandal-plagued Stonecipher and professing that he was going to clean up Boeing's ethics, McNerney had an opportunity to make a clean break from the MDC merger and from Stonecipher's GE upbringing. As a Boeing board member, he warned against too much cost cutting in the 787 program. But he didn't make this break. Instead, he doubled down on *his* Welch-dominated GE career. McNerney remained chairman and CEO of Boeing for ten years. His track record at the company speaks for itself.

If a finger must be pointed at one person, Jim McNerney is the one at the top of many people's lists. But the real culprit is Jack Welch.

34

The Way Back

"Let's work together to live our values and behaviors, uphold them, and return Boeing to the company that we all know we can be."

—KELLY ORTBERG IN AN APRIL 17, 2025, MESSAGE TO EMPLOYEES

HOW DOES THE BOEING COMPANY MAKE ITS WAY BACK to being legacy Boeing?

As has been discussed throughout this book, the answers involve returning to engineering excellence, fixing the balance sheet, returning to profitability in the company's commercial and defense units, repairing relationships with its unions and its supply chain, and launching a new airplane program. There's no need to repeat these issues. It's time to look forward.

Following the fifty-three-day strike at Boeing in 2024 by the International Association of Machinists District 751 (IAM 751) union and Boeing's missteps in how it handled its best and final offer to the union, Ortberg suffered a setback in his ambition to "reset" labor relations. Members of IAM 751 and of Boeing's engineering union, the Society of Professional Engineering Employees in Aerospace (SPEEA), remain suspicious of the company's efforts to ensure that workers who participate in Boeing's Speak Up (reporting) program will be respected and protected. Gaining employee confidence in this program will be a long, hard task.

Ortberg did not meet with SPEEA leadership until February 2025, six months after he assumed the CEO role. In fairness, he had his hands full, much like California firefighters battling thousands of acres of uncontrolled blazes. Additionally, SPEEA's contract isn't up until late 2026, so there wasn't an immediate need to rush to a meeting.

There have been signs, however, that Boeing's battered relationship with its supply chain is improving. Boeing had been at war with its supply chain ever since former CEO Jim McNerney launched his Partnering for Success program, which continued through Dennis Muilenburg's regime. Then came the MAX grounding, the pandemic, the suspension of 787 deliveries for twenty months, indefinite delays in the certification of the 777X, and the IAM 751 strike, all making supplier planning impossible.

For nearly twenty years (!) Boeing has had strained relations with its suppliers. For a good number of these years, the anger and criticism over this issue spilled out at the annual Pacific Northwest Aerospace Alliance (PNAA) conference, of which Boeing was a main sponsor and participant. Tension between PNAA and Boeing increased over time, as did the criticism and reporting of the way Boeing handled things, until Boeing boycotted PNAA for two years (2022 and 2023). It returned to the conference in February 2024, one month after the Alaska accident. It was a rare showing of humility.

At the 2025 February conference, the head of Boeing's Commercial Airplanes (BCA) supply unit, Ihssane Mounir, went out of his way to praise and apologize to the supply chain. He outlined a series of actions Boeing took post-Alaska to help suppliers, to meet with them, and to hear their concerns. Mounir also praised PNAA for acting as a facilitator with some suppliers. In my own reporting of the event, I noted that in contrast to 2023, when supplier anger toward Boeing permeated the conference, this time there was hope rather than anger. Skepticism remained about Boeing's timeline for increasing production rates, but this was rooted in past broken goals, as could be expected. In his report of Mounir's address, *Seattle Times* reporter Dominic Gates titled his article "Boeing Hugs Its Suppliers Instead of Squeezing Them for Money."[163] It was a very different Boeing. Coming from Mounir, the contrast was especially significant.

How much of the attitude change originates with Ortberg is unknown. Coming from Rockwell Collins, a major Boeing supplier, he was on the receiving end of the Partnering for Success program. But he joined Boeing toward the end of 2024, and this influence may have been limited.

It will take years if not a decade or more to turn the culture around at Boeing.

For many, the "only" way back is for Boeing to launch a new airplane program. Earlier parts of this book have already explained why this can't happen in the near future, so the reasons don't need to be repeated. The real question is what kind of airplane will Boeing produce and when does it get launched?

What kind of airplane is the easier question to answer. A 737 replacement won't be coming any time soon. As of this writing, Boeing has a backlog of 4,800 737s (over 5,000 without accounting for iffy orders). Production is basically filled into 2030 and continues well into the next decade. The 737 is where Boeing's largest cash flow and profits are gen-

---

163. Dominic Gates, "Boeing Hugs Its Suppliers Instead of Squeezing Then for Money," *Seattle Times* (February 7, 2025), https://www.seattletimes.com/business/boeing-aerospace/
boeing-hugs-its-suppliers-instead-of-squeezing-them-for-money/.

erated. Boeing simply has to protect this return on investment until it's healthy again. The minute a replacement aircraft is announced, the profits and cash flow of the MAX program will be negatively affected. Sure, Boeing may lose some additional market share in the medium run, but the alternative is to lose money—which will hurt its ability to launch any new airplane program.

So, what's next? The New Midmarket Airplane (NMA) or a lighter variation thereof may be the next choice. There is a middle-of-the-market gap in which there are still aging 767-300ERs and some A330ceos in service. Airbus's A321s and Boeing's MAX 10s should finish off the remaining 757s in operation today. Boeing doesn't want to build any more 787-8s (and today there are only around thirty orders remaining for this sub-type), so an NMA can grow a bit to slide in under the 787-9 and A330-900, making up for market potential lost at the lower end.

An NMA, or a revision of it, still needs a new engine in the 40,000-pound thrust category. CFM International doesn't have one, and Pratt & Whitney today is focused on fixing its GTF engine. Rolls-Royce has the Ultra Fan under development, and this is the logical prospect. With the work already done on the engine, it will still take perhaps five years or so to fully develop and certify it. Boeing already has done a lot of research and development on the NMA, so these efforts may be applied to the next airplane. For all sorts of analytical reasons, it seems likely that Boeing couldn't have an NMA-like airplane ready to enter service until 2035. This airplane will protect the investment, profits, and cash flow of the MAX. It also would serve as the proving ground for the moonshot production and design techniques needed for a MAX replacement.

Any announcement by Boeing of a new airplane seems unlikely before 2027— a date that would still fall within the new IAM 751 contract requirement that the next airplane be built in the Seattle area. It's also right about the time that the company's balance sheet should be back in shape and production rates should be back to near-2018 (pre-MAX grounding) levels, producing prodigious amounts of cash flow and profits at BCA.

Boeing's way back presumes, of course, that events outside its control won't derail the progress that needs to be made on a timely basis. Geopolitical events and unpredictable economic policies from the Trump Administration could upset all well-laid plans for Boeing and other manufacturers.

When the COVID-19 pandemic was underway, Boeing received several contracts from the U.S. Department of Defense (DOD). The company was under financial pressure from the MAX grounding and the pandemic, which had dried up nearly all its commercial deliveries, so the back-to-back-to-back contracts from the Pentagon had the look and feel of an assist from DOD. Whether contracts were awarded on the merits or based on a desire to help one of the top three defense contractors stay in business is a matter of conjecture. But on March 21, 2025, Boeing won a huge contract that took some analysts and observers by surprise.

Boeing and Lockheed Martin filed competing proposals with the U.S. Air Force for its sixth-generation fighter plane. Boeing had never built a fighter; its fighter aircraft came over from the 1997 McDonnell Douglas merger. Lockheed, along with Northrop Grumman, had been the Pentagon's fighter suppliers. On paper, Lockheed was the better bet. But Boeing won the Engineering and Manufacturing Development (EMD) contract for what in Pentagon-ese was called the Next Generation Air Dominance (NGAD) Platform. The new fighter was named the F-47. In an unusual move, the President of the United States made the award announcement—such things are usually handled solely by the Pentagon and the relevant service. Cynics asserted that the plane's name/number was an homage to Trump, the forty-seventh president. However, the Air Force was founded in 1947, so the name may be an homage to Trump, to the Air Force, or to both.

Defense Secretary Pete Hegseth said, "the F-47 represents a significant advancement over the F-22, which is currently the U.S. Air Force's primary air superiority fighter."

"The F-47 is designed to integrate next-generation stealth, sensor fusion, and long-range strike capabilities to counter the most sophisticated adversaries in contested environments. Its adaptability and modular design ensure seamless integration with emerging technologies, positioning it as a dominant platform for decades to come," a spokesperson for the Air Force said.

Significantly, the multi-billion-dollar contract is a cost-plus contract, not a fixed-price contract; the latter type of contract has cost Boeing many billions of dollars across each of several previous defense programs. Although the contract was awarded under Boeing's CEO Kelly Ortberg, his predecessor, David Calhoun, was clear that the days of the fixed-price contract were over when he became chief executive officer in January 2020.

Goldman Sachs's aerospace analyst noted, "This award comes at a pivotal time for Boeing, as it has not been awarded the prime contractor role on a U.S. fighter jet in decades. Long-term growth in its defense segment had been a question, along with substantial recent cost overruns on other development programs."

RBC Capital called the contract "a bit of a surprise for investors. We believe the award is a signal from the Air Force that it wants to ensure at least two fighter companies in the industrial base. Lockheed Martin produces the F-35. Northrop Grumman is the contractor for the new B-21 bomber."

If Boeing can execute on this contract—a big "if" considering how it's messed up on just about every one of its recent defense and space programs—it will be another step in the Way Back to Legacy Boeing.

Yet, like it has been so many times in the past, Boeing seems caught up in disasters not of its own making. There were the Iraq invasion of Kuwait and the 1991 Persian Gulf War; the Asian SARS epidemic; 9/11 and the resulting war on terror; and the COVID-19 pandemic, to name a few of the larger global upsets. While President Trump gave Boeing what some considered a gift with the F-47, he also gave Boeing—and the world—potentially crushing tariffs, which upset global trade in a matter of *days*. The tariff game is still being played out at the time of this writing.

Since this book's primary aim is to examine Boeing, I won't go into the macro issue of tariffs and the larger impacts of Trump's actions. For Boeing, Trump's announcements on tariffs were potentially disastrous. At the outset, there was way too much ambiguity over what, exactly, the tariffs would apply to. The president initially announced that there would be no exemptions or exceptions. Historically, commercial aviation largely has been immune to tariffs. The global supply chain for aircraft is just too intricate to efficiently apply a tax—and this is what a tariff is—to just the foreign content of an airplane. And this selective application of tariffs is what is called for in Trump's policy. Only foreign content is to be taxed. But Trump seemed to infer that the tariffs would apply to the total purchase price of aircraft. As of this writing, there has been no clarity on the matter.

Even on Boeing airplanes delivered domestically, the fact that they contain foreign content—including in engines, interiors, systems, and other airplane components (like the Chinese-made rudder on the 737 and nearly all the fuselage and wings on the 787) —means that tariffs can be levied. Globally, from 2025 through 2028 (just shy of the end of Trump's term in office), Airbus is scheduled to deliver just under 800 airplanes to U.S. customers—all subject to tariffs at some level. During the same period, Boeing is scheduled to deliver more than 2,700 airplanes to customers outside the U.S., all potentially subject to reciprocal tariffs. Hundreds more are scheduled for delivery to U.S. airlines, each with foreign content.

In normal times, i.e., before the 737 MAX was grounded for twenty-one months beginning on March 10, 2019, followed by the pandemic and Boeing's self-inflicted back-to-back wounds well into 2024, Boeing was the largest U.S. exporter and the biggest contributor to reducing the balance of trade—a big Trump concern and the underlying impetus for the imposition of potentially onerous tariffs. Trump's tariffs could hurt Boeing far more than Airbus.

Such is the potential setback to Boeing's Way Back over which it has no control.

The larger problem facing Ortberg and Boeing involves changing the company's culture. Ortberg has made a few key executive changes and a handful of changes within the middle-management ranks of Boeing's Commercial Airplanes division (BCA). Efforts, such as they were, under Muilenburg and Calhoun to improve the culture and encourage rank-and-file employees to speak up without fear of retaliation or retribution fell well short of success when the Alaska Airlines flight 1282 door-plug blowout happened. Employees of the engineers' and touch-labor unions made it clear that retribution was still feared, and formal complaints were filed alleging such. Ortberg, in office as CEO only since August 8, 2024, has tried to further encourage what is called the Speak Up program. But it's taken Boeing decades to descend into cultural dysfunction, and it will take a lot more than the culture-change attempts started after the two MAX crashes in 2018 and 2019 to fix the massive problem.

In April 2025, I interviewed a former Boeing employee whose assignment was safety education within the company. He quit earlier in the year, frustrated that mid-level managers and executives rarely attended meetings for more than introductory remarks and that lower-level employees often left before the classes were completed, citing work requirements. The employee brought his concerns to his managers, who dismissed them. The employee filed a Speak Up report and received a form-letter-type response.

He has considered becoming a whistleblower with the Federal Aviation Administration and with Washington Senator Maria Cantwell and Washington Congressman Adam Smith—two members of Congress who have been highly critical of Boeing despite being from BCA's home state. But this employee remains afraid of retribution.

"I guarantee you that they'll circle the wagons and try to discredit me as being a disgruntled employee. I am a disgruntled employee. I was furloughed and flattened. I was threatened with layoffs and laughed at. I was cussed out," he told me. "That was my experience in just the first few months. It wasn't until the team got toxic that I said, 'I've had enough.'"

Two days before the one-year anniversary of the Alaska accident, Boeing issued a press release touting all it had achieved in improving safety since that scary day. Simultaneously, it continued to stonewall the engineers union, SPEEA, on a safety initiative that was by that point almost a year old.[164] Among the items listed by Boeing in its press release were the following:

- "Addressed over 70% of action items in commercial airplanes production based on employee feedback during Quality Stand Down sessions.
- Instituted new random quality audits of documented removals in high frequency areas to ensure compliance to process.

164. Scott Hamilton, "Boeing Touts Safety Progress But Opposes SPEEA Initiative," *Leeham News and Analysis* (January 3, 2025), https://leehamnews.com/2025/01/03/boeing-touts-safety-progress-but-opposes-speea-initiative/.

- Added hundreds of hours of new curriculum to training programs, including quality proficiency, Safety Management System (SMS) Positive Safety Culture, and critical skills.
- Mapped and prepared thousands of governance documents and work instructions for revision.
- Significantly reduced defects in 737 fuselage assembly at Spirit AeroSystems by increasing inspection points at build locations and implementing customer quality approval process."

This list is all well and good, but the company didn't provide detailed data to support its claims. For example, Boeing said that it "addressed over 70% of action items" yet provided no definition of what this statistic meant. How many "items" involved actions that implemented employee suggestions? How many employee suggestions were rejected? Were some supposedly "addressed" with the issuance of a kind of form letter, as the employee above outlined? Boeing initially told reporters that there would be a briefing, then canceled this event. It also declined to make anyone available to answer questions, and its corporate communications office did not respond to specific questions I posed as the editor of *Leeham News*.

Rich Plunkett, the director of strategic development for SPEEA, is the lead liaison between the union and Boeing. He's expressed continuing frustration with Boeing over union safety initiatives. Among the complaints is that Boeing's labor relations department—not its safety department—is negotiating with the union on behalf of the company. Months would go by with no meetings, and the company negotiators insisted that Boeing be the arbitrator over what safety complaints would be heard by a special committee proposed by SPEEA, which could include a member from the FAA.

In contrast, Spirit AeroSystems, at the time Boeing's leading outside supplier (it made the fuselage for the 737 and nose sections for the other Boeing commercial airliners), cooperatively and quickly adopted the same safety program and process that SPEEA proposed to Boeing.

When Ortberg first joined Boeing, he quickly met with the leadership of IAM 751, the union that assembles the airliners in the Renton and Everett factories and which represents employees at several other Boeing production sites. The company and this union were engaged in contract negotiations when Ortberg came on board, as recounted in previous chapters. Ortberg had a "fire" to put out before the "house" burned down. He met with SPEEA leadership, but not until February 7, 2025.

Plunkett said that the meeting was friendly. "It was a nice enough social event," he told me a few months later. "But nothing came of it. We brought forth a number of items, particularly around the layoffs." Boeing's increasing use of contract labor was another topic SPEEA brought up in the Ortberg meeting. Union leaders routinely request data from Boeing for negotiations, ideas, and related issues. "We can't even get data from Boeing," Plunkett complained. "They fight us on data."

Plunkett said that the 10 percent layoffs ordered by Ortberg upon his arrival to cut costs in some cases amounted to a shuffling between employees and contractors.

"Boeing now contracts with Monument Consulting LLC, who in turn goes to contract houses to get contingent labor for Boeing," Plunkett said. "To indemnify the employer, H-1B visas, for example, Boeing can use these people till the cows come home. And Boeing will never be H-1B-dependent because they're not employing these people, even indirectly, because they're going through Monument."

Boeing engaged in what some of its communications people called "litigation public relations" during the MAX accident and grounding crisis from March 2019 through the rest of that year, with General Counsel Michael Luttig calling the shots for then-CEO Muilenburg. After the latter was fired, Luttig retired. New CEO Calhoun was more forthcoming about Boeing's shortcomings at the time. But even today, the culture within the organization is to often tap dance around identifying and solving problems, some insiders (past and present) say.

In congressional testimony in April 2025, Ortberg admitted that "missteps" had been made at Boeing.

"How about, 'look, we fucked up,'" Plunkett suggested, continuing in Boeing's "voice," "'We gutted the infrastructure that was necessary to ensure communications effectively from top down and bottom up.'"

Rather than identifying and solving problems, along the lines of former BCA CEO Alan Mulally's famous process of green, yellow, and red charts and leadership meetings, the blame game remains a part of the culture, people say today.

To use an incendiary political term, changing the culture in Boeing's "deep state" of middle management is the key.

On April 17, 2025, Boeing released the results of a survey it completed among employees. Among the results:

- More than 82% of employees participated, the highest response of any Boeing employee survey since 2016.
- 67% feel proud to work at Boeing, compared to 91% in 2013.
- 27% would highly recommend Boeing as place to work – and at the same time employees remain committed to turning the company around: More than 92% of employees said they plan to stay for more than a year.
- 54% of employees felt inspired by the previous Boeing values, and most believe the company should do a better job of living those values and holding each other accountable.

- 75% of employees believe their direct managers are effective, but only 61% of employees feel their contributions are valued and recognized.
- 42% have confidence in their senior leader's ability to make decisions, communicate direction and respond to concerns raised by employees.

The results were a mixed report card, clearly showing a lot of work still was needed to fix Boeing's culture.

In short, the Way Back to Boeing's legacy entails a long to-do list: fixing BCA and Boeing's Defense, Space & Security (BDS) division; improving the company's quality-control and production-safety processes; repairing its relations with regulators, its supply chain, its commercial, space, and defense customers, and its labor unions; and so much more.

Boeing also needs to develop a deep bench in its executive ranks. When Jim McNerney was named CEO of The Boeing Company in 2005, he said that one of his first priorities was to develop good succession planning. It was one of his greatest failures. He passed over Alan Mulally, who wanted to be president and chief operating officer at the corporate level. Mulally went to Ford Motor Company as CEO and saved the firm from collapse and bankruptcy. Mulally's engineering expertise and his demand that bad news and problems be presented to him along with the good was sorely missed when the 787 and 747-8 programs went off the rails.

It's never been confirmed, but there was a belief that the Boeing Board of Directors made the decision in 2012 to name Muilenburg president and COO of the corporation and to designate him as the presumed successor to McNerney. Muilenburg became chairman and CEO in 2015. Given Muilenburg's handling of the MAX crisis four years later, it would be fair to say that he was not the best choice.

David Calhoun, Muilenburg's successor, was always going to be a transition CEO. He was supposed to fix Boeing and position it for the future. Calhoun named Stephanie Pope as executive vice president (EVP) and COO of the corporation, elevating her from her position as president and CEO of Boeing Global Services (BGS). To many, Pope was an odd choice given that her background was, in the scheme of things, rather limited. Her entire career had been in finance; being CEO of BGS was her first leadership position. She had no experience in airliner sales, nor did she have a defense background. When what was termed the "Monday Morning Massacre" happened, Pope was named CEO of BCA in addition to her role as EVP and COO of the corporation. Once again, her appointment was an odd choice, as she had no technical background to deal with the Alaska 1282 crisis and all the fallout that came after it.

Ortberg quickly replaced the CEO of BDS, but eight months after his appointment (at the time of this writing), he hadn't named a new leader at BCA. Within Boeing and outside the company, few could understand why not. The leading theory was that once Boeing re-acquired Spirit AeroSystems, expected to happen by mid-year 2025, Spirit's CEO Pat Shanahan would be named CEO of BCA. Shanahan had been a Boeing lifer before being tapped to be deputy secretary of defense in the first Trump Administration. Shanahan was tapped by the Spirit board of directors to solve the company's quality control and production problems. A return to Boeing would make a lot of sense and has a lot of merit, although Shanahan would not be a universally popular choice.[165]

Ortberg was 64 when he was named Boeing's CEO. He and the board agreed that he could serve as CEO for a total of seven years, based on one-year renewal options. Assuming he stays the full seven years, exactly how much of the twenty-eight years of GEntrification of The Boeing Company he can unwind in one-fourth the time remains to be seen.

But this is Boeing's way back.

---

165. By the time this book is published, this theory is likely to be proved or disproved, since the re-acquisition of Spirit should be completed by then.

POSTSCRIPT

AS THIS BOOK WAS IN FINAL EDITING REVIEW, Air India flight 171 crashed on June 12 on take-off from Ahmedabad Airport, India, bound for London, England. The 11-year-old Boeing 787-8 was airborne for about 40 seconds. Immediately after takeoff, the pilot radioed a Mayday and said he had lost engine power.

There were 242 people on board; all but one died as the plane pancaked into a densely developed area. Nearly three dozen more were killed on the ground and sixty were injured.

As this book goes to press, India's Aircraft Accident Investigation Bureau (AAIB) hasn't released any meaningful information about the accident. Unlike the U.S. National Transportation Safety Board (NTSB), which gives frequent briefings following an accident, the AAIB gave only one shortly after the accident. The public doesn't know if the AAIB analyzed the cockpit voice and flight data recorders and if so, what was discovered.

Little is definitively known. The airplane took most of the 11,500 foot runway to take off. It never reached more than 625 feet, recorded by the pressure altitude. The airport's elevation is about 200 feet, so the flight may not have gotten much higher than about 425 feet above the ground. Video of the airplane showed a steady descent, suggesting the pilot had control as the plane lost altitude. The Ram Air Turbine (RAT) deployed, and the landing gear was down. There are about eight reasons the RAT would deploy. The cause isn't known and presumably will be revealed following analysis of the recorders.

Did the flight truly lose engine power? If so, how much? Were the flaps and slats properly set for take-off? Was the flight management computer properly programmed for take-off under the hot and humid conditions at the airport? The recorders should reveal all.

This was the first fatal accident involving a 787. Given Boeing's safety and quality control history, some immediately suggested Boeing is at fault. Given the lack of any information from the AAIB, this is pure speculation. However, if the cause of the accident is traced to a Boeing design problem,

Boeing's way back will suffer. If the cause of the accident is traced to the engine, made by GE Aerospace, Boeing may come out of this relatively unscathed. If there is a joint cause, much will depend on how much is Boeing's responsibility and how much is GE's. If something else entirely is the cause (pilot error, for example), then Boeing's way back should proceed uninhibited by the accident.

The other last minute development as this book was in final preparation for publication was the determination by the NTSB that Boeing bore primary responsibility for the Alaska 1282 accident. The NTSB also tagged the Federal Aviation Administration with culpability for failure to thoroughly oversee Boeing. The NTSB's conclusion was expected. No further damage to Boeing's reputation comes from the Alaska accident.

APPENDIX

Whistleblower Account of What Happened Aboard the Alaska Airlines 737-9 MAX Accident Aircraft

Author's note: The whistleblower's post is presented in its entirety. It has been lightly edited for clarity.

✳ ✳ ✳ ✳ ✳

Current Boeing employee here. I will save you waiting two years for the NTSB [National Transportation Safety Board] report to come out and give it to you for free: the reason the door blew off is stated in black and white in Boeing's own records. It is also very, very stupid and speaks volumes about the quality culture at certain portions of the business.

A couple of things to cover before we begin:

(Q1) Why should we believe you?

A) You shouldn't. I'm some random throwaway account, do your own due diligence. Others who work at Boeing can verify [if] what I say is true, but all I ask is [for] you consider the following based on its own merits.

(Q2) Why are you doing this?

(A) Because there are many cultures at Boeing, and while the executive culture may be thoroughly compromised since we were bought by Mc-Donnell Douglas, there are many other people who still push for a quality product with cutting-edge design. My hope is that this is the wake up call that finally forces the board [of directors] to take decisive action and remove the executives that are resisting the necessary cultural changes to return to a company that values safety and quality above schedule.

WHY DID THIS HAPPEN?

With that out of the way . . Why did the left hand (LH) mid-exit door plug blow off of the 737-9 registered as N704AL?

Simple. As has been covered in a number of articles and videos across aviation channels, there are 4 bolts that prevent the mid-exit door plug from sliding up off of the door stop fittings that take the actual pressurization loads in flight, and these 4 bolts were not installed when Boeing delivered the airplane. Our own records reflect this.

The mid-exit doors on a 737-9 of both the regular and plug variety come from Spirit [AeroSystems] already installed in what is supposed to be the final configuration in the Renton factory. There is a job for the doors team to verify this "final" install and rigging meets drawing requirements. In a healthy production system, this would be a "belt and suspenders" sort of check, but the 737 production system is quite far from healthy. It's a rambling, shambling, disaster waiting to happen.

As a result, this check job that should find minimal defects has in the past 365 calendar days recorded 392 nonconforming findings on 737 mid-fuselage door installations (so both actual doors for the high-density config[uration]s, and plugs like the one that blew out). That is a hideously high and very alarming number.

If our quality system on 737 was healthy, it would have stopped the line and driven the issue back to [the] supplier after the first few instances. Obviously, this did not happen.

THE ACCIDENT AIRCRAFT

Now, on the incident aircraft this check job was completed on 31 August 2023, and did turn up discrepancies, but on the RH [right-hand] side door, not the LH [left-hand side door] that actually failed. I could blame the team for missing certain details, but given the enormous volume of defects they were already finding and fixing, it was inevitable something would slip through. And on the incident aircraft, something did. I know what you are thinking at this point, but grab some popcorn because there is a plot twist coming up.

The next day, on 1 September 2023, a different team (remember: 737s flow through the factory quite quickly; 24 hours completely changes who is working on the plane) wrote up a finding for damaged and improperly installed rivets on the LH mid-exit door of the incident aircraft.

A brief aside to explain two of the record systems Boeing uses in production. The first is a program called CMES, which stands for something boring and unimportant, but what is important is that CMES is the sole authoritative repository for airplane build records (except on 787, which uses a different program). If a build record in CMES says something was built, inspected, and stamped in accordance with the drawing, then the airplane damn well better be per drawing.

The second is a program called SAT, which also stands for something boring and unimportant, but what is important is that SAT is *not* an authoritative records system. It's a bulletin board where various things affecting the airplane build get posted about and updated with resolutions. You can think of it sort of like a idiot's version of Slack or something.

Wise readers will already be shuddering and wondering how many consultants were involved, because, yes SAT is a *management visibility tool*. Like any good management visibility tool, SAT can generate metrics, lots of metrics, and Boeing managers love their metrics. As a result, SAT postings are the primary topic of discussion at most daily status meetings, and the whole system is perceived as being extremely important despite, I reiterate, it holding no actual authority at all.

FIXING THE ACCIDENT AIRCRAFT

We now return to our incident aircraft, which was written up for having defective rivets on the LH mid-exit door. Now, as is standard practice in Renton (but not to my knowledge in Everett on wide bodies), this write-up happened in two forms, one in CMES, which is the correct venue, and once in SAT to "coordinate the response" but really as a behind-covering measure so the manager of the team that wrote it can show his boss he's shoved the problem onto someone else.

Because there are so many problems with the Spirit build in the 737, Spirit has teams on site in Renton performing warranty work for all of their shoddy quality, and this SAT promptly gets shunted into their queue as a warranty item.

Lots of bickering ensues in the SAT messages, and it takes a bit [of time] for Spirit to get to the work package. Once they have finished, they send it back to a Boeing QA [Quality Assurance] for final acceptance, but then Malicious Stupid Happens! The Boeing QA writes another record in CMES (again, the correct venue) stating (with pictures) that Spirit has not actually reworked the discrepant rivets, they *just painted over the defects*. In Boeing production speak, this is a "process failure." For an A&P [Airframe and Powerplant certificated] mechanic at an airline, this would be called "federal crime."

Presented with evidence of their malfeasance, Spirit reopens the package and admits that not only did they not rework the rivets properly, there is a damaged pressure seal they need to replace (who damaged it, and when it was damaged is not clear to me). The big deal with this seal, at least according to frantic SAT postings, is [that] the part is not on hand and will need to be ordered, which is going to impact schedule, and (reading between the lines here) Management Is Not Happy.

PRESSURE-SEAL ISSUE

However, more critical for purposes of the accident investigation, [is that] the pressure seal is unsurprisingly sandwiched between the plug and the fuselage, and you cannot replace it without opening the door plug to gain access.

All of this conversation is documented in increasingly aggressive posts in the SAT, but finally we get to the damning entry which reads something along the lines of "coordinating with the doors team to determine if the door will have to be removed entirely, or just opened. If it is removed then a Removal will have to be written." Note: a Removal is a type of record in CMES that requires formal sign off from QA that the airplane been restored to drawing requirements.

If you have been paying attention to this situation closely, you may be able to spot the critical error: regardless of whether the door is simply opened or removed entirely, the 4 retaining bolts that keep it from sliding off of the door stops have to be pulled out.

A Removal should be written in either case for QA to verify install, but as it turns out, someone (exactly who will be a fun question for investigators) decides that the door only needs to be opened, and no formal Removal is generated in CMES (the reason for which is unclear—and a major process failure).

Therefore, in the official build records of the airplane, a pressure seal that cannot be accessed without opening the door (and thereby removing retaining bolts) is documented as being replaced, but the door is never officially opened and thus no QA inspection is required.

VERIFICATION JOB NOT OPENED

This entire sequence is documented in the SAT, and the nonconformance records in CMES address the damaged rivets and pressure seal, but at no point is the verification job reopened or . any record of removed retention bolts created, despite this being a physical impossibility.

Finally, with Spirit completing their work to Boeing QA's satisfaction, the two rivet-related records in CMES are stamped complete, and the SAT closed on 19 September 2023. No record or comment regarding the retention bolts is made.

I told you it was stupid.

So, where are the bolts? Probably sitting forgotten and unlabeled (because there is no formal record number to label them with) on a work-in-progress bench, unless someone already tossed them in the scrap bin to tidy up.

There's lots more to be said about the culture that enabled this to happened, but that's the basic details of what happened. The NTSB report will say it in more elegant terms in a few years.

FAA Letter Regarding Alaska Airlines Door-Plug Incident

U.S. Department
of Transportation
**Federal Aviation
Administration**

Aviation Safety
Aircraft Certification Service

800 Independence Ave., S.W.
Washington, D.C. 20591

January 10, 2024

File Number: EIR2024NM420001

The Boeing Company
Attn: Ms. Carole Murray
Vice President, Total Quality, Boeing Commercial Airplanes
P.O. Box 3707, MC 0H-325
Seattle, WA 98124-2207

Dear Ms. Murray:

The Federal Aviation Administration (FAA) is conducting an investigation concerning an in-service incident on a Boeing Model 737-9 MAX aircraft. The subject aircraft lost a "plug" type passenger door commor to an unused emergency exit location. After the incident, the FAA was notified of additional discrepancies on other Boeing 737-9 airplanes. This investigation is being performed to ensure compliance with Title 14 Code of Federal Regulations (14 CFR) and your FAA approved quality system.

REQUIREMENTS:

Part 21 CERTIFICATION PROCEDURES FOR PRODUCTS, ARTICLES, AND PARTS, Subpart G--Production Certificates, Sec. 21.146, Responsibility of holder, states in part, "The holder of a production certificate must…(c) Ensure that each completed product or article for which a production certificate has been issued … presented for airworthiness certification or approval conforms to its approved design and is in a condition for safe operation;"

BCA Quality Manual, Revision I dated June 26, 2023, section 8.5.1 Inspection and Testing states in part, "Appropriate inspection and test activities are conducted … post-delivery activities are conducted in accordance with contract or regulatory requirements."

ALLEGED NONCOMPLIANCE:

The above-described circumstances indicate that Boeing may have failed to ensure its completed products conformed to its approved design and were in a condition for safe operation in accordance with quality system inspection and test procedures.

This letter is to inform you that the FAA is investigating this matter. We would appreciate receiving any evidence or statements you might care to make concerning this matter within ten (10) business days of receipt of this letter. Any discussions or written statements will be given consideration in the final conclusion of our investigation. However, if we do not hear from you within the specified time, our report will be processed without the benefit of your statement.

Your response should contain the root cause of the encountered condition(s), products/articles affected, service impacts, the extent of any immediate/long-term action taken to correct and preclude its recurrence, and any mitigating circumstances which you believe may be relevant to this case.

Sincerely,

Digitally signed by BRIAN
T KNAUP
Date: 2024.01.10
13:32:48 -08'00'

for

John Piccola
Aviation Safety
Director for Integrated Certificate Management Division
Federal Aviation Administration

Boards of Directors, The Boeing Company

1996 directors who would vote for or against
the McDonnell Douglas merger
(1997 Proxy Statement)

Name	Position	Age	Director Since
Frank Shrontz	Chairman Emeritus, Boeing	65	1988
George Weyerhaeuser	Chairman, Weyerhaeuser Co.	70	1962
Harold Haynes	Chairman, Chevron (Ret.)	71	1974
John Bryson	Chairman, Edison International	53	1995
Philip Condit	Chairman, Boeing	55	1992
John Fery	Chairman, Boise Cascade (Ret.)	67	1989
Paul Gray	President Emeritus, Professor, Electrical Engineering, M	65	1990
Donald Peterson	Chairman, Ford (Ret.)	70	1990
Charles Piggott	Chairman Emeritus, Paccar	67	1972
Rozanne Ridgway	Former Assistant Secretary of State for Canada	61	1992

1997 directors,
following the merger with McDonnell Douglas
(1998 Proxy Statement)

Name	Position	Age	Director Since
John Biggs	Chairman, Teachers Insurance and Annuity Association	61	Aug. 1997
John Bryson	Chairman, Edison International	54	1995
Charles Pigott	Chairman Emeritus, Paccar	68	1972
Rozanne Ridgway	Former Assistant Secretary of State for Canada	62	1992
Phil Condit	Chairman, Boeing	56	1992
Kenneth Duberstein	Chairman, The Duberstein Group	53	Aug. 1997
John Fery	Chairman, Boise Cascade (Ret.)	68	1989
John McDonnell	Chairman, McDonnell Douglas	60	Aug. 1979
Paul Gray	President Emeritus, Professor, Electrical Engineering, MIT	66	1990
William Perry	Professor, School of Engineering, Stanford University	70	Nov. 1997
Donald Peterson	Chairman, Ford (Ret.)	71	1990
Harry Stonecipher	President, Boeing	61	Aug. 1997
George Weyerhaeuser	Chairman, Weyerhaeuser Co. (Ret.)	71	1962

2003 directors
(Condit resigns, Stonecipher becomes Chairman)
(2004 Proxy Statement)

Name	Position	Age	Director Since
John Biggs	Chairman, Teachers Insurance and Annuity Assn. (Ret.)	67	1997
John Bryson	Chairman, Edison International	60	1995
Linda Cook	President, Shell Canada	45	2003
Kenneth Duberstein	Chairman, The Duberstein Group	59	1997
James McNerney	Chairman, 3M Co.	54	2001
Lewis Platt	Non-Executive Chairman, Boeing	62	1999
Rozanne Ridgeway	Former Assistant Secretary of State for Canada	68	1992
John McDonnell	Chairman, McDonnell Douglas (Ret.)	66	1997
John Shalikashvili	Chairman, U.S. Joint Chiefs of Staff (Ret.)	67	2000
Harry Stonecipher	President, Boeing	67	1997

2004 directors
(Stonecipher fired March 2005)
(May 2005 Proxy Statement)

Name	Position	Age	Director Since
Kenneth Duberstein	Chairman, The Duberstein Group	60	1997
James McNerney	Chairman, 3M Co.	55	2001
Lewis Platt	Non-Executive Chairman, Boeing	63	1999
Mike Zafirovski	Former President, Motorola	51	2004
John McDonnell	Chairman, McDonnell Douglas (Ret.)	67	1997
Richard Nanula	Chief Financial Officer, Amgen	44	2005
John Shalikashvili	Chairman, U.S. Joint Chiefs of Staff (Ret.)	68	2000
John Biggs	Chairman, Teachers Insurance and Annuity Association (Ret.)	68	1997
John Bryson	Chairman, Edison International	61	1995
Linda Cook	Executive Director, Royal Dutch Petroleum Co.	46	2003
Rozanne Ridgway	Former Assistant Secretary of State for Canada	69	1992

2005 directors (McNerney is now chairman);
terms become one-year vs. staggered three-year terms.
(2006 Proxy Statement)

Name	Position	Age	Director Since
John Biggs	Former Chairman. Teachers Insurance and Annuity Association	69	1997
John Bryson	Chairman, Edisor International	62	1995
Linda Cook	Executive Director, Royal Dutch Shell	47	2003
William Daley	Chairman Midwest Region, JP Morgan Chase	57	2006
Kenneth Duberstein	Chairman, The Duberstein Group	61	1997
John McDonnell	Chairman, McDonnell Douglas (Ret.)	68	1997
Richard Nanula	Chief Financial Officer, Amgen	45	2005
Rozanne Ridgway	Former Assistant Secretary of State for Canada	70	1992
Mike Zafirovski	Director, President, Nortel	52	2004
James McNerney	Chairman, Boeing	56	2001

2009 directors
(Calhoun joins the board)
(April 2010 Proxy Statement)

Name	Position	Age	Director Since
John Biggs	Former Chairman, Teachers Insurance and Annuity Association	73	1997
John Bryson	Senior Advisor, KKR	66	1995
David Calhoun	Chairman, The Nielson Co.	52	2009
Arthur Collins	Senior Advisor, Oak Hill Capital Partners	62	2007
Linda Cook	Executive Director, Royal Dutch Shell (Ret.)	51	2003
William Daley	Chairman, JP Morgan Chase Midwest	61	2006
Kenneth Duberstein	Chairman, The Duberstein Group	65	1997
Edmund Giambastiani	7th Vice Chairman, U.S. Joint Chiefs of Staff (Ret.)	60	2009
John McDonnell	Chairman, McDonnell Douglas (Ret.)	71	1997
James McNerney	Chairman, Boeing	60	2001
Susan Schwab	Professor, University of Maryland School of Public Policy	54	2010
Mike Zafirovski	Former President, Nortel	56	2004

2015 directors
(McNerney retires, Muilenburg becomes chairman)
(May 2016 Proxy Statement)

Name	Position	Age	Director Since
David Calhoun	Senior Managing Director, Blackstone Group	58	2009
Arthur Collins	Senior Advisor, Oak Hill Capital Partners	68	2007
Kenneth Duberstein	Chairman, The Duberstein Group	71	1997
Edmund Giambastiani	7th Vice Chairman, U.S. Joint Chiefs of Staff (Ret.)	67	2009
Lynn Good	Chairman, Duke Energy Corp.	56	2015
Lawrence Kellner	President, Emerald Creek Group	57	2011
Edward Liddy	Former Chairman, Allstate	70	2010
Dennis Muilenburg	Chairman, Boeing	52	2015
Susan Schwab	Professor, University of Maryland School of Public Policy	60	2010
Randall Stephenson	Chairman, AT&T	55	2016
Ron Williams	Former Chairman, Aetna	66	2010
Mike Zafirovski	Executive Advisor, Blackstone Group	62	2004

2018 directors
(2019 Proxy Statement)

Name	Position	Age	Director Since
Robert Bradway	Chairman, Amgen	56	2016
David Calhoun	Senior Managing Director, Blackstone Group	61	2009
Arthur Collins	Senior Advisor, Oak Hill Capital Partners	71	2007
Edmund Giambastiani	7th Vice Chairman, U.S. Joint Chiefs of Staff (Ret.)	70	2009
Lynn Good	Chairman, Duke Energy Corp.	59	2015
Nikki Haley	Former U.S. Ambassador to the UN	47	2018
Lawrence Kellner	President, Emerald Creek Group	60	2011
Caroline Kennedy	Former U.S. Ambassador to Japan	61	2017
Edward Liddy	Former Chairman, Allstate Insurance	73	2010
Dennis Muilenburg	Chairman, The Boeing Co.	55	2015
Susan Schwab	Professor, University of Maryland School of Public Policy	63	2010
Ronald Williams	Former Chairman, Aetna Insurance	69	2010
Mike Zafirovski	Executive Advisor, Blackstone Group	65	2004

2020 directors
(After rejecting a shareholder motion at the April 2019 shareholders meeting to separate the board chairman and president positions,
the board of directors did just that in October 2019.
Larry Kellner was named chairman. Kellner joined the board in 2011.
Muilenburg is fired in December 2019, and
Calhoun is named president and CEO.)

Name	Position	Age	Director Since
Robert Bradway	Chairman, Amgen	57	2016
David Calhoun	President, Boeing	62	2009
Arthur Collins	Senior Advisor, Oak Hill Capital Partners	72	2007
Edmund Giambastiani	7th Vice Chairman, U.S. Joint Chiefs of Staff (Ret.)	71	2009
Lynn Good	Chairman, Duke Energy Corp.	60	2015
Nikki Haley	Former U.S. Ambassador to the UN	48	2019
Akhil Johri	Special Advisor to Chairman, United Technologies	58	2020
Lawrence Kellner	President, Emerald Creek Group; Non-Executive Chairman, Boeing	61	2011
Caroline Kennedy	Former U.S. Ambassador to Japan	62	2017
Steven Moellenkopf	Chief Executive Officer, Qualcomm	51	2020
John Richardson	31st Chief of Naval Operations (Ret.)	59	2019
Susan Schwab	Professor, University of Maryland School of Public Policy	64	2010
Ronald Williams	Chairman, RW2 Enterprises (Ret.)	70	2010

2022 directors (David Joyce joins the board)

Name	Position	Age	Director Since
Robert Bradway	Chairman, Amgen	59	2016
David Calhoun	President, Boeing	64	2009
Lynne Doughtie	Former Chairman, KPMG	59	2021
Lynn Goode	Chairman, Duke Energy Corp.	62	2015
Stacy Harris	Former Inspector General, U.S. Air Force; Former United Airlines Pilot	62	2021
Akhil Johri	Former Executive Vice President, CFO, United Technologies	60	2020
David Joyce	Former President, GE Aviation	65	2021
Lawrence Kellner	Non-Executive Chairman, Boeing	63	2011
Steven Mollenkopf	Former CEO, Qualcomm	53	2020
John Richardson	31st Chief of Naval Operations (Ret.)	61	2019
Ronald Williams	Former Chairman, Aetna	72	2010

Significant events during the tenures of Boeing CEOs from Philip Condit through Kelly Ortberg

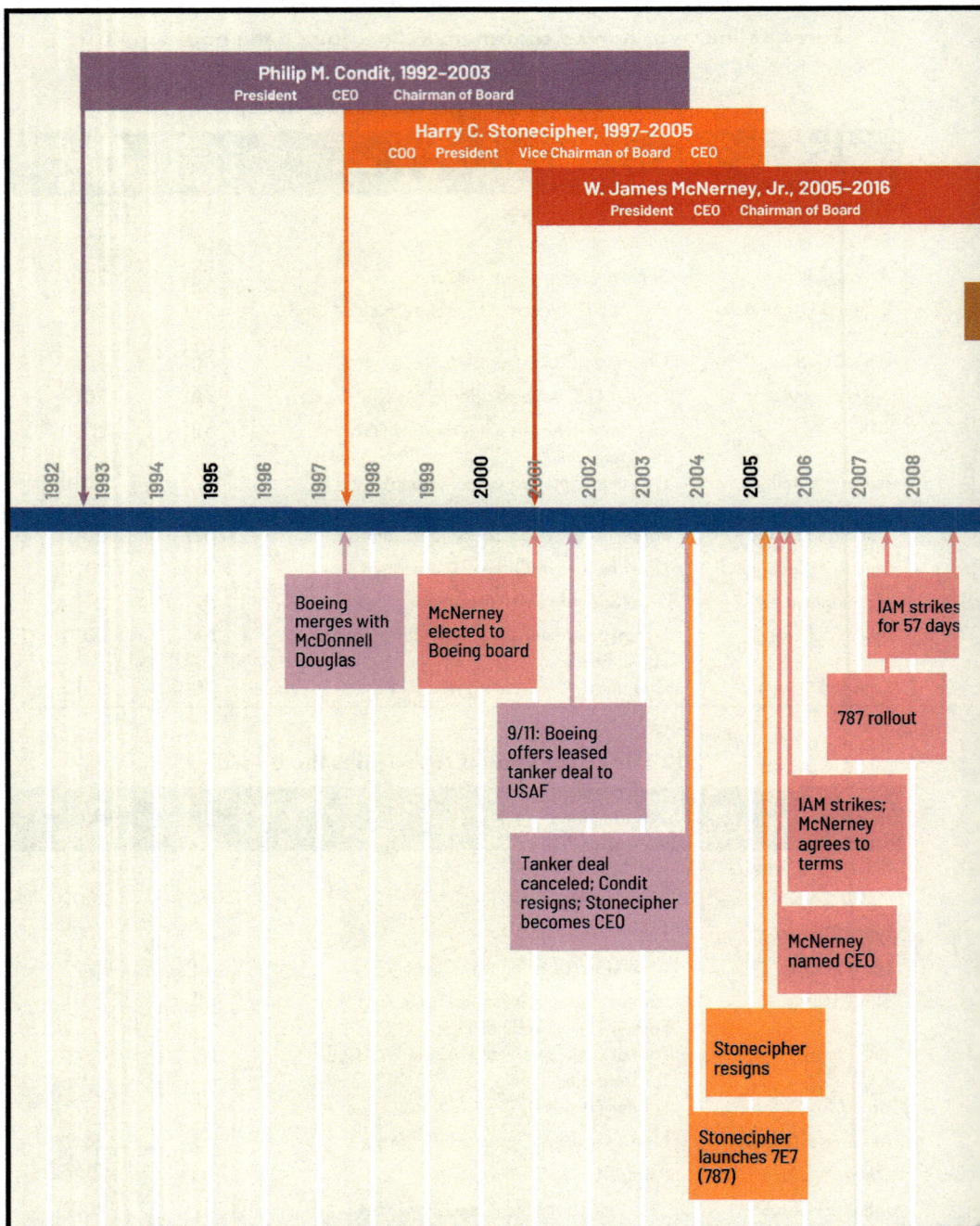

Philip M. Condit, 1992–2003
President   CEO   Chairman of Board

Harry C. Stonecipher, 1997–2005
COO   President   Vice Chairman of Board   CEO

W. James McNerney, Jr., 2005–2016
President   CEO   Chairman of Board

1992 1993 1994 **1995** 1996 1997 1998 1999 **2000** 2001 2002 2003 2004 **2005** 2006 2007 2008

Boeing merges with McDonnell Douglas

McNerney elected to Boeing board

9/11: Boeing offers leased tanker deal to USAF

Tanker deal canceled; Condit resigns; Stonecipher becomes CEO

IAM strikes for 57 days

787 rollout

IAM strikes; McNerney agrees to terms

McNerney named CEO

Stonecipher resigns

Stonecipher launches 7E7 (787)

Credit: chart by Scott Hamilton.

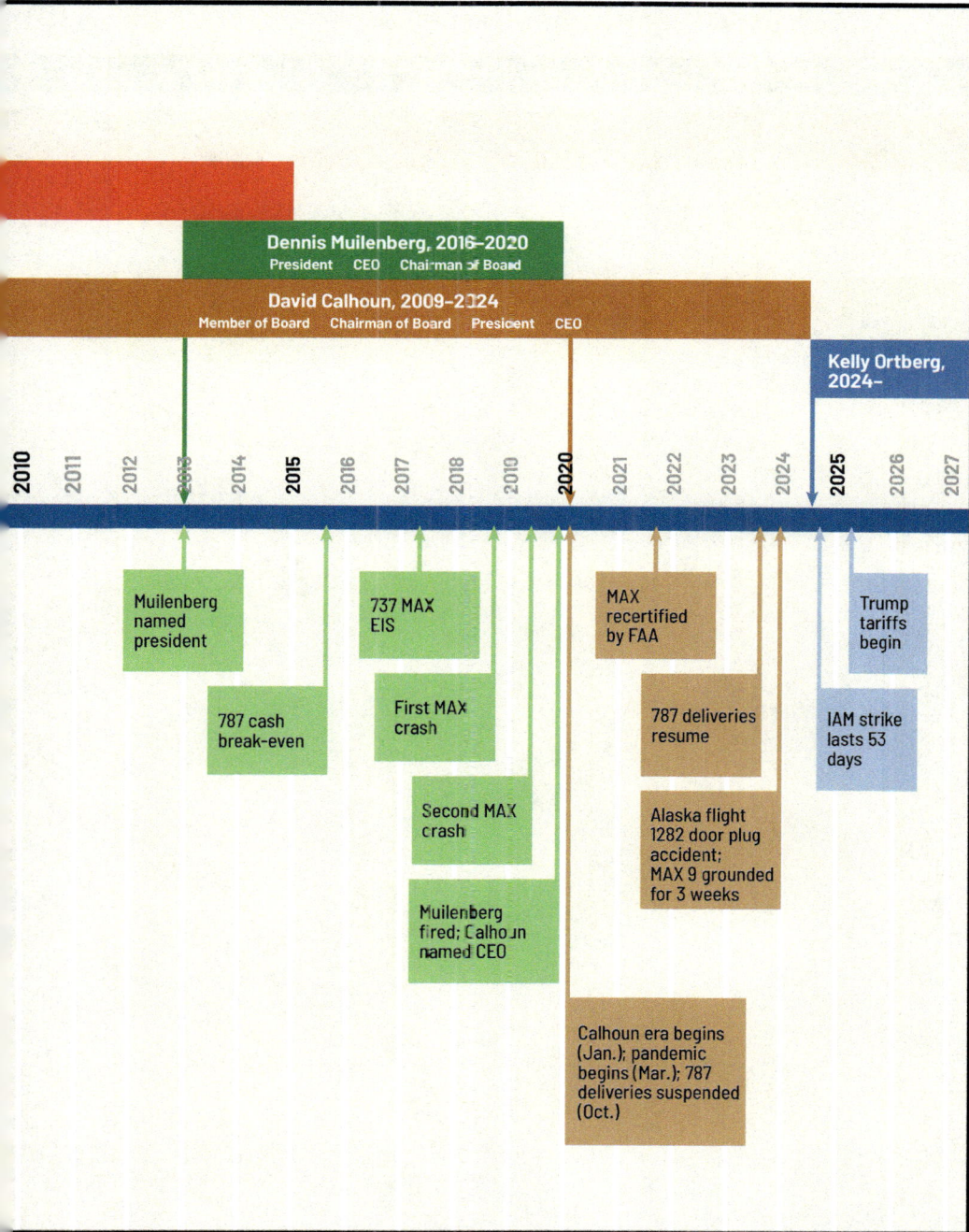

Dennis Muilenberg, 2016–2020
President   CEO   Chairman of Board

David Calhoun, 2009–2024
Member of Board   Chairman of Board   President   CEO

Kelly Ortberg, 2024–

2010 2011 2012 2013 2014 2015 2016 2017 2018 2019 2020 2021 2022 2023 2024 2025 2026 2027

Muilenberg named president

787 cash break-even

737 MAX EIS

First MAX crash

Second MAX crash

Muilenberg fired; Calhoun named CEO

Calhoun era begins (Jan.); pandemic begins (Mar.); 787 deliveries suspended (Oct.)

MAX recertified by FAA

787 deliveries resume

Alaska flight 1282 door plug accident; MAX 9 grounded for 3 weeks

Trump tariffs begin

IAM strike lasts 53 days

Boeing's Closing Stock Prices, 2004–2024,

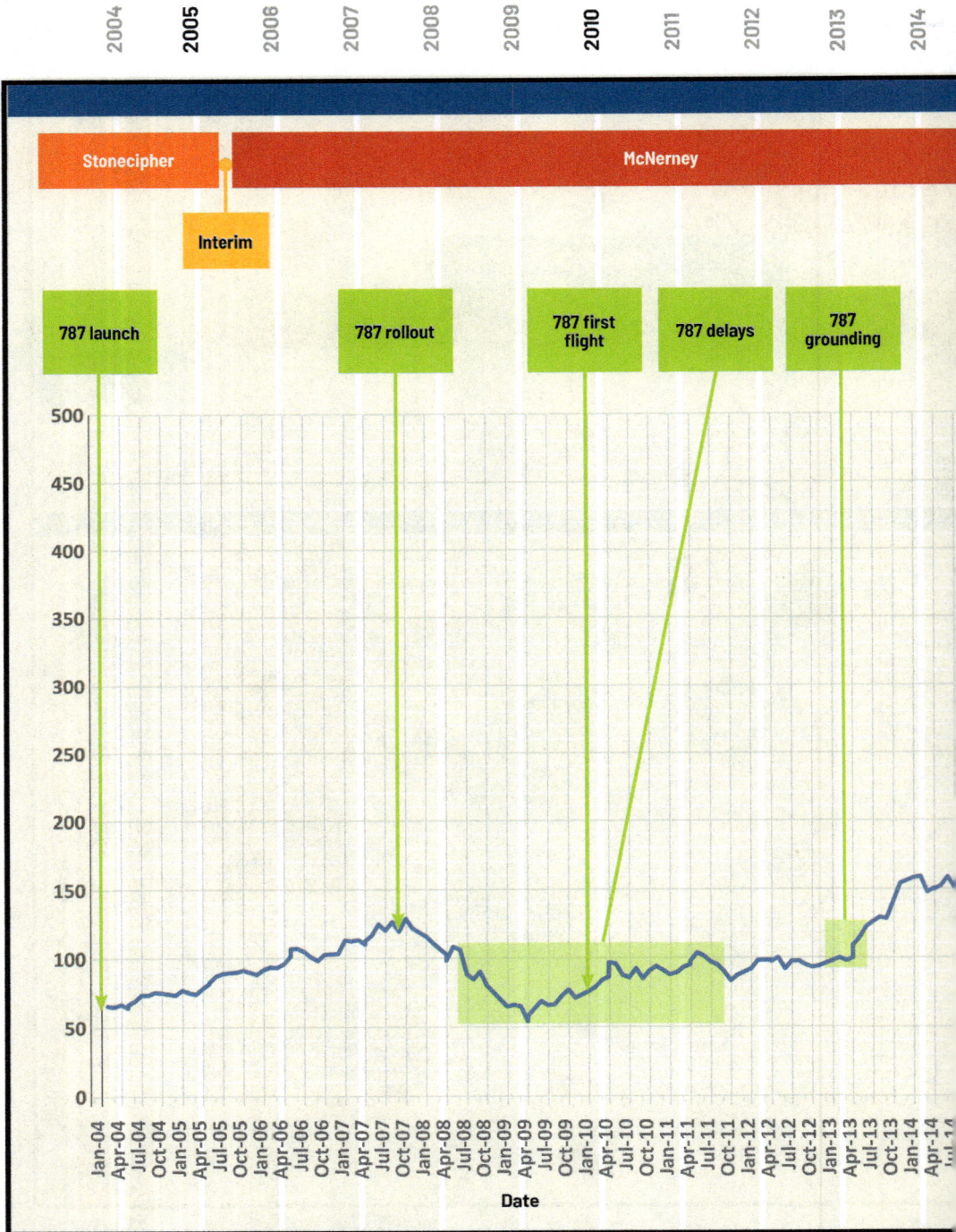

Sources: Investing.com, "Stock Prices"; Leeham News and Analysis (provided additional data, created chart).

Reflecting CEO Tenures and Key Company Events

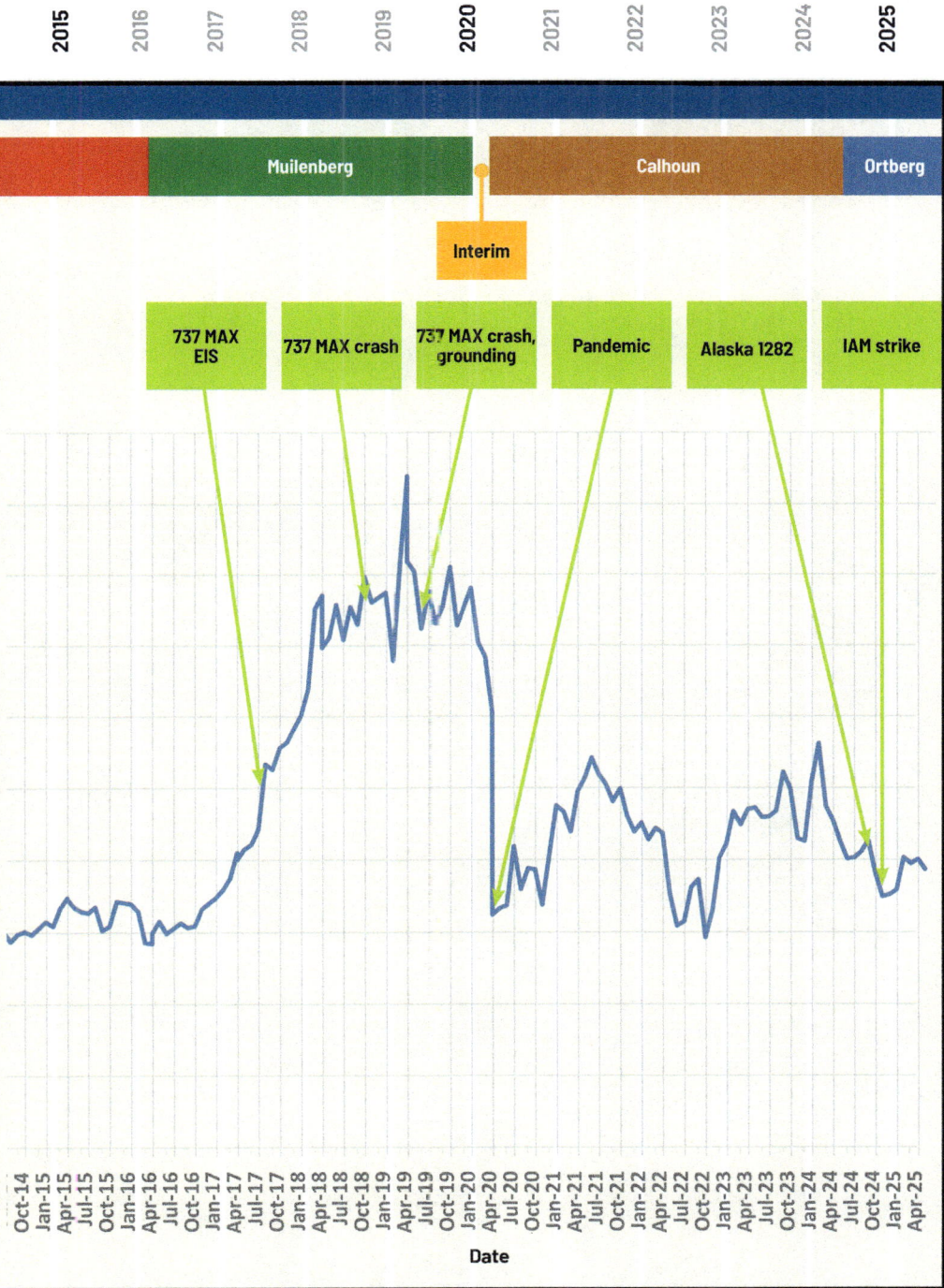

2015 2016 2017 2018 2019 2020 2021 2022 2023 2024 2025

Muilenberg | Interim | Calhoun | Ortberg

737 MAX EIS · 737 MAX crash · 737 MAX crash, grounding · Pandemic · Alaska 1282 · IAM strike

Date

Index

Acknowledgments

As with my first book, *Air Wars*, this publication is the result of cooperation from a lot of people. Most who were interviewed for *Air Wars* were happy to be identified by name. Some preferred anonymity. For this book, most requested anonymity. In a validation of all that has been printed in newspapers and aired on news programs, those who cooperated for *The Rise and Fall of Boeing* feared retaliation for critical comments, insights, and whistleblowing. Under Boeing's standard exit process, pensions can be revoked if critical comments are aired, to say nothing if confidential information is revealed. The atmosphere of retribution and retaliation, even among Boeing retirees, is alive and well. As a result, those named here constitute only a partial list of those to whom I am grateful.

First, a personal note about Robert Spingarn, to whom this book is dedicated. Rob was one of my best friends in the business world and a prince of a fellow. He had a very, very rare blood cancer that is always fatal. His illness is believed to have been traced to the environmental fallout of 9/11; he worked on Wall Street at the time but not in the Twin Towers.

Rob was one of the best aerospace analysts on Wall Street. We shared information we gained in our lines of work, and several times at the Farnborough and Paris Air Shows, Rob asked me to be his dinner speaker with his clients. We'd often connect when he was in Seattle visiting Boeing. Rob provided a lot of information for this book and is cited frequently.

Rob battled his cancer for five years, trying experimental treatments that in the end only prolonged his life. His final year was a real struggle. All of us who knew Rob will miss him.

Among others who helped, and in one way or another are able to be recognized publicly, are Richard Aboulafia, Larry Brown, Phil Condit, Bryan Corliss, John Feren, Ray Goforth, Jon Holden, John Leahy, Michel Merluzeau, Kevin Michael, Jon Ostrower, Rich Plunkett, Kiran Rao, and Don Shuper. The following members of my writing and partner staff at *Leeham News* and Leeham Co. also deserve recognition, either for contributions to *Leeham News* that provided information reported in this book or covering for me at *Leeham News* while I devoted time to *Rise and Fall:* Tom Batchelor, Bjorn Fehrm, Colleen Mondor, Judson Rollins, Gery Van Dessel, and Frank Ziegler. Two of our vendors do many of our airplane illustrations: Henry Lam, an Australian artist, and Guilhem Renier, of France (La Livery).

In addition, there are many aerospace analysts who, over the years, generously provided me with their analyst reports. Some information found the way into *Air Wars* and this book. Much information provided general analysis and insight as to what they were thinking about Boeing, Airbus and the commercial aviation industry. These include Charles Armitage, Ken Herbert, Douglas Harned, Scott Mikus, Robert Stallard, and Cai Von Rohmer.

I've already ambiguously mentioned those current and former Boeing employees who helped. The same goes for current and former members of the Boeing and Airbus supply chain. Like the former Boeing employees who required anonymity out of fear or retaliation or retribution, the suppliers also required anonymity for the same reasons. This speaks volumes about Boeing's sensitivities. One company that publicly criticized Boeing a few years ago saw a six figure contract canceled as a result.

In writing my first book, *Air Wars, The Global Combat Between Airbus and Boeing,* some of those who cooperated with that book show up in this book via references back to *Air Wars*. I was grateful to them then and grateful that their contributions to *Air Wars* were also useful for *Rise and Fall*.

My book editor was Melissa Twomey and my book designer was Michael Brady.

Scott Hamilton

September 2025